Revenue Statistics in Africa

1990-2014

Statistiques des recettes publiques en Afrique

1990-2014

Please cite this publication as:
OECD/ATAF/AUC (2016), *Revenue Statistics in Africa*, OECD Publishing, Paris.
http://dx.doi.org/10.1787/9789264253308-en-fr

Merci de citer cet ouvrage comme suit :
OCDE/ATAF/CUA (2016), *Statistiques des recettes publiques en Afrique*, Éditions OCDE, Paris.
http://dx.doi.org/10.1787/9789264253308-en-fr

ISBN 978-92-64-25190-8 (print/*imprimé*)
ISBN 978-92-64-25330-8 (PDF)

Corrigenda to OECD publications may be found on line at: *www.oecd.org/about/publishing/corrigenda.htm*.
Les corrigenda des publications de l'OCDE sont disponibles sur : *www.oecd.org/about/publishing/corrigenda.htm*.

Foreword

Revenue Statistics in Africa is a joint publication by the OECD Centre for Tax Policy and Administration, the OECD Development Centre, the African Tax Administration Forum and the African Union Commission, with the technical support of the African Development Bank, the World Customs Organisation and the *Centre de rencontres et d'études des dirigeants des administrations fiscales*. It presents detailed, internationally comparable data on both tax and non-tax revenues for eight African countries. Its approach is based on the well-established methodology of the OECD Revenue Statistics database, which has become an essential reference source for OECD member countries and many more. Comparisons are also made with the average for OECD economies and for the economies featured in *Revenue Statistics in Latin America and the Caribbean*.

The term "taxes" in this publication is confined to "compulsory, unrequited payments to general government". As outlined in the Interpretative Guide to the Revenue Statistics, taxes are "unrequited" in the sense that benefits provided by government to taxpayers are not normally in proportion to their payments. The OECD methodology classifies a tax according to its base: income, profits and capital gains (classified under heading 1000), payroll (heading 3000), property (heading 4000), goods and services (heading 5000) and other taxes (heading 6000). Compulsory social security contributions paid to general government are treated as taxes, and classified under heading 2000. Much greater detail on the tax concept and the classification of taxes are set out in the OECD Interpretative Guide in Annex A.

The term "non-tax revenue" includes all general government revenue that does not meet the OECD definition of taxation. Revenues that do not constitute taxation include grants (e.g. foreign aid), returns on government market investments, rents on the extraction of resources from public lands, sales of government-produced goods and services, and the collection of fines and forfeits. More details on these types of revenues, as well as an explanation of the use of cash or accrual basis of reporting in the publication are available in Annex B.

The report provides an overview of the main revenue trends in the eight participating African countries. It examines changes in the level of both tax and non-tax revenues as a percentage of GDP and the structure of these revenue streams between 1990 and 2014.

Avant-propos

Les *Statistiques des recettes publiques en Afrique* est une publication conjointe du Centre de politique et d'administrations fiscales de l'OCDE, du Centre de développement de l'OCDE, du Forum africain sur l'administration fiscale (ATAF), et de la Commission de l'Union africaine, avec l'assistance technique de la Banque africaine de développement, de l'Organisation mondiale des douanes et du Centre de rencontres et d'études des dirigeants des administrations fiscales. Elle fournit des données détaillées et comparables à l'échelle internationale, sur les recettes fiscales et non fiscales de huit pays africains. La démarche suivie repose sur la méthodologie bien établie des statistiques des recettes publiques de l'OCDE, devenue une source de référence essentielle pour les pays membres de l'Organisation et au-delà. Des comparaisons sont également effectuées avec la moyenne des économies de l'OCDE et avec celle des économies couvertes par les *Statistiques des recettes publiques en Amérique latine et dans les Caraïbes.*

Dans cette publication, le terme « impôts » fait référence uniquement aux « versements obligatoires sans contrepartie aux administrations publiques ». Comme indiqué dans le Guide d'interprétation de l'OCDE, les impôts sont « sans contrepartie » en ce sens que les prestations fournies par les administrations aux contribuables ne sont pas normalement proportionnelles à leurs paiements. La méthodologie de l'OCDE consiste à classer les impôts en fonction de l'assiette : le revenu, les bénéfices et les gains en capital (rubrique 1000), les salaires et la main-d'œuvre (rubrique 3000), le patrimoine (rubrique 4000), les biens et services (rubrique 5000) et autres impôts (rubrique 6000). Les cotisations obligatoires de sécurité sociale versées aux administrations publiques sont aussi traitées comme des impôts et classées dans la rubrique 2000. Des informations plus détaillées sur la notion d'impôt et sur la classification des impôts sont présentées dans le Guide d'interprétation figurant à l'annexe A.

Le terme « recettes non fiscales » recouvre toutes les recettes des administrations publiques qui ne sont pas considérées comme des « impôts » selon la définition de l'OCDE. Les recettes non fiscales incluent les dons (l'aide exterieure), les rendements d'investissements publics, les rentes tirées de l'extraction de ressources naturelles, les produits de la vente de biens et de services produits par le secteur public, les amendes et confiscations. On trouvera, à l'annexe B, des informations plus détaillées sur ces catégories de recettes ainsi qu'une explication de l'utilisation de l'enregistrement sur la base des décaissements ou des droits constatés.

Le présent rapport offre une vue d'ensemble des grandes tendances des recettes dans les huit pays d'Afrique couverts par la publication. Les auteurs examinent les variations des niveaux des recettes fiscales et non fiscales en pourcentage du PIB ainsi que leurs composantes entre 1990 et 2014.

Acknowledgements

Revenue Statistics in Africa has been jointly produced by the Organisation for Economic Co-operation and Development (OECD) Centre for Tax Policy and Administration (CTP), the OECD Development Centre (DEV), the African Tax Administration Forum (ATAF) and the African Union Commission (AUC), with the technical support of the African Development Bank (AfDB), the World Customs Organisation (WCO) and the *Centre de rencontres et d'études des dirigeants des administrations fiscales* (CREDAF). The staff from these organisations with responsibility for producing the publication were: Emmanuelle Modica, Maurice Nettley, and Jocelyn Pierre of CTP under the supervision of the Director Pascal Saint-Amans, Deputy Director Grace Perez-Navarro and the Head of the Tax Policy and Tax Statistics Division David Bradbury; Sébastien Markley and Luis Padilla of DEV under the supervision of the Director Mario Pezzini and the Head of the Africa Unit Henri-Bernard Solignac-Lecomte; Nara Monkam, Director of Research at ATAF; Policy Officer Patrick Ndzana Olomo and Acting Head of Statistics Division/MDGs Team Coordinator Dossina Yeo at AUC under the Director of Economic Affairs Dr. René N'guettia Kouassi; Statistician Koua Louis Kouakou at AfDB under the Division Manager of Economic and Social Statistics Beejaye Kokil; Technical Officer Thomas Cantens at WCO under the direction of Head of Research and Strategies Unit Robert Ireland; Secretary General Didier Cornillet of CREDAF. Elizabeth Nash and Delphine Grandrieux at DEV ensured the production of the publication in both paper and electronic forms.

The authors would like to thank their colleagues working in national entities with whom they have consulted regularly. These institutions include the finance ministries and national tax agencies of Cameroon, Côte d'Ivoire, Mauritius, Morocco, Rwanda, Senegal, South Africa, and Tunisia. They also wish to give their appreciation to the Government of Tunisia for the secondments of Rihab Ben Challadia and Raja el Haj Khalifa at CTP, and to DEV and CTP colleagues for commenting on drafts and providing technical assistance.

Finally, the partners would like to thank the European Commission, the AUC and Moroccan authorities that hosted and funded the technical workshops in Addis Ababa, Ethiopia (November 2014) and Rabat, Morocco (February 2015).

Remerciements

La publication des *Statistiques des recettes publiques en Afrique* a été produite conjointement par le Centre de politique et d'administration fiscales (CPAF) de l'Organisation de coopération et de développement économiques (OCDE), le Centre de développement de l'OCDE (DEV), le Forum africain sur l'administration fiscale (ATAF), et la Commission de l'Union africaine (CUA), avec l'assistance technique de la Banque africaine de développement (BAfD), l'Organisation mondiale des douanes (OMD) et le Centre de rencontres et d'études des dirigeants des administrations fiscales (CREDAF). Les agents de ces organisations auxquels la responsabilité de la publication a été confiée sont : Emmanuelle Modica, Maurice Nettley et Jocelyn Pierre, sous la supervision de Pascal Saint-Amans, Directeur du CPAF, Grace Perez-Navarro, Directrice adjointe du CPAF, et David Bradbury, Chef de la Division des politiques fiscales et statistiques ; Sébastien Markley et Luis Padilla, sous la supervision de Mario Pezzini, Directeur du Centre de développement, et Henri-Bernard Solignac-Lecomte, Chef de l'Unité Afrique ; Nara Monkam, Directrice de recherche à l'ATAF ; Patrick Ndzana Olomo, Chargé de mission, et Dossina Yeo, Chef par intérim de la Division statistique du Département des affaires économiques et Coordinateur de l'équipe ODD de la CUA, sous la supervision de René N'guettia Kouassi, Directeur des affaires économiques ; Koua Louis Kouakou, statisticien à la BAfD, sous la supervision de Beejaye Kokil, Directeur de la Division des statistiques économiques et sociales ; Thomas Cantens, Administrateur technique à l'OMD, sous la direction de Robert Ireland, Chef de l'Unité Recherche et stratégies ; Didier Cornillet, Secrétaire général du CREDAF. Elizabeth Nash et Delphine Grandrieux ont assuré la parution de la publication sous forme imprimée et électronique.

Les auteurs tiennent à remercier leurs collègues des institutions nationales avec lesquels des consultations ont eu lieu régulièrement. Ces institutions sont notamment les ministères des Finances et les administrations fiscales nationales de l'Afrique du Sud, du Cameroun, de la Côte d'Ivoire, du Maroc, de Maurice, du Rwanda, du Sénégal et de la Tunisie. Ils souhaitent également exprimer leur reconnaissance au gouvernement tunisien qui a accepté que Rihab Ben Challadia et Raja el Haj Khalifa soient envoyées en détachement auprès du CPAF, ainsi qu'aux agents du CPAF et de DEV pour leurs commentaires sur les projets de texte et leur assistance technique.

Enfin, les partenaires ont à cœur de remercier la Commission européenne, la CUA et les autorités marocaines d'avoir accueilli et financé les ateliers techniques organisés à Addis Abeba (Éthiopie) en novembre 2014 et Rabat (Maroc) en février 2015.

Table of contents

Table des matières

LIST OF TABLES/LISTE DE TABLEAUX

Chapter 1/Chapitre 1

Tax and non-tax revenue trends 1990-2014/Tendances des recettes fiscales et non fiscales, 1990-2014

Chapter 3/Chapitre 3

Tax levels and tax structures, 1990-2014/Niveaux et structures des impôts, 1990-2014

Chapter 4/Chapitre 4

Country tables 1990-2014 - Tax revenues/Tableaux par pays, 1990-2014 - Recettes fiscales

Chapter 5/Chapitre 5

Non-tax revenue: Levels and structures, 1997-2014

Recettes non fiscales: Niveaux et structures des impôts, 1990-2014

Non-tax revenue: Country tables 1990-2014

Recettes non fiscales : Tableaux par pays, 1990-2014

LIST OF FIGURES/LISTE DE GRAPHIQUES

Chapter 1/Chapitre 1

Tax and non-tax revenue trends 1990-2014/Tendances des recettes fiscales et non fiscales, 1990-2014

Chapter 3/Chapitre 3
Tax levels and tax structures, 1990-2014/Niveaux et structures des impôts, 1990-2014

Editorial

Revenue Statistics in Africa is a significant step towards enhancing the comparability, quality and accessibility of public revenue data on the continent. Co-operation and transparency guided the compilation of this first edition. African and international organisations, working in partnership, invited African governments to share their statistics and collaborated closely with officials from tax administrations and statistics offices. A time-tested methodology and process reclassified the figures, leading to a new set of detailed, country-specific data for wide public dissemination.

Through this process, African tax and customs policy makers made their own data comparable with that collected for OECD member countries and an increasing number of other countries in Asia, Latin America and the Caribbean. This has resulted in an improved information base for undertaking policy analysis, measuring or forecasting the impacts of reforms, devising common policies within regional economic communities, identifying best practices, engaging in international dialogue and peer learning, and reporting to citizens and their elected representatives. By integrating international standards in the reporting of a country's public revenues, this collaborative process reinforces the capacity of national administrations to develop further their own data methodologies and tax policy analysis.

This work contributes to the financial chapter of the African Charter on Statistics in rolling out the Strategy for the Harmonisation of Statistics in Africa. It also supports the first ten-year implementation plan (2014-2023) of the African Union's Agenda 2063, which aims to "develop and implement frameworks for Policies on Revenue Statistics and Fiscal Inclusiveness for Africa." At the global level, our work will support the Sustainable Development Goals' target 17.1 to "improve domestic capacity for tax and other revenue collection" and target 17.19 to "support statistical capacity building in developing countries."

Congratulations to all eight participating countries for volunteering to be in this first edition, and we thank all of them for the quality of the technical exchanges. They have paved the way for other countries to join, and we look forward to broadening coverage in future annual editions. We also extend our gratitude to our partners – the African Development Bank, the World Customs Organisation and the *Centre de rencontres et d'études des dirigeants des administrations fiscales* – for providing unlimited access to their expertise and networks.

We hope that this publication is a valuable new resource for tax policy makers and analysts and we trust that this and future editions will contribute to making the revenue statistics of African countries a public good available to all.

René N'Guietta Kouassi
Director
Department of Economic Affairs,
African Union Commission

Mario Pezzini
Director
OECD Development Centre

Pascal Saint-Amans
Director
OECD Centre for Tax Administration and Policy

Logan Wort
Executive Secretary
African Tax Administration Forum

Éditorial

La publication des *Statistiques des recettes publiques en Afrique* marque une étape importante dans l'amélioration de la comparabilité, de la qualité et de l'accessibilité des données relatives aux recettes publiques sur le continent africain. La coopération et la transparence sont les principes fondateurs de cette première édition. Des organisations africaines et internationales œuvrant en partenariat ont invité les États africains à partager leurs statistiques et collaboré étroitement avec les responsables des administrations fiscales et des offices statistiques de ces pays. Les chiffres ont été reclassés à l'aide d'une méthodologie et d'une procédure bien établies, ce qui a permis de créer une nouvelle base de données destinée à être largement diffusée, contenant des données détaillées par pays.

Grâce à ce processus, les hauts responsables des services fiscaux et douaniers de plusieurs pays d'Afrique ont permis que leurs données deviennent comparables avec celles recueillies par les pays membres de l'OCDE et un nombre croissant de pays d'Asie, d'Amérique latine et des Caraïbes. Leurs efforts ont ainsi permis d'améliorer le vivier d'informations indispensable pour analyser les politiques publiques, mesurer ou prévoir les effets de réformes, concevoir des politiques communes au sein des Communautés économiques régionales, identifier les bonnes pratiques, nourrir le dialogue et l'apprentissage par les pairs au niveau international, et rendre compte aux citoyens et à leurs élus. Ce processus collaboratif aide les administrations nationales à intégrer les normes internationales dans leur production de données sur les recettes publiques et renforce ainsi leur capacité à affiner leurs propres méthodologies et leurs propres analyses.

Les travaux menés contribuent au chapitre financier de la Charte africaine de la statistique élaborée dans le cadre du déploiement de la Stratégie pour l'harmonisation des statistiques en Afrique. Ils viennent en outre appuyer le premier plan de mise en œuvre sur dix ans (2014-2023) de l'Agenda 2063 de l'Union africaine visant à définir et appliquer des cadres dans lesquels devront s'inscrire les politiques conduites en Afrique en matière de statistiques sur les recettes publiques et d'intégration budgétaire. Au niveau mondial, ils serviront l'Objectif de développement durable 17.1, « renforcer les capacités nationales de collecte de l'impôt et d'autres recettes » et l'objectif 17.19, « appuyer le renforcement des capacités statistiques des pays en développement ».

Nous tenons à féliciter les huit pays qui ont participé à la première édition des *Statistiques des recettes publiques en Afrique* et à les remercier pour la qualité des échanges techniques entre nos équipes. Ils ouvrent la voie à d'autres, et nous espérons voir s'élargir la couverture des prochaines parutions annuelles. Nous souhaitons également exprimer toute notre gratitude à nos partenaires – la Banque africaine de développement, l'Organisation mondiale des douanes et le Centre de rencontres et d'études des dirigeants des administrations fiscales – de nous avoir offert un accès illimité à leurs compétences et à leurs réseaux.

Nous sommes confiants que cette publication constituera une nouvelle ressource précieuse pour les responsables et analystes des politiques fiscales et que cette édition comme les suivantes contribuera à faire des statistiques sur les recettes publiques des pays d'Afrique un bien public accessible à tous.

René N'Guietta Kouassi
Directeur, Département des affaires économiques, Commission de l'Union africaine

Mario Pezzini
Directeur, Centre de développement de l'OCDE

Pascal Saint-Amans
Directeur, Centre de politique et d'administration fiscales de l'OCDE

Logan Wort
Secrétaire exécutif, Forum africain sur l'administration fiscale

Executive summary

This first edition of *Revenue Statistics in Africa* presents internationally comparable revenue data for eight African countries. These countries account for almost a quarter of Africa's total GDP. The administrations of Cameroon, Côte d'Ivoire, Mauritius, Morocco, Rwanda, Senegal, South Africa, and Tunisia contributed to the project and worked closely with the OECD, the African Tax Administration Forum and the African Union Commission, with the technical support of the African Development Bank, the World Customs Organisation and the *Centre de rencontres et d'études des dirigeants des administrations fiscales*.

These new data respond to a demand from governments, citizens and international policy makers for reliable and comparable tax data to inform fiscal policy and provide a basis for planning, implementing and evaluating reforms. The importance of these data is not only their wide public availability, but that they can be used for comparisons with other countries in Africa and the rest of the world, thereby encouraging policy dialogue and greater political co-operation.

Taxes are "compulsory, unrequited payments to the general government", according to the OECD definition and non-tax revenues refer simply to all revenues paid to general government that are not defined as taxes. Non-tax revenue includes grants (e.g. foreign aid), returns on government market investments, rents on the extraction of resources from public lands, sales of government-produced goods and services, and the collection of fines and forfeits.

Based on their 2014 tax to GDP ratios, the countries included in this publication fall into two groups. One group has tax to GDP ratios ranging from 28% to 31% of GDP (Morocco, South Africa and Tunisia) and the other group has ratios ranging between 16% and 20% (Cameroon, Côte d'Ivoire, Mauritius, Rwanda and Senegal). All these countries have ratios below the OECD average of 34.4%.

Countries with higher levels of GDP per capita are more likely to have higher tax to GDP ratios. This relationship is generally reflected in the revenue data presented in this publication for the participating African countries.

Tax to GDP ratios have been increasing in these African countries as they have undertaken reforms and modernised their tax systems and administrations. Increases of around 4.5 percentage points or more occurred in Morocco, Rwanda, South Africa and Tunisia between 2000 and 2014. There were upward movements for the other four countries at a lower rate. This compared with a corresponding increase of four percentage points in the Latin American and the Caribbean (LAC) country average, while there was no significant change in the OECD average across the same time period.

This growth has mainly been driven by increases in taxes on incomes and profits as a percentage of GDP and more specifically by increases in corporate income tax revenue. The latter are a relatively important source of revenue in these African countries. In most of the African countries, the share of corporate income tax to total tax revenues is higher than the OECD average of 8.5% and in Cameroon and South Africa it is close to double that level.

There were also substantial increases in VAT revenues (which represent another important source of revenue for African countries) and social security contributions in some countries. On the other hand, specific consumption taxes (mainly excises and import duties) have shown either substantial decreases or only relatively small increases since African countries have increasingly opened their economies and reduced trade barriers as part of the global trade liberalisation.

Some of the countries benefit from substantial non-tax revenues paid to general government that supplement their tax receipts. The main sources of non-tax revenues are grants (predominantly foreign aid) and property income. These income streams tend to be much more volatile than those from tax revenues as observed over time.

Key findings

Tax ratios

- The tax to GDP ratios in 2014 for the eight African countries range from 16.1% to 31.3% (the OECD average is at 34.4%).
- Tunisia has the highest tax to GDP ratio at 31.3%, followed by Morocco (28.5%).
- Cameroon and Rwanda have the lowest tax to GDP ratios at 16.1% followed by Côte d'Ivoire (17.8%). All three countries have a relatively low GDP per capita.
- All eight countries saw increasing tax to GDP ratios between 2000 and 2014. The size of these increases ranged from 0.8 percentage points in Mauritius to 6.7 percentage points in Tunisia. Morocco, Rwanda and South Africa had increases of around 5-6 percentage points.
- Increases in taxes on income and profits (mainly corporate income tax) were the biggest drivers of the overall tax to GDP ratio growth between 2000 and 2014 across the eight African countries. In that period, corporate income tax revenue increased by more than 2 percentage points of GDP in the three countries displaying the highest tax ratios. The OECD average for these taxes decreased by 0.4 percentage points throughout the same period.

Tax structure

- The share of taxes on incomes and profits in total tax revenues is highest in South Africa at 51.2 % in 2014. The share of personal income taxes in South Africa is higher than the OECD average whereas it is lower for the other participating African countries.
- The shares of corporate income tax revenue to total tax revenues are significantly higher than the OECD average of 8.5% in six of the African countries – ranging between 13% and 18%.
- Consumption taxes yield the largest share of the total tax revenue – over 55% – in Cameroon, Côte d'Ivoire, Mauritius, Rwanda and Senegal. In each of these countries, except for Côte d'Ivoire, more than half of this category of revenue is generated by VAT.
- Tunisia and Morocco display a tax mix with revenues more evenly distributed between categories compared with the other countries: around 30% of tax revenues from taxes on incomes and profits; around 35-40% from consumption taxes; and 20-28% from social security contributions. The share of social security contributions to total tax revenue is far smaller in the six Sub-Saharan countries, ranging from 1.5% in South Africa to 11.3% in Côte d'Ivoire.

Non-tax revenues

- The total non-tax revenues collected as a percentage of GDP in 2014 range from 0.6% of GDP in South Africa to 9.5% of GDP in Rwanda.
- The countries for which the biggest source of non-tax revenue is grants are Rwanda (7.8% of GDP), Senegal (3.3% of GDP) and Côte d'Ivoire (1.8% of GDP).
- Cameroon obtains 3.6% of its GDP from resource rents, which is over 85% of its total non-tax revenue.

Résumé

Cette première édition des *Statistiques des recettes publiques en Afrique* présente des données comparables à l'échelle internationale relatives aux recettes publiques de huit pays africains qui représentent près du quart du PIB total de l'Afrique. Les administrations de l'Afrique du Sud, du Cameroun, de la Côte d'Ivoire, du Maroc, de Maurice, du Rwanda, du Sénégal et de la Tunisie ont participé à ce projet en coopération étroite avec l'OCDE, le Forum africain sur l'administration fiscale (ATAF) et la Commission de l'Union africaine, avec l'assistance technique de la Banque africaine de développement, l'Organisation mondiale des douanes et le Centre de rencontres et d'études des dirigeants des administrations fiscales (CREDAF).

Ces nouvelles données répondent aux attentes des administrations, des citoyens et des décideurs en matière de politiques publiques, qui doivent disposer de données fiscales à la fois fiables et comparables tant pour orienter les décisions budgétaires que pour programmer, mettre en œuvre et évaluer les programmes de réforme. Ces données revêtent un intérêt particulier, non seulement parce qu'elles sont publiques et facilement consultables, mais aussi parce qu'elles permettent aux pays concernés d'établir des comparaisons avec d'autres pays d'Afrique ou du reste du monde, ouvrant ainsi la voie à des échanges constructifs et à une coopération renforcée entre les responsables des politiques publiques.

Les taxes sont des "versements obligatoires sans contrepartie aux administrations publiques", selon la définition de l'OCDE tandis que les recettes non fiscales se réfèrent simplement à toutes les recettes versées aux administrations publiques qui ne sont pas définies comme des taxes. Les recettes non fiscales incluent les dons (l'aide étrangère), les retours sur investissements, les rentes tirées de l'extraction de ressources naturelles, les produits de la vente de biens et de services par le secteur public, les amendes et confiscations.

En 2014, les huit pays étudiés se divisent en deux grands groupes en ce qui concerne les ratios de recettes fiscales rapportées au PIB. Le premier groupe correspond aux pays dont les niveaux d'imposition sont compris entre 28 % et 31 % du PIB (Afrique du Sud, Maroc et Tunisie), et le second réunit ceux dont les ratios s'échelonnent de 16 % à 20 % (Cameroun, Côte d'Ivoire, Maurice, Rwanda et Sénégal). Le taux de pression fiscale de chacun des pays est en dessous du niveau moyen de la zone OCDE, qui s'élève à 34.4 %.

Les pays dans lesquels le PIB par habitant est le plus élevé sont les plus susceptibles de présenter également un taux de pression fiscale plus important. Cette relation se vérifie en règle générale pour les pays africains étudiés dans la présente publication.

Les recettes fiscales exprimées en pourcentage du PIB ont progressé dans ces pays africains sous l'effet de l'adoption de réformes et de la modernisation des systèmes fiscaux et des administrations concernées. Sur la période 2000-14, la hausse a ainsi avoisiné ou dépassé les 4.5 points de pourcentage en Afrique du Sud, au Maroc, au Rwanda et en Tunisie. Les quatre autres pays étudiés ont également bénéficié d'évolutions à la hausse, toutefois plus modérées. À titre de comparaison, pendant la même période, le taux de pression fiscale progressait de quatre points de pourcentage dans les pays de la région

Amérique latine et Caraïbes, tandis qu'il restait globalement inchangé dans la zone de l'OCDE.

Cette augmentation s'explique principalement par la hausse des recettes provenant des impôts sur le revenu et les bénéfices en pourcentage du PIB, et plus précisément par la progression des recettes fiscales liées aux impôts sur les bénéfices des sociétés. Cette dernière catégorie représente une fraction assez significative des recettes fiscales totales dans les pays d'Afrique de cette publication. En effet, la part des recettes issues de l'impôt sur les bénéfices des sociétés dans le total des recettes fiscales dépasse la valeur moyenne de 8.5 % relevée dans l'OCDE, elle est même proche du double en Afrique du Sud et au Cameroun.

Les recettes liées à la TVA (autre composante importante des recettes publiques dans les pays africains) ont également connu une augmentation marquée, au même titre que les cotisations de sécurité sociale dans certains pays. À l'inverse, les recettes issues des impôts spécifiques sur la consommation (principalement les droits d'accise et les droits à l'importation) ont enregistré soit de fortes baisses, soit des hausses relativement limitées, dans la mesure où les pays africains ont ouvert davantage leurs économies et limité les barrières aux échanges commerciaux dans un contexte de libéralisation du commerce mondial.

Dans certains pays, les recettes non fiscales perçues par les administrations publiques qui complètent les recettes fiscales, atteignent des montants importants. Ces recettes non fiscales sont générées pour l'essentiel par les dons (l'aide étrangère) et par les revenus de la propriété. L'analyse de ces flux de recettes montre qu'ils présentent fréquemment une volatilité bien plus forte que les recettes fiscales.

Principales conclusions

Niveau d'imposition

- En 2014, les ratios des recettes fiscales rapportées au PIB des huit pays étudiés s'échelonnent de 16.1 % à 31.3 % (la moyenne de l'OCDE s'élève à 34.4 %).
- La Tunisie présente le niveau d'imposition le plus élevé en 2014, avec 31.3 %, suivie du Maroc (28.5 %).
- En 2014, les trois pays avec les niveaux d'imposition en pourcentage du PIB les plus bas sont le Cameroun, le Rwanda (16.1 % dans les deux cas), et la Côte d'Ivoire (17.8 %). Ces trois pays disposent d'un PIB par habitant relativement faible.
- Entre 2000 et 2014, les huit pays couverts par l'étude ont enregistré une augmentation des niveaux d'imposition. Chaque pays a enregistré une progression différente, selon des hausses qui s'échelonnent de 0.8 point à Maurice à 6.7 points de pourcentage en Tunisie. En Afrique du Sud, au Maroc et au Rwanda, la hausse a avoisiné 5-6 points de pourcentage.
- Entre 2000 et 2014, les augmentations des recettes tirées des impôts sur le revenu et les bénéfices (qui ont concerné avant tout l'impôt sur les bénéfices) ont constitué le principal facteur de l'augmentation globale des ratios des recettes fiscales rapportées au PIB. Durant cette période, les recettes issues de l'impôt sur les bénéfices ont augmenté de plus de 2 points de pourcentage du PIB dans les pays présentant les niveaux d'imposition les plus élevés. Dans le même temps, ces recettes reculaient en moyenne de 0.4 point dans la zone OCDE.

Structure fiscale

- En 2014, la contribution des impôts sur le revenu et les bénéfices aux recettes fiscales totales est la plus élevée en Afrique du Sud, avec 51.2 %. Concernant l'apport relatif de l'impôt sur le revenu des personnes physiques, l'Afrique du Sud se place au dessus de la moyenne de l'OCDE, alors que les autres pays étudiés se situent en dessous.
- Dans six des huit pays couverts par la publication, les recettes issues de l'impôt sur les sociétés en proportion des recettes fiscales totales dépassent largement la valeur moyenne de 8.5 % relevée dans l'OCDE – les ratios étant compris entre 13 % et 18 %.
- Les impôts sur la consommation ont représenté la majeure partie des recettes fiscales totales – à savoir, plus de 55 % – au Cameroun, en Côte d'Ivoire, à Maurice, au Rwanda et au Sénégal. Dans ces pays, à l'exception de la Côte d'Ivoire, la TVA génère plus de la moitié du montant de cette catégorie.
- En Tunisie et au Maroc, les contributions relatives des différentes catégories de recettes fiscales présentent des différences moins accusées que dans les autres pays : les impôts sur le revenu et les bénéfices génèrent environ 30 % des recettes fiscales ; les impôts sur la consommation contribuent au total à hauteur de 35 % à 40 % environ ; les cotisations de sécurité sociale représentent environ 20 % à 28 %. La part des cotisations de sécurité sociale rapportée au total des recettes fiscales est beaucoup plus modeste dans les six pays d'Afrique subsaharienne, allant de 1.5 % en Afrique du Sud à 11.3 % en Côte d'Ivoire.

Recettes non fiscales

- Pour l'année 2014, les recettes non fiscales totales exprimées en pourcentage du PIB s'échelonnaient de 0.6 % en Afrique du Sud à 9.5 % au Rwanda.
- Les pays dans lesquels les aides constituent la première composante des recettes non fiscales sont le Rwanda (avec 7.8 % du PIB), le Sénégal (3.3 %) et la Côte d'Ivoire (1.8 %).
- Au Cameroun, les recettes tirées des ressources naturelles atteignent 3.6 % du PIB et dépassent 85 % du total des recettes non fiscales.

CHAPTER 1

TAX AND NON-TAX REVENUE TRENDS 1990-2014

CHAPITRE 1

TENDANCES DES RECETTES FISCALES ET NON FISCALES, 1990-2014

TAX AND NON-TAX REVENUE TRENDS 1990-2014

Introduction

The purpose of this annual *Revenue Statistics in Africa* (RSIA) publication is to present internationally comparative statistics on both tax and non-tax revenues for eight African countries (Cameroon, Côte d'Ivoire, Mauritius, Morocco, Rwanda, Senegal, South Africa, and Tunisia). It includes internationally comparable data for all levels of government on tax and non-tax revenues as percentage of GDP as well as the structures of these revenues. It also describes some of the factors behind their evolution in the years 1990-2014.

Cross-country comparisons of revenue data for the RSIA countries are presented here, along with comparisons with OECD and Latin America and Caribbean (LAC) averages. Because countries from all three groups follow the OECD classification of taxes, their revenue data can be compared both at an overall level, and within individual revenue categories. The eight RSIA countries do not form a basis on which to calculate a meaningful average for African countries, but averages for both LAC and the OECD are published and are included here for reference. There are, however, no corresponding OECD or LAC figures for non-tax revenues. The revenue statistics for RSIA and LAC countries are presented on a cash basis, while the majority of the data for OECD countries are on an accrual basis.

Taxes are "compulsory, unrequited payments to general government", according to the OECD definition and non-tax revenues refer simply to all revenues paid to general government that are not defined as taxes. Taxes are unrequited in the sense that benefits provided by government to taxpayers are not normally in proportion to their payments. Revenue, which includes that from taxes, is an increase in net worth resulting from a transaction.

It is important to compile and analyse non-tax revenues for African countries in order to produce a more balanced picture of their finances. The OECD produces other publications on revenue statistics, including *Revenue Statistics*, *Revenue Statistics in Latin America and the Caribbean*, and *Revenue Statistics in Asian Countries*, but *Revenue Statistics in Africa* is the only one to include data on non-tax revenue.

The data for the eight RSIA countries are presented in a standardised framework based upon the OECD classification of taxes. In the OECD classification, taxes are classified by the tax base:

- Income, profits and capital gains (heading 1000)
- Payroll and workforce (heading 3000)
- Property (heading 4000)
- Goods and services (heading 5000)
- Other (heading 6000)
- Compulsory social contributions paid to general government are treated as taxes (heading 2000)

Non-tax revenues fall under the following general categories:

- Grants
- Property income
- Sales of goods and services
- Fines, penalties and forfeits
- Other non-tax revenue

Much greater detail on the tax classification is set out in the OECD Interpretative Guide at Annex A of this Report. More information about data on non-tax revenues and the way they are compiled and classified in this report is included at Annex B.

TAX REVENUES

1.1. Tax ratios

The tax to GDP ratio is a key indicator of a country's current collection of funds through taxation to finance public goods and services and to invest in the infrastructure. Raising revenue through taxes is an important factor in ensuring a country's economic emergence (OECD, 2014). The appropriate level of taxation gives governments the capacity to make the investments necessary to achieve growth. It also enables developing countries to become less dependent on international aid and grants, allowing them to develop their political autonomy and build effective and accountable states (OECD, 2014). Many emerging countries recognise that tax revenues provide more predictable revenue streams than the often uncertain and more volatile non-tax revenues from oil and commodities that some countries have come to rely on.

Tax ratios in 2014

In 2014, the tax revenues as a ratio of GDP for the eight RSIA countries (Cameroon, Côte d'Ivoire, Mauritius, Morocco, Rwanda, Senegal, South Africa, and Tunisia) were lower than the OECD average of 34.4% (see Table 1.1). For five of the eight countries, the measure was also lower than the Latin American and Caribbean (LAC[1]) average of 21.7%.

Table 1.1. **Total tax revenue as percentage of GDP**

	1997	2000	2005	2008	2009	2010	2011	2012	2013	2014
Cameroon	10.9	12.8	13.5	14.8	15.0	14.0	14.8	15.3	15.8	16.1
Côte d'Ivoire[1]	17.1	15.4	15.7	18.4	17.2	16.8	16.1	18.4	18.3	17.8
Mauritius	17.8	19.1	18.8	19.4	20.1	19.8	19.6	20.2	19.9	20.0
Morocco[2]	..	23.6	24.8	30.5	27.3	27.1	28.7	29.7	28.5	28.5
Rwanda[3]	10.3	10.2	12.1	13.5	12.9	13.3	14.0	14.6	15.6	16.1
Senegal[4,5]	15.3	16.8	19.3	19.0	18.9	19.8	19.9	19.5	19.2	20.1
South Africa	22.6	22.4	25.2	27.7	25.7	25.6	26.3	26.7	27.3	27.8
Tunisia[3]	..	24.6	24.4	27.0	26.9	27.3	29.2	29.2	30.1	31.3
LAC average[6,7]	16.9	17.2	19.0	20.6	19.9	20.0	20.8	21.4	21.5	21.7
OECD average[7]	33.9	34.2	33.9	33.6	32.7	32.8	33.3	33.8	34.2	34.4

Notes: The figures exclude local government tax revenues for Cameroon, Côte d'Ivoire, Rwanda, Senegal and Tunisia as the data are not available. Local and provincial data prior to 2003 are not available for South Africa.

1. The tax to GDP ratio contains rents and royalties and sales of public goods and services normally classified as non-tax revenues in the OECD classification. These are considered tax revenues in Côte d'Ivoire. The inclusion of these elements represents 0.5% of GDP in 2014, and between 0.1% and 1.5% in the period from 2000 to 2014.
2. Estimated figures for years 2013 and 2014 and prior to 2005.
3. Rwanda and Tunisia do not include social security contributions in their tax to GDP ratio as neither country classifies them as taxes. They are included as tax revenue in this publication.
4. Estimated figures for years prior to 2006.
5. Figures include social security contributions from the Institution de prévoyance retraite du Sénégal (IPRES) and exclude the data from the Caisse de Sécurité Sociale (CSS) as they are not available.
6. Represents a group of 22 Latin American and Caribbean countries (LAC).
7. Represents the unweighted average for the LAC and OECD countries.

Source: Table 3.1.

StatLink http //dx.doi.org/10.1787/888933344347

The eight countries in this report form two distinct groups with respect to their tax to GDP ratios. The first group (Morocco, South Africa and Tunisia) had tax ratios ranging from around 28% to 31% of GDP in 2014 and those of the second group (Cameroon, Côte D'Ivoire, Mauritius, Rwanda and Senegal) were between 16% and 20%. As shown in Table 1.1 and Figure 1.1, Tunisia had the highest tax to GDP ratio in 2014 with 31.3% followed by Morocco (28.5%). The higher ratios for these countries featured a relatively high level of social security contributions, exceeding 5% of GDP, compared with 2% of GDP or less in the other African countries in this publication. The three countries with the lowest tax to GDP ratios in 2014 were Cameroon, Côte d'Ivoire and Rwanda. The tax to GDP ratios in Cameroon and Rwanda were both 16.1%, below the West African Economic and Monetary Union (WAEMU) convergence criterion of 17%. Côte d'ivoire's was slightly higher than this criterion, at 17.8%.

Evolution of tax ratios since 2000

All the African countries featured here have experienced an increase in tax revenues as percentage of GDP between 2000 and 2014 while over this period the OECD average has remained relatively stable. Both Figure 1.1 and Table 1.1 show how tax revenues as percentage of GDP have mostly been rising, aside from some temporary interruptions in the years following the global financial crisis of 2007-08. Each one of these countries saw their tax to GDP ratios increase by more than 3 percentage points between 2000 and 2014, except for Côte d'Ivoire and Mauritius which experienced more modest increases (2.4 percentage points and 0.8 percentage points respectively) (Figure 1.2). Increases in tax to GDP ratios of over 4.5 percentage points occurred in Morocco, Rwanda, South Africa[2] and Tunisia. In contrast, the OECD average tax ratio was only 0.2 percentage points higher than its level in 2000, while the average LAC country has seen its tax to GDP ratios grow by more than 4 percentage points.

Figure 1.1. **Total tax revenue as percentage of GDP, 1990-2014**

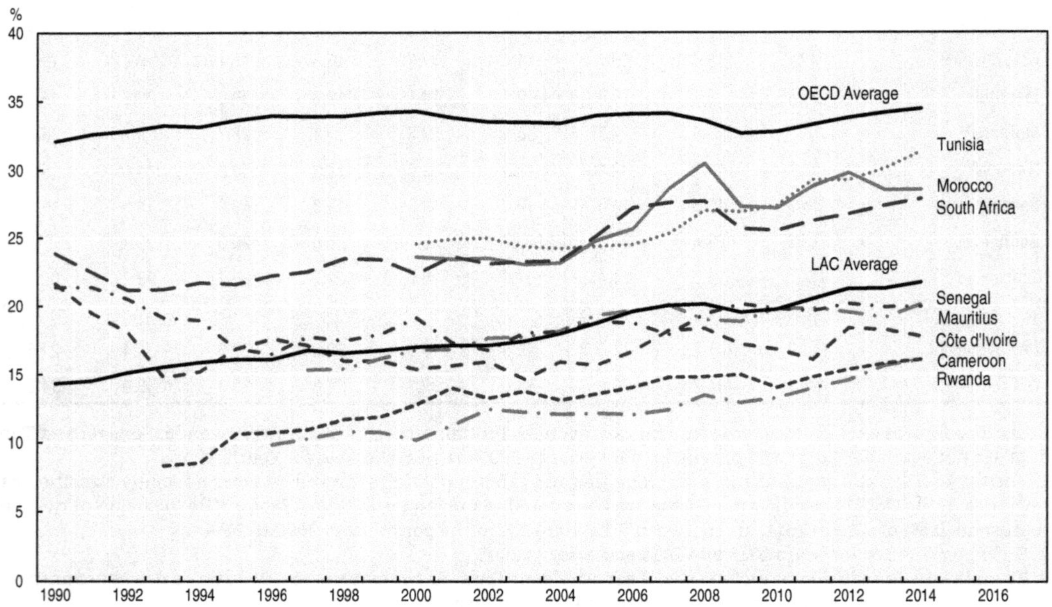

Note: The LAC and OECD averages are unweighted. The LAC average represents a group of 22 Latin American and Caribbean countries.

Source: Table 3.1.

StatLink http://dx.doi.org/10.1787/888933343626

The growth in tax revenues occurred during a period in which African countries adopted major structural reforms in their tax administrations and undertook significant changes to their tax systems. For many countries, the reforms were aimed at strengthening tax administrations and included the establishment of taxpayer offices that specialise in large and/or medium-sized companies and the modernisation of the structure of tax administrations. Initiatives such as self-assessment systems, taxpayer segmentation and modern risk management were introduced (Kloeden, 2011; Fossat and

Bua, 2013). Some countries undertook tax reforms to expand their tax base, eliminating certain exemptions and simplifying the tax legislation. As the *African Economic Outlook 2010* explains, "many countries have successfully enlarged their tax bases. Tunisia's has increased its own at a yearly average of 3.5%, South Africa has more than doubled it, ..., while Côte d'Ivoire has rebuilt its tax base after civil war" (AfDB/OECD/UNECA, 2010). These changes were often accompanied by programmes put in place to educate taxpayers about tax systems and to improve taxpayer services.

Figure 1.2. **Change in tax to GDP ratios between 2000 and 2014**

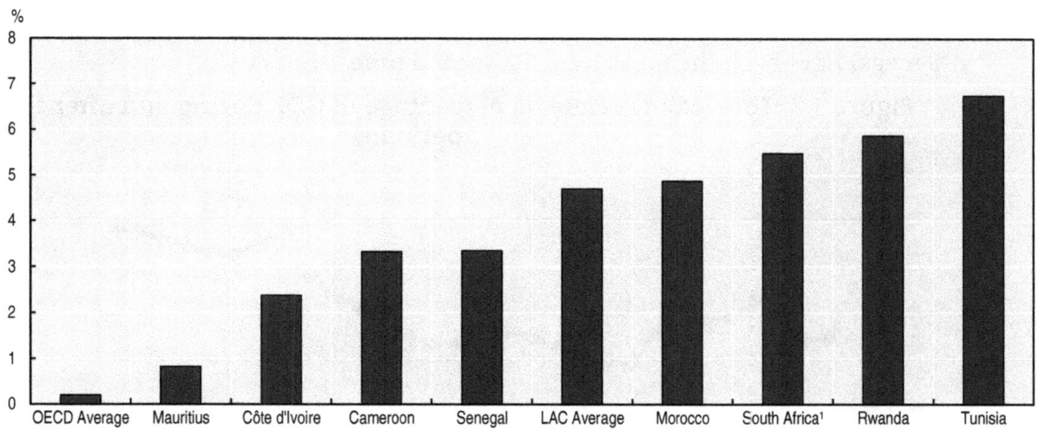

1. South Africa tax to GDP ratio includes provincial and local taxes for 2014 but not for 2000, when those figures were not available. This accounts for 1.3 percentage points of the difference between the two years.

Source: Table 3.1.

StatLink http://dx.doi.org/10.1787/888933343636

Box 1.1. **Tax system and tax administration reforms in Rwanda**

Tax collection in Rwanda has become more effective since 2000, due to significant fiscal and administrative reforms together with other initiatives (AfDB, 2010).The objective of the government was to expand the tax base by registering informal businesses and simplifying compliance processes. Rwanda established the Small and Medium Taxpayers Office in 2006 and implemented the block management system (designed to manage the tax affairs of Small and Medium Taxpayers by segmenting the businesses into manageable blocks). These reforms have had a major impact in increasing tax revenues. The compliance rate of large taxpayers has improved significantly to reach 97%. This is an important development considering that these taxpayers contribute around 75% of total domestic tax revenues. Other reforms contributing to the increase of tax revenues included the introduction of a VAT in 2001 and new income tax laws and tax rates in 2005 and in 2006. The compliance enforcement system was also strengthened, enabling better identification of risks and more systematic tax inspections and penalties. In addition, the tax authorities strengthened their internal processes, leading to efficiency improvements and a reduction in the cost of collection. Other non-fiscal measures also had an impact on tax revenues such as the increase of expenditure on priority agriculture and infrastructure projects.

The financial crisis in the years 2007 to 2010 marked a turning point in the evolution of tax to GDP ratios, although the tax to GDP ratios for the African countries followed very different trajectories. The accompanying global economic downturn coincided with a marked drop in tax to GDP ratios in OECD countries. Considering that these countries represent 63% of GDP[3], it would not be surprising if the forces that drove down tax to GDP ratios in those countries also had an impact on African government revenues as well. Indeed, every RSIA country saw falls in their tax to GDP ratios in the first years of the global financial crisis. These amounted to 0.5 percentage points or less in Mauritius, Rwanda and Tunisia and of 0.9 percentage points or more in all the remaining countries. Figure 1.3 shows the evolution of the tax to GDP ratio in each RSIA country from the pre-crisis peak to 2014. Côte d'Ivoire[4], Morocco and South Africa saw the biggest changes in the level of tax revenues. They registered falls of more than 2 percentage points of GDP during the period of the crisis. Other countries show less substantial declines ranging from 0.1 percentage points in Tunisia to 1.2 percentage points in Senegal. All the countries saw a recovery in the tax to GDP ratios, though Morocco, Côte d'Ivoire, and Senegal have seen the measure fall a second time.

Figure 1.3. **Total tax revenue as percentage of GDP during and after the crisis period**

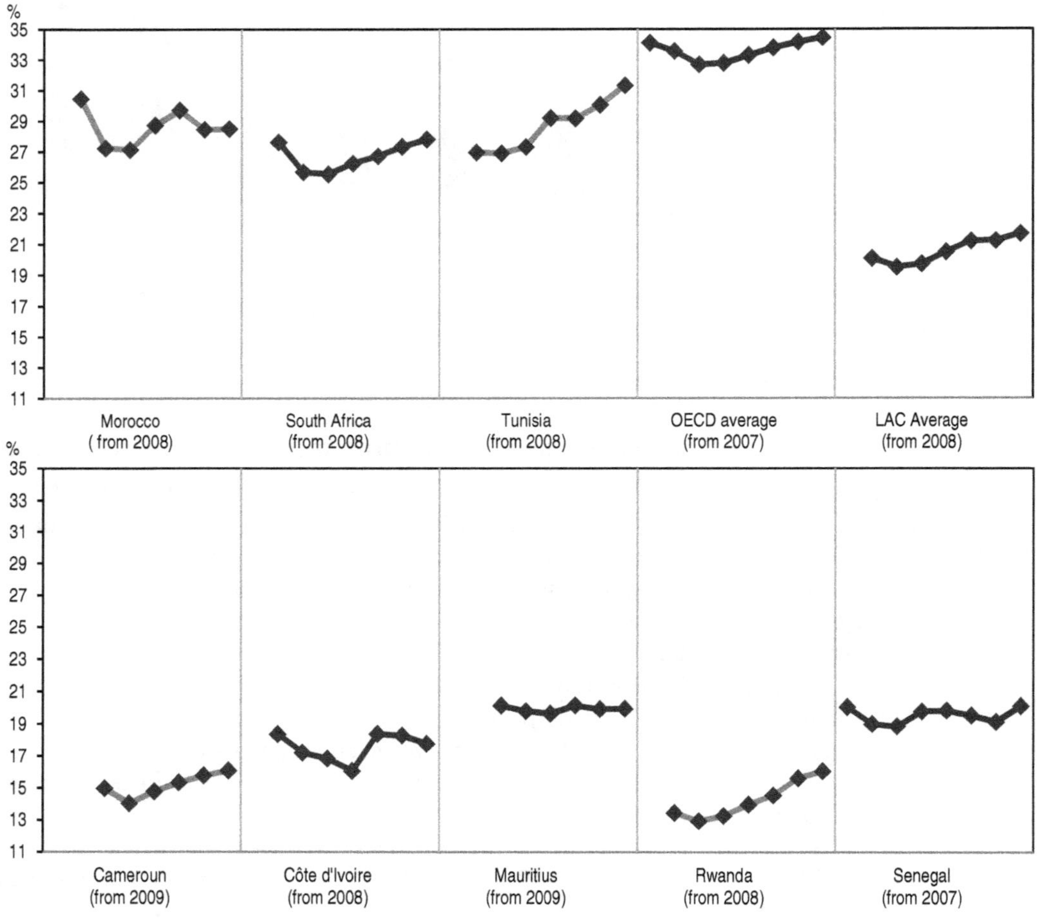

Source: Table 3.1.

StatLink http://dx.doi.org/10.1787/888933343643

After the crisis the tax to GDP ratios increased for all eight countries and by 2014, five of the eight countries had recovered their pre-crisis levels. Cameroon, Rwanda and Tunisia showed strong recoveries after the crisis and their tax to GDP ratios in 2014 are now well above their pre-crisis level. More particularly Rwanda and Tunisia have shown quite substantial increases after the crisis from their lowest point (3.1 percentage points and 4.4 percentage points respectively). It is important to note that Tunisia did not have to recover from as large a fall as the other RSIA countries. The Tunisian authorities have been able to mitigate the impact of the financial crisis thanks to cautious macroeconomic policies and a set of reforms (IMF, 2010). Senegal and South Africa have just reached their pre-crisis level in 2014. On the other hand the Moroccan tax to GDP ratio increased rapidly following its downturn, but its growth has slowed in the last two years.

Factors influencing tax to GDP ratios

The RSIA countries, on average, are much poorer than the OECD countries. The GDP per capita – a measure of the average amount of income in the country per person – for the average OECD country in 2014 was over twice as high as the RSIA country with the highest GDP per capita and 22 times higher than that for Rwanda. In addition the average LAC country had a higher GDP-per-capita than every RSIA country, except for Mauritius and South Africa.

Tax to GDP ratios tend to be higher in high-income countries. Figure 1.4 shows a scatterplot of the tax to GDP ratio and GDP per-capita of countries in the OECD compared with LAC countries and African countries. The OECD countries are to the top right hand of the figure, representing countries that are comparatively wealthier and also collect higher tax revenues from their populations. Countries in Africa are to the lower left quarter of the figure, representing countries that are both poorer and less able to mobilise domestic resources. With lower GDP per capita, Cameroon, Côte d'Ivoire, Rwanda and Senegal are well within the main cluster of African countries, while Mauritius, Morocco, South Africa, and Tunisia are more to the middle of the cluster of Latin American countries (i.e. well above and to the right of the African average). This means that although these countries are poor compared to OECD countries, they are wealthier than African countries in general. Mauritius is well to the left of the other three high-income RSIA countries having higher GDP per capita and yet lower tax to GDP ratios.

Figure 1.4. **GDP per capita in PPP dollars and tax to GDP ratios for countries in Africa, Latin America and the Caribbean and the OECD, 2014**

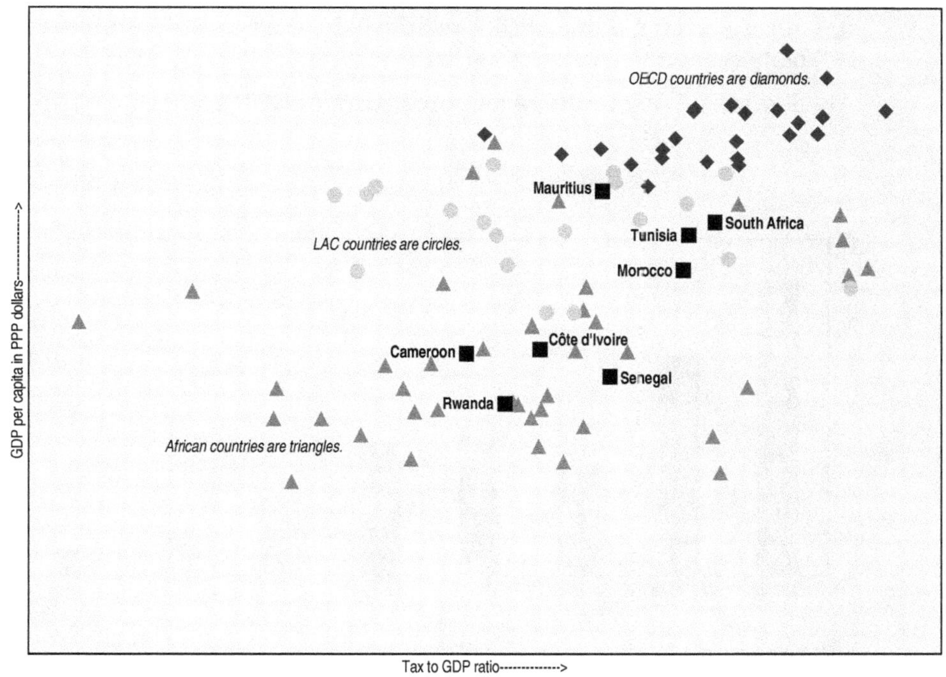

Note: The y axis is on a logarithmic scale. The tax to GDP ratio does not include social security contributions in this dataset.

Source: *World Economic Outlook*, October 2015, International Monetary Fund.

StatLink http://dx.doi.org/10.1787/888933343659

Tax to GDP ratios are influenced by many factors both domestic and international, and both economic and structural. Economic factors that can have influence on tax to GDP ratios include the importance of agriculture in the economy, whether the country is considered "resource-rich", openness to trade and the extent of the informal economy. In addition, foreign governments can have an impact on tax to GDP ratios by setting competitive tax rates or engaging in aggressive tax practices such as transfer pricing. All of these factors can undermine a country's ability to raise revenues (Mascagnani, Moore and McCluskey, 2014). The structure of tax collection also plays a role: the power of tax administrations, the levels of corruption and tax morale (or willingness of people to pay taxes) are all strongly linked to the level of tax revenue (OECD, 2014). Finally, geographic location and historical factors can also have an influence on tax to GDP ratios: for example landlocked countries are less able to impose taxes on goods and services at the port of entry than coastal countries.

The three RSIA countries with the lowest tax to GDP ratios are also those with the highest share of agriculture in their economies (over 20%) as shown in Figure 1.5. A higher percentage of GDP attributed to agriculture has generally been found to be associated with lower tax to GDP ratios (Addison and Levin, 2012) and this is consistent with the data for the eight African countries. One reason for this is thought to be that there is less taxation of the agricultural sector in Africa due to a high level of informality and a low level of monetisation. Payments are often made in cash or in kind by African farmers as opposed to through banks and almost none of them keep good business accounts (AfDB/OECD/UNECA, 2010). In addition to low tax compliance, the agricultural sector in Africa has many tax exemptions. For example, in Rwanda, agricultural enterprises are exempt from paying VAT on agricultural inputs and products. There are also VAT exemptions in Côte d'Ivoire and Senegal. The agricultural sector is large enough in many African countries for these factors to have an impact on the government's financial affairs, whereas in the OECD countries, the share of agriculture in GDP is no more than 2% on average. However, it should be noted that Mauritius, an island nation, has a small agricultural sector, along with a relatively low tax to GDP ratio and Morocco has over 15% of its economy devoted to agriculture with a relatively large tax to GDP ratio (28.5%).

Figure 1.5. **Agriculture as percentage of GDP and tax to GDP ratios, 2014**

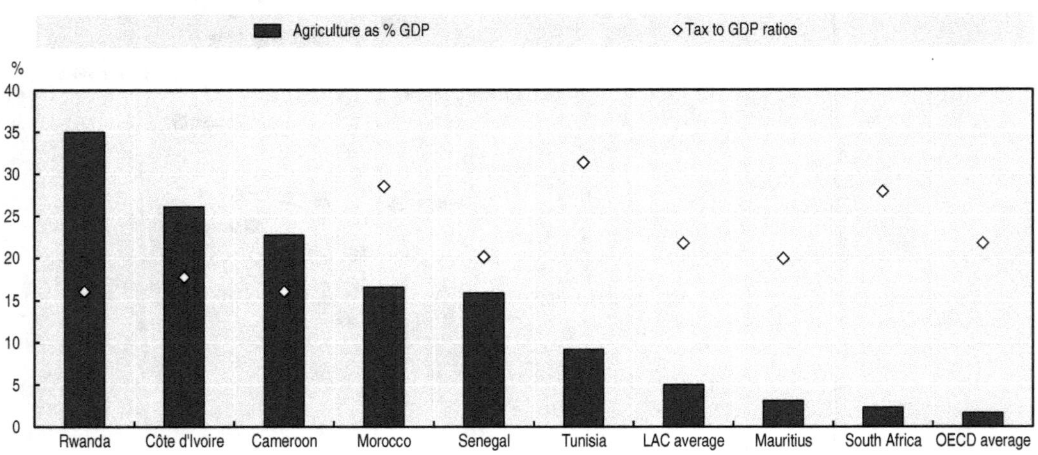

Note: The indicator "Agriculture as % of GDP" includes forestry, hunting, and fishing, as well as cultivation of crops and livestock production. The LAC average includes developing Latin American and Caribbean countries only.

Source: Table 1.1; AfDB/OECD/UNECA (2015), *African Economic Outlook 2015: Regional Development and Spatial Inclusion*; World Bank data.

StatLink http://dx.doi.org/10.1787/888933343666

Côte d'Ivoire and Cameroon receive substantial revenues from oil exports and exhibit low tax ratios due to narrow tax bases. Cameroon and Côte d'Ivoire have been classified by the International Monetary Fund as "resource-rich"[5] countries. Their main exports of mineral resources are petroleum (AfDB/OECD/UNDP, 2015). Countries with more revenues from natural resources tend to resort less to more politically demanding forms of taxation such as income taxes (AfDB/OECD/UNECA, 2010) and to have relatively narrow tax bases. In Cameroon and Côte d'Ivoire, small pools of taxpayers bear the vast majority of the tax burden. For example, in Cameroon, 55% of all corporate taxes in 2013 were paid by only ten companies (IMF, 2014b). The size of the informal sector in Côte d'Ivoire is estimated at 90% (UNDP, 2013). As a result the tax ratios of both countries are at the lower end of the scale. During the 2000's both these countries put in place various initiatives to address the over-exploitation of the available tax base (AfDB/OECD/UNECA, 2010). Côte d'Ivoire has reduced preferential measures to priority sectors and those sectors particularly affected by the 2002 crisis. Cameroon's government put in place programs in 2009 and 2010 to bring in new taxpayers from the informal sector. In recent years both countries have continued to strengthen tax policy and administrations with a view to expanding their tax base (IMF, 2013; IMF, 2014b).

Although Mauritius among RSIA countries most resembles an OECD nation in terms of its income and economic profile, its tax to GDP ratio of 20% remains low with respect to OECD countries as a consequence of fiscal decisions. Mauritius has some of the lowest tax rates in Africa (Sokeechand and Hussen, 2013). There are single rates of 15% for corporate tax, income tax and VAT. In contrast, the corporate tax rate is above 25% in the other seven RSIA countries and above 30% in Cameroon, Morocco, Rwanda and Senegal. Global companies residing in Mauritius can also claim a tax credit of 80% against Mauritian tax, thus resulting in an effective tax rate of 3%. The tax credit for foreign companies is either far less generous or non-existent in the remaining seven RSIA countries. Finally, Mauritius does not tax capital gains or dividends, and corporations are exempt from a number of taxes such as real property tax, stamp duties and transfer tax (Sokeechand and Hussen, 2013).

The impact of key taxes on overall tax ratios

The growth of tax revenue since 2000 has mainly been driven by increases in taxes on income and profits whereas these taxes have declined for the OECD countries on average. As shown in Table 1.2, seven countries showed increases in taxes on income and profits as percentage of GDP ranging from 1.4 percentage points in Senegal to 4.4 percentage points in Tunisia. Côte d'Ivoire was the only country that registered a small decline. The average amount of revenue collected by OECD countries through these taxes has also declined by 0.5 percentage points since 2000. However, the average level of taxes on income and profits as percentage of GDP in OECD countries remained well above the ratio of every RSIA country except for South Africa which had a ratio of 14.3%. In 2014, revenues from taxes on income and profits represented less than 6.0% of GDP in Cameroon, Côte d'Ivoire, Mauritius, Rwanda and Senegal, and between 8% and 10% in Morocco and Tunisia compared to nearly 12% for OECD countries (Figure 1.6).

Table 1.2. **Changes in tax to GDP ratios by type of tax between 2000 and 2014**

	Taxes on income and profits (1000)	Social security contributions (2000)	Taxes on payroll (3000)	Taxes on property (4000)	Taxes on goods and services (5000)	Other taxes (6000)	Total tax revenue
Cameroon	1.5	0.0	0.3	-0.1	1.4	0.2	3.3
Côte d'Ivoire	-0.1	0.7	0.0	0.0	1.7	0.0	2.4
Mauritius	2.3	0.0	-0.1	-0.1	-1.4	0.0	0.8
Morocco	2.5	2.0	0.0	0.6	-0.4	0.1	4.9
Rwanda	3.3	0.5	0.0	0.0	2.0	0.0	5.9
Senegal	1.4	0.3	0.0	0.2	1.4	0.0	3.3
South Africa	1.6	0.4	0.3	1.0	2.5	-0.3	5.5
Tunisia	4.4	3.4	0.0	0.1	-1.4	0.3	6.7

Note: South Africa tax to GDP ratio includes provincial and local taxes for 2014 but not for 2000, when those figures were not available. This accounts for 1.3 percentage points of the difference between the two years.

StatLink http://dx.doi.org/10.1787/888933344359

Figure 1.6. **Taxes on income and profits as percentage of GDP, 2014**

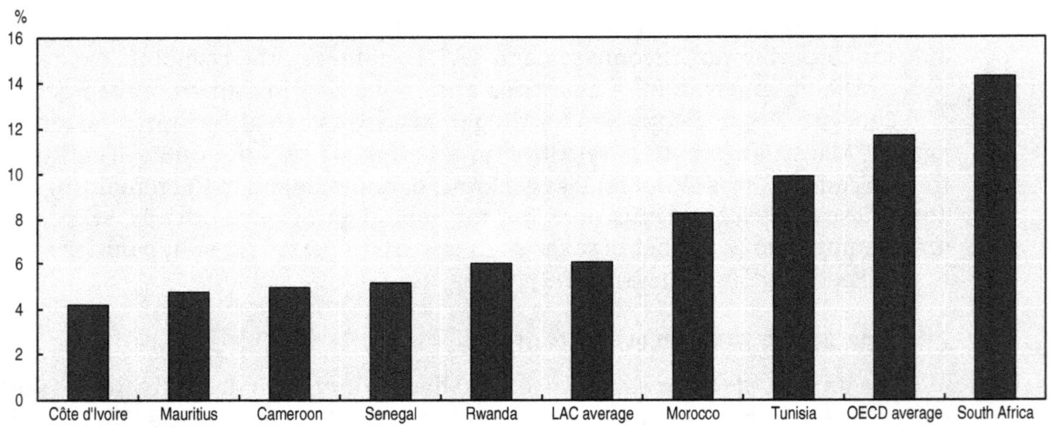

Source: Table 3.2.

StatLink http://dx.doi.org/10.1787/888933343678

In the seven countries that experienced growth in tax revenues from income and profits, the growth of corporate tax revenues outweighed that of personal income taxes except in Rwanda and Senegal. All these countries have shown increases in corporate tax revenues between 2000 and 2014 (Table 1.3). The three countries with higher overall tax ratios also experienced increases in the corporate income tax to GDP ratio of more than 2 percentage points during the period. On the other hand, the personal income tax to GDP ratio increased in all of the countries except in Cameroon and South Africa. In most countries, the magnitude of the increases for corporate income tax was much larger than that for personal income tax. However the reverse was observed in Rwanda and Senegal as the personal income tax ratio grew much more strongly (2.6 percentage points and 1.2 percentage points respectively) than that for corporate income tax (0.7 percentage points and 0.2 percentage points).

Table 1.3. **Changes in revenue from taxes on income and profits as percentage of GDP by sub-category between 2000 and 2014**

	Taxes on income and profits (1000)	Taxes on incomes (1100)	Taxes on profits (1200)	Unallocable (1300)
Cameroon	1.5	-0.2	1.1	0.6
Mauritius	2.3	0.5	1.5	0.3
Morocco	2.5	0.2	2.3	0.0
Rwanda	3.3	2.6	0.7	0.0
Senegal	1.4	1.2	0.2	0.0
South Africa	1.6	-0.3	2.3	-0.4
Tunisia	4.4	1.5	2.8	0.0

Note: Data for Cameroon needs to be interpreted with caution given the relatively high proportion of unallocable revenue figures in the total for taxes on income and profits.

StatLink http://dx.doi.org/10.1787/888933344360

Social security contributions were a major component of the increases in tax to GDP ratios in three countries whereas in South Africa, property tax played a greater role. Social security contributions were an important part of the increases in tax to GDP ratios between 2000 and 2014 in Morocco and Tunisia and to a lesser degree in Côte d'Ivoire (Table 1.2). Tunisia registered the biggest increase in social security contributions as percentage of GDP with 3.4 percentage points. This growth was the second ranked contributor to the overall increase in tax to GDP ratio in Tunisia after taxes on income and profits. Property taxes significantly contributed to the increase in tax to GDP ratio in South Africa and to a lesser extent in Morocco. On the other hand, the revenues from payroll taxes and other taxes remained largely unchanged.

The growth between 2000 and 2014 on revenues from taxes on goods and services as percentage of GDP varied greatly across countries. This source of revenue increased in five countries (Cameroon, Côte d'Ivoire, Rwanda, Senegal and South Africa) by 1.4 percentage points or more and decreased in three countries (Mauritius, Morocco and Tunisia). While the increases in revenues from taxes on goods and services as percentage of GDP were lower than that for taxes on income and profits in Cameroon, Rwanda and Senegal, this was not the case in Côte d'Ivoire and South Africa. Increases in the ratio of taxes on goods and services to GDP were the primary factor in the overall increases in the tax ratios in the two latter countries.

Within taxes on goods and services, taxes on general consumption have contributed substantially to the increase in tax revenues for six RSIA countries. As shown in Table 1.4, taxes on general consumption (mainly value-added taxes) as percentage to GDP increased in all RSIA countries. Rwanda experienced the biggest increase since 2000 (3.1 percentage points) as their sales tax was replaced by VAT in 2001. Morocco had an increase of 2.9 percentage points that has largely been attributed to an important VAT reform in 2005. This reform aligned the Moroccan tax system with international best practice by reducing exemptions, broadening their tax base (to cover the retail and service sectors) and reducing the number of tax rates (Cruce, 2011). In addition Mauritius increased VAT rates from 12% to 15% in 2003, which has contributed to the increase in the taxes on general consumption as percentage of GDP.

Table 1.4. **Changes in revenue from taxes on goods and services, taxes on general consumption and taxes on specific consumption as percentage of GDP between 2000 and 2014**

	Taxes on goods and services (5000)	Taxes on general consumption (5110)	Taxes on specific consumption (5120)
Cameroon	1.4	1.2	0.2
Côte d'Ivoire	1.7	0.2	1.4
Mauritius	-1.4	2.0	-3.5
Morocco	-0.4	2.9	-3.3
Rwanda	2.0	3.1	-1.1
Senegal	1.4	0.6	0.8
South Africa	2.5	1.3	1.0
Tunisia	-1.4	0.4	-1.8

StatLink http://dx.doi.org/10.1787/888933344372

Revenues from taxes on specific consumption (mainly excises and import duties) have shown either substantial decreases or relatively small increases as percentage of GDP. Between 2000 and 2014, Mauritius, Morocco, Rwanda and Tunisia registered decreases in revenues from taxes on specific consumption. These were wholly compensated by increases in revenues from taxes on general consumption in Rwanda and partially compensated in the other three countries. On the other hand, Cameroon, Côte d'Ivoire, Senegal and South Africa have shown increases in revenues from taxes on specific consumption as percentage of GDP. The decreases of tax revenues from import duties were partly due to trade liberalisation that took the form of reductions of tariffs and new trade agreements (AfDB/OECD/UNECA, 2010). Trade liberalisation resulted in the decline of import duties and to the near extinction of export taxes as a source of revenue over the past decades. Côte d'Ivoire is a notable exception to these trends. Revenue from export taxes remains a major component in Côte d'Ivoire's budget and import duties as percentage of GDP has actually increased since the year 2000. This is reflected in the relatively large increase of revenues from taxes on specific consumption[6] as percentage of GDP.

Figure 1.7. **Taxes on income and profits as percentage of GDP in countries with lower tax to GDP ratios, 2000-14**

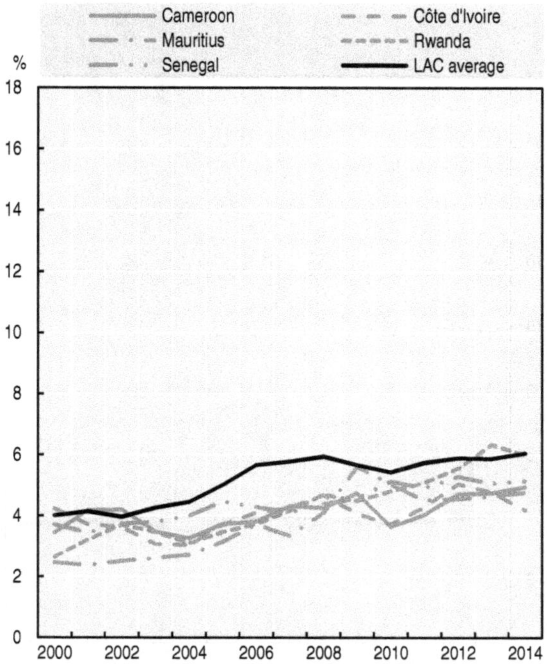

Source: Table 3.4.

StatLink http://dx.doi.org/10.1787/888933343681

Figure 1.8. **Taxes on goods and services as percentage of GDP in countries with lower tax to GDP ratios, 2000-14**

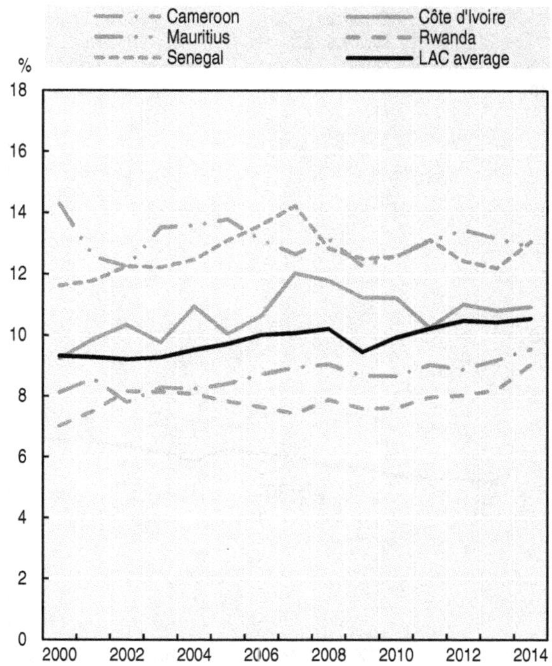

Source: Table 3.4.

StatLink http://dx.doi.org/10.1787/888933343691

Figure 1.9. **Taxes on income and profits as percentage of GDP in countries with higher tax to GDP ratios, 2000-14**

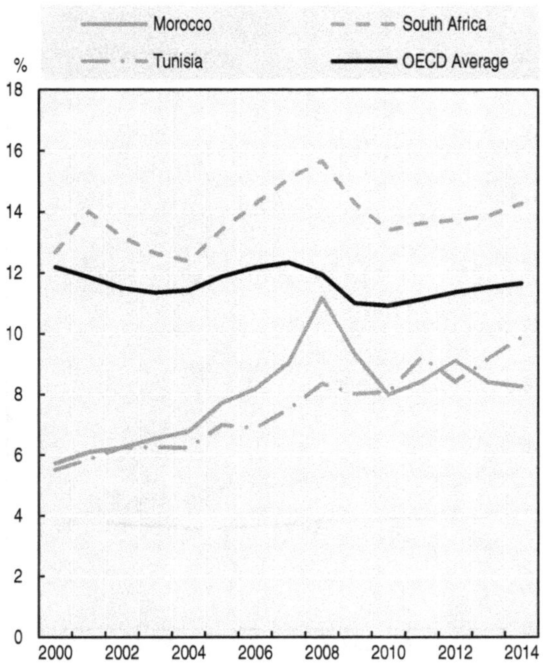

Source: Table 3.4.

StatLink http://dx.doi.org/10.1787/888933343706

Figure 1.10. **Taxes on goods and services as percentage of GDP in countries with higher tax to GDP ratios, 2000-14**

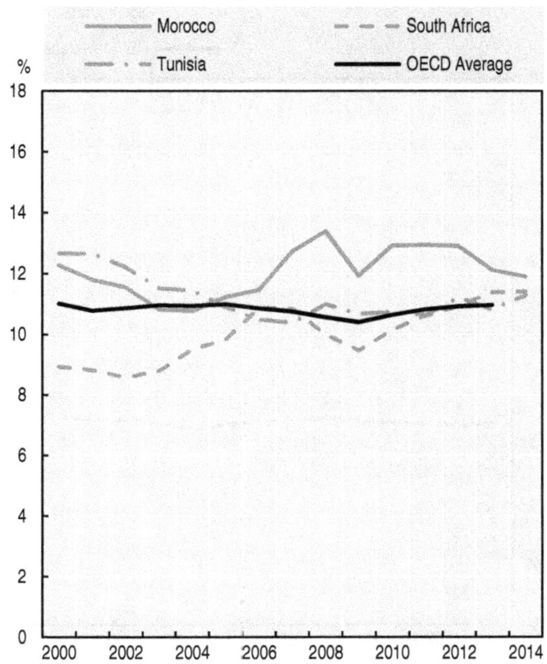

Source: Table 3.4.

StatLink http://dx.doi.org/10.1787/888933343715

Figure 1.11. **Taxes on general consumption as percentage of GDP in countries with lower tax to GDP ratios, 2000-14**

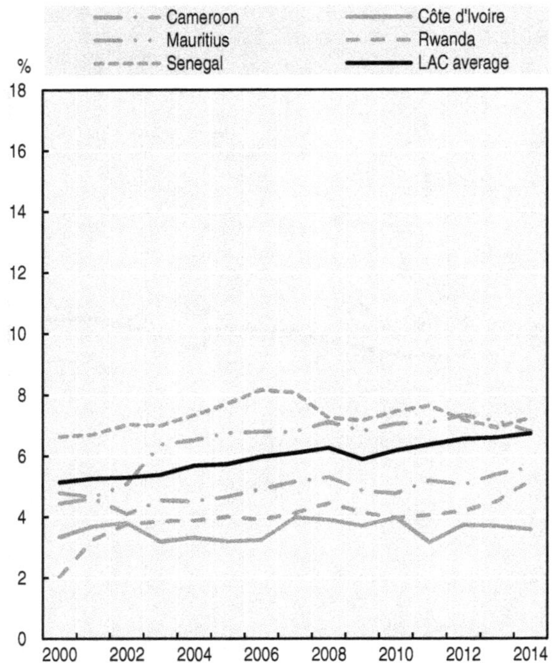

Source: Table 3.12.

StatLink http://dx.doi.org/10.1787/888933343728

Figure 1.12. **Taxes on specific consumption as percentage of GDP in countries with lower tax to GDP ratios, 2000-14**

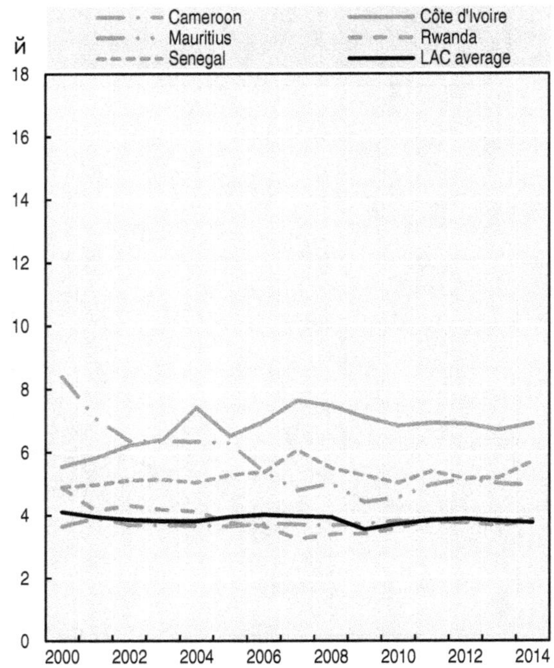

Source: Table 3.12.

StatLink http://dx.doi.org/10.1787/888933343738

Figure 1.13. **Taxes on general consumption as percentage of GDP in countries with higher tax to GDP ratios, 2000-14**

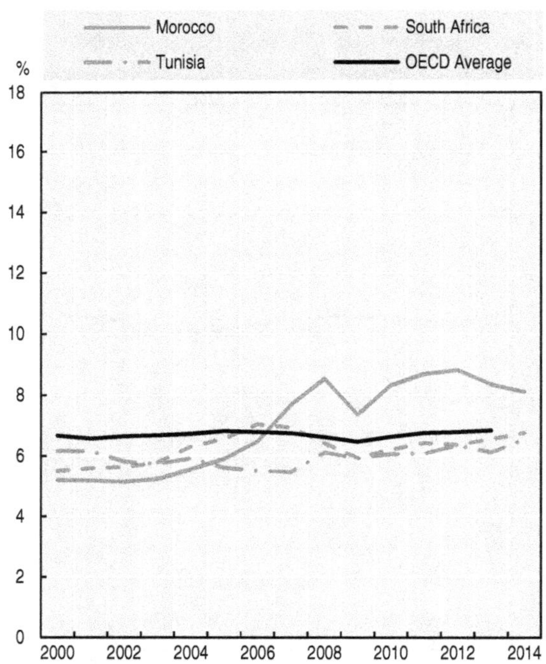

Source: Table 3.12.

StatLink http://dx.doi.org/10.1787/888933343747

Figure 1.14. **Taxes on specific consumption as percentage of GDP in countries with higher tax to GDP ratios, 2000-14**

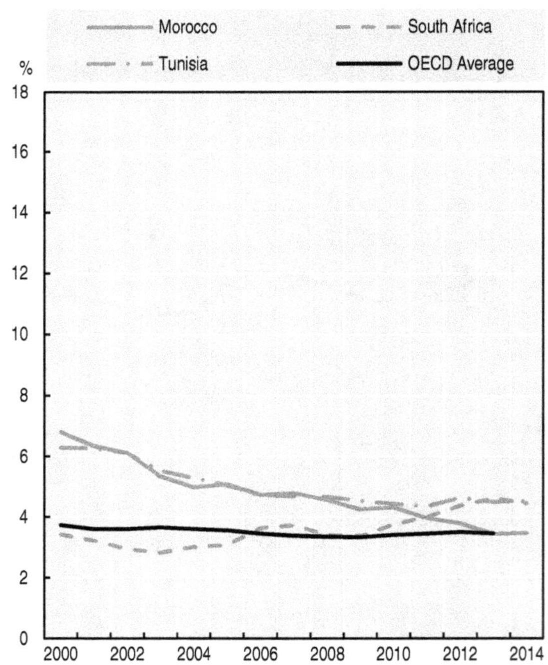

Source: Table 3.12.

StatLink http://dx.doi.org/10.1787/888933343757

1.2. Tax structures

The monitoring of the structures of tax systems in individual countries in addition to level of total revenues provides insights into how governments choose to collect their revenues. It also helps to understand the country's social and political system. There are several types of tax, each with their own strengths and weaknesses in terms of political costs, revenue potential, and their impacts on the economy. Each of these different taxes is also affected differently by economic changes. Tax structures are the result of social and political choices reflecting the balance of economic and political interests in the country.

Analysing the breakdown in tax revenues by sub-categories of taxes can help gain insight into tax policy priorities, the effects of tax reforms or the aftermath of economic events. The OECD tax classification distinguishes between different kinds of taxes in a way that is widely accepted as meaningful by tax policy analysts. By calculating the percentage of total taxation attributed to each category of tax, we can examine the mixture of taxes that makes up each country's tax base and make comparisons across countries and overtime. These spatial and temporal differences will reflect the different factors driving tax policy.

Tax structures in 2014

In 2014, RSIA countries show a great variation in tax structures and can be divided into three groups (Figure 1.15). The first group formed by Tunisia and Morocco, demonstrated a relatively balanced tax mix. South Africa is the only country relying heavily on taxes on income and profits that represented about half of their tax revenues. The third group including countries with lower tax ratios obtained more than half of tax revenues from consumption taxes.

Figure 1.15. **Tax structures, 2014**

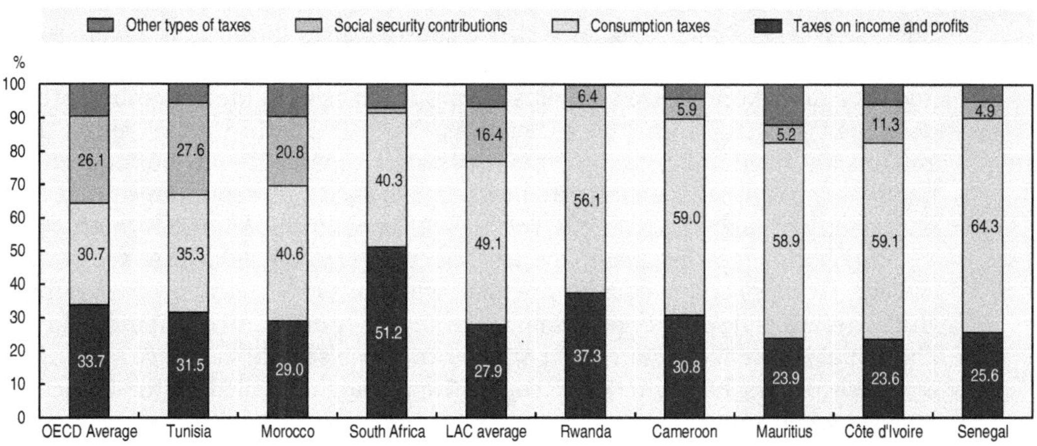

Note: 2013 data for the OECD.
Source: Table 3.2.

StatLink http://dx.doi.org/10.1787/888933343765

Tunisia and Morocco, in comparison with OECD countries in general, displayed a relatively even breakdown of revenues between the main categories of taxes (Figure 1.15). OECD countries tend to have a balanced tax mix, because it is generally believed that more revenues can be raised at lower cost with this type of tax system (AfDB/OECD/UNECA, 2010). Although there is a great deal of variation in tax mixes for OECD countries, on average, the bulk of tax revenue can be divided into three roughly equal parts: one third from taxes on income and profits, one quarter from social security contributions, and about 30% from consumption taxes. Outside these three main categories, other taxes make up about 10% of total tax revenue. The tax mix is similar to this in both Morocco and Tunisia. However in 2014, the share of consumption taxes in their total tax revenues was slightly higher than the OECD average of 30.7%.

South Africa obtains half of its tax revenues from taxes on income and profits, a far greater share than that collected by other countries in this report, and far greater than the average for OECD countries. However this is offset by the fact that it collects very little revenue from social security contributions. Revenue from taxes on income and profits were 30-40% in Cameroon, Morocco, Rwanda and Tunisia and 23-26% in Côte d'Ivoire, Mauritius and Senegal compared with about 34% in the OECD countries on average (Figure 1.15).

In 2014, consumption taxes (mainly VAT, excises and import duties) represented the largest share of the total tax revenue for countries with lower tax ratios. In Côte d'Ivoire, Cameroon, Mauritius, Rwanda and Senegal over 55% of revenues in 2014 came from consumption taxes. These are similar levels to those found in the LAC countries, which on average levy around 50% of their tax revenues from these types of tax. This is typical of emerging countries and poorer countries (Besley and Persson, 2013).

VAT, excises and import duties are often a bigger component of revenue collection in lower-income countries in Africa because they are generally less costly to collect than other types of tax. Import duties are also less costly to administer, since they only require the government to record trade transactions at major border crossings. In contrast, personal income taxes are collected from millions of individuals requiring the government to invest heavily in enforcement and compliance structures (Besley and Persson, 2013). Wealthier countries such as Morocco, South Africa and Tunisia have consumption taxes that represent 35-40% of GDP. In OECD countries, this ratio is around 30% of GDP on average.

The importance of social security contributions varies greatly across the eight RSIA countries.[7] The share of social security contributions in total tax revenue is highest in Tunisia (27.6%) and Morocco (20.8%) and relatively close to the OECD average of 26.1%. Social security contributions are a far smaller proportion of total tax revenue in the remaining countries, ranging from 1.5% in South Africa to 11.3% in Côte d'Ivoire. This variation reflects the diversity of the social security programmes and contributions rates in the RSIA countries that have often inherited their social security programmes from the countries that colonised them. For example, social security contributions in South Africa consist only of contributions to the Unemployment Insurance Fund (UIF). Other social risks, such as old age, sickness and maternity, are dealt with via social assistance programmes – which differ from social security programmes in that they are non-contributory. In South Africa the social insurance system is far smaller than the social assistance system. In contrast, social security schemes in Morocco and Tunisia are modelled on the French system and cover a wider range of risks including old-age, disability, sickness and maternity, work injury (Tunisia), unemployment (Morocco) and family benefits (SSA, 2015).

RSIA countries vary on the relative sizes of corporate income tax and personal income tax revenues. As shown in Figure 1.16, personal income tax revenues are higher than those for corporate income tax in Rwanda, Senegal, South Africa, Tunisia and for the average OECD country. The opposite is the case in Cameroon, Mauritius, Morocco and the average LAC country. The preference for one type of income taxation over the other does not appear to be related to a country's GDP or its overall tax ratio.

Figure 1.16. **Personal income tax and corporate income tax as percentage of total tax revenue, 2014**

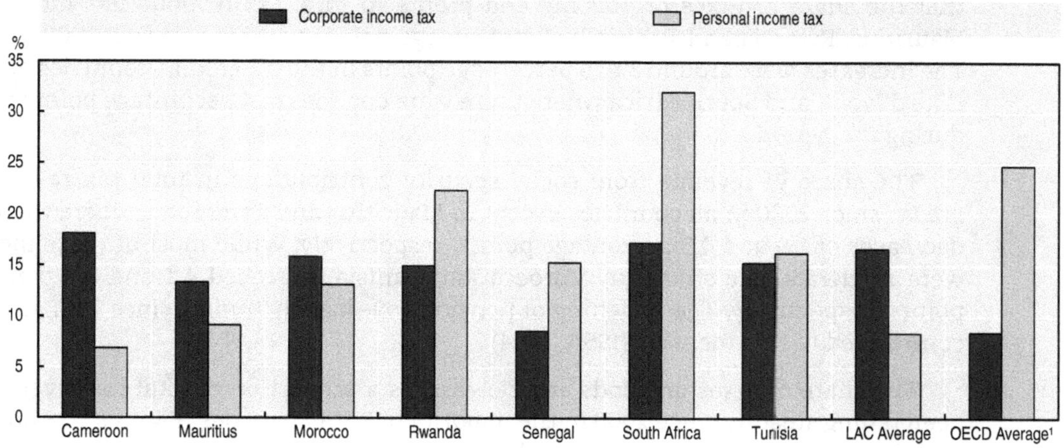

Note: Côte d'Ivoire is not shown here since income tax data cannot be disaggregated.
1. Data for 2013.
Source: Authors' calculations based on Tables 4.1-4.8.

StatLink http://dx.doi.org/10.1787/888933343774

Evolution of the tax structures since 2000

The overall tax structures of the eight RSIA countries have altered since the year 2000. In most of the countries, there has been an increase in the shares of revenues from taxes on income and profits and social security contributions as percentage of total tax revenues and a fall in the share of taxes on goods and services (Table 1.5). The table summarises the magnitude of these changes since 2000 and highlights in bold the exceptions to the general tendencies. These main trends were most clearly seen in Morocco, Rwanda, Senegal and Tunisia and were consistent with that of the LAC countries on average. Cameroon, Mauritius and South Africa followed the same trends to some extent, but each differed in one aspect. Côte d'Ivoire is the only country that has evolved in the opposite direction with an increase in the share of taxes on goods and services and a fall in the share of taxes on income and profits.

Table 1.5. **Changes in tax structure by type of tax between 2000 and 2014 (in percentage points)**

	Taxes on income and profits (1000)	Social Security contributions (2000)	Taxes on payroll (3000)	Taxes on property (4000)	Taxes on goods and services (5000)	Other taxes (6000)
Cameroon	3.7	**-1.9**	1.8	-0.7	-4.2	1.3
Côte d'Ivoire	**-4.0**	2.5	-0.2	-0.1	**1.6**	0.2
Mauritius	11.0	**-0.3**	-0.3	-0.5	-10.1	0.2
Morocco	4.7	4.1	0.0	1.3	-10.2	0.1
Rwanda	11.3	1.4	0.0	-0.2	-12.5	0.0
Senegal	3.4	0.9	-0.1	0.5	-4.3	-0.4
South Africa	**-5.5**	1.5	0.8	3.3	1.1	-1.1
Tunisia	9.1	6.1	-0.3	0.0	-15.5	0.7
LAC average	5.5	1.2	-0.3	0.4	-6.6	-0.2

Note: Numbers in bold are exceptions to the general tendencies in the RSIA countries.

StatLink http://dx.doi.org/10.1787/888933344382

The importance of taxes on income and profits tends to grow as a country develops (Bird and Zolt, 2003). Figure 1.17 shows the clear upwards trend in revenues from taxes on income and profits in the countries with lower tax to GDP ratios. Table 1.5 shows that the share of taxes on income and profits in total tax revenue has increased in Mauritius, Rwanda and Tunisia by 9 percentage points or more between 2000 and 2014. The increases were around 3 to 5 percentage points in the other RSIA countries except in Côte d'Ivoire and South Africa where there were declines of 4 percentage points or more during the period.

The share of revenue from social security contributions in total tax revenue has grown since 2000 in all countries except in Mauritius and Cameroon, where there were decreases of 1.9 and 0.3 percentage points, respectively. While most of these increases were moderate, the shares in Morocco and Tunisia increased 4.1 and 6.1 percentage points, respectively. The widening of pension coverage in Tunisia since 2002 may have contributed to this increase (ISSA, 2014).

The share of taxes on goods and services as a proportion of total tax revenues has been falling steadily since 2000 in the majority of RSIA countries (Figures 1.18 and 1.20), mainly driven by the decline in the share of revenues from specific consumption taxes. As shown in Table 1.6, the share of taxes on goods and services out of total taxation has declined in each RSIA country except in Côte d'Ivoire and South Africa. It decreased by between 10 and 16 percentage points in Mauritius, Morocco, Rwanda and Tunisia. This was wholly driven by declines in the share of specific consumption taxes in Mauritius, Morocco and Rwanda and mainly by this factor in Tunisia. In these four countries falls in the share of specific consumption taxes amounted to between 11 and 24 percentage points. These patterns were also observed in LAC countries where the share of taxes on goods and services declined 7 percentage points and the share of specific consumption taxes fell 8 percentage points.

Table 1.6. **Changes in the share of taxes on goods and services, taxes on general consumption and taxes on specific consumption between 2000 and 2014 (in percentage points)**

	Taxes on goods and services (5000)	Taxes on general consumption (5110)	Taxes on specific consumption (5120)
Cameroon	-4.2	0.1	-4.4
Côte d'Ivoire	1.6	-1.6	2.9
Mauritius	-10.1	9.1	-19.2
Morocco	-10.2	6.4	-16.6
Rwanda	-12.5	12.3	-24.0
Senegal	-4.3	-3.6	-0.9
South Africa	1.1	-0.3	0.7
Tunisia	-15.5	-4.2	-11.2
LAC average	-6.6	0.9	-7.7

StatLink http://dx.doi.org/10.1787/888933344393

The share of general consumption taxes (mainly VAT) has increased in four countries and decreased in four. Mauritius, Rwanda and Morocco have seen strong increases in the share of general consumption taxes as percentage of the total tax revenues since 2000. Rwanda experienced the biggest increase (12.3 percentage points) followed by Mauritius (9.1 percentage points) and Morocco (6.4 percentage points). On the other hand, Côte d'Ivoire, Senegal, South Africa and Tunisia have demonstrated declines in the share of general consumption taxes ranging from 0.3 percentage points in South Africa to 4.2 percentage points in Tunisia.

Figure 1.17. **Taxes on income and profits as percentage of total tax revenue in countries with lower tax to GDP ratios, 2000-14**

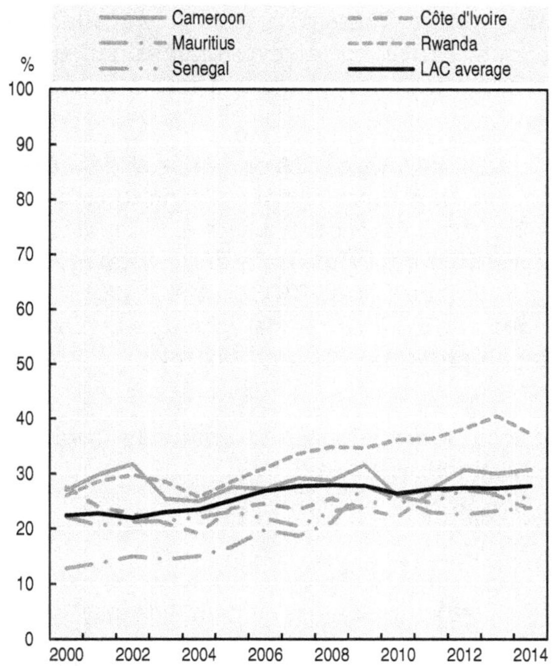

Source: Table 3.3.

StatLink http://dx.doi.org/10.1787/888933343787

Figure 1.18. **Taxes on goods and services as percentage of total tax revenue in countries with lower tax to GDP ratios, 2000-14**

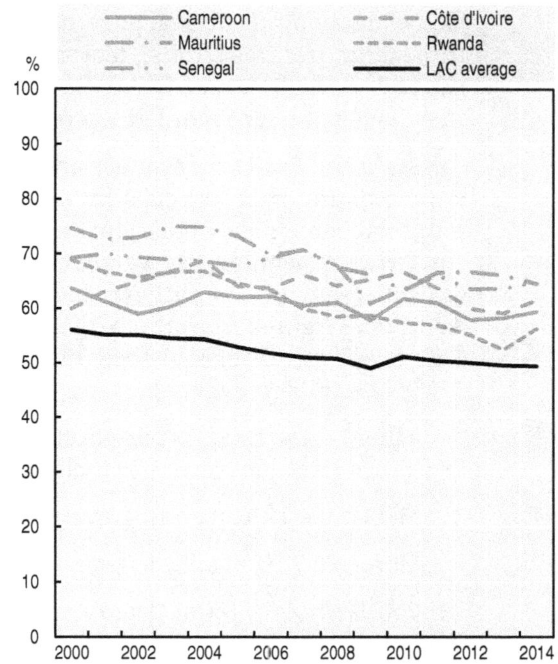

Source: Table 3.3.

StatLink http://dx.doi.org/10.1787/888933343799

Figure 1.19. **Taxes on income and profits as percentage of total tax revenue in countries with higher tax to GDP ratios, 2000-14**

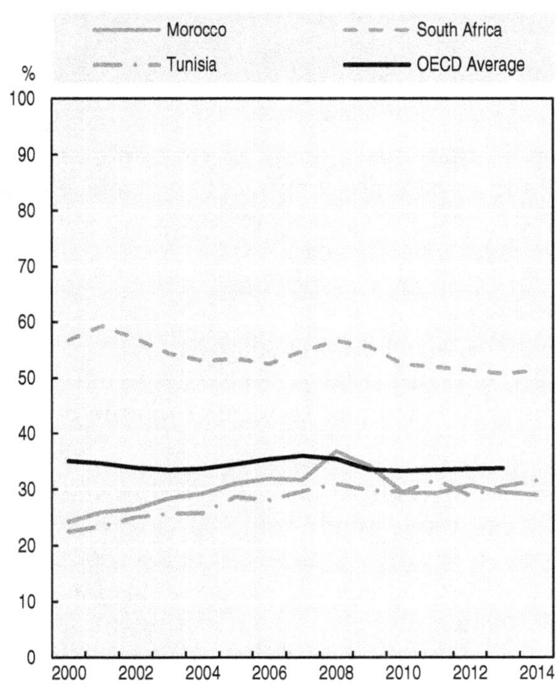

Source: Table 3.3.

StatLink http://dx.doi.org/10.1787/888933343806

Figure 1.20. **Taxes on goods and services as percentage of total tax revenue in countries with higher tax to GDP ratios, 2000-14**

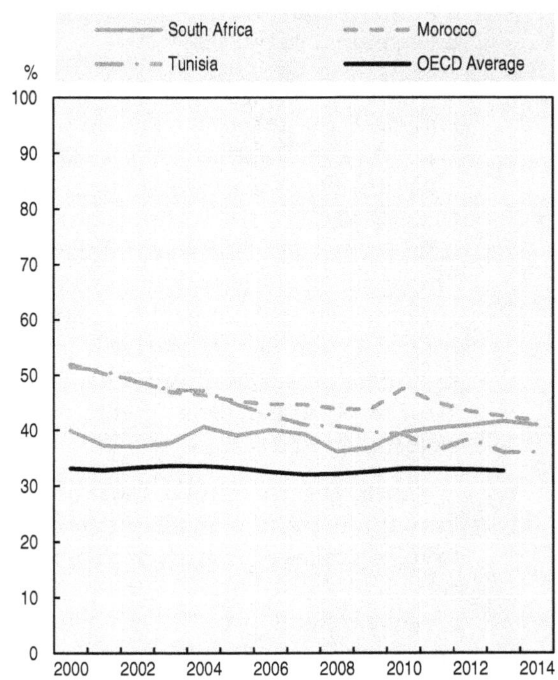

Source: Table 3.3.

StatLink http://dx.doi.org/10.1787/888933343814

1.3. Taxes by level of government

The analysis of taxation by level of government in this publication is limited by a lack of data on sub-central government tax revenues. These data were only available in three countries: Mauritius[8], Morocco and South Africa. Local government finances are not always well-tracked in Africa. In some countries, where financial statements exist, they have not been recorded electronically.

State and local tax revenues are considered to be low in RSIA countries. Where there is no existing data, officials invariably believe that these revenues constitute only a marginal percentage of total tax revenues. The *African Economic Outlook 2015* reports that "in Africa on average, the weight of local government revenue is 7% of the total revenue of local, regional and national governments combined" (AfDB/OECD/UNDP, 2015: 190). Additional figures from the African Development Bank show that local tax revenue in Côte d'Ivoire and Senegal accounts for a small proportion of total tax revenue (around 3-4%[9] of total tax revenue).

Where data exist, reported state and local tax revenues are relatively low. Sub-central government revenues included in this publication are:

Mauritius: 1.1% of all tax revenues in 2014 falling from 1.8% in 2000.

Morocco: 3.1% of all tax revenues in 2014 falling from 3.7% in 2000.

South Africa: 4.8% of tax revenues in 2014, which is equal to what it was in 2010.

Revenues from property taxes are an important source for sub-central governments in Mauritius, Morocco and South Africa. They represent about 80% of the total in South Africa, about 75% in Morocco and about 50% in Mauritius. Most of the remainder relates to taxes on goods and services. Property taxes generally contribute more to local government revenues in Africa's English speaking countries than in its French-speaking ones (AfDB/OECD/UNDP, 2015). There are wide discrepancies in this context in Africa and many countries do not levy any local taxes on buildings and landholdings, or even on economic activities.

Sub-central governments generally have limited tax collection responsibilities and most tax revenue collection remains principally at the central government level. The *African Economic Outlook 2015* observed that "many local governments receive a significant share of their total revenues from central government transfers (AfDB/OECD/UNECA, 2015)". This is partly because local tax systems in Africa are a legacy from French and English administrations and have hardly changed since independence. This is particularly true in Francophone Africa. In French-speaking countries, such as Morocco, Senegal, Côte d'Ivoire and Cameroon, local revenues are often collected by the central government on the local government's behalf whereas in South Africa, in general, local revenues come from their own collection (89% in 2007) (Fjeldstad, Chambas and Brun, 2014). Local governments in Mauritius rely heavily on transfers from the central government (IMF, 2014a).

Local governments in most of sub-Saharan Africa have limited resources and their tax administrations' instruments are inefficient, obsolete and not appropriately equipped to collect taxes efficiently or to properly account for them. This results in high collection costs and an extensive number of low-yield taxes. Moreover the processing of data on revenue collection and the exchange of information with other public institutions is poor and there is usually little co-operation with the central government. This leads to the duplication of taxes or taxes that are contrary to national objectives (such as local taxes on export crops). Outside of South Africa, appropriate property registers are lacking, which is a real challenge for the collection of property taxes (Fjeldstad, Chambas and

Brun, 2014). In Mauritius, for instance, property tax provides a low yield partly due to outdated cadastres and valuations of property (IMF, 2014a).

Although African countries in general and the RSIA countries in particular have undertaken major reforms of their central tax legislations and central tax administrations over the last decades, little has been done at the local government level. Central government taxation has been a greater priority because the need to reduce national fiscal deficits has been felt more at the national level. It is also easier and less costly to reform central tax legislation and systems than those for local taxes and the potential benefits of tax reform in terms of higher revenue are greater. Morocco has been engaged in reforming local government tax systems and administrations since 2007 to strengthen local tax revenue (Boisard, de Freitas and Hidouci, 2014). Other RSIA countries in this publication, such as Cameroon, Côte d'Ivoire (AfDB/OECD/UNECA, 2010) and recently Tunisia (World Bank, 2015) have started processes of fiscal decentralisation intended to empower local governments and improve tax revenue collection. South Africa, for example, has successfully decentralised urban property tax collection and has developed a modern system to collect property tax revenue. Municipal governments there benefit from appropriate expertise and resources. "In South Africa, provincial governments provide local authorities with additional administrative support and training to assist with valuation, issuing bills and collection" (Monkam and Moore, 2015).

1.4 Comparative figures

Figure 1.21. **Total tax revenues as percentage of GDP, 2014**[1]

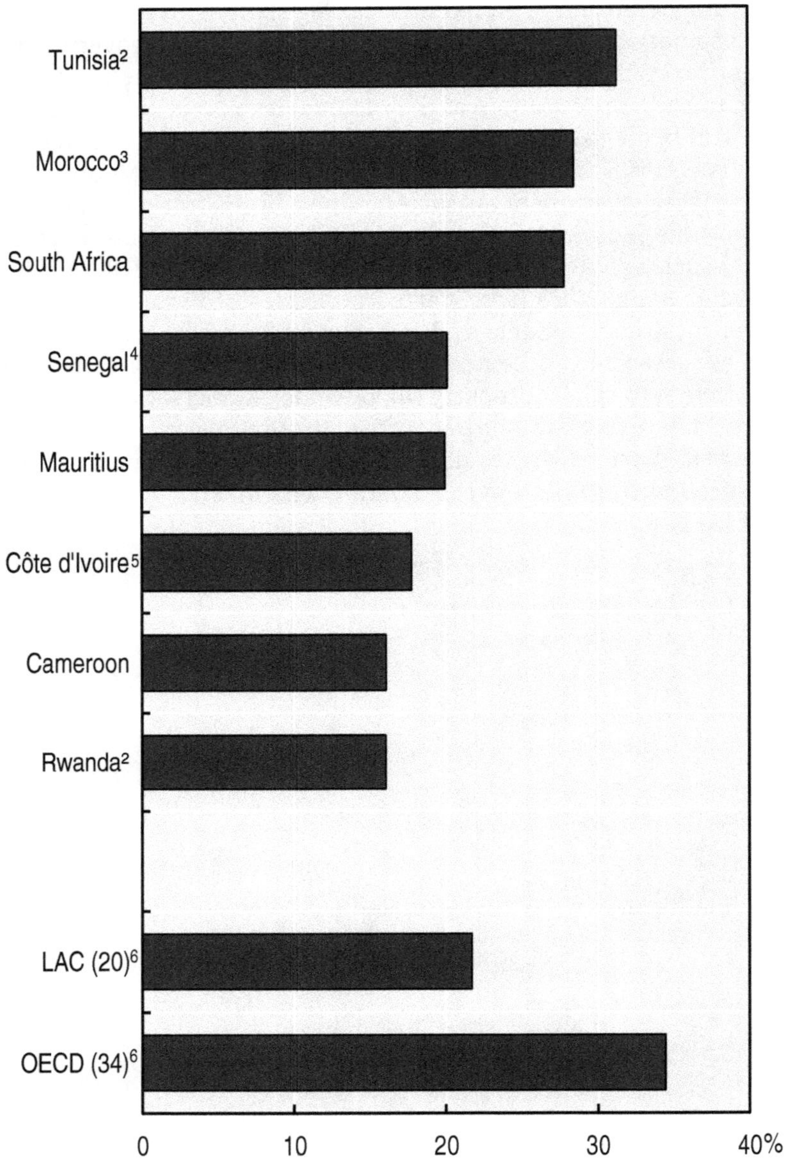

1. Countries have been ranked by their total tax revenue to GDP ratios.

2. Rwanda and Tunisia do not include social security contributions in their tax to GDP ratio as they don't consider them as taxes. They are included in this publication.

3. Estimated figures.

4. Figures include social security contributions from the Institution de prévoyance retraite du Sénégal (IPRES) and exclude the data from the Caisse de Sécurité Sociale (CSS) as they are not available.

5. The tax to GDP ratio contains rents and royalties and sales of public goods and services normally classified as non-tax revenues in the OECD classification. These are considered tax revenues in Côte d'Ivoire. The inclusion of these elements represents 0.5% of GDP in 2014.

6. Represents the unweighted average for OECD member countries and LAC countries.

Source: Table 3.1.

StatLink http://dx.doi.org/10.1787/888933343826

Figure 1.22. **Changes in tax to GDP ratios, 2000-14**

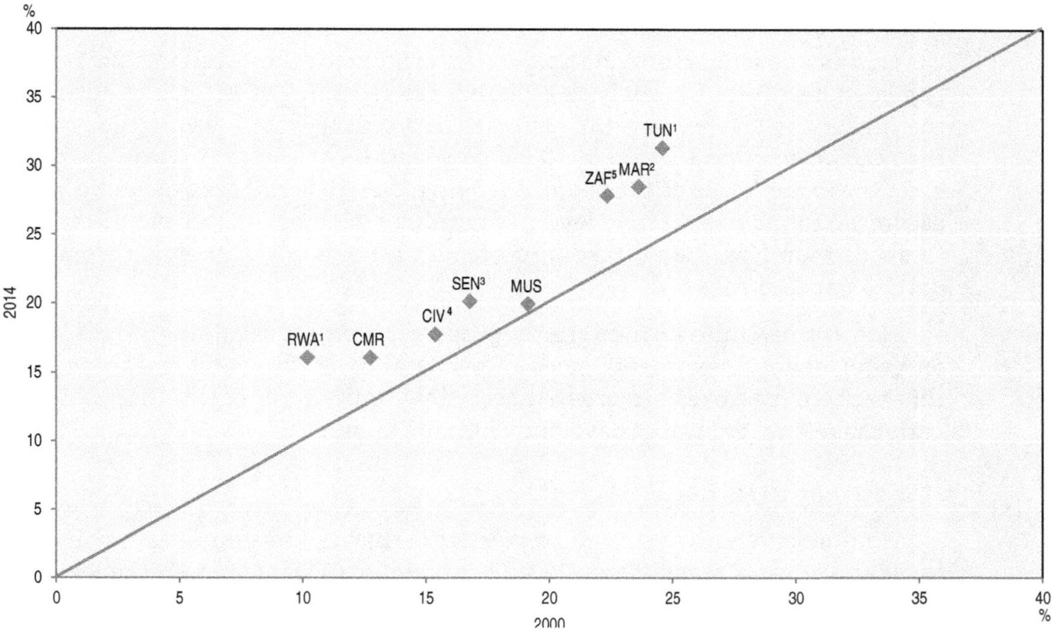

1. Rwanda and Tunisia do not include social security contributions in their tax to GDP ratio as neither country considers them as taxes. They are included as tax revenue in this publication.

2. Estimated figures.

3. Figures include social security contributions from the Institution de prévoyance retraite du Sénégal (IPRES) and exclude the data from the Caisse de Sécurité Sociale (CSS) as they are not available.

4. The tax to GDP ratio contains rents and royalties and sales of public goods and services normally classified as non-tax revenues in the OECD classification. These are considered tax revenues in Côte d'Ivoire. The inclusion of these elements represents 0.5% of GDP in 2014.

5. Local data are included in the 2014 figures and not in 2000 (local and provincial data are only available from 2003).

Source: Table 3.1.

StatLink http://dx.doi.org/10.1787/888933343836

NON-TAX REVENUES

Introduction

Non-tax revenues provide important context to the levels of tax revenues. This has been a priority for analysts studying the revenues of African countries. Logically, the higher the level of non-tax revenues in a country, the lower is the rate of taxation required to maintain the same level of government services. Two governments may have the same levels of taxes and spending, but their finances could be very different according to their respective levels of non-tax revenues. A clear picture of government finances therefore should take into account all of a government's revenues including both tax and non-tax.

Non-tax revenues include grants, property income (e.g. mining royalties and returns on government investment), sales of goods and services, and fines and penalties. In this section, countries are ordered according to their per capita GDP to make revenue patterns related to level of development more apparent.

1.5. Non-tax revenues as percentage of GDP

Non-tax revenues are much more volatile than tax revenues, especially in countries for which non-tax revenues are large compared to GDP (Table 1.7). The levels of non-tax revenues to GDP in 2014 reported by the countries ranged from 9.5% in Rwanda to 0.6% in South Africa. However, Rwanda raised only 6.0 % of GDP in 1998 and as much as 12.7% in both 2005 and 2008. In Cameroon, there was a peak of 9.2% of GDP in 2008, falling to 4.2% in 2014. Non-tax revenue for Côte d'Ivoire was 1.0% of GDP in 2011, but it was over three times higher only two years previously.

Table 1.7. **Total non-tax revenue as percentage of GDP**

	1997	2000	2005	2008	2009	2010	2011	2012	2013	2014
Rwanda	7.5	11.8	12.7	12.7	12.1	12.5	12.5	9.0	11.3	9.5
Senegal	2.4	2.7	2.3	3.4	3.6	3.2	2.9	3.8	4.1	5.7
Cameroon	5.3	8.0	6.9	9.2	4.6	4.8	6.2	5.0	4.9	4.2
Côte d'Ivoire[1]	1.3	1.1	2.2	2.3	3.2	1.3	1.0	1.0	1.8	2.2
Morocco	0.0	2.2	2.9	3.0	3.4	3.2	3.6	3.4	3.9	3.5
Tunisia	0.0	2.3	2.4	3.5	3.1	2.7	3.9	3.4	3.4	2.2
South Africa	0.3	0.5	0.5	0.6	0.4	0.6	0.7	0.7	0.7	0.6
Mauritius[2]	4.4	3.3	2.5	3.0	4.3	3.8	3.5	3.1	3.2	2.4

Note: The figures exclude local government tax revenues for Cameroon, Côte d'Ivoire, Rwanda, Senegal and Tunisia as the data are not available. Local and provincial data for South Africa are not available prior to 2003.

1. The non-tax revenues as a percentage of GDP excludes rents, royalties and fees for public services as these are considered to be tax revenues in Côte d'Ivoire. The inclusion of these elements represents 0.5% of GDP in 2014 and between 0.1% and 1.5% in the period from 2000 to 2014.
2. Estimated figures for 2013 and 2014.

StatLink http://dx.doi.org/10.1787/888933344402

This volatility is largely due to the instability of grant and property revenues, which generally constitute the majority of non-tax revenues. The levels of grants change according to the priorities of donors which can shift substantially over time. Property income can change sharply due to movements in mineral prices, or when a major new mine opens up, bringing about a surge of mineral production. This contrasts with the more stable level of variation in the reported tax revenues of RSIA countries. A high reliance on non-tax revenues means that these countries have had less stable finances over the past two decades.

Figure 1.23. **Total non-tax revenue as percentage of GDP**

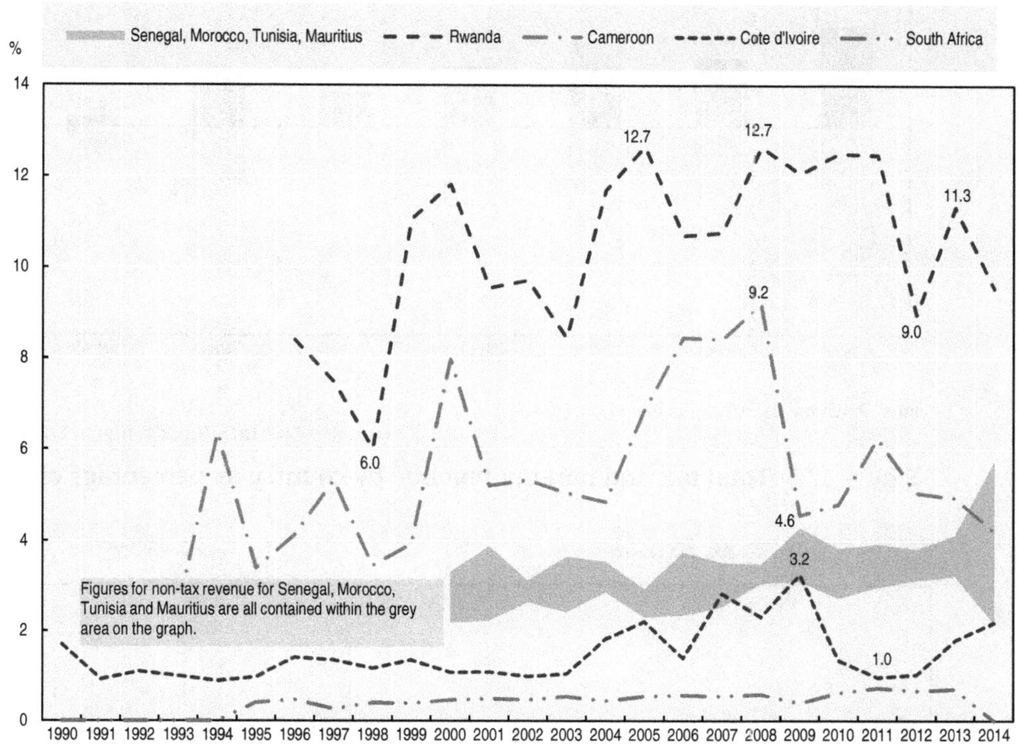

Source: Table 5.1.

StatLink http://dx.doi.org/10.1787/888933343840

Non-tax revenues can also change sharply from one year to the next (Figure 1.24). Cameroon saw a drop in non-tax revenues of 4.6 percentage points of GDP (between 2008 and 2009) while Rwanda saw an increase of 2.4 percentage points of GDP (between 2012 and 2013) and a fall of 2.5 percentage points of GDP (between 2011 and 2012). In contrast, Morocco and South Africa had relatively stable levels of non-tax revenues in the decade to 2014.

The countries with higher GDP per capita tended to have higher tax to GDP ratios, but lower ratios of non-tax revenue to GDP ratios. Figure 1.25 shows the total tax and non-tax revenues for each country as a percentage of GDP in 2014. The countries are presented in order from the country with the lowest per-capita GDP in 2014, Rwanda, to the country with the highest in 2014, Mauritius. The four countries with lower GDP per capita on the left hand side of the figure show both lower tax revenue and with the exception of Côte d'Ivoire, higher non-tax revenue than the countries with higher GDP per capita on the right. The general rule that richer countries have higher tax revenue (see Figure 1.4 in the discussion on tax ratios) seems to be reversed when it comes to non-tax revenue for the countries in this report.

Figure 1.24. **Largest year-on-year change in non-tax revenues as percentage of GDP, between 2005 and 2014**

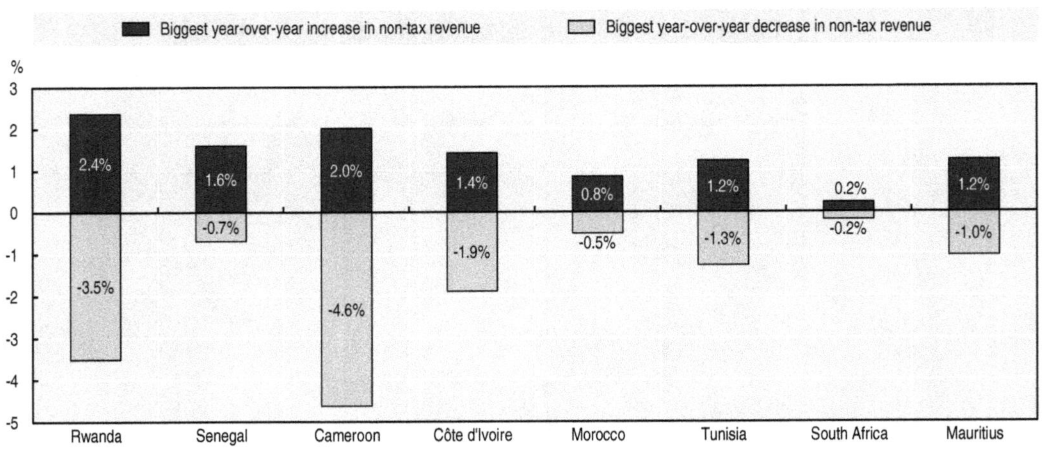

Source: Authors' calculations based on Table 5.1.

StatLink http://dx.doi.org/10.1787/888933343851

Figure 1.25. **Total tax and non-tax revenue by country as percentage of GDP, 2014**

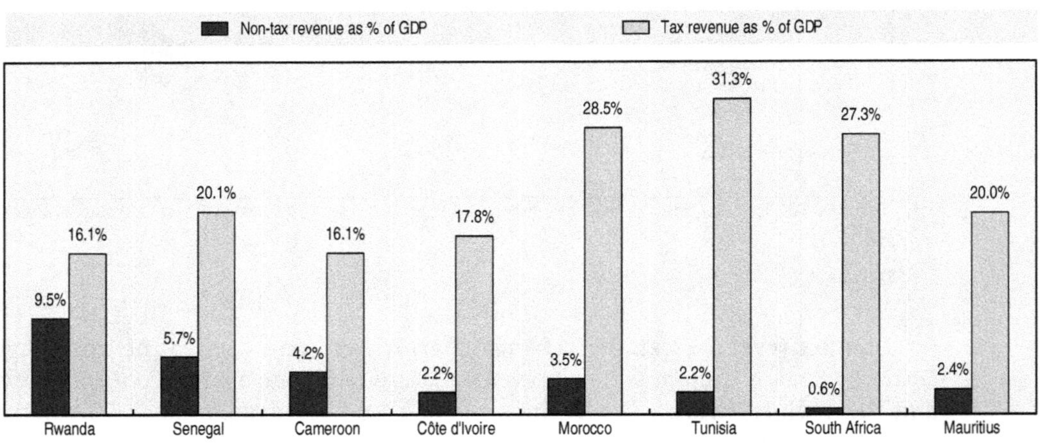

Source: Tables 3.1 and 5.1.

StatLink http://dx.doi.org/10.1787/888933343863

Box 1.2. **Non-tax revenues – data quality issues**

Data on non-tax revenues are more difficult to obtain and classify than tax revenues because they are not as readily available, less transparent and less scrutinised. In this publication, non-tax revenue statistics are less detailed than for tax revenues, making verification more difficult. For example, some countries have values for total non-tax revenues in some years, with no breakdown beyond grants and other non-tax revenues. In addition, the revenue totals even at the most granular level may also not fit exactly with the OECD classification. Some countries have different ways of classifying items such as fees for service than the OECD. Finally, many of these revenues are not part of the main budgeting process and are therefore not subject to the same types of oversight and scrutiny as tax revenues. The compulsory nature of taxation may be an incentive for more public scrutiny of government that is not as present when it comes to non-tax revenues.

Non-tax payments to governments are sometimes the result of negotiations between governments and corporations. There are risks of a loss of transparency in making settlements and therefore the amount of information available for analysis. Grants, legal settlements, and mining and oil contracts often involve very large payments by powerful external entities such as multinational corporations and foreign governments. Some aspects of these deals may be kept secret, for example when large contracts with resource extraction companies contain strong confidentiality causes (AfDB/OECD/UNECA, 2010). In addition, some countries negotiate large payments that cover many categories of revenue, making detailed breakdowns less reliable.

The concept of non-tax revenue is also broader than the concept of tax revenue, which could make accounting less clear. A tax liability is generally defined in terms of the national currency either before or after payment. In contrast, this is not the case for non-tax revenues where payments can be made in terms of non-financial assets which are not necessarily valued in the national currency at the time of transaction.

1.6. Structure of non-tax revenues

Table 1.8. **Sub-categories of non-tax revenue as percentage of total non-tax revenue, 2014**

Country	Grants	Property income	Sale of goods and services	Fines, penalties	Miscellaneous and unidentified revenue[1]
Rwanda[2]	82	..	..	..	18
Senegal	57	29	0	11	2
Cameroon	4	87	8	1	1
Côte d'Ivoire[3]	82	6	7	0	5
Morocco[4]	0	37	41	2	21
Tunisia	21	56	1	11	11
South Africa	9	82	4	5	0
Mauritius[5]	4	57	30	4	6

Note: The figures exclude local government tax revenues for Cameroon, Côte d'Ivoire, Rwanda, Senegal and Tunisia as the data are not available. Local and provincial data for South Africa are not available prior to 2003.

1. Including capital transfers not elsewhere classified and voluntary transfers other than grants.
2. Data for property income, sales of goods and services and fines, penalties and forfeits are included in miscellaneous and unidentified revenue.
3. The "Property income" heading excludes rents and royalties and the "Sales of goods and services" heading excludes fees for user goods and services. These are considered as tax revenues in Côte d'Ivoire.
4. Data for 2013.
5. Estimated figures for the headings "Property income" and "Sales of goods and services".

StatLink http://dx.doi.org/10.1787/888933344416

There is substantial variation in the structure of non-tax revenues in the RSIA countries. In 2014, about 82% of non-tax revenues in Côte d'Ivoire and Rwanda and 57% in Senegal came from grants. In contrast, the majority of non-tax revenues reported by Cameroon, Mauritius, South Africa and Tunisia were classified as property income (Table 1.8). In the case of Cameroon, property income was mostly related to rents and royalties whereas for Mauritius, South Africa and Tunisia, it was mostly interest and dividends. Côte d'Ivoire received considerable revenues from their oil industry however this resource-based revenue was mostly classified as taxation in this publication, rather than rent. Morocco was the only country with revenue from sales of goods and services (including administrative fees) being the largest category of non-tax revenue.

1.7. Non-tax revenue by sub-category

In this section each sub-category of non-tax revenue is analysed separately. Each of these types of revenue has a different impact not only on public finances but also on governance issues in general. Table 1.9 shows the contribution of each sub-category of non-tax revenue to the total non-tax revenue as percentage of GDP for each RSIA country.

Table 1.9. **Non-tax revenue sub-categories as percentage of GDP, 2014**

Category	Rwanda[1]	Senegal	Cameroon	Côte d'Ivoire[2]	Morocco[3]	Tunisia	South Africa	Mauritius[4]
Total non-tax revenue	**9.5**	**5.7**	**4.2**	**2.2**	**3.9**	**2.2**	**0.6**	**2.4**
Grants	7.8	3.3	0.2	1.8	0.0	0.5	0.1	0.1
Property income	..	1.7	3.7	0.1	1.4	1.2	0.5	1.4
Rents and royalties	..	0.3	3.6	0.1	0.6	0.4	0.1	0.3
Interest and dividends	..	0.7	0.1	0.1	0.9	0.8	0.2	0.4
Other property income	..	0.0	0.0	0.0	0.0	0.0	0.1	0.7
Sale of goods and services	..	0.0	0.3	0.2	1.6	0.0	0.0	0.7
Fines, penalties and forfeits	..	0.6	0.0	0.0	0.1	0.2	0.0	0.1
Miscellaneous and unidentified revenue[5]	1.7	0.1	0.0	0.1	0.8	0.2	0.0	0.1
Total tax revenue	*16.1*	*20.1*	*16.1*	*17.8*	*28.5*	*31.3*	*27.8*	*20.0*
Total sum of tax and non-tax revenue	*25.6*	*25.9*	*20.3*	*19.9*	*17.8*	*33.5*	*27.9*	*22.4*

Note: The figures exclude local government tax revenues for Cameroon, Côte d'Ivoire, Rwanda, Senegal and Tunisia as the data are not available. Local and provincial data for South Africa are not available prior to 2003.

1. Data for property income, sales of goods and services and fines, penalties and forfeits are included in miscellaneous and unidentified revenue.
2. The "Property income" heading excludes rents and royalties and the "Sales of goods and services" heading excludes fees for user goods and services. These are considered as tax revenues in Côte d'Ivoire.
3. Data for 2013.
4. Estimated figures for the headings "Property income" and "Sales of goods and services".
5. Including capital transfers not elsewhere classified and voluntary transfers other than grants.

StatLink http://dx.doi.org/10.1787/888933344421

Grants

The countries receiving the most in grants as percentage of GDP were countries with lower tax to GDP ratios. Three of the four countries that received the largest grant income in 2014, Côte d'Ivoire, Rwanda and Senegal, were among those with the lowest GDP per capita featured in Figure 1.26. Rwanda reported by far the largest amount of grants as percentage of GDP at 7.8%, followed by Senegal (3.3%) and Côte d'Ivoire (1.8%).

Figure 1.26. **Grants as percentage of GDP, 2014**

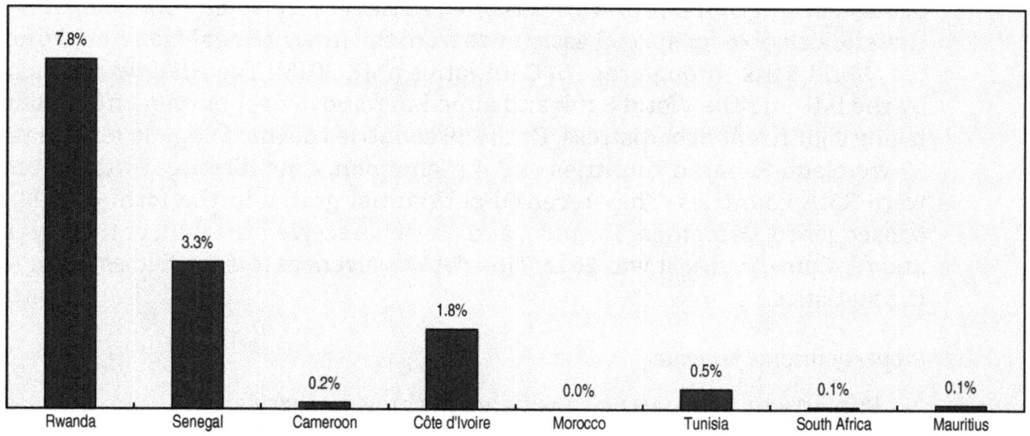

Source: Table 5.2.

StatLink http://dx.doi.org/10.1787/888933343878

Over the past two decades, grants as percentage of GDP has been fairly volatile, featuring periodic spikes. They have varied between 5 and 12 percentage points of GDP for Rwanda, while they were reported as being below 3.3% for the other countries in the publication (Figure 1.27). Rwandan grant revenues peaked in 2000, 2005, and 2010, and reached troughs in 1998, 2003, 2012 and 2014. Grants peaked in 2009 for Côte d'Ivoire and in 2007 for Cameroon while they have remained consistently between 1.5 and 3.3 percentage of GDP for Senegal. Grants for Tunisia have only been above 0.5 percentage points of GDP in 2012, when they rose to 0.9% which was three times higher than 2011 and 2013. Grants for Mauritius reached as high as 1% of GDP only once, in 2009, but this was five times higher than in the previous year.

Figure 1.27. **Grants as percentage of GDP, 1995-2014**

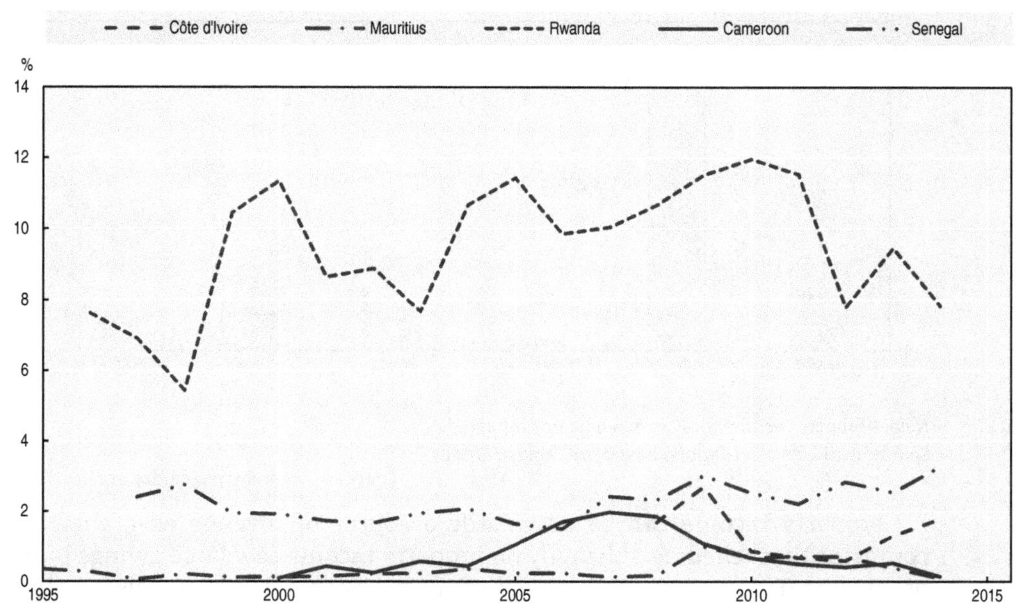

Source: Authors' calculations based on Tables 5.5-5.12.

StatLink http://dx.doi.org/10.1787/888933343888

A single international aid programme is responsible for some of the biggest spikes in grant funding to RSIA countries in recent years. Cameroon, Côte d'Ivoire, Rwanda, and Senegal belong to the countries classified as Heavily Indebted Poor Countries (HIPC) and therefore eligible for special assistance from the International Monetary Fund (IMF) and the World Bank through the HIPC initiative (IMF, 2015). The HIPC was launched in 1996 by the IMF and the World Bank and aimed to remove debt burdens from poor countries facing significant debt distress. Of the 39 countries deemed eligible for this programme, 33 were sub-Saharan countries and 4 (Cameroon, Côte d'Ivoire, Rwanda, and Senegal) were RSIA countries. They received substantial grants in the form of debt relief as a consequence. Cameroon, Rwanda, and Senegal received the bulk of their grants in 2006 and for Côte d'Ivoire, it was 2012. This debt forgiveness is classified as grant revenues in the statistics.

Property income revenue

Property income can be considered in three categories:

- Rents and royalties reflecting the renewable and non-renewable natural resources under government ownership
- Interest and dividends
- Other and unallocable property income

Rents and royalties are obtained by the government from prospecting and extracting minerals from public lands, or from harvesting government-owned farms and forests, while interest and dividends are returns on government-owned investments. In 2014, Cameroon reported the highest level of rents and royalties at 3.6% of GDP. 98% of this revenue was accounted for by rents and royalties (Figure 1.28). Mauritius, at 1.1% was the only other country with revenues from this source above 1% of GDP.

Figure 1.28. **Property income as percentage of GDP, 2014**

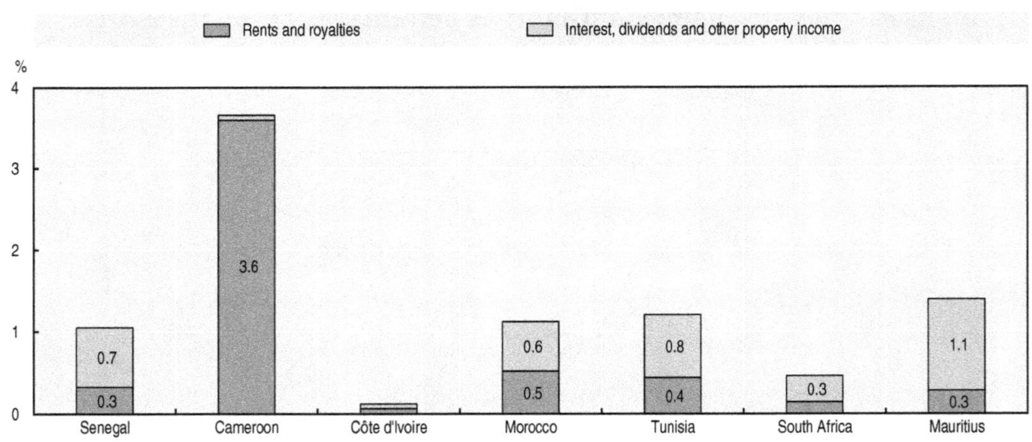

Note: Property income for Rwanda was not reported.
Source: Authors' calculations based on Tables 5.5-5.12.

StatLink http://dx.doi.org/10.1787/888933343899

Property income can be as volatile a source of revenue as grants. Three of the countries that relied most heavily on property income saw large swings in this category of revenue (Figure 1.29). Cameroon's property income, which consisted almost entirely of rents and royalties, displayed five large spikes in revenues within a 20-year span. The countries that relied more on interest, dividends and other property income had less variation in their revenues, although Tunisia did see its property income fall by two thirds within three years, from 2011 to 2014. The data from Mauritius also shows large fluctuations between 2006 and 2014, but comparisons over longer time scales are also impacted by changes in data classification in their time series. In contrast, Senegal, South Africa and Tunisia had variations of 1.0% or less.

Figure 1.29. **Property income as percentage of GDP, 1990-2014**

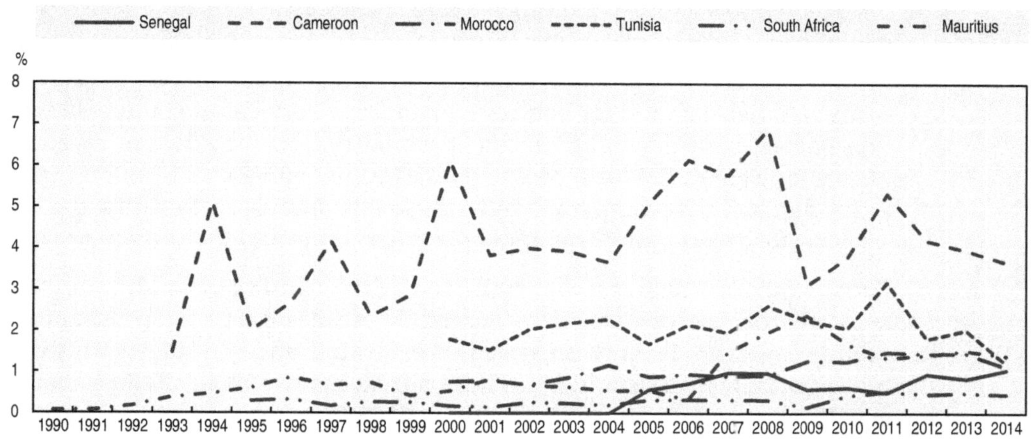

Source: Authors' calculations based on Tables 5.5-5.12.

StatLink http://dx.doi.org/10.1787/888933343907

Revenues from natural resources

Revenues from businesses focusing on the use of natural resources can have a significant impact on public finances, but they are accounted for in different ways depending on existing regulatory and fiscal policies and on the types of contracts these companies sign with the relevant authorities. Governments can obtain revenues through natural resource exploitation both through taxation and through non-tax revenues, but also by the spending on a country's infrastructure by the businesses that are involved. The following is a summary of the various ways that these revenues can impact government balance sheets:[10]

1. Rents and royalties are the most direct form of revenue relating to natural resource wealth. The government charges fees to companies and individuals in exchange for the right to access government lands. It does this in its capacity as landowner, and these fees are generally decided through negotiation. These are recorded under property income.
2. Payment for services provided by the government is another source of non-tax revenue paid for by businesses in the primary sector. This can include, for example, payments for environmental inspections by government officials, or payments for the construction of infrastructure. These are recorded under sales of goods and services.
3. Ownership of a corporation, public or other, that exploits natural resources on the government's behalf results in government revenues in the form of profits and dividends. These are recorded under property income.
4. Taxes or levies can be designed to target companies or individuals who access natural resources. It may sometimes be difficult to make a distinction between a tax on companies operating on public lands, and a royalty charged to such companies.

5. Taxes targeting the activity of natural resource exploitation could be introduced such as an excise tax on the sale of materials extracted from public lands, or a tax on mining that targets the activity, rather than the individual or company exploiting natural resources. These, too, will be recorded as taxes.
6. Companies and individuals exploiting natural resources are generally subject to all the same taxes (e.g. income taxes, VAT's) as the rest of the population. These general taxes will be included on government financial statements, but not necessarily attributed to sectors exploiting natural resources.
7. In addition, companies and individuals may use some of the wealth they obtain from natural resource extraction to build infrastructure or provide services. Where this satisfies demand for public investment or services, it could result in a savings on government expenditure, but it would not be recorded as revenue. In some cases, as a condition for access to publically owned natural resources, governments may demand that companies and individuals provide certain services, for example paying for at least part of the cost of constructing and maintaining roads to mines.

Rents and royalties are the main source of non-tax revenues from businesses focusing on the use of natural resources. These are part of the primary industries including renewable resources (agriculture, fishing and hunting) and non-renewable resources (mainly mining and oil). These have a major role in the RSIA countries with lower GDP per capita (Figure 1.30); the share of GDP of these industries is 37% in Rwanda, 33% in Côte d'Ivoire, 32% in Cameroon, 21% in Morocco and 18% in Senegal. In most of these countries, agriculture, fishing and hunting have a much larger share of GDP than mining and oil.

Figure 1.30. **Primary industries as percentage of GDP, 2014**

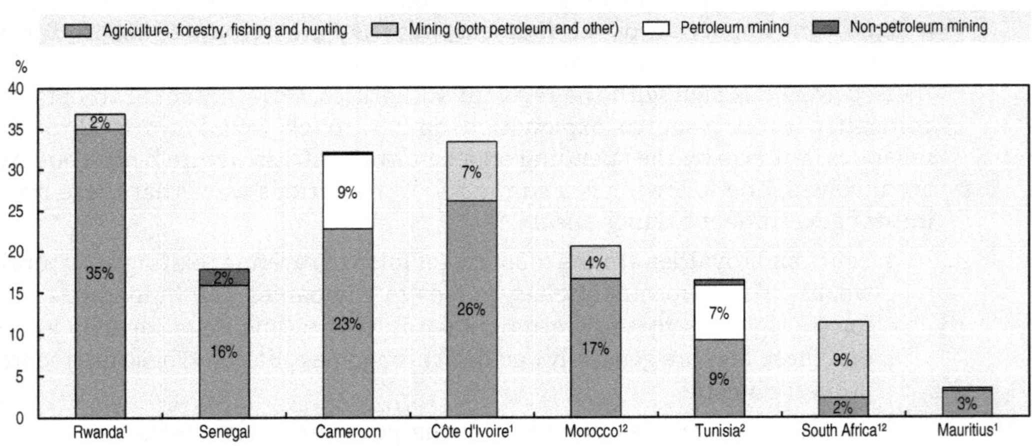

1. The distinction between oil and non-oil mining in the data for Rwanda, Côte d'Ivoire, Tunisia and South Africa is not available.

2. 2013 data.

Source: (AfDB/OECD/UNDP, 2015), *African Economic Outlook 2015: Regional Development and Spatial Inclusion.*

StatLink http://dx.doi.org/10.1787/888933343913

The four countries for which mining has the largest share of GDP are Cameroon, Côte d'Ivoire, South Africa and Tunisia. In these countries, mining contributed between 7% and 9% of GDP. In the other countries it was between 1% and 4% though this was not necessarily reflected in the size of revenues from rents and royalties. In Cameroon, government revenues from rents and royalties as percentage of GDP in 2014 were significant at 3.6% of GDP but they were 0.5% or less in all the other countries.

Natural resource revenues tend to be a risky source of financing. An IMF paper notes that mining projects are high risk, with high sunk costs, but high potential returns, meaning that with large revenues at stake, mistakes made on the part of the government can be very costly (IMF, 2011). A high dependence on the production of primary goods also increases exposure to the impact of swings in commodity prices (seen in Figure 1.31). For example, since 1990, the price of gold has risen as high as 35.8% over the previous year, and has plunged by as much as 15.4%. In addition, the price of oil was 57.1% higher in 2000 than it was a year earlier, while in 2009, it was 37.8% lower.

Figure 1.31. **Change in annual prices of oil and gold over previous year (%), 1990-2014**

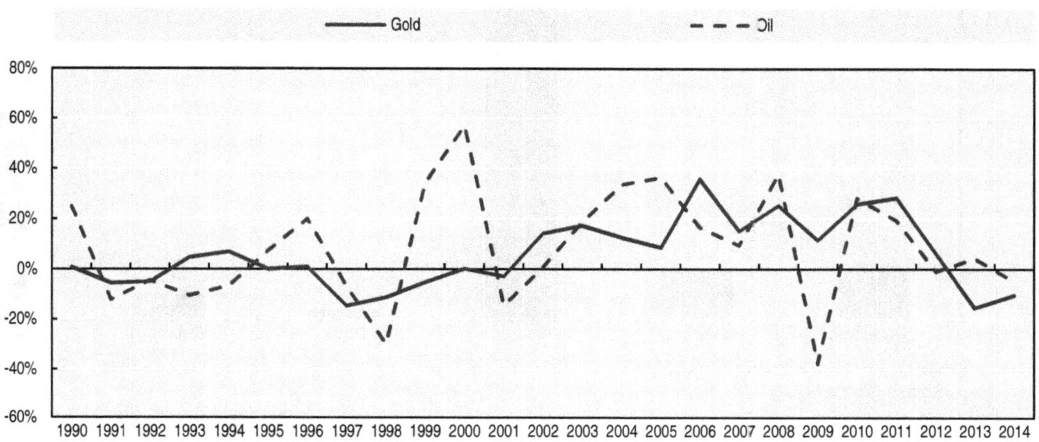

Source: Economic Research Division, Federal Reserve Bank of St. Louis.

StatLink http://dx.doi.org/10.1787/888933343925

Sales of goods and service revenue

Governments can produce goods and services both as a market and as a non-market participant. As a market participant, governments sometimes provide goods and services that can be obtained from private companies (such as selling food or providing transportation). At the same time, they can also provide services in the course of administrating programmes and executing laws that are unique to the function of government. Fees charged for these non-market services are generally classified as administrative fees and would typically include fees for registration and licenses, plus user or application fees.

Administrative fees are often difficult to classify since they occupy a grey area between payments for services (which are non-tax revenues) and compulsory unrequited payments collected during government operations (which are taxes).[11] When they are classified as taxes, they are typically assigned to one of the following categories:

- 4400 Taxes on financial and capital transactions
- 5200 Taxes on use of goods and performing activities
- 6000 Other taxes

Morocco (48% of total non-tax revenues) and Mauritius (29.5%) generate the largest percentage of their non-tax revenues through sales of goods and services and administrative fees (Figure 1.32). Of the other countries providing this data, the corresponding percentages range from 1.4% in Tunisia to 7.9% in Cameroon. Most revenue from sales of goods and services are collected at the local level in Morocco, and 38% involve sales of produced goods. In Mauritius non-tax revenue collected through sales of goods and services reported at the local level was negligible. It included a large number of different fees for various government services including route air navigation, police services, as well as receipts from the sale of a range of different products including ground water, animal feed and forest produce.

Figure 1.32. **Sales of goods and services and administrative fees as percentage of total non-tax revenues, 2014**

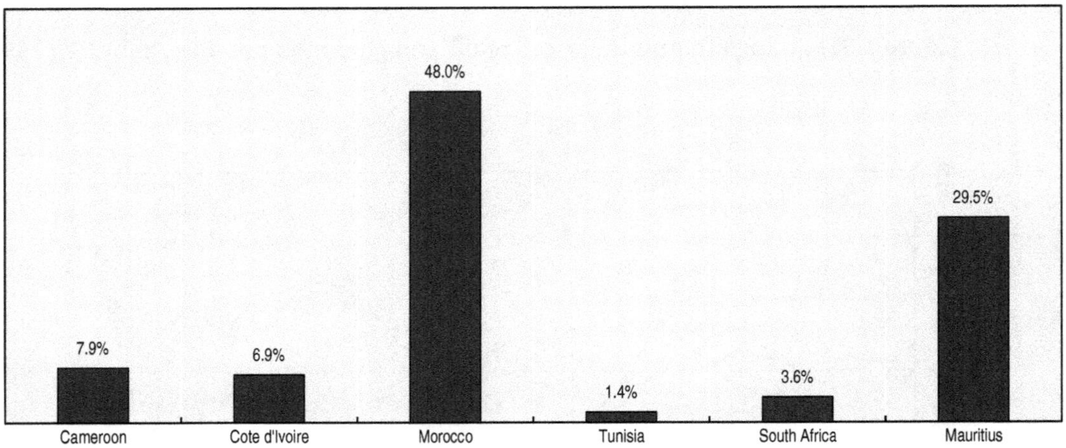

Source: Table 5.2.

StatLink http://dx.doi.org/10.1787/888933343933

Fines and forfeits

Fines and forfeits can sometimes be an important source of revenue but they are subject to volatility. Some small fines, such as speeding tickets, are obtained on a regular and a predictable basis. In some countries, a percentage of these revenues are used simply to finance policing activities and are therefore not reported in the statistics. Apart from that, these small fines are negligible in the context of the overall level of non-tax revenues. Larger fines such as a settlement with a multinational corporation or major penalties can provide a financial windfall but this will not necessarily be replicated in future years.

Figure 1.33. **Fines, penalties and forfeits as percentage of GDP**

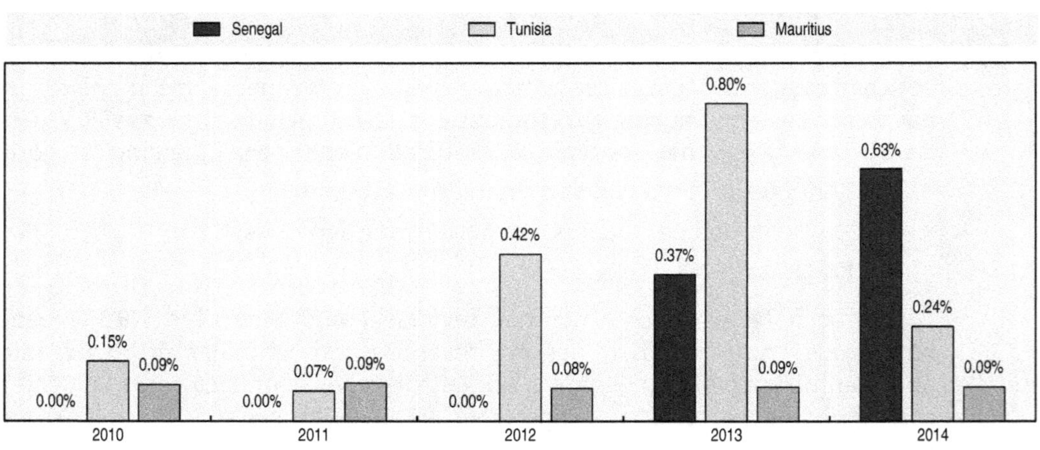

Source: Tables 5.5-5.12.

StatLink http://dx.doi.org/10.1787/888933343943

In general, most RSIA countries had negligible revenues from fines, forfeits and penalties; Tunisia and Senegal were exceptions (Figure 1.33). In Tunisia, the percentage of fines and penalties to GDP rose from 0.09% to 0.8% between 2011 and 2013 and then fell back to 0.24% in 2014. In Senegal, this ratio was 0.37% of GDP in 2013 and 0.63% in 2014 compared with negligible values in the three previous years.

Miscellaneous or unidentified revenue

There are some notable categories of non-tax revenue that do not fit in with any of the categories listed above. These include:

1. Capital transfers not included elsewhere.
2. Voluntary donations to government agencies from individuals or corporations.
3. Insurance claims paid to government agencies.
4. Payments covering different categories in the classification list where a breakdown is not available.
5. Payments whose proper classification is unknown due to a lack of data.

These revenues can be a significant component of non-tax revenues in specific years (Figure 1.34). In 2013, for example, 21% of Moroccan non-tax revenues were classified in this category. Other revenues that were under this heading include exceptional voluntary contributions to government in Tunisia, capital transfers from special statutory funds in Mauritius, and, in Morocco, payments made to government in exchange for the right to compete with state institutions in the provision of services.

Figure 1.34. **The year between 2010 and 2014 when miscellaneous or unidentified revenue as percentage of total non-tax revenue was highest**

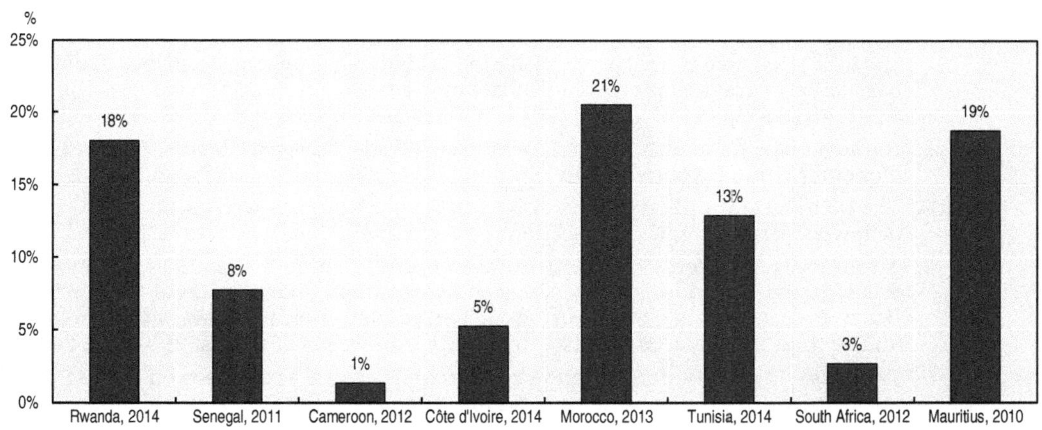

Source: Authors' calculations based on Tables 5.5-5.12.

StatLink http://dx.doi.org/10.1787/888933343952

Levels of unidentified revenue are generally variable, with periodic spikes (Figure 1.35). This could be due to large, one-time capital transfers, revenue streams that are short-lived, or funds that are reclassified as unidentified due to lack of information. Insufficient data is available for a proper analysis of this category, but the incidence of higher values for this category could reflect a greater degree of uncertainty as to the true amount of revenue within the other non-tax revenue classifications.

Figure 1.35. **Miscellaneous and unidentified revenue as percentage of total non-tax revenue, 2000-14**

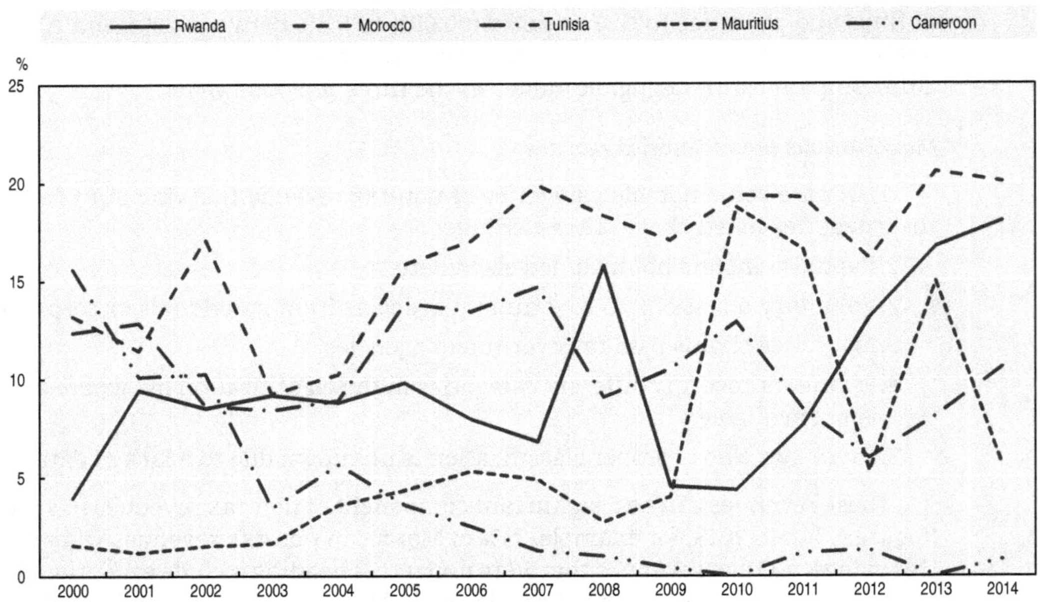

Source: Authors' calculations based on Tables 5.5-5.12.

StatLink http://dx.doi.org/10.1787/888933343965

Notes

1. LAC refers to the 22 countries featured in the 2016 edition of *Revenue Statistics in Latin America and the Caribbean.*
2. The difference between reported total tax to GDP ratio in 2014 and 2000 is 5.5% of GDP when provincial and local taxation data that are available in 2014 but that are not reported in 2000 are included in the calculations (local and provincial data are only available from 2003 onwards). The increase in the South African tax to GDP ratio is only 4.2% when local and provincial data is excluded.
3. Authors' calculations based on data from *World Economic Outlook Database*, International Monetary Fund, October 2015.
4. The political and military crisis of 2011 in Côte d'Ivoire, as well as the global financial crisis, deeply affected the country's economic environment and the tax to GDP ratio.
5. A country is considered rich in hydrocarbons and/or mineral resources if it meets either of the following criteria: i) an average share of hydrocarbon and/or mineral fiscal revenues in total fiscal revenue of at least 25% during the period 2000-05 or ii) an average share of hydrocarbon and/or mineral export proceeds in total export proceeds of at least 25 % (IMF, 2007).
6. The taxes on specific consumption contain rents, royalties and fees on the use of public goods and services usually classified as non-tax revenues in the OECD classification. The increase in these elements contributed nearly as much as import duties to the increase in taxes on specific consumption between 2000 and 2014 (0.8 percentage points).
7. The lack of data for some countries also contributes to the variation. For example the data from the Caisse de Sécurité Sociale (CSS) for Senegal are not available.
8. The data from Mauritius were derived from financial statements produced by Statistics Mauritius.
9. This figure probably includes other revenues such as fees for utilities services or for other public services such as road tolls that are not classified as tax revenue in this publication.
10. Mansour and Rota-Graziosi (2013) note that taxes on oil extraction can include corporate income tax, excise taxes on energy product, un-refunded sales taxes such as VATs and non-tax revenue can include royalties, profit sharing, dividends received from state enterprises, and dividends and other investment income received from government direct participation in extractive enterprises.
11. See paragraphs 9-13 of the OECD Interpretive Guide in Annex A for an explanation of how administrative fees are classified in this publication.

References

Addison, T. and J. Levin (2012), *The Determinants of Tax Revenue in Sub-Saharan Africa*, Swedish Business School at Örebro University, Örebro, Sweden, oru.diva-portal.org/smash/record.jsf?pid=diva2%3A570456&dswid=4207.

AfDB (2010), *Domestic Resource Mobilization for Poverty Reduction in East Africa: Rwanda case study*, African Development Bank, Abidjan, Côte d'Ivoire, www.afdb.org/fileadmin/uploads/afdb/Documents/Project-and-Operations/Rwanda%20case%20study%20paper%20final.pdf.

AfDB/OECD/UNDP (2015), *African Economic Outlook 2015: Regional Development and Spatial Inclusion*, OECD Publishing, Paris, http://dx.doi.org/10.1787/aeo-2015-en.

AfDB/OECD/UNDP (2014), *African Economic Outlook 2014: Global Value Chains and Africa's Industrialisation*, OECD Publishing, Paris, http://dx.doi.org/10.1787/aeo-2014-en.

AfDB/OECD/UNECA (2010), *African Economic Outlook 2010: Domestic Resource Mobilisation and Aid*, OECD Publishing, Paris, http://dx.doi.org/10.1787/aeo-2010-en.

Besley, T. and T. Persson (2013), "Taxation and Development", (chapter prepared for *Handbook of Public Economics*, edited by Auerbach, A., R. Chetty and M. Feldstein, and E. Saez), econ.lse.ac.uk/staff/tbesley/papers/TaxationAndDevelopment.pdf.

Bird, R. and E. Zolt (2003), *Introduction to Tax Policy Design and Development*, draft module prepared for a course on Practical Issues of Tax Policy in Developing Countries, World Bank, 28 April-1 May, www1.worldbank.org/publicsector/LearningProgram/PracticalIssues/papers/introduction%20to%20tax%20policy/WBI%20Module%201(Bird&Zolt)April10.doc.

Boisard, S., C. de Freitas and G. Hidouci (2014), *Renforcer les recettes fiscales locales pour financer le développement urbain*, FMDV, Paris, resolutionstofundcities.org/sites/default/files/docs/renforcer-les-recettes-fiscales-locales-pour-financer-le-developpement-urbain/etudefmdvfiscalitelocalevillesafrique.pdf.

Cruce, F. (2011), "Evaluating value added tax in Morocco," *Minor Field Study Series*, No. 209, Department of Economics at the University of Lund, Lund, https://liveatlund.lu.se/intranets/LUSEM/NEK/mfs/MFS/209.pdf.

Fjeldstad, O.H., G. Chambas and J.F. Brun (2014), "Local government taxation in Sub-Saharan Africa: a review and an agenda for research", *CMI Working Paper*, WP 2014: 2, CHR. Michelsen Institute, Bergen, www.cmi.no/publications/file/5098-local-government-taxation-in-sub-saharan-africa.pdf.

Fossat, P. and M. Bua (2013), "Tax administration reform in the francophone countries of sub-Saharan Africa", *IMF Working Paper*, WP/13/173, International Monetary Fund, Washington, DC, www.imf.org/external/pubs/ft/wp/2013/wp13173.pdf.

IMF (2015), "Debt Relief Under the Heavily Indebted Poor Countries (HIPC) Initiative", *International Monetary Fund Factsheet*, International Monetary Fund, Washington, DC, September, www.imf.org/external/np/exr/facts/hipc.htm.

IMF (2014a), "Mauritius: Article IV Consultation-staff report, press release and statement by the executive director for Mauritius", *IMF Country Report*, No. 14/107, International Monetary Fund, Washington, DC, www.imf.org/external/pubs/ft/scr/2014/cr14107.pdf.

IMF (2014b), "Cameroon: Article IV Consultation", *IMF Country Report*, No. 14/212, International Monetary Fund, Washington, DC, www.imf.org/external/pubs/ft/scr/2014/cr14212.pdf.

IMF (2013), "Côte d'Ivoire: Article IV Consultation and Fourth Review under the extended Credit Facility Arrangement," *IMF Country Report*, No. 13/367, International Monetary Fund, Washington, DC, www.imf.org/external/pubs/ft/scr/2013/cr13367.pdf.

IMF (2011), *Revenue Mobilization in Developing Countries*, International Monetary Fund, Washington, DC, https://www.imf.org/external/np/pp/eng/2011/030811.pdf.

IMF (2010), "Tunisie–Conclusions préliminaires de la mission de consultation au titre de l'article IV (2010)", International Monetary Fund, Washington, DC, https://www.imf.org/external/np/ms/2010/061510a.htm, (accessed January 7, 2015).

IMF (2007), *Guide on resource revenue transparency*, International Monetary Fund, Washington, DC, www.imf.org/external/np/pp/2007/eng/051507g.pdf.

ISSA (2014), *Africa: Strategic approaches to improve social security*, International Social Security Association, Geneva, www.issa.int/details?uuid=3c1e0654-a158-48db-a5dc-892b36b78ae3.

Kloeden, D. (2011), "Revenue Administration Reforms in Anglophone Africa Since the Early 1990s", *IMF Working Paper*, WP/11/162, International Monetary Fund, Washington, DC, www.imf.org/external/pubs/ft/wp/2011/wp11162.pdf.

Mansour M. and G. Rota-Graziosi (2013), "Tax Coordination, Tax Competition, and Revenue Mobilization in the West African Economic and Monetary Union", *IMF Working Paper* WP/13/163, International Monetary Fund, Washington, DC, https://www.imf.org/external/pubs/ft/wp/2013/wp13163.pdf.

Mascagnani, G., M. Moore and R. McCluskey (2014), *Tax revenue mobilisation in developing countries issues and challenge*, European Union, Brussels, www.europarl.europa.eu/RegData/etudes/etudes/join/2014/433849/EXPO-DEVE_ET%282014%29433849_EN.pdf.

Monkam, N. and M. Moore (2015), *How Property Tax Would Benefit Africa*, Africa Research Institute, London, UK, www.africaresearchinstitute.org/publications/property-tax-benefit-africa.

OECD (2014), *Development Co-operation Report 2014: Mobilising Resources for Sustainable Development*, OECD Publishing, Paris, http://dx.doi.org/10.1787/dcr-2014-en.

Sokeechand, K.R. and G. Hussen (2013), "The Mauritian experience", presentation prepared for regional workshop on "Effectiveness of and alternatives to tax incentives as instruments to generate employment and attract investments in Lusaka", 12-13 February, Zambia, International Tax Compact, www.taxcompact.net/documents/workshop-lusaka/2013-02-13_itc_Rambaksh-Sokeechand_MRA-MoF-Mauritius.pdf.

SSA (2015), "Social security through the world: Africa 2015", *SSA Publication* No. 13-11802, Social Security Administration, Washington DC, www.ssa.gov/policy/docs/progdesc/ssptw/2014-2015/africa/ssptw15africa.pdf.

UNDP (2013), *Rapport sur le développement humain 2013: Emploi, changements structurels et développement humain en Côte d'Ivoire*, United Nations Development Programme, New York, www.ci.undp.org/content/cote_divoire/fr/home/library/poverty/rndh_2013.html.

World Bank (2015), *Note d'orientation du financement des collectivités locales*, World Bank, Washington, DC, www-wds.worldbank.org/external/default/WDSContentServer/WDSP/IB/2015/10/13/090224b0831405d5/2_0/Rendered/PDF/Note0d0orienta0ollectivites0locales.pdf.

Further reading

AfDB (2010), "Senegal – Évaluation du potentiel de recettes publiques", www.afdb.org/fileadmin/uploads/afdb/Documents/Project-and-Operations/Pages%20from%20SENEGAL_%20Evaluation%20du%20potentiel%20des%20recettes%20publiques%20Eng.pdf.

IMF (2015), *Current challenges in revenue mobilization: Improving compliance*, International Monetary Fund, Washington, DC, https://www.imf.org/external/np/pp/eng/2015/020215a.pdf.

IMF (2014), *Government Finance Statistics Manual*, International Monetary Fund, Washington, DC.

John, J.D. (2009), "Taxation, Governance and Resource Mobilisation in Sub Saharan Africa: A Survey of Key Issues (WP)," *Sub-Saharan Africa Working Paper*, 49/2009, Real Instituto Elcano, Madrid, www.realinstitutoelcano.org/wps/portal/web/rielcano_en/contenido?WCM_GLOBAL_CONTEXT=/elcano/elcano_in/zonas_in/dt49-2009.

Keen, M. and M. Mansour (2009), "Revenue Mobilization in Sub-Saharan Africa: Challenges from Globalization", *IMF Working Paper*, WP/09/157, International Monetary Fund, Washington, DC, www.imf.org/external/pubs/ft/wp/2009/wp09157.pdf.

Lewis, C. and T. Alton (2015), "How can South Africa's tax system meet revenue raising challenges?", *OECD Economics Department Working Papers*, No. 1276, OECD Publishing, Paris, dx.doi.org/10.1787/5jrp1g0xztbr-en.

Thomas, A. and J.P. Treviño (2013), "Resource Dependence and Fiscal Effort in Sub-Saharan Africa," *IMF Working Paper*, WP/13/188, International Monetary Fund, Washington, DC, https://www.imf.org/external/pubs/ft/wp/2013/wp13188.pdf.

Wilson, P., A. Cobham and A. Goodall (2014), "The ICTD Government Revenue Dataset", *ICTD Working Paper* 19, Institute of Development Studies, Brighton, r4d.dfid.gov.uk/pdf/outputs/taxation/ICTD-WP19.pdf.

TENDANCES DES RECETTES FISCALES ET NON FISCALES, 1990-2014

Introduction

La publication annuelle, *Statistiques des recettes publiques en Afrique* (SRPA), consacrée aux statistiques des recettes publiques en Afrique présente des données permettant d'effectuer des comparaisons sur les recettes fiscales et non fiscales de huit pays africains (Afrique du Sud, Cameroun, Côte d'Ivoire, Maroc, Maurice, Rwanda, Sénégal et Tunisie). Elle contient des données comparables à l'échelle internationale sur les recettes fiscales et non fiscales, exprimées en pourcentage du PIB, pour tous les niveaux d'administration, ainsi que des données sur la composition de ces recettes. Cette publication fournit une description de quelques-uns des facteurs expliquant les évolutions observées pendant la période 1990-2014.

Les données sur les recettes des pays couverts par la publication donnent lieu à des comparaisons internationales de même qu'à des comparaisons avec la moyenne des pays de l'OCDE et celle des pays d'Amérique latine et des Caraïbes (ALC). Etant donné que les pays de ces trois groupes suivent la classification de l'OCDE, les données fournies sur les recettes peuvent être comparées tant au niveau global que par type d'impôts. Les huit pays ne constituent pas un échantillon suffisament large permettant de calculer une moyenne pertinente pour les pays d'Afrique, mais les moyennes d'une part des pays de l'OCDE et d'autre part des pays ALC y sont citées pour référence. En revanche les moyennes équivalentes concernant les recettes non fiscales pour les pays de l'OCDE et les pays ALC ne sont pas disponibles. Les statistiques des recettes publiques des pays d'Afrique et des pays ALC sont des données enregistrées sur la base des encaissements alors que la majorité des données sur les pays de l'OCDE sont enregistrées sur la base des droits constatés.

Les impôts sont des « versements obligatoires sans contrepartie aux administrations publiques » selon la définition de l'OCDE et les recettes non fiscales sont simplement l'ensemble des recettes perçues par les administrations publiques qui ne rentrent pas dans la définition des impôts. Les impôts sont sans contrepartie en ce sens que les prestations fournies par les administrations aux contribuables ne sont pas normalement proportionnelles à leurs paiements. Une recette, y compris lorsqu'elle est tirée d'un impôt, est une augmentation de la valeur nette qui résulte d'une transaction.

Il est important de présenter et d'analyser les recettes non fiscales des pays africains pour dresser un tableau équilibré de leurs finances. L'OCDE publie d'autres ouvrages sur les statistiques des recettes publiques, notamment les *Statistiques des recettes publiques*, les *Statistiques des recettes publiques en Amérique latine et dans les Caraïbes* et *Statistiques des recettes publiques dans les pays d'Asie*. Les *Statistiques des recettes publiques en Afrique* est la seule à proposer des données relatives aux recettes non fiscales.

Les données concernant les huit pays SRPA sont présentées dans un cadre harmonisé fondé sur la classification des impôts de l'OCDE. Dans cette classification, les impôts sont classés en fonction de l'assiette :

- revenus, bénéfices et gains en capital (rubrique 1000)
- salaires et main-d'œuvre (rubrique 3000)
- patrimoine (rubrique 4000)
- biens et services (rubrique 5000)
- autres (rubrique 6000)
- Les cotisations obligatoires de sécurité sociale versées aux administrations publiques sont considérées comme des impôts (rubrique 2000)

Les recettes non fiscales relèvent des catégories suivantes :

- dons
- revenus de la propriété
- ventes de biens et de services
- amendes, pénalités et confiscations
- autres recettes non fiscales

Des informations plus détaillées sur la classification des impôts sont présentées dans le Guide d'interprétation figurant à l'annexe A du présent rapport. D'autres informations sur les données des recettes non fiscales et sur leur classification figurent à l'annexe B.

RECETTES FISCALES

1.1. Niveau d'imposition

Le ratio des recettes fiscales en pourcentage du PIB est un indicateur essentiel qui mesure la proportion de fonds levés par l'impôt permettant de financer les biens et services publics et la construction d'infrastructures. L'aptitude d'un pays à recourir à la fiscalité pour mobiliser ses ressources est un facteur important pour son essor économique (OCDE, 2014). Appliquer une fiscalité appropriée est pour un État un moyen de mobiliser des recettes afin de pouvoir financer les investissements nécessaires à la croissance. C'est aussi un moyen, pour les pays en développement, de devenir moins dépendants des dons et de l'aide internationale et d'être ainsi en mesure de gagner en autonomie politique et de bâtir des États efficaces et aptes à rendre compte de leurs décisions devant les citoyens (OCDE, 2014). Un grand nombre de pays émergents reconnaissent que les recettes fiscales constituent des flux de ressources plus prévisibles que les recettes non fiscales. Les recettes non fiscales liées au pétrole et aux matières premières dont certains pays sont tributaires sont souvent incertaines et plus fluctuantes.

Niveaux d'imposition en 2014

En 2014, les recettes fiscales rapportées au PIB des huit pays SRPA (Afrique du Sud, Cameroun, Côte d'Ivoire, Maroc, Maurice, Rwanda, Sénégal et Tunisie) ont été inférieures à la moyenne de l'OCDE s'élevant à 34.4 % (voir tableau 1.1). Pour cinq d'entre eux, ce chiffre est même plus faible que la moyenne des pays d'Amérique latine et des Caraïbes[1] (ALC), s'élevant à 21.7 %.

Les huit pays de cette publication forment deux groupes distincts si l'on considère les ratios des recettes fiscales rapportées au PIB. Le premier groupe se compose de trois pays (Afrique du Sud, Maroc et Tunisie) qui ont enregistré des ratios s'échelonnant entre 28 % et 31 % en 2014 et le second groupe réunit des pays (Cameroun, Côte d'Ivoire, Maurice, Rwanda et Sénégal) affichant des ratios compris entre 16 % et 20 %. Comme le montrent le tableau 1.1 et le graphique 1.1, la Tunisie est le pays qui présentait le niveau d'imposition le plus élevé en 2014, soit 31.3 %, suivie du Maroc (28.5 %). Les résultats de ces pays s'expliquent par le niveau relativement élevé des cotisations de sécurité sociale, représentant plus de 5 % du PIB, contre moins de 2 % du PIB dans les autres pays SRPA. Les trois pays dans lesquels le niveau d'imposition en pourcentage du PIB a été le plus bas en 2014 sont le Cameroun, la Côte d'Ivoire et le Rwanda. Le Cameroun et le Rwanda ont tous deux un ratio de 16.1 %, inférieur au seuil de 17 % fixé comme critère de convergence par l'Union économique et monétaire ouest-africaine (UEMOA). La Côte d'Ivoire montre pour sa part un pourcentage légèrement supérieur à ce seuil, soit 17.8 %.

Tableau 1.1. Total des recettes fiscales en pourcentage du PIB

	1997	2000	2005	2008	2009	2010	2011	2012	2013	2014
Afrique du Sud	22.6	22.4	25.2	27.7	25.7	25.6	26.3	26.7	27.3	27.8
Cameroun	10.9	12.8	13.5	14.8	15.0	14.0	14.8	15.3	15.8	16.1
Côte d'Ivoire[1]	17.1	15.4	15.7	18.4	17.2	16.8	16.1	18.4	18.3	17.8
Maurice	17.8	19.1	18.8	19.4	20.1	19.8	19.6	20.2	19.9	20.0
Maroc[2]	..	23.6	24.8	30.5	27.3	27.1	28.7	29.7	28.5	28.5
Rwanda[3]	10.3	10.2	12.1	13.5	12.9	13.3	14.0	14.6	15.6	16.1
Sénégal[4,5]	15.3	16.8	19.3	19.0	18.9	19.8	19.9	19.5	19.2	20.1
Tunisie[3]	..	24.6	24.4	27.0	26.9	27.3	29.2	29.2	30.1	31.3
Moyenne ALC[6,7]	16.9	17.2	19.0	20.6	19.9	20.0	20.8	21.4	21.5	21.7
Moyenne de l'OCDE[7]	33.9	34.2	33.9	33.6	32.7	32.8	33.3	33.8	34.2	34.4

Note : Les chiffres excluent les recettes fiscales des collectivités locales pour le Cameroun, la Côte d'Ivoire, le Rwanda, le Sénégal et la Tunisie car les données ne sont pas disponibles. Les données des collectivités locales et provinciales ne sont pas disponibles pour l'Afrique du Sud avant 2003.

1. Le ratio des recettes fiscales au PIB comprend les loyers, les redevances et les ventes de biens et services publics normalement classés comme des recettes non fiscales dans la classification de l'OCDE. Ils sont considérés comme des recettes fiscales pour la Côte d'Ivoire. L'inclusion de ces éléments représente 0.5 % du PIB en 2014 et varie entre 0.1 % et 1.5 % pour la période 2000 à 2014.
2. Les chiffres sont estimés pour 2013 et 2014 ainsi que pour les années antérieures à 2005.
3. Le Rwanda et la Tunisie n'incluent pas les cotisations de sécurité sociale dans le ratio de pression fiscale car ces deux pays ne les considèrent pas comme des impôts. Elles sont incluses dans les recettes fiscales de cette publication.
4. Les chiffres sont estimés pour les années antérieures à 2006.
5. Les chiffres comprennent les cotisations de sécurité sociale de l'Institution de prévoyance retraite du Sénégal (IPRES) et excluent les cotisations de sécurité sociale de la Caisse de Sécurité Sociale (CSS) qui ne sont pas disponibles.
6. Représente un groupe de 22 pays d'Amérique latine et des Caraïbes (ALC).
7. Représente la moyenne non pondérée des pays ALC et OCDE.

Source : Tableau 3.1.

StatLink http://dx.doi.org/10.1787/888933344435

Évolution des niveaux d'imposition depuis 2000

Tous les pays d'Afrique de cette publication ont vu leurs recettes fiscales croître en pourcentage du PIB entre 2000 et 2014 alors que la moyenne de l'OCDE est restée relativement stable pendant cette période. Le graphique 1.1 et le tableau 1.1 montrent que les recettes fiscales rapportées au PIB ont suivi dans la plupart des pays une pente ascendante en dépit d'interruptions temporaires en 2009 et 2010 après la crise financière. Les niveaux d'imposition en pourcentage du PIB ont progressé de plus de 3 points de pourcentage entre 2000 et 2014 dans tous ces pays à l'exception de la Côte d'Ivoire et de Maurice où les hausses ont été plus modestes (2.4 points de pourcentage et 0.8 point de pourcentage respectivement) (graphique 1.2). L'Afrique du Sud[2], le Maroc, le Rwanda et la Tunisie ont affiché une augmentation du niveau d'imposition de plus de 4.5 points. Dans le même temps, les recettes fiscales rapportées au PIB dans la zone OCDE n'ont augmenté que de 0.2 point par rapport au niveau de 2000 tandis que dans la région ALC, elles ont gagné plus de 4 points.

Graphique 1.1. **Total des recettes fiscales en pourcentage du PIB, 1990-2014**

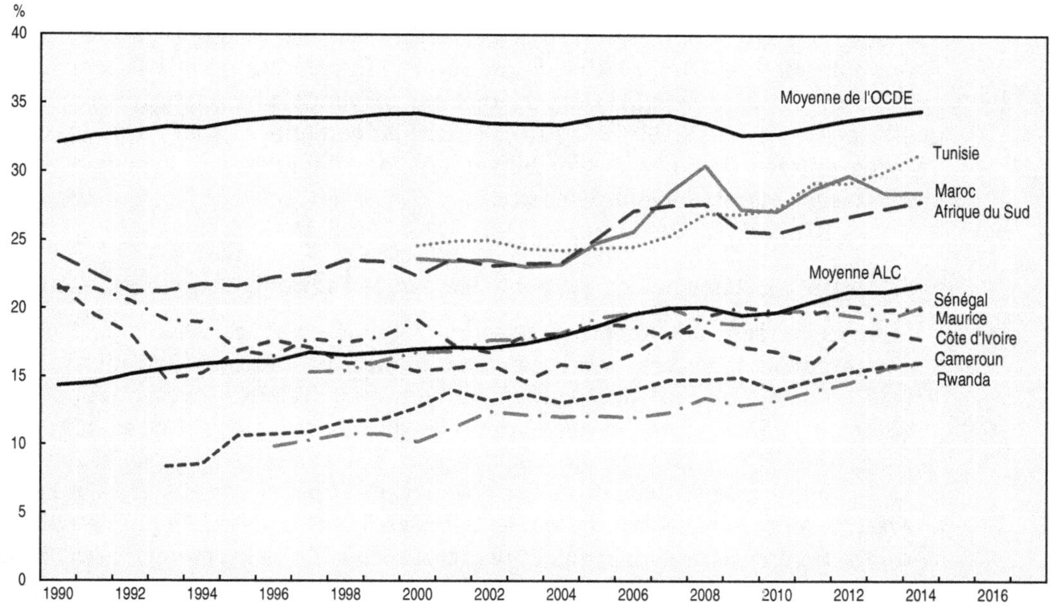

Note : Les moyennes de l'ALC et de l'OCDE ne sont pas pondérées. La moyenne de l'ALC représente un groupe de 22 pays d'Amérique latine et des Caraïbes.
Source : Tableau 3.1.

StatLink http://dx.doi.org/10.1787/888933343992

Graphique 1.2. **Variation du niveau d'imposition en pourcentage du PIB entre 2000 et 2014**

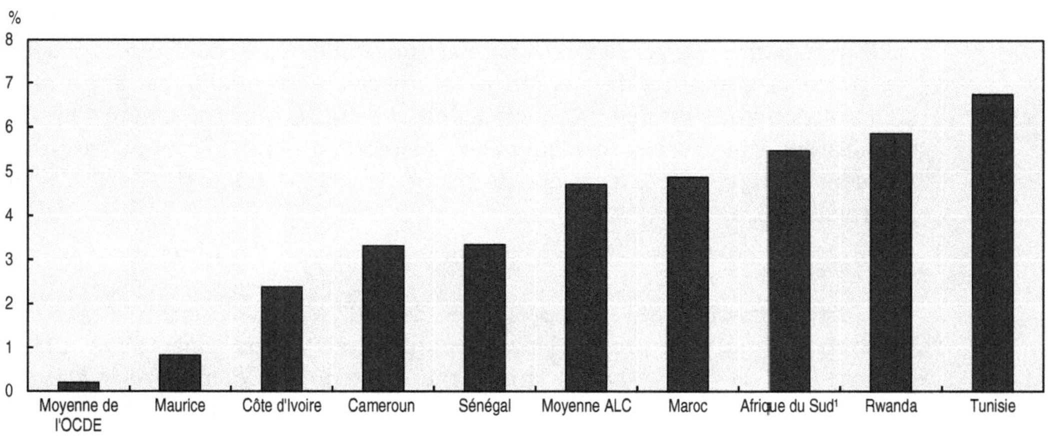

1. Le niveau d'imposition en pourcentage du PIB en Afrique du Sud inclut les recettes des collectivités locales and provinciales en 2014 et les exclut en 2000. La différence entre les deux années s'élève à 1.3 point de pourcentage.
Source : Tableau 3.1.

StatLink http://dx.doi.org/10.1787/888933344003

L'accroissement des recettes fiscales est survenu pendant une période au cours de laquelle les pays africains ont procédé à des réformes structurelles majeures au sein de leurs administrations fiscales et entrepris de modifier radicalement leurs systèmes fiscaux. Pour nombre de pays, les réformes ont eu pour but de renforcer les administrations fiscales et amener les gouvernements à créer des bureaux des gros contribuables et/ou des petits et moyens contribuables et à moderniser l'organisation des administrations fiscales. Des systèmes tels que l'impôt déclaratif, le ciblage des contribuables et une gestion moderne des risques ont été adoptés (Kloeden, 2011 ; Fossat et Bua, 2013). Certains pays ont engagé des réformes fiscales en vue d'élargir la base imposable, d'éliminer certaines exonérations et de simplifier la législation fiscale. Comme l'expliquent les *Perspectives Économiques en Afrique 2010* « De nombreux pays sont parvenus à élargir leur assiette fiscale. La Tunisie, par exemple, accroît la sienne au rythme annuel de 3.5 % ; l'Afrique du Sud et l'Égypte ont doublé la leur au cours des cinq dernières années ; et la Côte d'Ivoire est parvenue à reconstituer la sienne après la guerre civile (BAfD/OCDE/CEA, 2010). » Ces changements se sont souvent accompagnés de programmes destinés à sensibiliser les contribuables aux systèmes fiscaux et à améliorer les services à leur disposition.

Encadré 1.1. **Réformes du système fiscal et de l'administration fiscale au Rwanda**

Le recouvrement des impôts au Rwanda a gagné en efficacité depuis 2000 grâce à d'importantes réformes fiscales et administratives couplées à d'autres initiatives (BAfD, 2010). L'objectif des pouvoirs publics était d'élargir la base d'imposition en obtenant l'immatriculation des entreprises du secteur informel et en simplifiant les procédures imposées aux contribuables pour s'acquitter de leurs obligations fiscales. Le Rwanda a créé en 2006 le Bureau des moyens et petits contribuables et institué un système de gestion par bloc du fichier des contribuables (destiné à permettre de mieux traiter les dossiers des moyens et petits contribuables en regroupant les entreprises par blocs homogènes). Ces réformes ont eu des effets considérables en termes de hausse des recettes fiscales. Le taux de respect des obligations fiscales par les gros contribuables s'est sensiblement amélioré, jusqu'à atteindre 97 %. C'est une évolution importante si l'on considère que ces contribuables génèrent environ 75 % du montant total des recettes fiscales du pays. D'autres réformes ont contribué à l'accroissement des recettes fiscales, notamment l'adoption de la TVA en 2001 et l'application d'une nouvelle législation sur l'imposition des revenus et de nouveaux taux d'imposition en 2005 et 2006. Le système en place assurant le respect de la législation fiscale a été renforcé de façon à permettre un meilleur repérage des risques ainsi qu'une application plus systématique de vérifications fiscales et de pénalités. Par ailleurs, la consolidation des procédures internes de l'administration fiscale s'est traduite par une amélioration de son efficacité et par une réduction des coûts de recouvrement. D'autres mesures non fiscales ont également eu des effets sur les recettes fiscales, comme l'accroissement des dépenses consacrées à des projets prioritaires dans les domaines de l'agriculture et d'infrastructure.

La crise financière qui s'est prolongée de 2007 à 2010 a marqué un tournant dans l'évolution des taux de pression fiscale qui ont suivi des trajectoires différentes. Le ralentissement de l'activité économique mondiale qui a accompagné la crise a coïncidé avec un repli marqué des recettes fiscales rapportées au PIB dans les pays de l'OCDE. Sachant que ces pays représentent 63 % du PIB[3], il n'est pas surprenant de constater que les facteurs qui ont tiré vers le bas les taux de pression fiscale dans ces pays ont également eu des répercussions sur les recettes des États africains. De fait, tous les pays de la publication ont subi un recul de leurs recettes fiscales rapportées au PIB pendant les premières années de la crise financière mondiale. La baisse a été de 0.5 point de pourcentage, voire moins, à Maurice, au Rwanda et en Tunisie, et de 0.9 point, voire plus, dans les autres pays. Le graphique 1.3 illustre l'évolution de la pression fiscale en pourcentage du PIB dans chacun des pays depuis le pic précédant la crise jusqu'en 2014. L'Afrique du Sud, la Côte d'Ivoire[4] et le Maroc sont les pays qui ont enregistré les plus fortes variations du niveau de leurs recettes fiscales. Celles-ci, rapportées au PIB, se sont contractées de plus de 2 points pendant la crise. D'autres pays ont subi des replis moins marqués s'échelonnant entre 0.1 point en Tunisie et 1.2 point au Sénégal. Tous ont observé une augmentation de leurs recettes fiscales rapportées au PIB même si le Maroc, la Côte d'Ivoire et le Sénégal ont par la suite connu une nouvelle baisse.

Graphique 1.3. **Total des recettes fiscales en pourcentage du PIB pendant et après la période de crise**

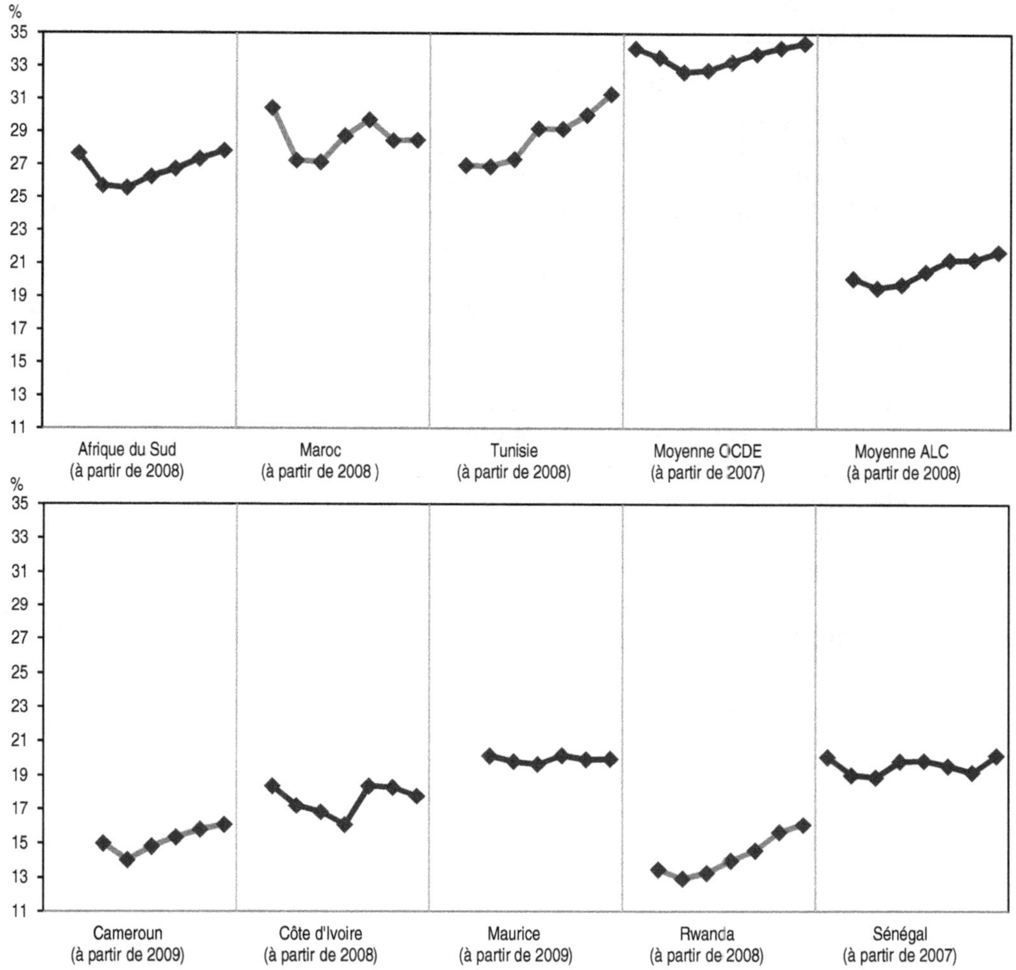

Source : Tableau 3.1.

StatLink http://dx.doi.org/10.1787/888933344016

Après la crise, les recettes fiscales rapportées au PIB ont progressé dans les huit pays et cinq d'entre eux avaient retrouvé en 2014 leur niveaux d'imposition d'avant la crise. Au Cameroun, au Rwanda et en Tunisie, un net redressement des niveaux d'imposition en pourcentage du PIB a été constaté après la crise. En 2014, ceux-ci étaient désormais nettement au-dessus de leur niveaux d'avant la crise. Le Rwanda et la Tunisie en particulier ont enregistré des hausses tout à fait considérables après la crise par rapport à leur niveau le plus bas (3.1 points de pourcentage et 4.4 points de pourcentage respectivement). Il est important de noter que la Tunisie n'avait pas à se remettre d'une chute de ses recettes aussi conséquente que celle des autres pays SRPA. Les autorités tunisiennes ont réussi à atténuer les effets de la crise financière en menant des politiques macroéconomiques prudentes ainsi qu'un ensemble de réformes (FMI, 2010). L'Afrique du Sud et le Sénégal viennent tout juste de retrouver en 2014 leurs taux de pression fiscale d'avant la crise. Au Maroc en revanche, le taux de pression fiscale s'est redressé rapidement après la crise, mais sa croissance s'est ralentie ces deux dernières années.

Facteurs ayant un effet sur les niveaux d'imposition

En moyenne, les pays SRPA sont beaucoup plus pauvres que ceux de l'OCDE. Le PIB par habitant – qui mesure le revenu moyen par personne dans le pays – était pour la moyenne des pays de l'OCDE en 2014 près de deux fois supérieur à celui du pays SRPA ayant le PIB par habitant le plus élevé. Il était 22 fois supérieur à celui du Rwanda. En outre, en moyenne, un pays ALC affichait un PIB par habitant supérieur à n'importe quel pays SRPA, à l'exception d'Afrique du Sud et de Maurice.

Les niveaux d'imposition sont généralement supérieurs dans les pays à haut revenu. Le graphique 1.4 illustre par un nuage de points le niveau d'imposition en pourcentage du PIB et le PIB par habitant des pays de l'OCDE en comparaison avec l'Amérique latine, les Caraïbes et l'Afrique. Les pays de l'OCDE se situent dans l'angle supérieur droit du graphique, qui réunit des pays relativement riches et qui collectent des recettes fiscales importantes auprès de leur population. Les pays d'Afrique se concentrent dans l'angle inférieur gauche du graphique, où se trouvent les pays à la fois plus pauvres et moins à même de mobiliser des ressources intérieures. Avec un faible PIB par habitant, le Cameroun, la Côte d'Ivoire, le Rwanda et le Sénégal se situent à l'intérieur du groupe principal de pays d'Afrique, tandis que l'Afrique du Sud, Maurice, le Maroc et la Tunisie se rapprochent davantage du milieu du groupe des pays d'Amérique latine et des Caraïbes (bien au dessus et à droite de la moyenne de l'Afrique). Cela signifie que ces pays, bien que plus pauvres que les pays de l'OCDE, sont plus riches que les pays africains en général. Maurice se positionne très à gauche des trois autres pays SRPA à revenu élevé. Ce pays se caractérise par un PIB par habitant élevé mais aussi par un niveau d'imposition faible par rapport à l'Afrique du Sud, le Maroc et la Tunisie.

Graphique 1.4. PIB par habitant en PPA (dollars) et niveau d'imposition en pourcentage du PIB dans les pays d'Afrique, d'Amérique Latine et des Caraïbes et de l'OCDE, 2014

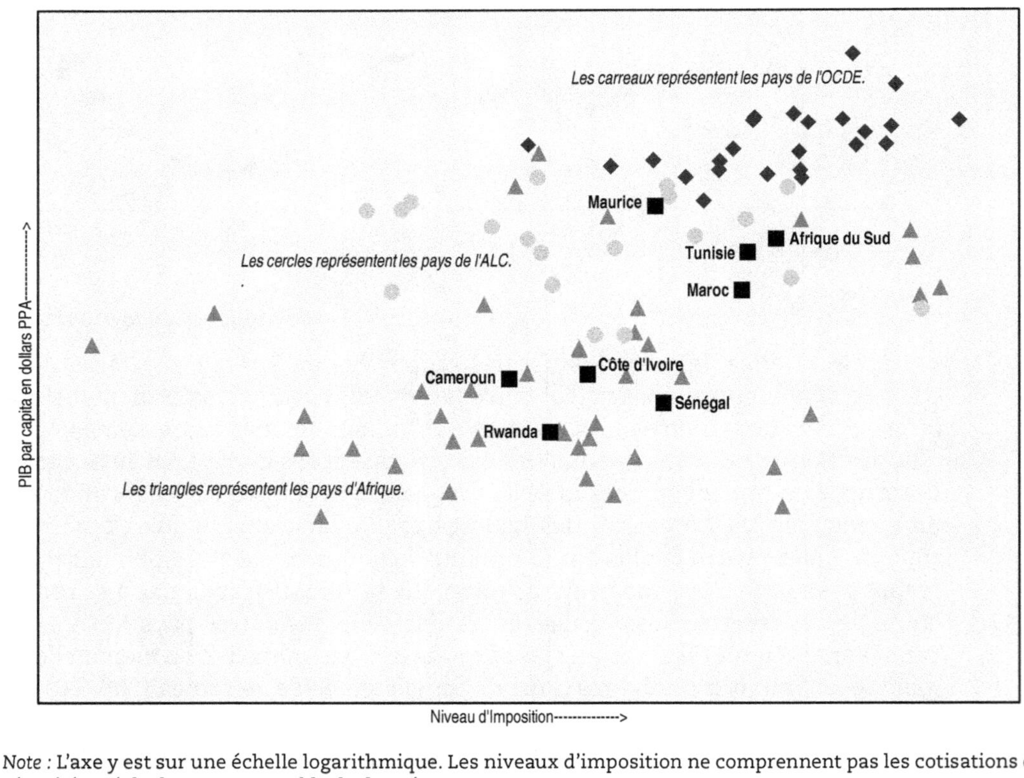

Note : L'axe y est sur une échelle logarithmique. Les niveaux d'imposition ne comprennent pas les cotisations de sécurité sociale dans cet ensemble de données.

Source : Perspectives de l'économie mondiale, octobre 2015, Fond monétaire international.

StatLink http://dx.doi.org/10.1787/888933344023

De nombreux facteurs, nationaux et internationaux et de nature à la fois économique et structurelle, influent sur les niveaux d'imposition. Les facteurs économiques susceptibles de se répercuter sur les niveaux d'imposition incluent l'importance de l'agriculture dans l'économie, la disponibilité de ressources naturelles, le degré d'ouverture au commerce international et l'ampleur de l'économie informelle. En outre, des pays extérieurs peuvent agir sur les niveaux d'imposition en fixant des taux d'imposition compétitifs ou en se livrant à des pratiques fiscales agressives: en manipulant les prix de transfert par exemple. Tous ces facteurs peuvent nuire à la capacité d'un pays de mobiliser des recettes (Mascagnani, Moore et McCluskey, 2014). La structure du système fiscal joue également un rôle : le pouvoir de l'administration fiscale, le niveau de corruption et le civisme fiscal (le consentement à l'impôt) sont aussi étroitement liés au niveau des recettes fiscales (OCDE, 2014). Enfin, l'emplacement géographique et des facteurs historiques peuvent exercer une influence sur les niveaux d'imposition : par exemple, les pays enclavés peuvent plus difficilement taxer les biens et services au port d'entrée que les pays ayant un accès à la mer.

Les trois pays SRPA qui enregistrent les niveaux d'imposition les plus faibles sont également ceux dans lesquels la prédominance de l'agriculture dans l'économie est la plus élevée (plus de 20 %), comme l'illustre le graphique 1.5. Une proportion élevée de l'agriculture en pourcentage du PIB est généralement associé à un taux de pression fiscale faible (Addison et Levin, 2012). Ce résultat est cohérent avec les données disponibles pour les huit pays africains. Cela s'expliquerait par le faible niveau des prélèvements dans le secteur agricole en Afrique en raison de l'ampleur de l'activité informelle et du faible degré de monétisation. Les exploitants agricoles africains effectuent souvent leurs paiements en espèces ou en nature, sans passer par le système bancaire, et peu tiennent une comptabilité en bonne et due forme (BAfD/OCDE/CEA, 2010). Outre le manque de discipline fiscale, le secteur agricole en Afrique bénéficie de nombreuses exemptions d'impôt. Au Rwanda, par exemple, les entreprises agricoles sont exonérées de la TVA sur les intrants et les produits agricoles. Il existe aussi des exonérations de TVA en Côte d'Ivoire et au Sénégal. Du fait de l'importance du secteur agricole dans de nombreux pays africains, ces facteurs ont des répercussions sur la situation financière des États, alors que dans les pays de l'OCDE, l'agriculture ne représente guère plus de 2 % du PIB en moyenne. Il faut toutefois remarquer que Maurice, État insulaire, compte un secteur agricole de petite taille et enregistre un taux de pression fiscale relativement faible, tandis qu'au Maroc, l'agriculture représente 15 % de l'économie et le taux de pression fiscale est relativement élevé (28.5 %).

La Côte d'Ivoire et le Cameroun tirent des recettes substantielles des exportations de pétrole et enregistrent des faibles niveaux d'imposition en pourcentage du PIB en raison d'une assiette imposable étroite. Le Cameroun et la Côte d'Ivoire sont classés par le Fonds monétaire international sur la liste des pays « riches en ressources naturelles ».[5] Leurs principales exportations de ressources minérales sont le pétrole (BAfD/OCDE/PNUD, 2015). Les pays qui tirent d'importantes recettes de leurs ressources naturelles ont généralement des taux de pression fiscale plus faibles que d'autres pays qui ne disposent pas de telles ressources. En effet, ils ont moins recours à des formes d'imposition plus politiquement contraignantes, comme l'impôt sur le revenu (BAfD/OCDE/CEA, 2010), et leurs bases d'imposition sont relativement étroites. Au Cameroun et en Côte d'Ivoire, un groupe restreint de contribuables supporte l'essentiel de la charge fiscale. Au Cameroun, par exemple, seulement dix entreprises ont payé 55 % du total des impôts sur les bénéfices des sociétés en 2013 (FMI, 2014b). On estime que le secteur informel en Côte d'Ivoire représente 90 % de l'économie (PNUD, 2013). Par conséquent, les taux de pression fiscale de ces deux pays se situent au bas de l'échelle. Au cours des années 2000, ces deux pays ont engagé diverses initiatives visant à remédier à la surexploitation de la base d'imposition disponible (BAfD/OCDE/CEA, 2010). La Côte d'Ivoire a décidé de limiter l'application de mesures préférentielles à des secteurs prioritaires et à ceux qui ont été particulièrement touchés par la crise de 2002. En 2009 et 2010, le gouvernement camerounais a mis en place des programmes destinés à mobiliser de nouveaux contribuables provenant du secteur informel (BAfD/OCDE/CEA, 2010). Ces dernières années, ces deux pays ont continué de renforcer leur politique et leur administration fiscales dans le but d'élargir leur base d'imposition (FMI, 2013 ; FMI, 2014).

Graphique 1.5. **Agriculture en pourcentage du PIB et niveau d'imposition en pourcentage du PIB, 2014**

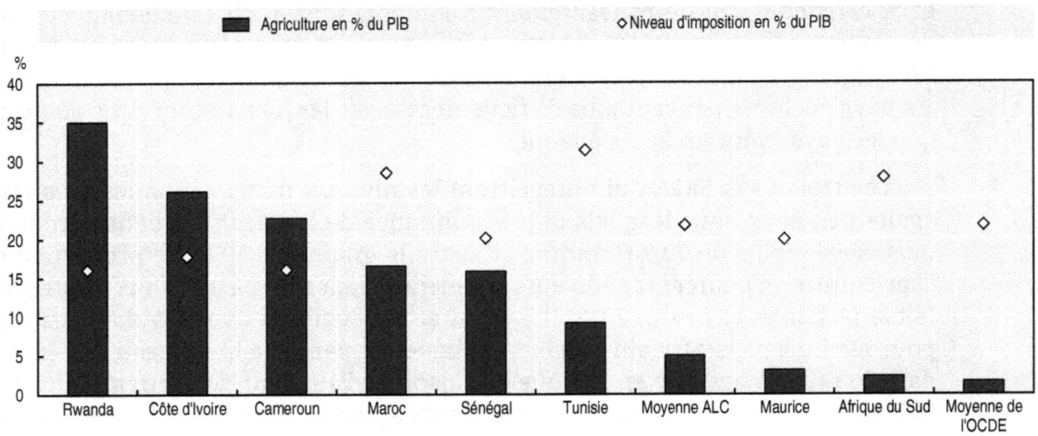

Note : L' indicateur agriculture en % du PIB comprend la silviculture, la chasse et la pêche, ainsi que la cultivation et la production animale. La moyenne de l'ALC comprend seulement les pays en développement de L'Amérique latine et des Caraïbes.

Source : Tableau 1.1; BAfD, OCDE et PNUD (2015), *Perspectives économiques en Afrique 2015: Développement territorial et inclusion spatiale*; Banque mondiale.

StatLink http://dx.doi.org/10.1787/888933344035

Le niveau d'imposition en pourcentage du PIB de Maurice s'élevant à 20 % reste faible comparé aux pays de l'OCDE, bien que Maurice soit le pays SRPA qui s'apparente le plus à un pays de l'OCDE de par la structure de ses revenus et son profil économique. Ce faible niveau d'imposition est en conséquence de décisions fiscales des autorités mauriciennes. En effet, Maurice est l'un des pays d'Afrique qui offre le régime fiscal le plus attractif (Sokeechand et Hussen, 2013), avec des taux uniques de 15 % pour l'impôt sur les sociétés, l'impôt sur le revenu des personnes physiques et la TVA. À l'inverse, le taux de l'impôt sur les sociétés dépasse 25 % dans les sept autres pays SRPA et atteint 30 % au Cameroun, au Maroc, au Rwanda et au Sénégal. Les entreprises multinationales établies à Maurice peuvent également prétendre à un crédit d'impôt de 80 % au titre de l'impôt mauricien, aboutissant à un taux effectif d'imposition de 3 %. Le crédit d'impôt en faveur des entreprises étrangères est soit beaucoup moins généreux, soit inexistant dans les sept autres pays. Enfin, Maurice ne taxe pas les gains en capital ou les dividendes, à la différence des autres pays, et les entreprises sont exonérées d'un certain nombre d'impôts tels que la taxe foncière, les droits de timbre et les droits de mutation (Sokeechand et Hussen, 2013).

L'impact des principaux impôts sur le niveau global d'imposition

La croissance des recettes fiscales intervenue depuis 2000 résulte principalement d'une hausse des impôts sur le revenu et sur les bénéfices, tandis que ces impôts ont baissé dans les pays de l'OCDE en moyenne. Ainsi que le tableau 1.2 l'indique, sept pays ont vu leurs impôts sur le revenu et sur les bénéfices augmenter en pourcentage du PIB, allant de 1.4 point au Sénégal à 4.4 points en Tunisie. La Côte d'Ivoire est le seul pays qui a enregistré une légère baisse. Le montant moyen des recettes recouvrées par les pays de l'OCDE grâce à ces impôts a lui aussi reculé de 0.5 point depuis 2000. Toutefois, il est resté bien supérieur à celui de tous les pays SRPA, à l'exception de l'Afrique du Sud dont le ratio s'élevait à 14.3 %. En 2014, les recettes tirées des impôts sur le revenu et sur les bénéfices représentaient moins de 6 % du PIB au Cameroun, en Côte d'Ivoire, à Maurice, au Rwanda et au Sénégal, et entre 8 % et 10 % au Maroc et en Tunisie, contre près de 12 % dans les pays de l'OCDE (graphique 1.6).

Tableau 1.2. **Variations du niveau d'imposition en pourcentage du PIB par type d'impôts entre 2000 et 2014**

	Impôts sur le revenu et les bénéfices (1000)	Cotisations de sécurité sociale (2000)	Impôts sur les salaires et la main-d'œuvre (3000)	Impôts sur le patrimoine (4000)	Impôts sur les biens et services (5000)	Autres impôts (6000)	Total des recettes fiscales
Afrique du Sud	1.6	0.4	0.3	1.0	2.5	-0.3	5.5
Cameroun	1.5	0.0	0.3	-0.1	1.4	0.2	3.3
Côte d'Ivoire	-0.1	0.7	0.0	0.0	1.7	0.0	2.4
Maurice	2.3	0.0	-0.1	-0.1	-1.4	0.0	0.8
Maroc	2.5	2.0	0.0	0.6	-0.4	0.1	4.9
Rwanda	3.3	0.5	0.0	0.0	2.0	0.0	5.9
Sénégal	1.4	0.3	0.0	0.2	1.4	0.0	3.3
Tunisie	4.4	3.4	0.0	0.1	-1.4	0.3	6.7

Note : Le niveau d'imposition en pourcentage du PIB en Afrique du Sud inclut les recettes des collectivités locales and provinciales en 2014 et les exclut en 2000. La différence entre les deux années s'élève à 1.3 point de pourcentage.

StatLink http://dx.doi.org/10.1787/888933344445

Graphique 1.6. **Impôts sur le revenu et les bénéfices en pourcentage du PIB, 2014**

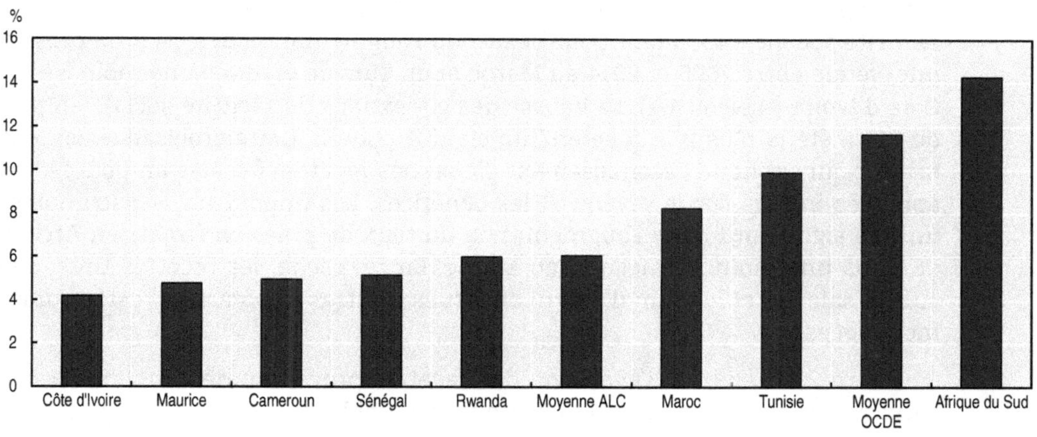

Source : Tableau 3.2.

StatLink http://dx.doi.org/10.1787/888933344049

Dans les sept pays où les recettes fiscales générées par les impôts sur le revenu et sur les bénéfices ont progressé, la croissance des recettes issues de l'impôt sur les sociétés a dépassé celle des recettes de l'impôt sur le revenu des personnes physiques, sauf au Rwanda et au Sénégal. Tous ces pays ont enregistré une progression des recettes de l'impôt sur les sociétés entre 2000 et 2014 (tableau 1.3). Les trois pays aux niveaux d'imposition les plus élevés ont vu leur ratio des impôts sur les bénéfices en pourcentage du PIB croître de plus de 2 points au cours de cette période. En revanche, le ratio des recettes de l'impôt sur le revenu des personnes physiques a augmenté dans tous les pays sauf en Afrique du Sud et au Cameroun. Dans la plupart des pays, l'ampleur des hausses des recettes provenant de l'impôt sur les bénéfices a été beaucoup plus prononcée que celle des recettes de l'impôt sur le revenu des personnes physiques. On observe toutefois la situation inverse au Rwanda et au Sénégal, où le ratio des recettes de l'impôt sur le revenu des personnes physiques a progressé beaucoup plus fortement (respectivement 2.6 points et 1.2 point) que celui de l'impôt sur les bénéfices des sociétés (0.7 point et 0.2 point).

Tableau 1.3. **Variations des recettes fiscales issues de l'impôt sur le revenu et des bénéfices en pourcentage du PIB par type d'impôts entre 2000 et 2014**

	Les impôts sur les revenus et les bénéfices (1000)	Impôts sur les revenus (1100)	Impôts sur les bénéfices (1200)	Non ventilable (1300)
Afrique du Sud	1.6	-0.3	2.3	-0.4
Cameroun	1.5	-0.2	1.1	0.6
Maurice	2.3	0.5	1.5	0.3
Maroc	2.5	0.2	2.3	0.0
Rwanda	3.3	2.6	0.7	0.0
Sénégal	1.4	1.2	0.2	0.0
Tunisie	4.4	1.5	2.8	0.0

Note : Les données pour le Cameroun doivent être interprétées avec prudence compte tenu de la proportion relativement élevée du montant non ventilable entre les impôts sur le revenu et les impôts sur les bénéfices dans le total des impôts sur le revenu et les bénéfices.

StatLink http://dx.doi.org/10.1787/888933344451

Les cotisations de sécurité sociale ont beaucoup contribué à la hausse des taux de pression fiscale dans trois pays, tandis qu'en Afrique du Sud, les impôts sur le patrimoine sont principalement à l'origine de cette évolution. Les cotisations de sécurité sociale expliquent pour beaucoup l'augmentation des taux de pression fiscale intervenue entre 2000 et 2014 au Maroc et en Tunisie et, dans une moindre mesure, en Côte d'Ivoire (tableau 1.2). La hausse des cotisations de sécurité sociale en pourcentage du PIB a été la plus marquée en Tunisie (3.4 points). Cette croissance est le deuxième facteur qui explique l'accroissement global des recettes fiscales en pourcentage du PIB après les impôts sur le revenu et les bénéfices. Les impôts sur le patrimoine ont joué un rôle significatif dans l'augmentation du taux de pression fiscale en Afrique du Sud et, dans une moindre mesure, au Maroc. En revanche, les recettes tirées des impôts sur les salaires et la main d'œuvre ou issues d'autres impôts sont restées pratiquement inchangées.

Entre 2000 et 2014, l'évolution des recettes provenant des impôts sur les biens et services, en pourcentage du PIB, a été très variable d'un pays à l'autre. Cette source de recettes a augmenté dans cinq pays (Afrique du Sud, Cameroun, Côte d'Ivoire, Rwanda et Sénégal) de 1.4 point ou plus et a diminué dans trois pays (Maurice, Maroc et Tunisie). Bien que la progression des recettes tirées des impôts sur les biens et services en pourcentage du PIB ait été inférieure à celle des impôts sur le revenu et sur les bénéfices au Cameroun, au Rwanda et au Sénégal, cela n'a pas été le cas en Afrique du Sud et en Côte d'Ivoire. L'accroissement du ratio des recettes issues des impôts sur les biens et services a été le principal facteur à l'origine de l'augmentation globale des niveaux d'imposition dans ces deux derniers pays.

Au sein de la catégorie des impôts sur les biens et services, les impôts généraux sur la consommation ont beaucoup contribué à la progression des recettes fiscales dans six pays SRPA. Comme le montre le tableau 1.4, les impôts généraux sur la consommation (principalement les taxes sur la valeur ajoutée), en pourcentage du PIB, se sont accrus dans tous les pays SRPA. Rwanda a enregistré la plus forte hausse depuis 2000 (3.1 points). Le pays a mis en place en 2001 un régime de TVA remplaçant ainsi la taxe sur les ventes. Au Maroc, l'augmentation de 2.9 points est imputable en grande partie à une réforme de la TVA de grande ampleur intervenue en 2005. Cette réforme a aligné le système fiscal marocain sur les meilleures pratiques internationales en supprimant des exemptions, élargissant la base d'imposition (pour couvrir les secteurs des services et de la vente au détail) et réduisant le nombre de taux d'imposition (Cruce, 2011). En outre, Maurice a relevé son taux de TVA de 12 % à 15 % en 2003, ce qui a contribué à la hausse des recettes issues des impôts généraux sur la consommation.

Tableau 1.4. **Variations des recettes des impôts sur les biens et services en pourcentage du PIB par sous-catégorie entre 2000 et 2014**

	Impôts sur les biens et services (5000)	Impôts généraux sur la consommation (5110)	Impôts sur les biens et services déterminés (5120)
Afrique du Sud	2.5	1.3	1.0
Cameroun	1.4	1.2	0.2
Côte d'Ivoire	1.7	0.2	1.4
Maurice	-1.4	2.0	-3.5
Maroc	-0.4	2.9	-3.3
Rwanda	2.0	3.1	-1.1
Sénégal	1.4	0.6	0.8
Tunisie	-1.4	0.4	-1.8

StatLink http://dx.doi.org/10.1787/888933344464

Les recettes provenant d'impôts spécifiques sur la consommation (principalement les droits d'accise et les droits à l'importation) ont enregistré soit de fortes baisses, soit une hausse relativement limitée, en pourcentage du PIB. Entre 2000 et 2014, Maurice, le Maroc, le Rwanda et la Tunisie ont vu leurs recettes tirées d'impôts spécifiques sur la consommation diminuer. Cette tendance a été compensée intégralement par une progression des recettes provenant des impôts généraux sur la consommation au Rwanda et partiellement dans les trois autres pays. En revanche, l'Afrique du Sud, le Cameroun, la Côte d'Ivoire et le Sénégal ont enregistré une augmentation des recettes générées par les impôts spécifiques sur la consommation en pourcentage du PIB. La dégradation des recettes fiscales provenant des droits à l'importation est due en partie à la libéralisation des échanges sous la forme de réductions des droits de douane et de nouveaux accords commerciaux (BAfD/OCDE/CEA, 2010). La libéralisation des échanges s'est traduite par une diminution des droits à l'importation et par la quasi-disparition des taxes à l'exportation comme source de recettes au cours des dernières décennies. La Côte d'Ivoire fait exception à ces tendances. Les recettes mobilisées par les taxes à l'exportation restent une composante essentielle du budget de la Côte d'Ivoire, et les droits à l'importation en pourcentage du PIB sont même en augmentation depuis l'année 2000. Cette augmentation est à l'origine de la hausse relativement importante des recettes tirées des impôts spécifiques sur la consommation[6] en pourcentage du PIB.

Graphique 1.7. **Impôts sur le revenu et les bénéfices en pourcentage du PIB dans les pays au niveau d'imposition plus faible, 2000-14**

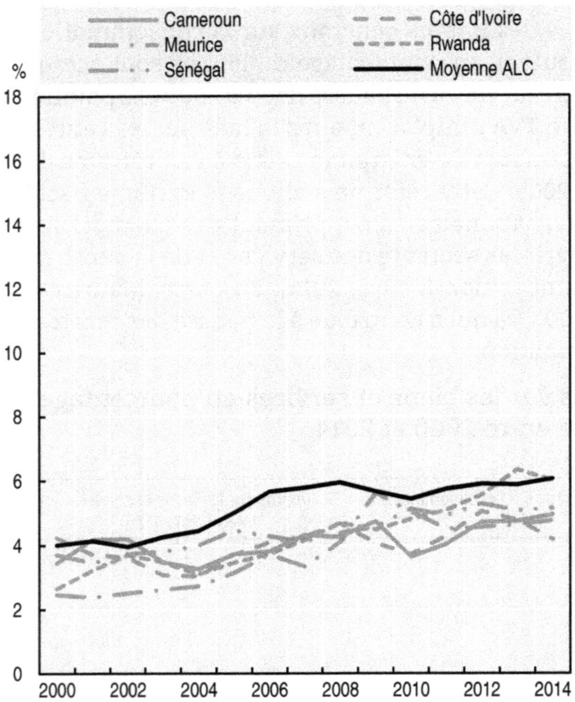

Source : Tableau 3.4.

StatLink http://dx.doi.org/10.1787/888933344056

Graphique 1.8. **Impôts sur les biens et services en pourcentage du PIB dans les pays au niveau d'imposition plus faible en pourcentage du PIB, 2000-14**

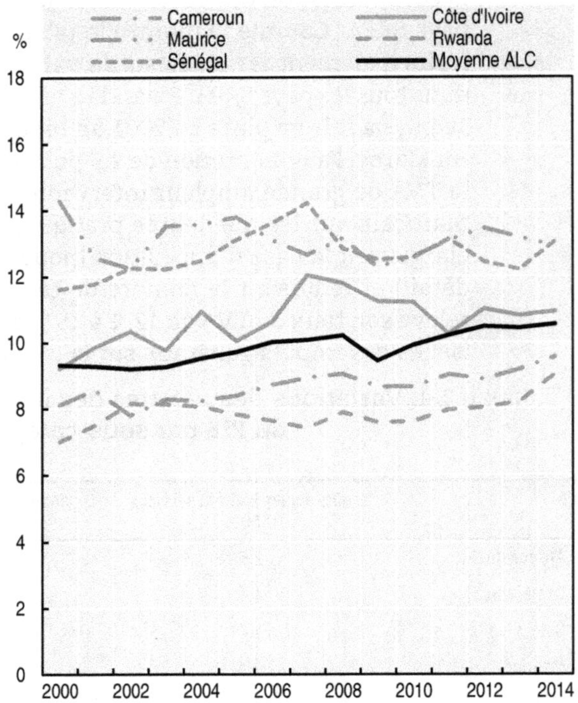

Source : Tableau 3.4.

StatLink http://dx.doi.org/10.1787/888933344063

Graphique 1.9. **Impôts sur le revenu et les bénéfices en pourcentage du PIB dans les pays au niveau d'imposition plus élevé en pourcentage du PIB, 2000-14**

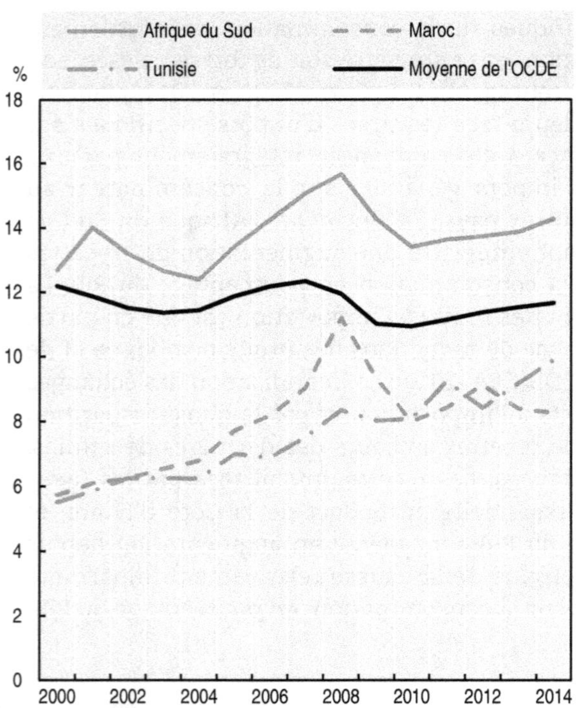

Source : Tableau 3.4.

StatLink http://dx.doi.org/10.1787/888933344079

Graphique 1.10. **Impôts sur les biens et services en pourcentage du PIB dans les pays au niveau d'imposition plus élevé en pourcentage du PIB, 2000-14**

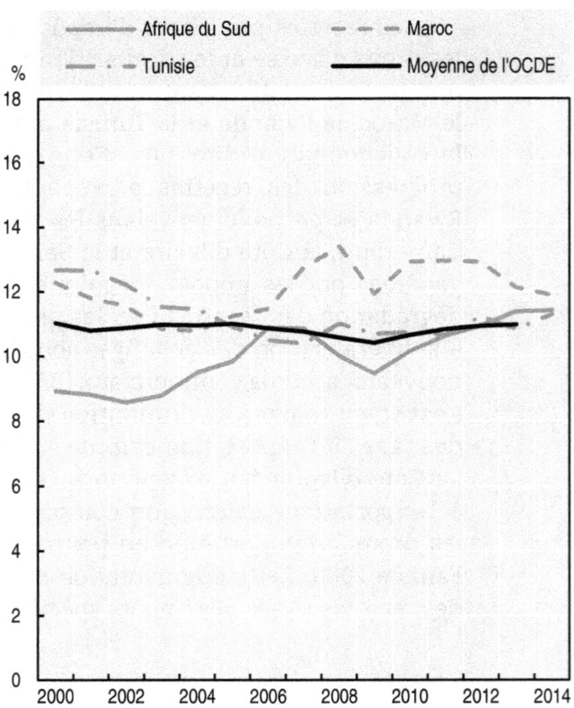

Source : Tableau 3.4.

StatLink http://dx.doi.org/10.1787/888933344080

Graphique 1.11. Impôts généraux sur la consommation en pourcentage du PIB dans les pays au niveau d'imposition plus faible par rapport au PIB, 2000-14

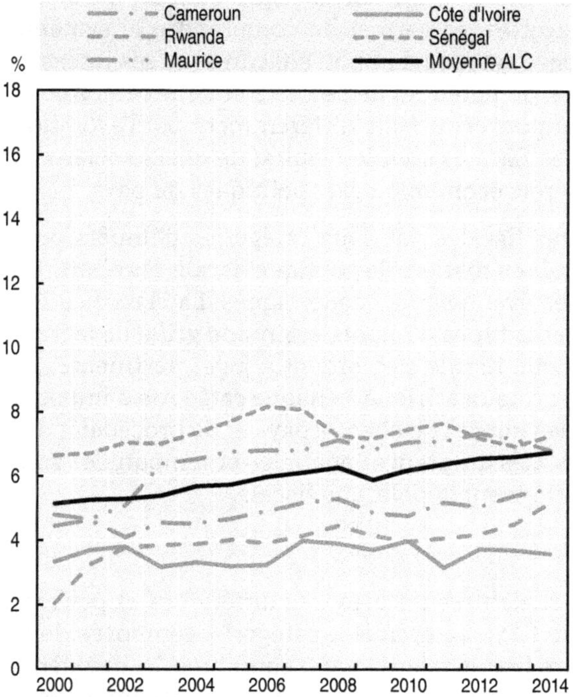

Source : Tableau 3.12.

StatLink http://dx.doi.org/10.1787/888933344095

Graphique 1.12. Impôts sur la consommation spécifique en pourcentage du PIB dans les pays au niveau d'imposition plus faible en pourcentage du PIB, 2000-14

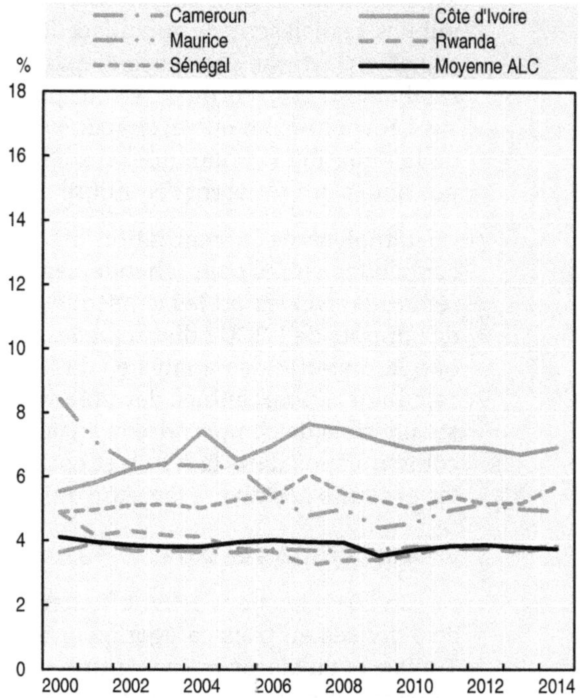

Source : Tableau 3.12.

StatLink http://dx.doi.org/10.1787/888933344105

Graphique 1.13. Impôts généraux sur la consommation en pourcentage du PIB dans les pays au niveau d'imposition plus élevé en pourcentage du PIB, 2000-14

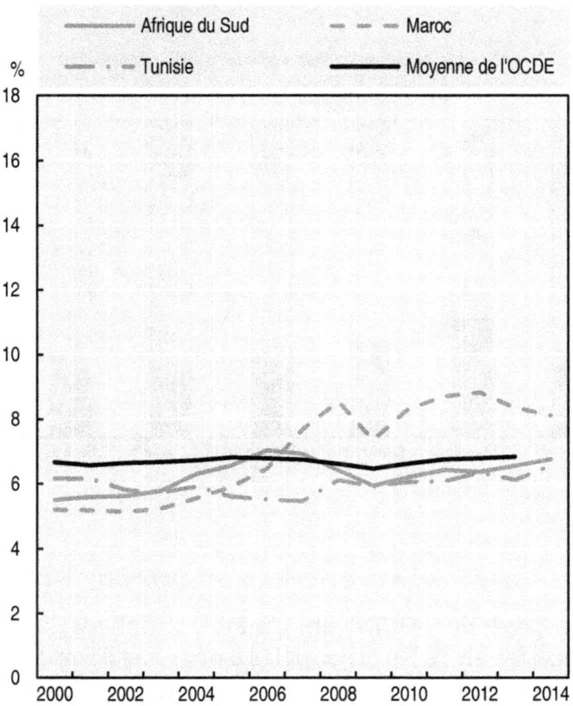

Source : Tableau 3.12.

StatLink http://dx.doi.org/10.1787/888933344117

Graphique 1.14. Impôts généraux sur la consommation en pourcentage du PIB dans les pays au niveau d'imposition plus élevé en pourcentage du PIB, 2000-14

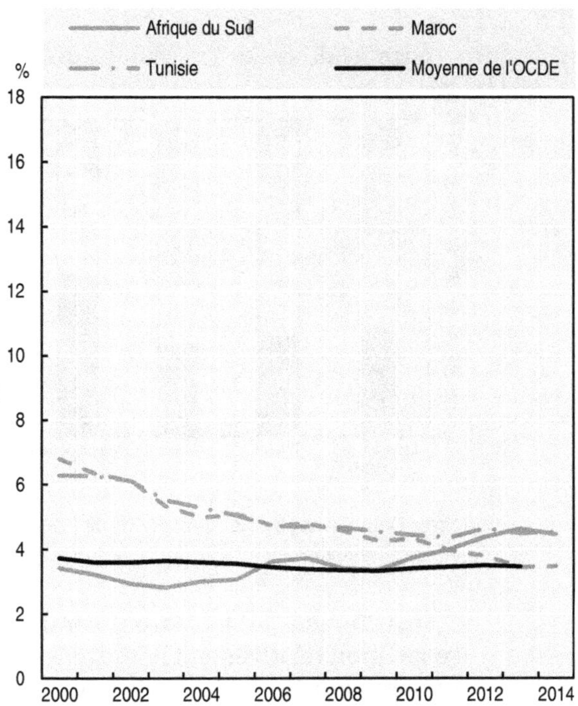

Source : Tableau 3.12.

StatLink http://dx.doi.org/10.1787/888933344122

1.2 Structures fiscales

L'examen des structures des systèmes fiscaux dans les différents pays, en conjonction avec celui de la pression fiscale, apporte un éclairage sur la façon dont les pouvoirs publics choisissent de mobiliser leurs recettes, et permet de comprendre le système social et politique d'un pays. Il existe plusieurs types d'impôt, chacun avec ses forces et ses faiblesses en termes de coût politique, de potentiel de recettes et de répercussions sur l'économie. En outre, chacun de ces impôts est affecté différemment par l'évolution de la situation économique. Les structures fiscales sont le résultat de choix sociaux et politiques qui reflètent l'équilibre des intérêts économiques et politiques du pays.

L'analyse de la ventilation des recettes fiscales par sous catégories d'impôts peut contribuer à mieux appréhender les priorités en matière de politique fiscale, les effets des réformes fiscales ou les conséquences des événements économiques. La classification des impôts de l'OCDE distingue les différents types d'impôts selon une grille de lecture que la majorité des analystes de la politique fiscale s'accordent à juger pertinente. En calculant le pourcentage des prélèvements totaux attribué à chaque catégorie d'impôt, il est possible de comprendre la structure des impôts de chaque pays et de procéder à des comparaisons dans la durée et entre pays. Ces différences spatiales et temporelles sont les produits des divers facteurs qui conditionnent la politique fiscale.

Structures fiscales en 2014

En 2014, les pays SRPA affichent des structures fiscales très différentes et peuvent être divisés en trois catégories (graphique 1.15). La première catégorie, composée de la Tunisie et du Maroc, présente une structure fiscale relativement équilibrée. La deuxième catégorie inclut uniquement l'Afrique du Sud, qui recourt massivement aux impôts sur les revenus et les bénéfices, puisqu'ils représentent près de la moitié de ses recettes fiscales. La troisième catégorie rassemble des pays ayant des pressions fiscales plus faibles et qui réalisent plus de la moitié de leurs recettes fiscales grâce aux impôts sur la consommation.

Graphique 1.15. **Structures fiscales, 2014**

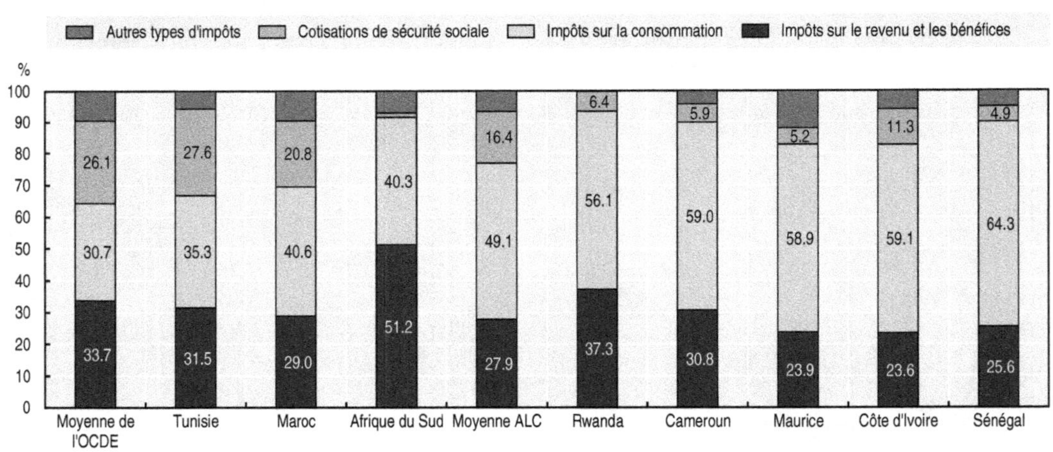

Note : Données 2013 pour la moyenne de l'OCDE.
Source : Tableau 3.2.

StatLink http://dx.doi.org/10.1787/888933344136

La Tunisie et le Maroc, comme les pays de l'OCDE en général, affichent une répartition relativement homogène des recettes entre les principales catégories d'impôts (graphique 1.15). Les pays de l'OCDE ont généralement mis en place une structure fiscale équilibrée, suivant l'idée répandu que ce système de système fiscal permet de mobiliser plus de recettes à moindre coût (BAfD/OCDE/CEA, 2010). En dépit des nombreuses différences observées dans les structures fiscales des pays de l'OCDE, la majeure partie des recettes fiscales se divise à parts globalement égales entre trois catégories : un tiers provient des impôts sur le revenu et sur les bénéfices, un quart des cotisations de sécurité sociale et environ 30 % des impôts généraux et spécifiques sur la consommation. Hormis ces trois principales catégories, les autres impôts représentent environ 10 % du total des recettes fiscales. On observe une structure fiscale analogue à ce modèle au Maroc et en Tunisie. Toutefois, en 2014, les recettes tirées des impôts sur la consommation y étaient légèrement supérieures à la moyenne de l'OCDE de 30.7 %.

L'Afrique du Sud obtient la moitié de ses recettes fiscales des impôts sur le revenu et les bénéfices, soit une fraction beaucoup plus importante que celle recouvrée par les autres pays de ce rapport et que la moyenne des pays de l'OCDE. Néanmoins, cette situation est contrebalancée par le fait qu'elle tire très peu de recettes des cotisations de sécurité sociale. Les recettes issues des impôts sur le revenu et les bénéfices oscillaient entre 30 % et 40 % au Cameroun, au Maroc, au Rwanda et en Tunisie, et entre 23 % et 26 % en Côte d'Ivoire, à Maurice et au Sénégal, contre 34 % environ dans les pays de l'OCDE en moyenne (graphique 1.15).

En 2014, les impôts sur la consommation (principalement la TVA, les droits d'accise et les droits à l'importation) ont constitué la majorité des recettes fiscales totales des pays ayant une faible pression fiscale. En Côte d'Ivoire, au Cameroun, à Maurice, au Rwanda et au Sénégal, plus de 55 % des recettes dégagées en 2014 provenaient des impôts sur la consommation. Ce sont des niveaux comparables à ceux enregistrés dans les pays ALC, qui collectent en moyenne la moitié environ de leurs recettes fiscales via ces impôts. Ce schéma est caractéristique des pays émergents et des pays pauvres (Besley et Persson, 2013).

La TVA, les droits d'accise et les droits à l'importation représentent souvent un plus fort pourcentage des recettes collectées dans les pays d'Afrique à bas revenu parce qu'ils sont généralement moins coûteux à recouvrer que d'autres types d'impôts. Les droits à l'importation sont eux aussi moins onéreux à administrer puisqu'ils requièrent uniquement de la part des pouvoirs publics l'enregistrement des opérations commerciales aux principaux points de passage aux frontières. À l'inverse, les impôts sur le revenu des personnes physiques sont collectés auprès de millions de personnes, ce qui oblige à procéder à des investissements considérables dans des structures de recouvrement et de contrôle (Besley et Persson, 2013). Dans les pays plus riches comme l'Afrique du Sud, le Maroc et la Tunisie, les impôts sur la consommation représentent 35 % à 40 % du PIB, contre environ 30 % dans les pays de l'OCDE.

L'importance des cotisations de sécurité sociale[7] est très variable entre les huit pays SRPA. La part des cotisations de sécurité sociale dans le total des recettes fiscales est la plus élevée en Tunisie (27.6 %) et au Maroc (20.8 %), où elle se rapproche de la moyenne de l'OCDE de 26.1 %. Elles occupent une place beaucoup plus modeste dans le total des recettes fiscales dans les autres pays, allant de 1.5 % en Afrique du Sud à 11.3 % en Côte d'Ivoire. Cette hétérogénéité reflète la diversité des régimes de sécurité sociale et des taux de cotisation dans les pays SRPA, qui en ont souvent hérité des pays qui les ont colonisés. Par exemple, les cotisations de sécurité sociale en Afrique du Sud se composent uniquement des cotisations au Fonds d'assurance chômage. Les autres risques sociaux, tels que la vieillesse, la maladie et la maternité, sont couverts par des programmes d'aide sociale – qui se distinguent des régimes de sécurité sociale en ce qu'ils sont non contributifs. En Afrique du Sud, le système de sécurité sociale est beaucoup moins développé que celui d'aide sociale. À l'inverse, les régimes de sécurité sociale marocain et tunisien sont calqués sur le système français et couvrent un éventail plus large de risques, y compris la vieillesse, l'incapacité, la maladie, la maternité, les accidents du travail (Tunisie), le chômage (Maroc) et les allocations familiales (SSA, 2015).

On observe des divergences entre les pays SRPA concernant l'importance relative des recettes issues de l'impôt sur les bénéfices des sociétés et de l'impôt sur le revenu des personnes physiques. Comme l'illustre le graphique 1.16, les recettes de l'impôt sur le revenu des personnes physiques sont plus élevées que celles de l'impôt sur les sociétés en Afrique du Sud, au Rwanda, au Sénégal et en Tunisie, ainsi que pour la moyenne des pays de l'OCDE. C'est l'inverse qui se produit pour le Cameroun, le Maroc, Maurice et la moyenne des pays ALC. La préférence pour un type d'impôt plutôt qu'un autre ne semble pas être liée au PIB du pays ou à sa pression fiscale globale.

Graphique 1.16. **Impôt sur le revenu des personnes physiques et des bénéfices des sociétés en pourcentage du total des recettes fiscales, 2014**

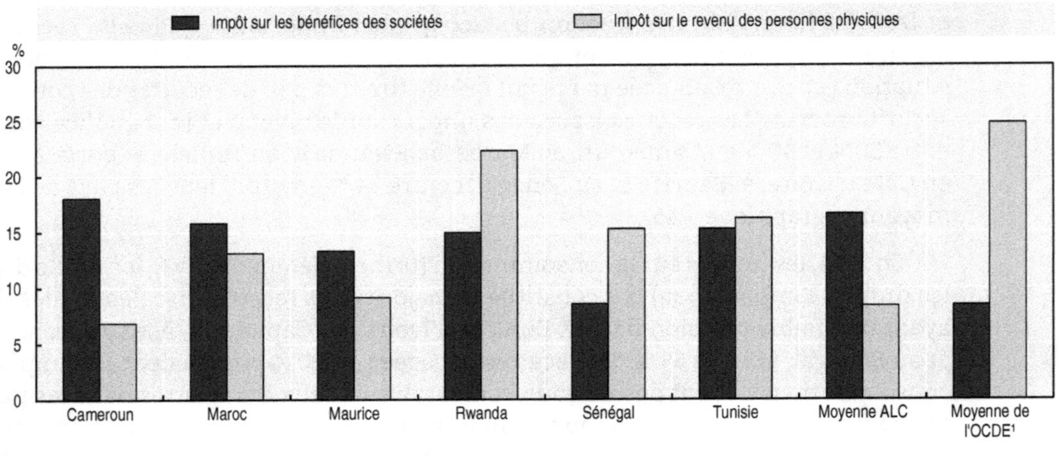

Note : La Côte d'Ivoire n'est pas incluse car leur données fiscales sur les impôts sur le revenu et les bénéfices ne peuvent pas être ventilées.

1. Données pour l'année 2013.

Source : Calculs des auteurs basés sur les tableaux 4.1-4.8.

StatLink http://dx.doi.org/10.1787/888933344145

Évolution des structures fiscales depuis 2000

Les structures fiscales globales des huit pays SRPA ont changé depuis l'année 2000. Dans la plupart des pays, on constate une augmentation des recettes tirées des impôts sur le revenu et les bénéfices et issues des cotisations de sécurité sociale, en pourcentage des recettes fiscales totales, ainsi qu'une baisse des recettes provenant des impôts sur les biens et services (tableau 1.5). Le tableau ci-dessous résume l'ampleur de ces changements depuis 2000 et les exceptions aux tendances globales sont indiquées en gras. Ces principales tendances ont été le plus clairement observées au Maroc, au Rwanda, au Sénégal et en Tunisie et rejoignent celles des pays ALC en moyenne. L'Afrique du Sud, le Cameroun et Maurice ont suivi la même évolution dans une certaine mesure, mais en y dérogeant sur un aspect. La Côte d'Ivoire est le seul pays qui a évolué dans la direction opposée, avec une progression de la part des impôts sur les biens et services et un recul de celle des impôts sur le revenu et les bénéfices.

L'importance des impôts sur le revenu et les bénéfices a tendance à se renforcer à mesure qu'un pays se développe (Bird et Zolt, 2003). Le graphique 1.17 illustre la nette augmentation des recettes tirées des impôts sur le revenu et les bénéfices dans les pays où les niveaux d'imposition sont faibles. Le tableau 1.5 montre que la part des impôts sur le revenu et les bénéfices s'est fortement accrue à Maurice, au Rwanda et en Tunisie, gagnant 9 points ou plus entre 2000 et 2014. Les hausses ont été de l'ordre de 3 à 5 points dans les autres pays, sauf en Côte d'Ivoire et en Afrique du Sud qui ont enregistré de fortes baisses de 4 points ou plus au cours de la même période.

La part des recettes issues des cotisations de sécurité sociale dans le total des recettes fiscales a progressé depuis 2000 dans tous les pays hormis le Cameroun et Maurice, qui ont enregistré des baisses de respectivement 1.9 point et 0.3 point. Bien que ces augmentations soient le plus souvent modérées, elles étaient de 4.1 points et 6.1 points respectivement au Maroc et en Tunisie. L'élargissement de la couverture du régime de retraite en Tunisie mis en œuvre depuis 2002 a vraisemblablement contribué à cette hausse (AISS, 2014).

Tableau 1.5. **Variation de la structure fiscale par type d'impôts entre 2000 et 2014 (en points de pourcentage)**

	Impôts sur le revenu et les bénéfices (1000)	Cotisations de sécurité sociale (2000)	Impôts sur les salaires et la main d'œuvre (3000)	Impôts sur le patrimoine (4000)	Impôts sur les biens et services (5000)	Autres impôts (6000)
Afrique du Sud	**-5.5**	1.5	0.8	3.3	1.1	-1.1
Cameroun	3.7	**-1.9**	1.8	-0.7	-4.2	1.3
Côte d'Ivoire	**-4.0**	2.5	-0.2	-0.1	**1.6**	0.2
Maurice	11.0	**-0.3**	-0.3	-0.5	-10.1	0.2
Maroc	4.7	4.1	0.0	1.3	-10.2	0.1
Rwanda	11.3	1.4	0.0	-0.2	-12.5	0.0
Sénégal	3.4	0.9	-0.1	0.5	-4.3	-0.4
Tunisie	9.1	6.1	-0.3	0.0	-15.5	0.7
Moyenne ALC	5.5	1.2	-0.3	0.4	-6.6	-0.2

Note : Les chiffres en gras sont des exceptions aux tendances générales dans les pays SRPA.

StatLink http://dx.doi.org/10.1787/888933344470

La part des impôts sur les biens et services, en proportion du total des recettes fiscales, recule constamment depuis 2000 dans la plupart des pays (graphiques 1.18 et 1.20), principalement sous l'effet de la baisse de la part des recettes issues des impôts spécifiques sur la consommation. Comme le montre le tableau 1.6, la part des impôts sur les biens et services s'est contractée dans tous les pays sauf en Afrique du Sud et en Côte d'Ivoire. Cette évolution est imputable en totalité au recul de la part des impôts spécifiques sur la consommation à Maurice, au Maroc et au Rwanda, et en partie à ce facteur en Tunisie. Dans ces quatre pays, la baisse de la part des impôts spécifiques sur la consommation oscillait entre 11 et 24 points. On observe les mêmes tendances dans les pays ALC où la part des impôts sur les biens et services s'est repliée de 7 points, et celle des impôts spécifiques sur la consommation a diminué de 8 points.

Tableau 1.6. **Variation de la proportion des recettes fiscales sur les biens et services en pourcentage du total des recettes fiscales (en points de pourcentage)**

	Impôts sur les biens et services (5000)	Impôts généraux sur la consommation (5110)	Impôts sur les biens et services déterminés (5120)
Afrique du Sud	1.1	-0.3	0.7
Cameroun	-4.2	0.1	-4.4
Côte d'Ivoire	1.6	-1.6	2.9
Maurice	-10.1	9.1	-19.2
Maroc	-10.2	6.4	-16.6
Rwanda	-12.5	12.3	-24.0
Sénégal	-4.3	-3.6	-0.9
Tunisie	-15.5	-4.2	-11.2
Moyenne ALC	-6.6	0.9	-7.7

StatLink http://dx.doi.org/10.1787/888933344482

Graphique 1.17. **Impôts sur le revenu et des bénéfices en pourcentage du total des recettes fiscales dans les pays au niveau d'imposition plus faible en pourcentage du PIB, 2000-14**

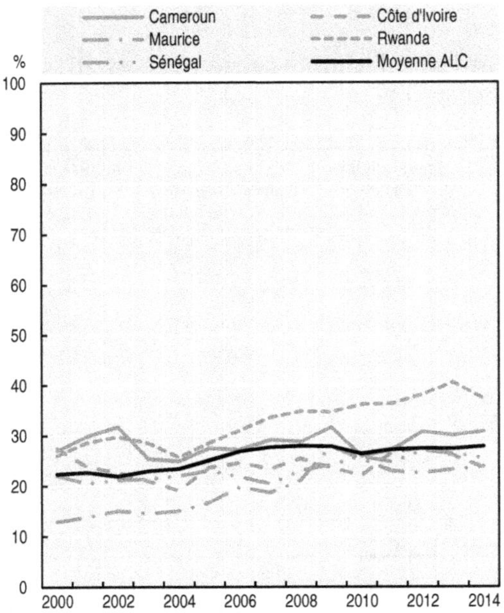

Source : Tableau 3.3.

StatLink http://dx.doi.org/10.1787/888933344156

Graphique 1.18. **Impôts sur les biens et services en pourcentage du total des recettes fiscales dans les pays au niveau d'imposition plus faible en pourcentage du PIB, 2000-14**

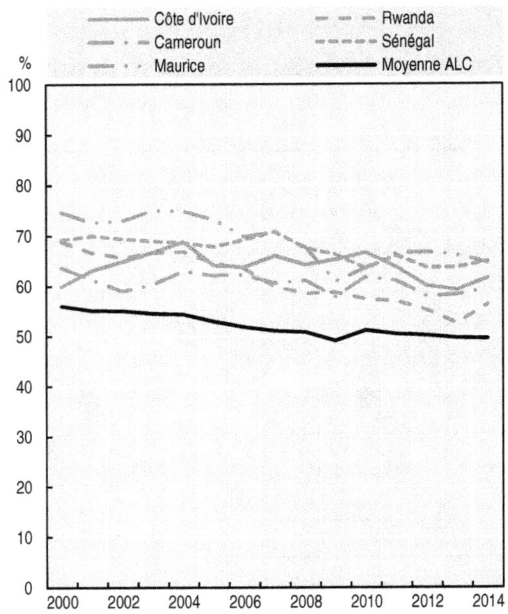

Source : Tableau 3.3.

StatLink http://dx.doi.org/10.1787/888933344164

Graphique 1.19. **Impôts sur le revenu et des bénéfices en pourcentage du total des recettes fiscales dans les pays au niveau d'imposition plus élevé en pourcentage du PIB, 2000-14**

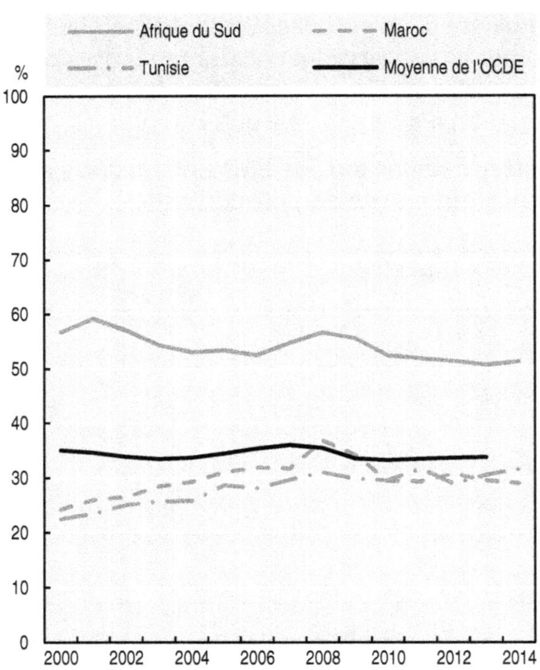

Source : Tableau 3.3.

StatLink http://dx.doi.org/10.1787/888933344176

Graphique 1.20. **Impôts sur les biens et services en pourcentage du total des recettes fiscales dans les pays au niveau d'imposition plus élevé en pourcentage du PIB, 2000-14**

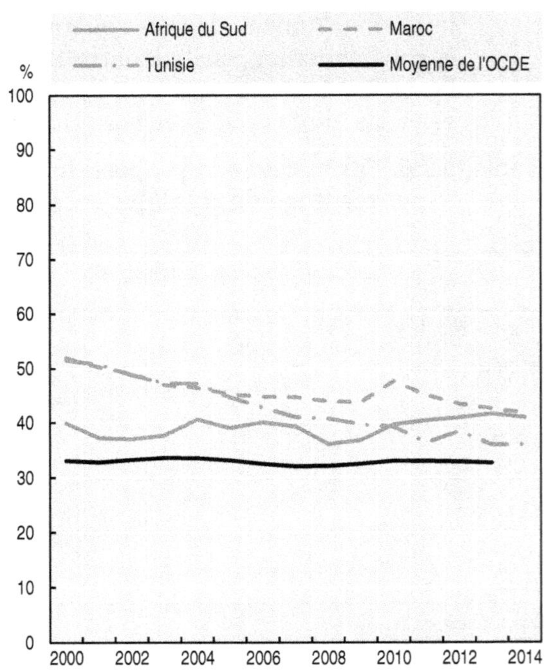

Source : Tableau 3.3.

StatLink http://dx.doi.org/10.1787/888933344187

La part des impôts généraux sur la consommation (principalement la TVA) s'est accrue dans quatre pays et a reculé dans les quatre autres pays. Maurice, le Rwanda et le Maroc ont enregistré de fortes hausses des impôts généraux sur la consommation en pourcentage du total des recettes fiscales depuis 2000. Le Rwanda a connu l'augmentation la plus sensible (12.3 points), suivi de Maurice (9.1 points) et du Maroc (6.4 points). À l'inverse, l'Afrique du Sud, la Côte d'Ivoire, le Sénégal et la Tunisie ont vu la part des impôts généraux sur la consommation reculer, dans des proportions comprises entre 0.3 point en Afrique du Sud et 4.2 points en Tunisie.

1.3. Impôts par niveaux d'administration

L'analyse de la répartition des impôts par niveaux d'administration effectuée dans cette publication est limitée par le manque de données sur les recettes fiscales perçues par les administrations infrarégionales. Ces données n'étaient disponibles que pour trois pays : Maurice[8], le Maroc et l'Afrique du Sud. Les finances des collectivités locales ne sont pas toujours bien suivies en Afrique. Dans certains pays, lorsque des états financiers existent, ils ne font pas l'objet d'un archivage électronique.

Les recettes fiscales des collectivités locales sont considérées comme faibles dans les pays SRPA. Lorsqu'il n'existe pas de données, les spécialistes estiment que ces recettes ne représentent qu'un pourcentage marginal du total des rentrées fiscales. D'après les *Perspectives économiques en Afrique 2015*, « en moyenne, les recettes de l'administration locale représentent 7 % des recettes cumulées des échelons de gouvernement local, régional et national » (BAfD/OCDE/PNUD, 2015: 214). Des chiffres supplémentaires émanant de la Banque africaine de développement montrent que les recettes des collectivités locales en Côte d'Ivoire et au Sénégal représentent une faible proportion du total des rentrées fiscales (de l'ordre de 3-4 %[9]).

Lorsque des données sont disponibles, elles montrent que les recettes de l'administration régionale et des collectivités locales restent minimes. Les recettes des administrations infranationales recensées dans cette publication sont les suivantes :

Maurice : 1.1 % du total des recettes fiscales en 2014, contre 1.8 % en 2000.

Maroc : 3.1 % du total des recettes fiscales en 2014, contre 3.7 % en 2000.

Afrique du Sud : 4.8 % des recettes fiscales en 2014, comme en 2010.

Les impôts sur le patrimoine constituent une source importante de revenu pour les administrations infrarégionales en Afrique du Sud, à Maurice et au Maroc. Ils représentent environ 80 % du total des recettes en Afrique du Sud, 75 % au Maroc et quelque 50 % à Maurice. Le reste se compose principalement des impôts sur les biens et services. Les impôts sur le patrimoine contribuent généralement plus aux recettes des collectivités locales dans les pays anglophones d'Afrique que dans les pays francophones. On observe de grandes disparités en la matière, et de nombreux pays ne lèvent aucune taxe locale sur les bâtiments et la propriété foncière, voire même sur les activités économiques (BAfD/OCDE/PNUD, 2015).

Les compétences fiscales dévolues aux administrations infrarégionales sont généralement limitées, et la responsabilité du recouvrement de l'impôt incombe avant tout à l'administration centrale. BAfD/OCDE/PNUD (2015) observent que « de nombreuses administrations locales perçoivent une fraction importante de leurs recettes totales grâce aux transferts opérés par l'administration centrale ». Cette situation tient en partie au fait que les systèmes fiscaux au niveau local ont été hérités des administrations française et anglaise et n'ont pratiquement pas été modifiés depuis l'indépendance. C'est notamment vrai en Afrique francophone. Dans les pays francophones comme le Maroc, le Sénégal, la Côte d'Ivoire et le Cameroun, les recettes sont souvent collectées par l'administration centrale pour le compte des administrations locales, tandis qu'en Afrique du Sud, elles le sont directement par les collectivités locales (89 % en 2007) (Fjeldstad, Chambas et Brun, 2014). Les administrations locales mauriciennes sont largement tributaires des transferts de l'administration centrale (FMI, 2014a).

Les collectivités locales dans la plupart des pays d'Afrique sub-saharienne se heurtent à des contraintes de ressources et les outils dont disposent leurs administrations fiscales sont inefficaces, obsolètes et inadaptés pour procéder à un recouvrement efficient des impôts et pour les comptabiliser correctement. Cette situation entraîne des coûts de recouvrement élevés et un grand nombre d'impôts peu productifs. En outre, le traitement des données relatives aux recettes collectées et l'échange de renseignements avec d'autres institutions publiques sont peu développés, et les administrations locales coopèrent généralement peu avec l'administration centrale. Cela se traduit par des impôts en double ou qui vont à l'encontre des objectifs nationaux (comme des taxes locales sur les cultures d'exportation). À l'exception de l'Afrique du Sud, les registres fonciers en bonne et due forme font défaut, ce qui entrave la collecte des impôts fonciers (Fjeldstad, Chambas et Brun, 2014). À Maurice, par exemple, la taxe foncière est peu productive en partie à cause de cadastres périmés et de valeurs de biens qui ne sont plus à jour (FMI, 2014a).

Bien que les pays africains en général et les pays SRPA en particulier aient entrepris de vastes réformes de leur administration fiscale centrale et de la législation correspondante au cours des dernières décennies, il n'y a guère eu d'initiatives de ce genre au niveau des administrations locales. La priorité a été donnée aux recettes perçues par l'administration centrale. En effet, la nécessité de réduire les déficits budgétaires au niveau national s'est imposée en premier lieu. Par ailleurs, il est plus simple et moins coûteux de réformer la législation et les systèmes fiscaux au niveau national qu'au niveau local, et les avantages potentiels de la réforme fiscale en termes d'accroissement des recettes sont plus importants. En 2007, le Maroc a lancé une réforme du système fiscal et des administrations fiscales locales en vue d'augmenter les recettes générées par les impôts locaux. (Boisard, de Freitas et Hidouci, 2014). D'autres pays de la publication *Statistiques des recettes publiques en Afrique* tels que le Cameroun, la Côte d'Ivoire (BAfD/OCDE/CEA, 2010) et plus récemment la Tunisie (Banque mondiale, 2015), ont engagé un processus de décentralisation fiscale destiné à promouvoir la capacité d'action des collectivités locales et améliorer la collecte des recettes fiscales. L'Afrique du Sud est un exemple de pays qui a décentralisé avec succès le processus de recouvrement de la taxe foncière urbaine. Elle a mis en place un système moderne de collecte des recettes de la taxe foncière et les autorités municipales reçoivent un appui approprié en termes d'expertise et de moyens. « En Afrique du Sud, les autorités provinciales apportent aux autorités locales un soutien administratif et une formation pour faciliter le calcul de l'impôt, l'émission des avis de recouvrement et la collecte » (Monkam et Moore, 2015).

1.4. Graphiques comparatifs

Graphique 1.21. Total des recettes fiscales en pourcentage du PIB, 2014[1]

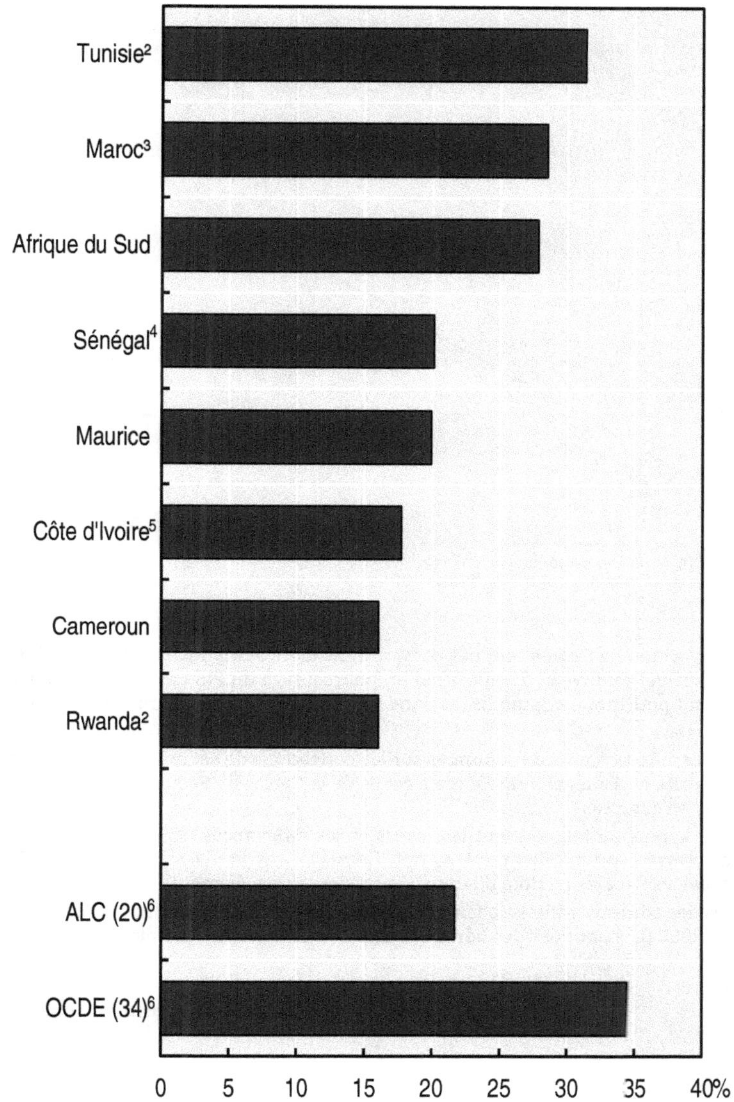

1. Les pays ont été classés selon leur niveau d'imposition en pourcentage du PIB.

2. Le Rwanda et la Tunisie ne tiennent pas compte dans leurs statistiques nationales des cotisations de sécurité sociale dans le calcul des recettes fiscales rapportées au PIB car ils ne les considèrent pas comme des impôts. Elles sont pourtant comptabilisées dans les recettes fiscales aux fins de la présente publication.

3. Chiffres estimés.

4. Les chiffres tiennent compte des données sur les cotisations de sécurité sociale provenant de l'Institution de prévoyance retraite du Sénégal (IPRES), mais celles de la Caisse de Sécurité Sociale (CSS) font défaut et ne sont donc pas prises en compte.

5. La taxe par rapport au PIB contient les loyers et les redevances et les ventes de biens et services publics normalement classés comme des recettes non fiscales dans la classification de l'OCDE. Ils sont considérés comme des recettes fiscales en Côte d'Ivoire. L'inclusion de ces éléments représente 0.5 % du PIB en 2014.

6. Représente la moyenne non pondérée des pays de l'ALC et de l'OCDE.

Source : Tableau 3.1.

StatLink http://dx.doi.org/10.1787/888933344199

Graphique 1.22. **Variation du niveau d'imposition en pourcentage du PIB, 2000-14**

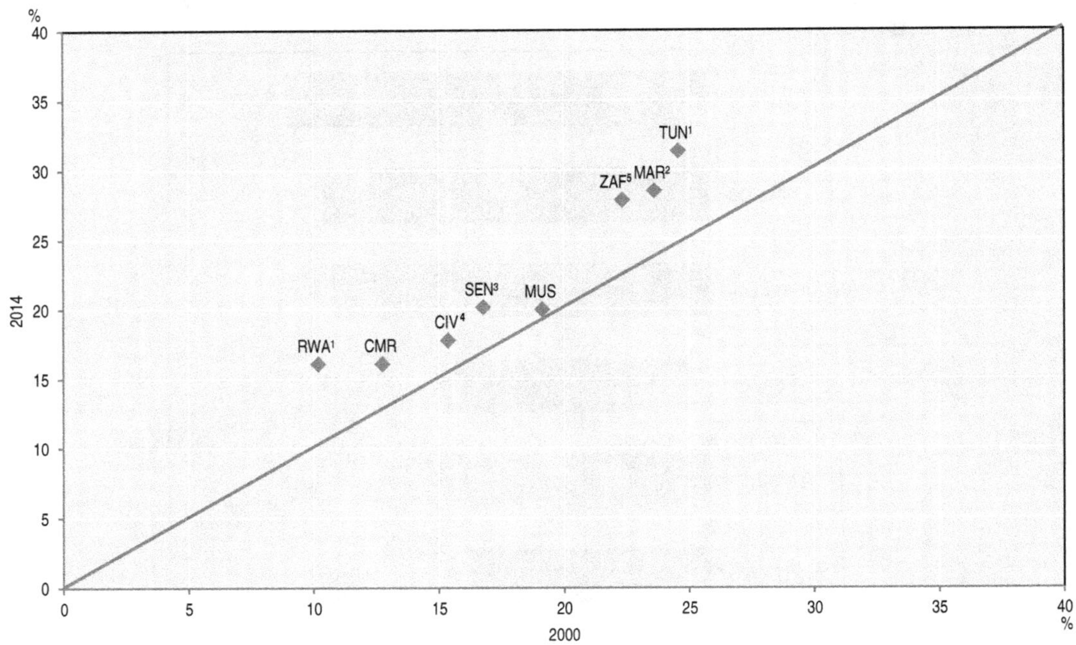

1. Le Rwanda et la Tunisie ne tiennent pas compte dans leurs statistiques nationales des cotisations de sécurité sociale dans le calcul du niveau d'imposition en pourcentage du PIB car ils ne les considèrent pas comme des impôts. Elles sont pourtant comptabilisées dans les recettes fiscales aux fins de la présente publication.
2. Chiffres estimés.
3. Les chiffres tiennent compte des données sur les cotisations de sécurité sociale provenant de l'Institution de prévoyance retraite du Sénégal (IPRES), mais celles de la Caisse de Sécurité Sociale (CSS) font défaut et ne sont donc pas prises en compte.
4. La taxe par rapport au PIB contient les loyers et les redevances et les ventes de biens et services publics normalement classés comme des recettes non fiscales dans la classification de l'OCDE. Ils sont considérés comme des recettes fiscales en Côte d'Ivoire. L'inclusion de ces éléments représente 0.5 % du PIB en 2014.
5. Les données des administrations locales et provinciales sont incluses dans les chiffres de 2014 mais pas dans les chiffres de 2000 (Les données des administrations locales et provinciales ne sont disponibles qu'à partir de 2003).

Source : Tableau 3.1.

StatLink http://dx.doi.org/10.1787/888933344205

RECETTES NON FISCALES

Introduction

Les recettes non fiscales représentent une toile de fond importante pour l'interprétation des taux de pression fiscale. À ce titre, leur analyse a constitué l'une des priorités des experts qui étudient les recettes publiques de pays africains. Le niveau d'imposition en pourcentage du PIB nécessaire pour assurer un niveau donné de services publics dans un pays sera d'autant plus faible que les recettes non fiscales y seront importantes. Ainsi, deux pays peuvent afficher des niveaux d'imposition et de dépenses identiques alors que leur situation financière peut différer grandement selon leurs niveaux respectifs de recettes non fiscales. En conséquence, il convient de tenir compte de l'ensemble des recettes publiques, fiscales et non fiscales, pour obtenir une vision précise de la situation financière d'une administration.

Les recettes non fiscales englobent les aides sous forme de dons (aide étrangère), les revenus de la propriété (notamment les redevances minières et les retours sur investissements des administrations publiques), les ventes de biens et de services, et les amendes. Dans la présente section, les pays dans tous les tableaux et graphiques sont présentés classés en ordre croissant de PIB par capita pour démontrer le lien entre les niveaux de développement et ratios des revenues fiscales en pourcentage du PIB.

1.5. Recettes non fiscales exprimées en pourcentage du PIB

La volatilité des recettes non fiscales est bien plus marquée que celle des recettes fiscales, en particulier dans les pays où les recettes non fiscales représentent une part importante du PIB (tableau 1.7). Pour l'année 2014, les recettes non fiscales rapportées par les pays et exprimées en pourcentage du PIB s'échelonnaient de 0.6 % en Afrique du Sud à 9.5 % au Rwanda. Cependant, dans le cas du Rwanda, ces recettes ne représentaient que 6.0 % du PIB en 1998 et ont atteint 12.7 % à deux reprises, en 2005 et 2008. Au Cameroun, elles ont enregistré un taux maximum de 9.2 % du PIB en 2008, avant de tomber à 4.2 % en 2014. En Côte d'Ivoire, les recettes non fiscales s'établissaient à 1.0 % du PIB en 2011, alors qu'elles dépassaient 3 % deux ans plus tôt seulement.

Cette volatilité découle en grande partie de la forte instabilité des deux catégories qui représentent en règle générale l'essentiel des recettes non fiscales, à savoir les aides sous forme de dons et les revenus de la propriété. Le niveau des aides varie en fonction des priorités retenues par les donneurs, lesquelles évoluent parfois de manière conséquente au fil des ans. Quant aux revenus de la propriété, ils peuvent varier brutalement selon les cours des minéraux, ou au début de l'exploitation d'une nouvelle mine qui entraîne une forte croissance de la production. À l'inverse, les niveaux des recettes fiscales déclarées par les pays SRPA sont plus stables, et une dépendance élevée à l'égard des recettes non fiscales signifie que la situation financière des pays concernés a été moins stable au cours des deux dernières décennies.

Tableau 1.7. **Total des recettes non fiscales en pourcentage du PIB**

	1997	2000	2005	2008	2009	2010	2011	2012	2013	2014
Rwanda	7.5	11.8	12.7	12.7	12.1	12.5	12.5	9.0	11.3	9.5
Sénégal	2.4	2.7	2.3	3.4	3.6	3.2	2.9	3.8	4.1	5.7
Cameroun	5.3	8.0	6.9	9.2	4.6	4.8	6.2	5.0	4.9	4.2
Côte d'Ivoire[1]	1.3	1.1	2.2	2.3	3.2	1.3	1.0	1.0	1.8	2.2
Maroc	0.0	2.2	2.9	3.0	3.4	3.2	3.6	3.4	3.9	3.5
Tunisie	0.0	2.3	2.4	3.5	3.1	2.7	3.9	3.4	3.4	2.2
Afrique du Sud	0.3	0.5	0.5	0.6	0.4	0.6	0.7	0.7	0.7	0.6
Maurice[2]	4.4	3.3	2.5	3.0	4.3	3.8	3.5	3.1	3.2	2.4

Note : Les chiffres excluent les recettes fiscales des collectivités locales pour le Cameroun, la Côte d'Ivoire, le Rwanda, le Sénégal et la Tunisie car les données ne sont pas disponibles. Les données des collectivités locales et provinciales ne sont pas disponibles pour l'Afrique du Sud avant 2003.

1. Le ratio des recettes non-fiscales au PIB ne comprend pas les loyers, les redevances et les frais d'usage des services publics car ils sont considérés comme des recettes fiscales en Côte d'Ivoire. Ces éléments représentent 0.5 % du PIB en 2014 et varient entre 0.1 % et 1.5 % pour la période 2000 à 2014.
2. Les chiffres sont estimés pour 2013 et 2014.

StatLink http://dx.doi.org/10.1787/888933344496

Graphique 1.23. **Total des recettes non fiscales en pourcentage du PIB**

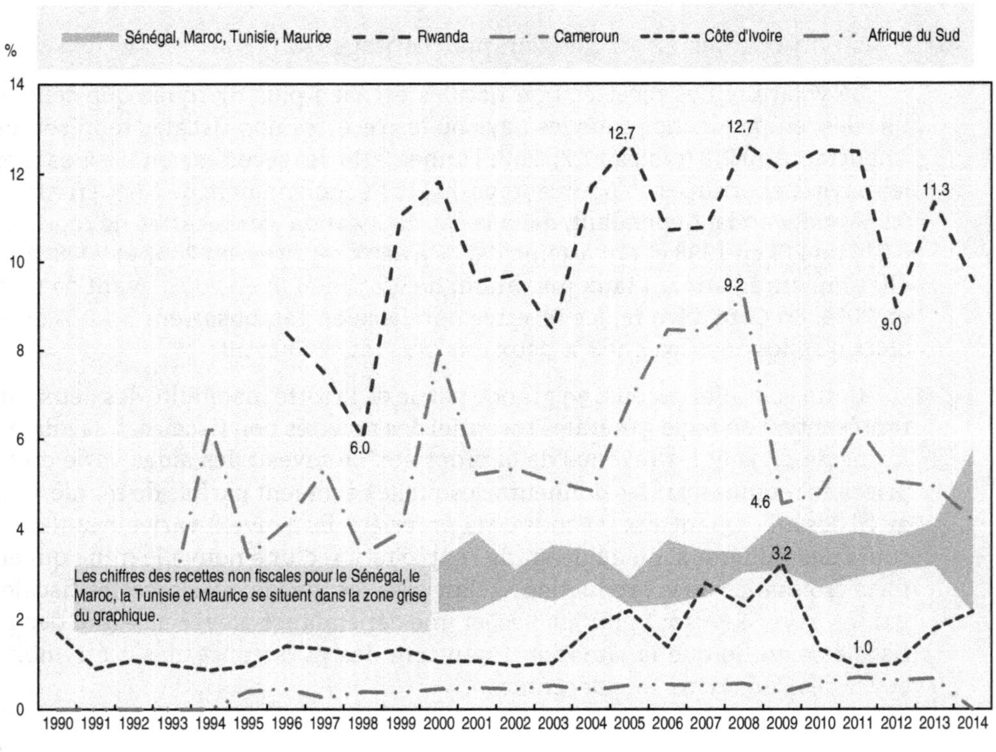

Source : Tableau 5.1.

StatLink http://dx.doi.org/10.1787/888933344215

Les recettes non fiscales peuvent en outre varier brutalement d'une année à l'autre. Le Cameroun a vu ses recettes non fiscales exprimées en pourcentage du PIB chuter de 4.6 points de pourcentage (entre 2008 et 2009) alors qu'au Rwanda, si elles ont connu une hausse de 2.4 points (entre 2012 et 2013), elles avaient précédemment chuté de 2.5 points (entre 2011 et 2012). À l'inverse, le Maroc et l'Afrique du Sud ont enregistré des niveaux de recettes non fiscales relativement stables durant la période 2004-14.

Graphique 1.24. **Variation annuelle maximale des recettes non fiscales en pourcentage du PIB entre 2005 et 2014**

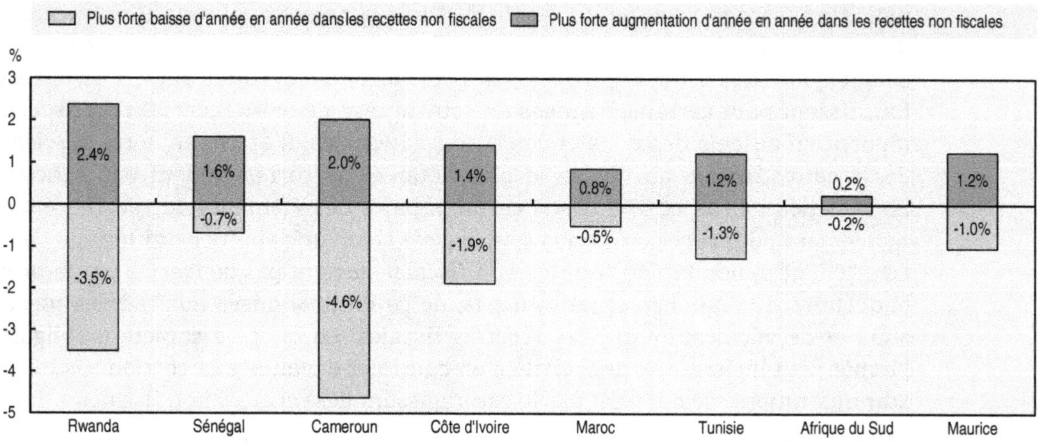

Source : Calculs des auteurs basés sur le tableau 5.1.

StatLink http://dx.doi.org/10.1787/888933344223

Dans les pays où le PIB par habitant est plus élevé, on observe en général que le ratio des recettes fiscales en pourcentage du PIB est également plus élevé, tandis que celui des recettes non fiscales est plus faible. Le graphique 1.25 présente les recettes fiscales et non fiscales totales de chaque pays en pourcentage du PIB pour l'année 2014. Les pays figurent dans l'ordre croissant du PIB par habitant en 2014, depuis le Rwanda jusqu'à Maurice. Dans la partie gauche du graphique, les quatre pays dont les PIB par habitant sont les plus faibles montrent à la fois des niveaux de recettes fiscales en pourcentage du PIB plus faibles et, à l'exception de la Côte d'Ivoire, des niveaux de recettes non fiscales en pourcentage du PIB supérieurs à ceux des pays de la partie droite du graphique, dont les PIB par habitant sont plus importants. La règle générale selon laquelle les pays plus riches ont des taux de pression fiscale plus élevés (voir le graphique 1.4 dans la partie consacrée aux taux de pression fiscale) semble s'inverser lorsque l'on analyse les recettes non fiscales des pays étudiés dans le présent rapport.

Graphique 1.25. **Total des recettes fiscales et non fiscales en pourcentage du PIB par pays, 2014**

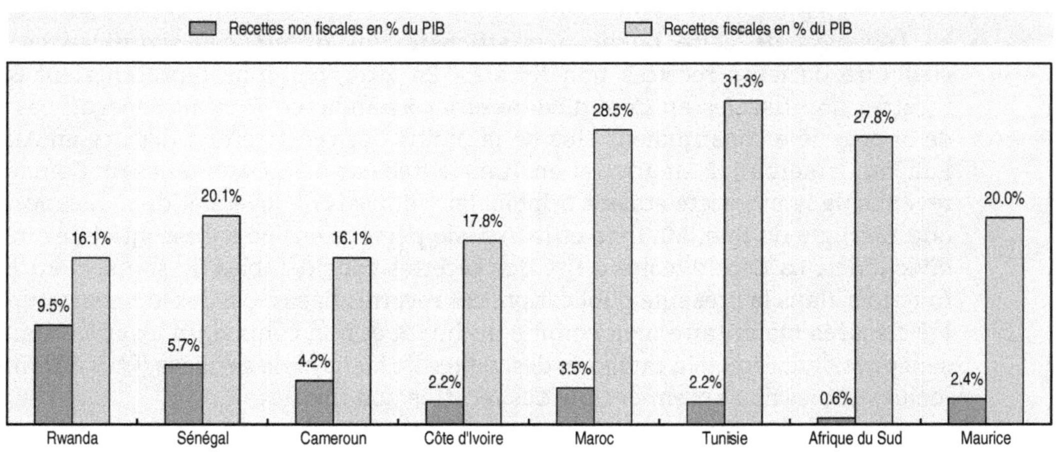

Source : Tableaux 3.1 et 5.1.

StatLink http://dx.doi.org/10.1787/888933344233

Encadré 1.2. **Les problèmes de qualité propres aux données des recettes non fiscales**

Les données relatives aux recettes non fiscales sont plus difficiles à recueillir et à classer que celles portant sur les recettes fiscales, car elles sont moins aisément disponibles, moins transparentes et moins vérifiées. Dans la présente publication, les statistiques des recettes non fiscales sont moins détaillées que celles concernant les recettes fiscales, ce qui ajoute à la difficulté d'opérer des vérifications. Certains pays, à titre d'exemple, fournissent pour certaines années un total agrégé de leurs recettes non fiscales, sans répartition au-delà des dons et des autres catégories. Il arrive en outre que les totaux des recettes, même au niveau le plus détaillé, ne correspondent pas exactement à la classification de l'OCDE. Dans certains pays, des éléments de revenu tels que les redevances pour services rendus sont classés selon une approche différente de celle de l'OCDE. Enfin, nombre de recettes non fiscales ne sont pas couvertes par la procédure budgétaire de référence et ne sont pas, de ce fait, soumises aux mêmes mesures de suivi et de vérification que les recettes fiscales. En effet, le caractère obligatoire de l'impôt peut inciter la société civile à en contrôler davantage la gestion assurée par les administrations, ce qui n'est pas le cas s'agissant des recettes non fiscales.

Les payments constituant les recettes non fiscales reposent occasionellement sur des negociations entre l'État et entreprises. Les risques de perte de transparence qui entourent la conclusion de ces négociations peuvent limiter les données disponibles aux fins d'analyse. Les dons, les règlements de différends juridiques, les contrats d'exploitation minière ou pétrolière donnent souvent lieu à des versements très importants de la part de grandes entités extérieures telles que des entreprises multinationales ou des administrations. Certaines dispositions de tels accords peuvent être tenues secrètes, par exemple lorsqu'un contrat important signé avec une entreprise exploitant des ressources naturelles est assorti de clauses de confidentialité très strictes (BAfD/OCDE/CEA, 2010). De plus, la fiabilité des données détaillées est amoindrie dès lors qu'un pays négocie un versement qui recouvre de nombreuses catégories de recettes.

De plus, la notion de recettes non fiscales est plus large que celle de recettes fiscales, ce qui peut affecter la précision de la comptabilisation. Une créance fiscale détenue par l'État est le plus souvent comptabilisée en monnaie nationale, que ce soit avant ou après son paiement. À l'inverse, ce n'est pas le cas pour certaines recettes non fiscales qui peuvent donner lieu à des paiements réalisés au moyen d'actifs non financiers qui ne sont pas toujours valorisés dans la monnaie nationale à la date de la transaction.

1.6. Structure des recettes non fiscales

Les pays de cette publication affichent des différences significatives dans la structure de leurs recettes non fiscales. En 2014, les dons représentaient 82 % des recettes non fiscales en Côte d'Ivoire et au Rwanda, et 57 % au Sénégal. Les revenus de la propriété constituaient plus de la moitié des recettes non fiscales en Afrique du Sud, au Cameroun, à Maurice et en Tunisie (tableau 1.8). Dans le cas du Cameroun, ces revenus de la propriété étaient principalement issus de loyers et de redevances, tandis que l'Afrique du Sud, Maurice et la Tunisie percevaient pour l'essentiel des intérêts et dividendes. La Côte d'Ivoire a tiré des recettes considérables de son secteur pétrolier, toutefois, dans la présente publication, ces recettes liées à des ressources naturelles ont été classées majoritairement comme un impôt et non comme un loyer. Le Maroc est le seul pays dans lequel la catégorie des ventes de biens et de services (frais administratifs inclus) se hissait au premier rang des recettes non fiscales.

Tableau 1.8. Recettes non fiscales par sous-catégorie en pourcentage du total des recettes non fiscales, 2014

Pays	Dons	Revenus de la propriété	Ventes de biens et de services	Amendes, pénalités et confiscations	Recettes diverses et non identifiées[1]
Rwanda[2]	82	..	..	..	18
Sénégal	57	29	0	1	2
Cameroun	4	87	8	1	1
Côte d'Ivoire[3]	82	6	7	0	5
Maroc[4]	0	37	41	2	21
Tunisie	21	56	1	11	11
Afrique du Sud	9	82	4	5	0
Maurice[5]	4	57	30	4	6

Note : Les chiffres excluent les recettes fiscales des collectivités locales pour le Cameroun, la Côte d'Ivoire, le Rwanda, le Sénégal et la Tunisie car les données ne sont pas disponibles. Les données des collectivités locales et provinciales ne sont pas disponibles pour l'Afrique du Sud avant 2003.

1. Y compris transferts de capitaux non compris ailleurs et transferts volontaires autres que les dons des gouvernements et institutions étrangers.
2. Les données des revenus de la propriété, ventes de biens et de services, pénalités et confiscations sont incluses dans la catégorie "Recettes diverses et non identifiées".
3. La catégorie "Revenus de la propriété" ne comprend pas les loyers et les redevances et la catégorie "Ventes de biens et de services" ne comprend pas les frais pour l'utilisation des biens et services. Ceux-ci sont classés comme des recettes fiscales en Côte d'Ivoire.
4. Données pour 2013.
5. Les chiffres sont estimés pour les catégories "Revenus de la propriété" et "Ventes de biens et de services".

StatLink http://dx.doi.org/10.1787/888933344503

1.7. Recettes non fiscales par sous-catégories

La présente section propose une analyse de chaque sous-catégorie de recettes non fiscales. Chacune de ces catégories a des retombées différentes non seulement sur les finances publiques mais aussi sur les questions de gouvernance de manière générale. Le tableau 1.9 montre la part respective de chacune d'entre elles, exprimées en pourcentage du PIB, dans le total des recettes non fiscales de chaque pays SRPA.

Tableau 1.9. Recettes non fiscales par sous-catégorie en pourcentage du PIB, 2014

Catégories	Rwanda[1]	Sénégal	Cameroun	Côte d'Ivoire[2]	Maroc[3]	Tunisie	Afrique du Sud	Maurice[4]
Total des recettes non fiscales	**9.5**	**5.7**	**4.2**	**2.2**	**3.9**	**2.2**	**0.6**	**2.4**
Dons	7.8	3.3	0.2	1.8	0.0	0.5	0.1	0.1
Revenus de la propriété	..	1.7	3.7	0.1	1.4	1.2	0.5	1.4
Loyers et redevances	..	0.3	3.6	0.1	0.6	0.4	0.1	0.3
Intérêts et dividendes	..	0.7	0.1	0.1	0.9	0.8	0.2	0.4
Autres revenus de la propriété	..	0.0	0.0	0.0	0.0	0.0	0.1	0.7
Ventes de biens et de services	..	0.0	0.3	0.2	1.6	0.0	0.0	0.7
Amendes, pénalités et confiscations	..	0.6	0.0	0.0	0.1	0.2	0.0	0.1
Recettes diverses et non identifiées[5]	1.7	0.1	0.0	0.1	0.8	0.2	0.0	0.1
Total des recettes fiscales	*16.1*	*20.1*	*16.1*	*17.8*	*28.5*	*31.3*	*27.8*	*20.0*
Total des recettes fiscales et non fiscales	*25.6*	*25.9*	*20.3*	*19.9*	*17.8*	*33.5*	*27.9*	*22.4*

Note : Les chiffres excluent les recettes fiscales des collectivités locales pour le Cameroun, la Côte d'Ivoire, le Rwanda, le Sénégal et la Tunisie car les données ne sont pas disponibles. Les données des collectivités locales et provinciales ne sont pas disponibles pour l'Afrique du Sud avant 2003.

1. Les données des revenus de la propriété, ventes de biens et de services, pénalités et confiscations sont incluses dans la catégorie "Recettes diverses et non identifiées".
2. La catégorie "Revenus de la propriété" ne comprend pas les loyers et les redevances et la catégorie "Ventes de biens et de services" ne comprend pas les frais pour l'utilisation des biens et services. Ceux-ci sont classés comme des recettes fiscales en Côte d'Ivoire.
3. Données pour 2013.
4. Les chiffres sont estimés pour les catégories "Revenus de la propriété" et "Ventes de biens et de services".
5. Y compris transferts de capitaux non compris ailleurs et transferts volontaires autres que les dons des gouvernements et institutions étrangers.

StatLink http://dx.doi.org/10.1787/888933344519

Dons

Les pays qui ont reçu le plus de dons en pourcentage du PIB sont ceux qui présentent les taux de pression fiscale les plus faibles. Trois des quatre pays ayant eu les plus fortes recettes au titre de dons en pourcentage du PIB en 2014, à savoir la Côte d'Ivoire, le Rwanda et le Sénégal, figuraient aussi parmi ceux dont les PIB par habitant étaient les plus faibles, comme le montre le graphique 1.26. Le Rwanda se situe largement en tête quant au montant d'aide reçue en pourcentage du PIB, avec un taux de 7.8 %, il est suivi du Sénégal (3.3 %) et de la Côte d'Ivoire (1.8 %).

Graphique 1.26. **Dons en pourcentage du PIB, 2014**

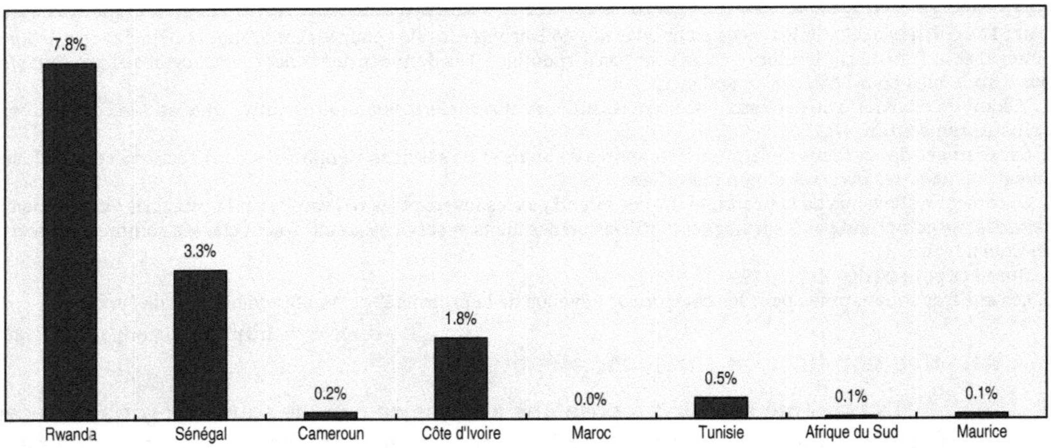

Source : Tableau 5.2.

StatLink http://dx.doi.org/10.1787/888933344247

Au cours des deux dernières décennies, le montant des aides est resté plutôt volatile, affichant périodiquement des variations brutales. Leur montant a ainsi fluctué entre 5 % et 12 % du PIB au Rwanda, tandis que, dans les autres pays étudiés, il restait en dessous de 3.3 % (graphique 1.27). Au Rwanda, les recettes liées aux dons ont atteint des pics en 2000, 2005 et 2010, tandis que les années 1998, 2003, 2012 et 2014 ont été marquées par des niveaux très bas. En Côte d'Ivoire et au Cameroun, des pics ont été enregistrés en 2009 et 2007 respectivement, tandis qu'au Sénégal, les montants sont restés dans la fourchette de 1.7 % à 3.3 % du PIB. En Tunisie, le montant des dons n'a dépassé le seuil de 0.5 % du PIB qu'en 2012, où il a atteint 0.9 %, soit trois fois plus que les niveaux comptabilisés pour 2011 et 2013. Dans le cas de Maurice, cette catégorie de recettes ne s'est élevée à 1 % du PIB qu'une seule fois, en 2009, qui correspondait à un montant multiplié par cinq par rapport à 2008.

Graphique 1.27. **Dons en pourcentage du PIB, 1995-2014**

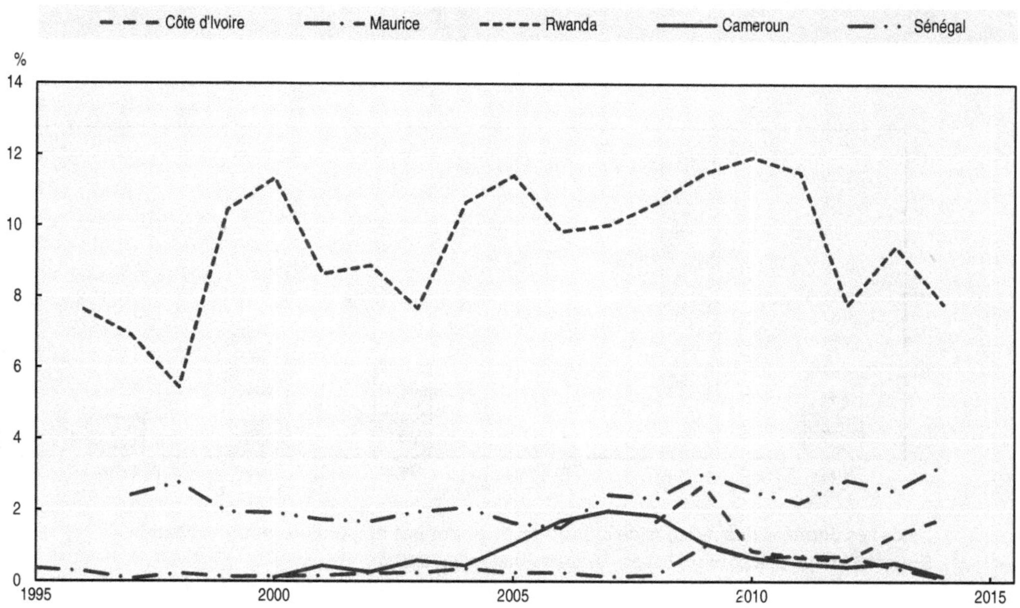

Source : Calculs des auteurs basés sur les tableaux 5.5-5.12.

StatLink http://dx.doi.org/10.1787/888933344256

Certaines des plus fortes variations du montant des dons reçus par les pays SRPA ces dernières années trouvent leur origine dans un seul et même programme d'aide internationale. Le Cameroun, la Côte d'Ivoire, le Rwanda et le Sénégal appartiennent à la catégorie des pays dits Pays Pauvres Très Endettés (PPTE) et bénéficient à ce titre d'une aide spéciale de la part du Fonds monétaire international (FMI) et de la Banque mondiale par l'intermédiaire de l'Initiative PPTE (FMI, 2015a). L'Initiative PPTE, lancée en 1996 par le FMI et la Banque mondiale, a pour objectif d'alléger le fardeau de la dette de pays pauvres surendettés. Parmi les 39 pays éligibles à cette initiative figuraient 33 pays de l'Afrique sub-saharienne, dont quatre pays SRPA (Cameroun, Côte d'Ivoire, Rwanda et Sénégal). Ces pays ont reçu à ce titre des aides importantes sous forme d'allégement de la dette. Le Cameroun, le Rwanda et le Sénégal ont perçu l'essentiel de cette aide en 2006, tandis que la Côte d'Ivoire en a bénéficié en 2012. Dans nos statistiques, ces annulations de dette sont classées parmi les dons.

Revenus de la propriété

On distingue ici trois grandes sous-catégories de recettes :

- les loyers et redevances correspondant à l'exploitation de ressources naturelles renouvelables ou non renouvelables qui appartiennent à l'État ;
- les intérêts et dividendes ;
- les autres revenus de la propriété non attribuables.

L'État perçoit des loyers et des redevances en contrepartie d'activités de prospection et d'exploitation de resources naturelles sur des terres appartenant au domaine public, ou de l'exploitation de fermes et de forêts détenues par l'État, tandis que les intérêts et dividendes sont des retours sur investissements réalisés par les pouvoirs publics. En 2014, c'est au Cameroun que le montant des loyers et redevances était le plus élevé, avec 3.6 % du PIB. Ce montant correspondait pour 98 % à des loyers et redevances (graphique 1.28). Avec 1.1 % du PIB, Maurice est le seul autre pays SRPA dans lequel cette catégorie de recettes a dépassé 1 % du PIB.

Graphique 1.28. **Revenus de la propriété en pourcentage du PIB, 2014**

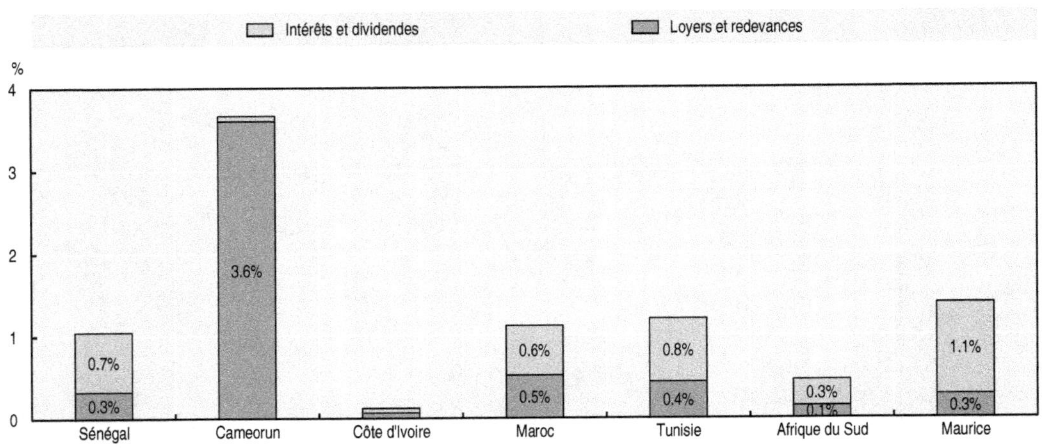

Note : Les données des revenus de la propriété ne sont pas disponibles pour le Rwanda.
Source : Calculs des auteurs basés sur les tableaux 5.5-5.12.

StatLink http://dx.doi.org/10.1787/888933344268

La volatilité des revenus de la propriété comme celle des recettes provenant des dons peut être aussi très forte. Parmi les pays les plus dépendants de ce type de recettes, trois pays ont enregistré des variations importantes des montants perçus (graphique 1.29). Au Cameroun, les revenus de la propriété, qui étaient presqu'exclusivement constitués de loyers et redevances, ont connu en vingt ans cinq épisodes de fluctuation considérable. Les pays qui dépendaient plus des intérêts, dividendes et autres types de revenus de la propriété ont connu des variations moindres de ces recettes, hormis la Tunisie, qui a enregistré une baisse égale aux deux tiers de ses revenus de la propriété en trois ans, entre 2011 et 2014. Les données relatives à Maurice montrent aussi des écarts importants entre 2006 et 2014 ; il est important de noter que les changements apportés aux classifications des données dans les séries temporelles affectent les comparaisons qui couvrent des périodes plus longues. À l'inverse, l'Afrique du Sud, le Sénégal et la Tunisie ont connu des variations de 1.0 point de pourcentage, voire moins.

Graphique 1.29. **Revenus de la propriété en pourcentage du PIB, 1990-2014**

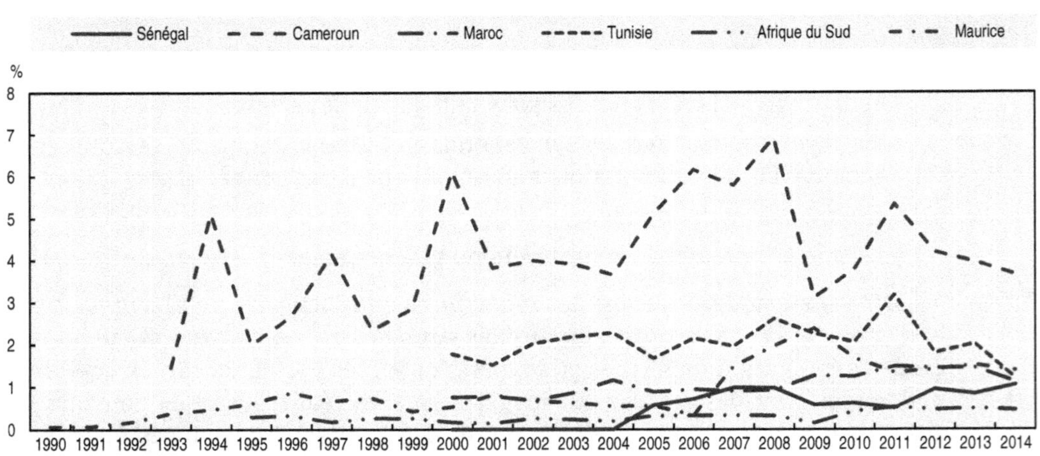

Source : Calculs des auteurs basés sur les tableaux 5.5-5.12.

StatLink http://dx.doi.org/10.1787/888933344277

Recettes issues de ressources naturelles

Les recettes provenant des entreprises qui ont pour principale activité l'exploitation de ressources naturelles peuvent avoir des retombées importantes sur les finances publiques, cependant, les pays suivent plusieurs méthodes de comptabilisation selon leur cadre budgétaire et réglementaire et selon le type de contrat conclu avec les entreprises concernées. Les revenus que les administrations publiques perçoivent au titre de l'exploitation de ressources naturelles peuvent être non seulement des recettes fiscales et non fiscales, mais aussi découler d'investissements dans des infrastructures nationales effectués par des entreprises qui réalisent ces activités d'exploitation. Ces revenus peuvent produire des effets dans les comptes publics de diverses manières, que l'on peut résumer comme suit[10]:

1. Les recettes au titre de loyers et redevances présentent le lien le plus direct avec la richesse en ressources naturelles d'un pays. L'État perçoit des rémunérations acquittées par des entreprises et des particuliers en contrepartie d'un droit d'accès à des terres appartenant au domaine public. Il agit en sa qualité de propriétaire des terrains concernés, et les montants versés sont en règle générale fixés à l'issue d'une négociation. Ces recettes sont ensuite rattachées aux revenus de la propriété.
2. Les paiements pour services fournis par les administrations publiques est une autre source de recettes non fiscales émanant d'entreprises du secteur primaire. Cette sous-catégorie regroupe notamment les paiements au titre de contrôles environnementaux réalisés par des agents de l'administration, ou les paiements pour la construction d'infrastructure. Ces recettes sont incluses dans la catégorie des ventes des biens et de services.
3. Les participations au capital de sociétés, publiques ou non, qui exploitent des ressources naturelles au nom de l'État, génèrent des recettes sous forme de bénéfices et dividendes. Ces recettes constituent des revenus de la propriété.
4. Il est possible d'instituer des taxes ou des droits conçus de manière à cibler les sociétés ou les particuliers qui ont accès à des ressources naturelles. Il peut s'avérer difficile de différencier un impôt appliqué aux entreprises qui exploitent des terres appartenant à l'État d'une redevance acquittée par ces mêmes entreprises.
5. Des taxes et des droits ciblant l'exploitation de ressources naturelles peuvent être mis en place, notamment un droit d'accise sur les matières premières extraites de terres appartenant au domaine public, ou une taxe minière ciblant l'activité d'exploitation des ressources naturelles plutôt que le particulier ou la société qui réalise cette activité. Les revenus correspondants sont alors classés parmi les recettes fiscales.
6. Les sociétés et les particuliers qui exploitent des ressources naturelles acquittent le plus souvent les mêmes impôts et taxes que le reste de la population (par exemple : imposition sur le revenu, TVA). Ces impôts et taxes de nature générale sont enregistrés dans les comptes publics, mais ne sont pas nécessairement attribués à une catégorie sectorielle spécifique.
7. De plus, des sociétés et des particuliers sont susceptibles de consacrer une partie de la richesse qu'ils retirent de l'extraction de ressources naturelles à la construction d'infrastructures ou à la prestation de services. Dès lors que ces infrastructures ou services répondent à une demande d'investissements ou de services publics, il peut en résulter une économie de dépenses publiques, qui toutefois ne sera pas comptabilisée comme une recette dans les comptes publics. Dans certains cas, l'État impose que les entreprises et particuliers concernés fournissent certains services comme condition à l'accès aux ressources naturelles dont il est propriétaire, par

exemple en prenant à leur charge une partie au moins du coût de construction et d'entretien des routes desservant les mines.

Graphique 1.30. **Part des secteurs de l'industrie primaire en pourcentage du PIB, 2014**

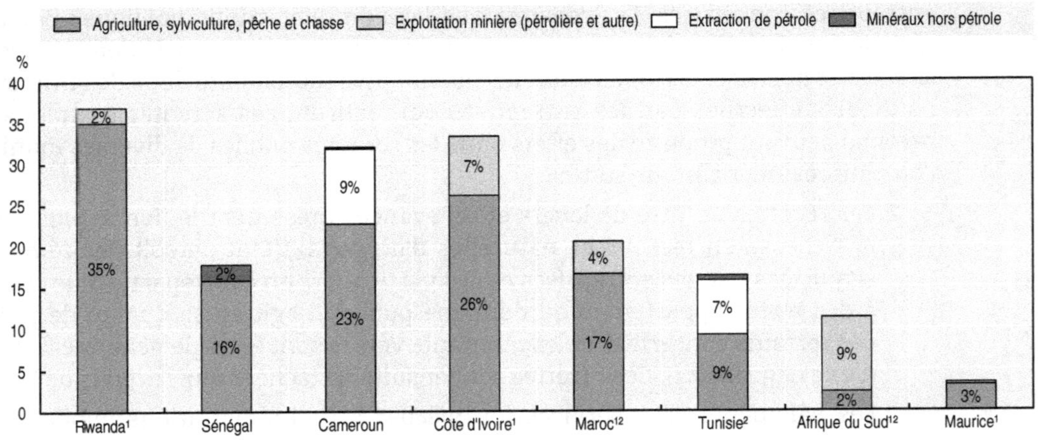

1. La distinction entre l'exploitation minière pétrolière et non pétrolière dans les données du Rwanda, de la Cote d'Ivoire, de la Tunisie et de l'Afrique du Sud n'est pas disponible.

2. Données de 2013.

Source : (BafD/OCDE/PNUD, 2015), *Perspectives économiques en Afrique 2015: Développement territorial et inclusion spatiale.*

StatLink http://dx.doi.org/10.1787/888933344287

Les loyers et redevances constituent la première source de recettes non fiscales émanant des entreprises dont l'activité est principalement centrée sur l'exploitation de ressources naturelles. Les activités concernées correspondent à une partie du secteur primaire en incluant les ressources naturelles renouvelables (agriculture, pêche, chasse) et les ressources non renouvelables (principalement l'exploitation minière et pétrolière). Ces activités jouent un rôle important dans les pays SRPA qui présentent les PIB par habitant les plus faibles (graphique 1.30) ; leur poids dans le PIB total atteint ainsi 37 % au Rwanda, 33 % en Côte d'Ivoire, 32 % au Cameroun, 21 % au Maroc et 18 % au Sénégal. Les graphiques ci-dessous montrent que l'agriculture, la pêche et la chasse contribuent largement plus au PIB que l'exploitation minière et pétrolière.

Les quatre pays dans lesquels la contribution des activités minières au PIB est la plus élevée sont le Cameroun, la Côte d'Ivoire, l'Afrique du Sud et la Tunisie. Dans ces pays, le secteur minier représente entre 7 % et 9 % du PIB. Dans les autres pays, cette part est comprise entre 1 % et 4 %, bien que le montant des recettes liées aux loyers et redevances ne reflète pas toujours cette réalité. En 2014, les recettes publiques découlant des loyers et redevances exprimées en pourcentage du PIB représentaient au Cameroun 3.6 % du PIB, ce qui n'est pas négligeable, mais elles étaient limitées à 0.5 %, voire moins, dans tous les autres pays.

Les recettes tirées des ressources naturelles sont une source de financement non exempte de risques. Selon un document du FMI, les risques entourant les projets miniers sont élevés, avec non seulement des coûts irrécupérables importants, mais aussi des rendements potentiellement hauts. En d'autres termes, le montant des recettes en jeu est considérable, et toute erreur de la part de l'administration peut se révéler très coûteuse (FMI, 2011). Par ailleurs, une forte dépendance à l'égard de la production de biens primaires accroît la vulnérabilité face aux fluctuations des prix des produits de base (voir graphique 1.31). À titre d'exemple, depuis 1990, les plus fortes variations interannuelles du cours de l'or ont atteint 35.8 % à la hausse et 15.4 % à la baisse. De plus, les prix du pétrole ont successivement connu une flambée de 57.1 % en 2000 par rapport à l'année antérieure, avant de chuter de 37.8 % entre 2008 et 2009.

Graphique 1.31. **Variations des prix annuels du pétrole et de l'or par rapport à l'année précédente (%), 1990-2014**

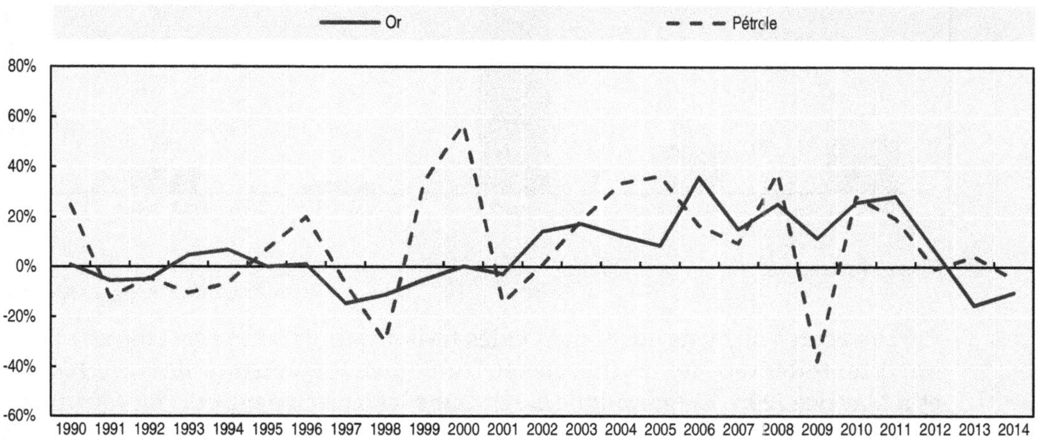

Source : La division de la recherche économique de la Banque fédérale de réserve de St. Louis.

StatLink http://dx.doi.org/10.1787/888933344295

Ventes de biens et de services

Les administrations peuvent produire des biens et des services aussi bien dans le secteur marchand que non marchand. Dans le secteur marchand, les administrations publiques vendent parfois des biens et services qui sont aussi fournis par des entreprises privées (tels que la vente d'aliments ou la prestation de services de transport). En parallèle, elles peuvent assurer, au titre de la gestion de programmes ou de l'application du droit, différents services qui sont du seul ressort d'un État. Les frais correspondant à ces services non marchands, qui sont le plus souvent classés en tant que frais administratifs, recouvrent habituellement les droits d'enregistrement et d'octroi de licence, ainsi que les droits d'utilisation et autres frais de traitement des démarches administratives.

Les frais administratifs sont souvent difficiles à classer, car ils se situent dans une zone grise, à mi-chemin entre les rémunérations de services (qui sont des recettes non fiscales) et les prélèvements obligatoires effectués sans contrepartie versés aux administrations publiques (qui sont des recettes fiscales)[11]. Lorsqu'elles sont classées comme des recettes fiscales, elles sont traditionnellement rattachées à l'une des catégories suivantes :

- 4400 – Impôts sur les transactions mobilières et immobilières
- 5200 – Impôts sur l'utilisation des biens et l'autorisation d'exercer des activités
- 6000 – Autres impôts

Graphique 1.32. **Ventes de biens et de services et frais administratifs en pourcentage du total des recettes non fiscales, 2014**

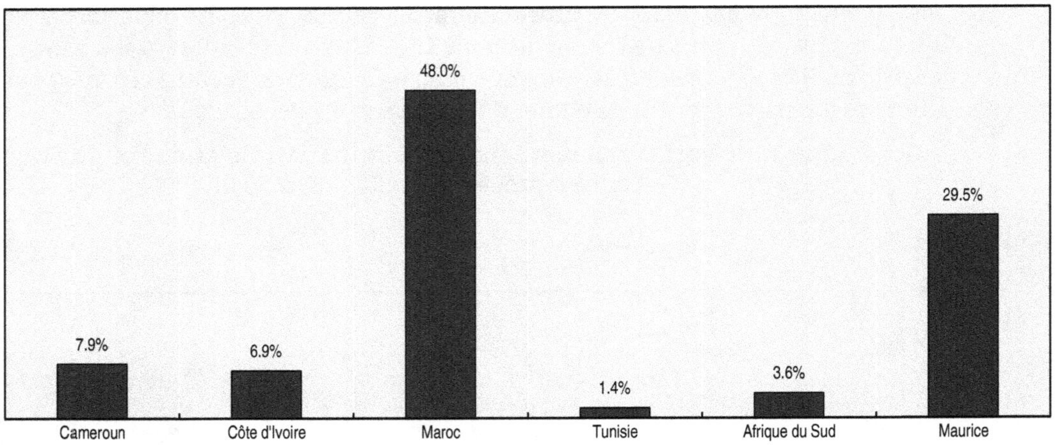

Source : Tableau 5.2.

StatLink http://dx.doi.org/10.1787/888933344303

Les ventes de biens et services et les frais administratifs représentent la part la plus importante des recettes non fiscales au Maroc (avec 48 % du total des recettes non fiscales) et à Maurice (29.5 %) (graphique 1.32). Dans les autres pays qui ont fourni les données concernées, les pourcentages varient de 1.4 % en Tunisie à 7.9 % au Cameroun. Au Maroc, les recettes liées aux ventes de biens et de services sont perçues majoritairement par des administrations locales et correspondent pour 38 % du total à des ventes de biens. À Maurice, les recettes non fiscales liées aux ventes de biens et de services qui sont perçues à l'échelon local sont négligeables. Ces recettes sont générées par un ensemble de frais perçus au titre de différents services assurés par les administrations publiques, allant du contrôle de la navigation aérienne aux services de police, ainsi que par la vente d'une gamme de produits tels que les eaux souterraines, des aliments pour animaux et des produits forestiers.

Amendes et confiscations

Si les amendes et confiscations peuvent représenter une source importante de revenus, elles restent très volatiles. Certaines amendes de montants modestes, comme celles liées aux contraventions pour excès de vitesse, constituent des recettes régulières et prévisibles. Dans certains pays, une fraction de ces recettes est affectée simplement au financement de missions de la police, et ne sont pas comptabilisées dans les statistiques. Ces petites amendes de faibles montants sont négligeables au regard du montant total des recettes non fiscales. Des amendes plus substantielles, comme le règlement d'un différend avec une entreprise multinationale ou le recouvrement de pénalités importantes peuvent se traduire par une manne financière ponctuelle mais et non négligeable, mais difficile à renouveler pour les années suivantes.

Graphique 1.33. **Amendes, pénalités et confiscations en pourcentage du PIB**

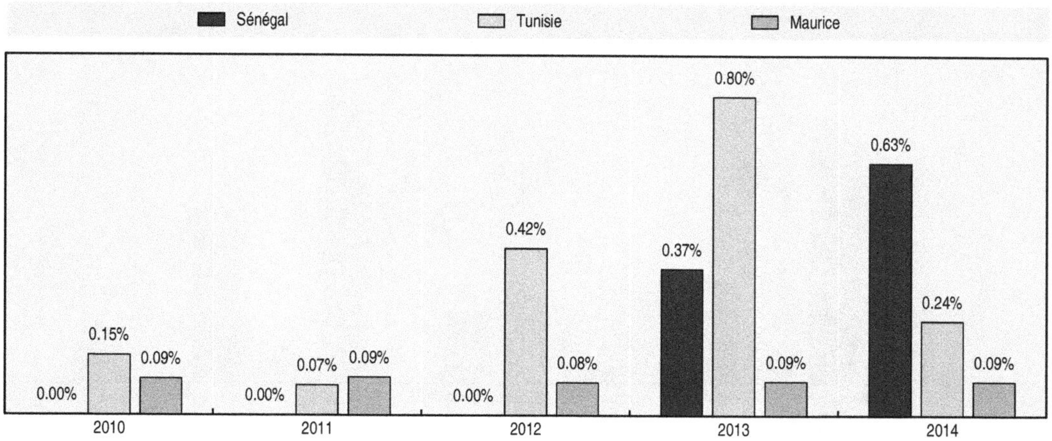

Source : Tableaux 5.5-5.12.

StatLink http://dx.doi.org/10.1787/888933344312

Les recettes tirées des amendes, confiscations et pénalités sont restées négligeables dans la plupart des pays SRPA ; la Tunisie et le Sénégal en sont deux exceptions (graphique 1.33). En Tunisie, la valeur des amendes et pénalités en pourcentage du PIB a progressé, passant de 0.09 % en 2011 à 0.8 % en 2013, avant de retomber à 0.24 % en 2014. Au Sénégal, cette part a atteint 0.37 % du PIB en 2013 et 0.63 % en 2014 alors qu'elle était restée négligeable au cours des trois années qui ont précédé.

Recettes diverses ou non identifiées

Certaines recettes non fiscales représentent des montants significatifs mais ne s'inscrivent dans aucune des catégories citées ci-dessus. Cela concerne notamment :

1. les transferts en capital non inclus par ailleurs.
2. les dons volontaires à des organismes publics de la part de particuliers ou de sociétés.
3. les indemnités d'assurance versées aux administrations publiques.
4. les versements couvrant différentes catégories de la classification et pour lesquels aucune ventilation n'est disponible.
5. les paiements dont la classification appropriée n'est pas identifiable faute de données pertinentes.

Les montants concernés peuvent représenter une part importante des recettes non fiscales durant certaines années spécifiques (graphique 1.34). À titre d'exemple, en 2013, 21 % des recettes non fiscales du Maroc ont été classifiées dans cette catégorie. Parmi les autres recettes susceptibles d'entrer dans cette rubrique figurent les contributions volontaires versées à l'administration en Tunisie, les transferts en capital depuis des fonds statutaires spéciaux à Maurice et, au Maroc des montants versés à l'administration en contrepartie du droit à entrer en concurrence avec des institutions publiques pour la prestation de services.

Graphique 1.34. **Année entre 2010 et 2014 où le montant des recettes diverses et non identifiées en pourcentage du total des recettes non fiscales est le plus élevé**

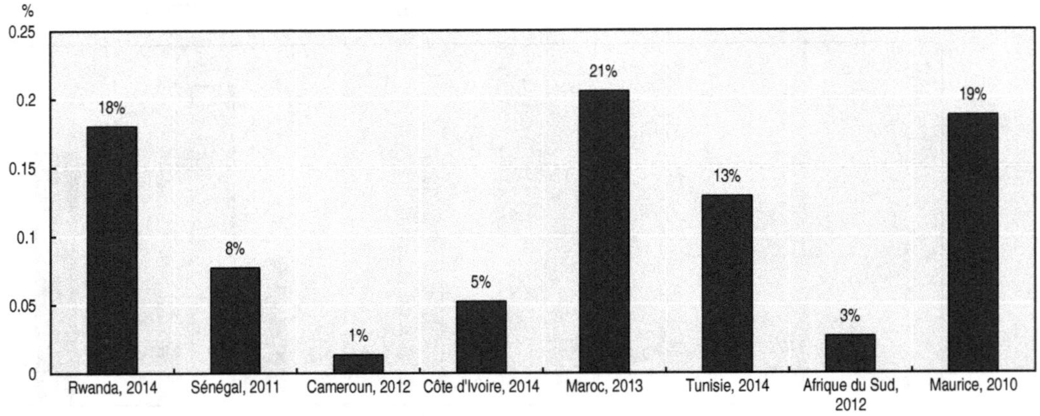

Source : Calculs des auteurs basés sur les tableaux 5.5-5.12.

StatLink http://dx.doi.org/10.1787/888933344326

Le montant des recettes non identifiées est le plus souvent variable et connaît périodiquement des écarts importants (graphique 1.35). Dans certains cas, ces variations sont liées à des transferts en capital importants mais ponctuels, à des entrées de recettes éphémères, ou à des reclassifications de fonds dans la catégorie des recettes non identifiées en raison de l'absence de données. Les données disponibles sont insuffisantes pour mener une analyse concluante de cette catégorie, mais la présence de montants élevés dans cette rubrique peut conduire à s'interroger sur la précision des montants inscrits dans les autres catégories de recettes non fiscales.

Graphique 1.35. **Recettes diverses et non identifiées en pourcentage du total des recettes non fiscales, 2000-14**

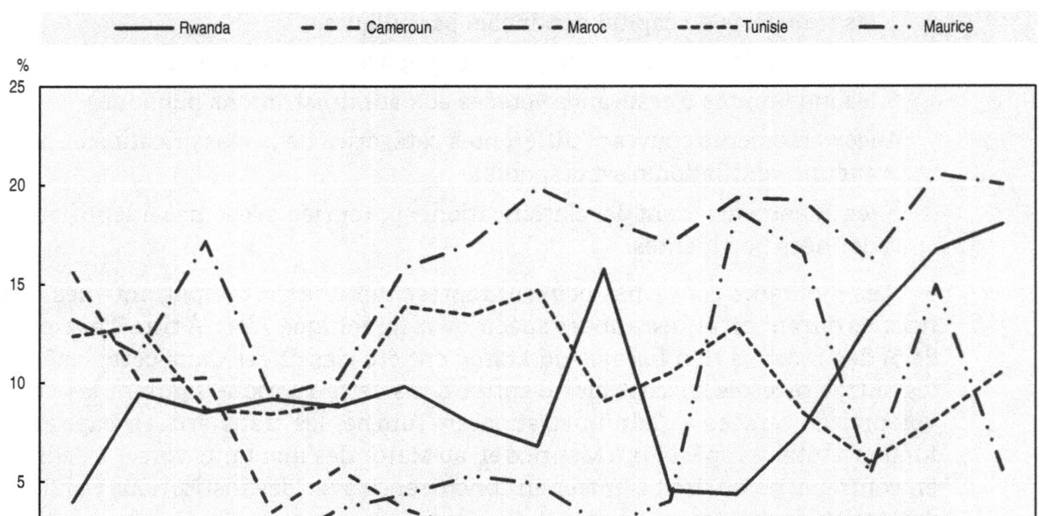

Source : Calculs des auteurs basés sur les tableaux 5.5-5.12.

StatLink http://dx.doi.org/10.1787/888933344333

Notes

1. L'acronyme ALC renvoie aux 22 pays figurant dans l'édition 2016 des *Statistiques des recettes publiques en Amérique latine et dans les Caraïbes*.
2. En Afrique du Sud, la hausse de 5.5 points de pourcentage du taux de pression fiscale entre 2000 et 2014 s'explique en partie par le fait que les recettes fiscales des administrations locales et provinciales sont prises en compte dans les chiffres de 2014 alors qu'elles ne le sont pas dans les chiffres de 2000 (les données concernant les administrations locales et provinciales ne sont disponibles qu'à partir de 2003). La hausse du taux de pression fiscale est de 4.2 points de pourcentage en excluant les données relatives aux administrations locales et provinciales.
3. Calculs des auteurs basés sur la base de données *Perspectives de l'économie mondiale*, octobre 2015, Fonds monétaire international.
4. La crise politico-militaire en 2011 en Côte d'Ivoire en plus de la crise financière mondiale a affecté très lourdement l'environnement économique du pays et le niveau de ses recettes fiscales en pourcentage du PIB.
5. Un pays est considéré comme riche en hydrocarbures et/ou en ressources minérales s'il remplit un ou plusieurs des critères suivants : i) la part moyenne des recettes tirées des hydrocarbures et/ou des ressources minérales dans le total des recettes fiscales est d'au moins 25 % au cours de la période 2000-05 ou ii) la part moyenne des recettes d'exportations d'hydrocarbures et/ou de ressources minérales dans le total des recettes d'exportation est d'au moins 25 % (FMI, 2007).
6. Les impôts spécifiques sur la consommation uniquement pour la Côte d'Ivoire englobent les loyers, redevances et droits sur l'utilisation de biens et services publics généralement considérés comme des recettes non fiscales dans la classification de l'OCDE. L'augmentation de ces recettes en particulier a contribué presque autant que les droits à l'importation à la hausse des impôts spécifiques sur la consommation entre 2000 et 2014 (0.8 point).
7. L'absence de données pour certains pays explique en partie ces différences. Par exemple, les données provenant de la Caisse de Sécurité Sociale (CSS) au Sénégal ne sont pas disponibles.
8. Les données concernant Maurice proviennent des états financiers établis par le Bureau des statistiques de Maurice.
9. Ce chiffre inclut probablement d'autres recettes, telles que les charges de services publics et d'autres services d'utilité publique tels que les péages routiers qui ne sont pas assimilés à la catégorie des recettes fiscales dans cette publication.
10. Mansour et Rota-Graziosi (2013) indiquent que les recettes fiscales liées à l'extraction pétrolière peuvent englober l'impôt sur les bénéfices des sociétés, les droits indirects sur des produits énergétiques ainsi que des montants non remboursés de taxes sur les ventes comme la TVA, tandis que les recettes non fiscales peuvent correspondre à des redevances, des participations aux bénéfices, des dividendes et d'autres revenus d'investissements perçus au titre de participations directes de l'administration au capital des entreprises qui réalisent des activités d'extraction.
11. Pour plus de précisions sur la classification des recettes fiscales et non fiscales utilisée dans la présente publication, consulter, en annexe A, les paragraphes 9 à 13 du Guide d'interprétation de l'OCDE.

Références

Addison, T. et J. Levin (2012), *The Determinants of Tax Revenue in Sub-Saharan Africa*, Swedish Business School at Örebro University, Örebro, Sweden, oru.diva-portal.org/smash/record.jsf?pid=diva2%3A570456&dswid=4207.

AISS (2014), *Approches stratégiques pour renforcer la sécurité sociale, Association internationale de la sécurité sociale*, Genève, www.issa.int/details?uuid=3c1e0654-a158-48db-a5dc-892b36b78ae3.

BAfD (2010), *Domestic Resource Mobilization for Poverty Reduction in East Africa: Rwanda case study*, Banque africaine de développement, Abidjan, Côte d'Ivoire, www.afdb.org/fileadmin/uploads/afdb/Documents/Project-and-Operations/Rwanda%20case%20study%20paper%20final.pdf.

BAfD, OCDE et PNUD (2015), *Perspectives économiques en Afrique 2015: Développement territorial et inclusion spatiale*, Éditions OCDE, Paris, http://dx.doi.org/10.1787/aeo-2015-fr.

BAfD, OCDE et PNUD (2014), *Perspectives économiques en Afrique 2014: Les chaînes de valeur mondiales et l'industrialisation de l'Afrique*, Éditions OCDE, Paris, http://dx.doi.org/10.1787/aeo-2014-fr.

BAfD, OCDE et CEA (2010), *Perspectives économiques en Afrique 2010: la mobilisation des ressources publiques et l'aide*, Éditions OCDE, Paris, http://dx.doi.org/10.1787/aeo-2010-fr.

Banque mondiale (2015), *Note d'orientation du financement des collectivités locales*, Banque mondiale, Washington DC, www-wds.worldbank.org/external/default/WDSContentServer/WDSP/IB/2015/10/13/090224b0831405d5/2_0/Rendered/PDF/Note0d0orienta0ollectivites0locales.pdf.

Besley, T. et T. Persson (2013), *Taxation and Development*, (chapitre préparé pour le Handbook of Public Economics, édité par Auerbach, A., R. Chetty, M. Feldstein et E. Saez), econ.lse.ac.uk/staff/tbesley/papers/TaxationAndDevelopment.pdf.

Bird R. et E. Zolt (2003), *Introduction to Tax Policy Design and Development, module brouillon préparé pour un cours sur les questions pratiques de la politique fiscale dans les pays en développement*, Banque Mondiale, 28 April-1 May, www1.worldbank.org/publicsector/LearningProgram/PracticalIssues/papers/introduction%20to%20tax%20policy/WBI%20Module%201(Bird&Zolt)April10.doc.

Boisard, S., C. de Freitas et G. Hidouci (2014), *Renforcer les recettes fiscales locales pour financer le développement urbain*, FMDV, Paris, resolutionstofundcities.org/sites/default/files/docs/renforcer-les-recettes-fiscales-locales-pour-financer-le-developpement-urbain/etudefmdvfiscalitelocalevillesafrique.pdf.

Cruce, F. (2011), "Evaluating value added tax in Morocco," *Minor Field Study Series*, No. 209, Department of Economics at the University of Lund, Lund, https://liveatlund.lu.se/intranets/LUSEM/NEK/mfs/MFS/209.pdf.

Fjeldstad, O.H., G. Chambas et J.F. Brun (2014), "Local government taxation in Sub-Saharan Africa: a review and an agenda for research", *CMI Working Paper*, WP 2014: 2, CHR. Michelsen Institute, Bergen, www.cmi.no/publications/file/5098-local-government-taxation-in-sub-saharan-africa.pdf.

FMI (2015), "Allégement de la dette au titre de l'initiative en faveur des pays pauvres très endettés (PPTE)", *International Monetary Fund Factsheet*, mars, Fonds monétaire international, Washington, DC, https://www.imf.org/external/np/exr/facts/fre/pdf/hipcf.pdf.

FMI (2014a), "Mauritius: Article IV Consultation- staff report, press release and statement by the executive director for Mauritius", *IMF Country Report*, No. 14/107, Fonds monétaire international Washington, DC, www.imf.org/external/pubs/ft/scr/2014/cr14107.pdf.

FMI (2014b), Cameroun: Consultations de 2014 au titre de l'article IV", *Rapport du FMI*, No. 14/212, Fonds monétaire international, Washington, DC, www.imf.org/external/french/pubs/ft/scr/2014/cr14212f.pdf.

FMI (2013), "Côte d'Ivoire : Consultations de 2013 au titre de l'Article IV et quatrième revue de l'accord au titre de la facilité élargie de credit", *Rapport du FMI* No. 13/367, Fonds monétaire international , Washington, DC, www.imf.org/external/french/pubs/ft/scr/2013/cr13367f.pdf.

FMI (2011), *Mobilisation des recettes dans les pays en développement*, Fonds monétaire international, Washington, DC, http://www.imf.org/external/french/np/pp/2011/030811f.pdf.

FMI (2010), *Tunisie – Conclusions préliminaires de la mission de consultation au titre de l'article IV (2010)*, Fonds monétaire international, Washington, DC, www.imf.org/external/french/np/ms/2010/061510af.htm (accessed 7 January 2015).

FMI (2007), *Guide sur la transparence des recettes des ressources naturelles*, Fonds monétaire international, Washington, DC, https://www.imf.org/external/np/fad/trans/fre/guidef.pdf.

Fossat, P. et M. Bua (2013), "Tax Administration Reform in the Francophone Countries of Sub-Saharan Africa", *IMF Working Paper*, WP/13/173, Fonds monétaire international, Washington, DC, www.imf.org/external/pubs/ft/wp/2013/wp13173.pdf.

Kloeden, D. (2011), "Revenue Administration Reforms in Anglophone Africa Since the Early 1990s", *IMF Working Paper*, WP/11/162, Fonds monétaire international, Washington, DC, www.imf.org/external/pubs/ft/wp/2011/wp11162.pdf.

Mansour M. et G. Rota-Graziosi (2013), "Tax Coordination, Tax Competition, and Revenue Mobilization in the West African Economic and Monetary Union", *IMF Working Paper* WP/13/163, Fonds monétaire international, Washington, DC, https://www.imf.org/external/pubs/ft/wp/2013/wp13163.pdf

Mascagnani, G., M. Moore et R. McCluskey (2014), *Tax revenue mobilisation in developing countries issues and challenge*, Union européenne, Bruxelles, www.europarl.europa.eu/RegData/etudes/etudes/join/2014/433849/EXPO-DEVE_ET%282014%29433849_EN.pdf.

Monkam, N. et M. Moore (2015), *How Property Tax Would Benefit Africa*, Africa Research Institute, London, www.africaresearchinstitute.org/publications/property-tax-benefit-africa.

OCDE (2014), *Coopération pour le développement 2015, Mobiliser les ressources au service du développement durable*, Éditions OCDE, Paris, http://dx.doi.org/10.1787/dcr-2014-fr.

PNUD (2013), *Rapport sur le développement humain 2013: Emploi, changements structurels et développement humain en Côte d'Ivoire*, Programme des Nations Unies pour le développement, New York, www.ci.undp.org/content/cote_divoire/fr/home/library/poverty/rndh_2013.html.

Sokeechand, K.R. et G. Hussen (2013), "The Mauritian experience", presentation prepared for regional workshop on "Effectiveness of and alternatives to tax incentives as instruments to generate employment and attract investments in Lusaka", 12-13 February, Zambia, International Tax Compact, www.taxcompact.net/documents/workshop-lusaka/2013-02-13_itc_Rambaksh-Sokeechand_MRA-MoF-Mauritius.pdf.

SSA (2015), "Social security through the world: Africa 2015", *SSA Publication* No. 13-11802, Social Security Administration, Washington DC, www.ssa.gov/policy/docs/progdesc/ssptw/2014-2015/africa/ssptw15africa.pdf..

Pour en savoir plus

BAfD (2010), "Senegal- Évaluation du potentiel de recettes publiques", www.afdb.org/fileadmin/uploads/afdb/Documents/Project-and-Operations/Pages%20from%20SENEGAL_%20Evaluation%20du%20potentiel%20des%20recettes%20publiques%20Eng.pdf

FMI (2015), *Current challenges in revenue mobilization: Improving tax compliance*, Fonds monétaire international, Washington, DC, https://www.imf.org/external/np/pp/eng/2015/020215a.pdf.

FMI (2014), *Government Finance Statistics Manual*, Service des publications du Fonds monétaire international, Washington, DC, www.imf.org/external/Pubs/FT/GFS/Manual/2014/gfsfinal.pdf.

John, J.D. (2009), "Taxation, Governance and Resource Mobilisation in Sub-Saharan Africa: A Survey of Key Issues (WP)," *Sub-Saharan Africa Working Paper*, 49/2009, Real Instituto Elcano, Madrid, www.realinstitutoelcano.org/wps/portal/web/rielcano_en/contenido?WCM_GLOBAL_CONTEXT=/elcano/elcano_in/zonas_in/dt49-2009.

Keen, M. et M. Mansour (2009), "Revenue mobilization in sub-Saharan Africa: Challenges from globalization ", *IMF Working Paper*, WP/09/157, Fonds monétaire international, Washington, DC, www.imf.org/external/pubs/ft/wp/2009/wp09157.pdf.

Lewis, C. et T. Alton (2015), "How can South Africa's tax system meet revenue raising challenges?", *Documents de travail du Département des affaires économiques*, No. 1276, Éditions OCDE, Paris, http://dx.doi.org/10.1787/5jrp1g0xztbr-en.

Thomas, A. et J.P. Treviño (2013), "Resource Dependence and Fiscal Effort in Sub-Saharan Africa," *IMF Working Paper*, WP/13/188, Fonds monétaire international, Washington, DC, https://www.imf.org/external/pubs/ft/wp/2013/wp13188.pdf.

Wilson, P., A. Cobham et A. Goodall (2014), "ICTD Working Paper 19: The ICTD Government Revenue Dataset", Institute of Development Studies, Brighton, r4d.dfid.gov.uk/pdf/outputs/taxation/ICTD-WP19.pdf.

CHAPTER 2

SPECIAL FEATURE

The benefits and limitations of comparing revenue statistics: What does this mean for Africa?

CHAPITRE 2

ÉTUDE SPÉCIALE

Atouts et limites de la comparaison des statistiques des recettes publiques : quelles implications pour l'Afrique ?

SPECIAL FEATURE

The benefits and limitations of comparing revenue statistics: What does this mean for Africa?

Availability of comparative public revenue statistics

For Africa, as for the rest of the world, taxes are an instrument of social justice and economic prosperity. The 2008 global economic and financial crisis gave new momentum to initiatives and calls for taxation to be more effective, more investment-attractive, more transparent, more progressive, simpler and more stable in order to return to more robust and fairer growth. The stakes are all the greater in the countries of Africa. On one hand, from a budgetary point of view, in a context of strong demographic growth, governments and local authorities are struggling to provide quality public and social services to their citizens. The financing needs for infrastructure that will attract investors and unlock the productive potential of the continent's economies are colossal. On the other hand, from the institutional point of view, taxation is a fundamental instrument to build and consolidate a modern state. By promoting fair circulation of wealth in a society, it constitutes a democratic lever for good governance and an engine for broader reforms.

Setting up effective and fair taxation, and allowing governments and citizens to debate these issues requires, at the very least, making information on public revenue accessible. A few simple, relevant, permanently available indicators are then able to meet users' demand for rigour and objectivity, and referring to them could become routine. If in addition, the collection and classification methods of such statistics are sufficiently detailed and transparent, then leaders, researchers and citizens can easily adapt, refer to, enhance, model and/or aggregate them. In short, revenue statistics could become a public good. There are several examples of good practices in this area on the African continent, such as in South Africa.[1] The majority of economies, however, still have many steps to take to achieve this goal.

The pan-African ambition of greater economic and political integration, leading to harmonised public policies, requires building an efficient statistical tool and using common methodologies. Where taxation is concerned, such harmonisation is an explicit goal of the Strategy for the Harmonization of Statistics in Africa (SHaSA) promoted by the African Union Commission (AUC), the African Development Bank (AfDB) and the Economic Commission for Africa (ECA).[2] This ambition is also regarded as an instrument for stronger co-operation amongst African tax authorities, actively encouraged by the African Tax Administration Forum (ATAF).

Responding to these needs, in particular that of comparability, is what this first report of the Revenue Statistics in Africa project endeavours to do. The aim of the partners in this initiative is to publish, on a regular basis, the public revenue data of the continent's economies according to a common format in order to provide information, in particular on the evolution and the positioning of their levels of revenue compared to that of other countries. They have therefore invited African countries to share their data on a voluntary basis by using a methodology developed for tax purposes by the OECD, in order to make their data comparable with that of other African countries and with the statistics of other geographical regions. The project has laid the foundations of a database intended to cover the greater number of the continent's economies and to allow national, regional and international organisations, governmental or not, to speak the same language. It capitalises on 40 years of experience in OECD member states, as well as on that of a growing number of countries in Latin America and Asia that have been involved in similar initiatives for several years.

There are particular difficulties in measuring tax revenues, however – and even more so in making these measurements comparable – which this project has strived to surmount. Ever-increasing international exchanges and the deployment of automated information systems are facilitating the production of figures and the standardisation of international comparisons in every field of collective action. These sometimes obscure the fact that the premises used to build any new measuring system need to be looked at carefully. For example, measuring comparative revenue statistics can be based on several dimensions shared by the various national administrations (e.g. tax base, type of taxpayer, level of government, etc.), but in doing that other dimensions are not considered and certain specificities are concealed (level of wealth, ownership of capital, nature of government, etc.). As with any single measuring tool, this statistical tool thus has both the virtues of a common language and the limits of "one size fits all".

This special feature aims to highlight what is at stake in making the comparability of tax systems a priority objective, in order to clarify the expected benefits and limits.[3] Its conclusion is based on the two principles underpinning the Revenue Statistics in Africa initiative, namely co-operation and transparency.

The benefits of comparison

The primary objective of this project is to speak a common language by sharing tables and charts containing comparative figures that are useful to all countries as well as to international organisations, governmental or not.

What does comparison mean and how did we carry it out?

Making the world measurable and its elements comparable constitutes the main added value of multilateralism. Thus, as of the first edition of this work in 1972, the OECD claimed comparison itself to be the end-purpose of comparison:

> "*Limitations on the coverage and international comparability of existing data on governments have come increasingly to be felt as a drawback at a time when governments and international organisations are having to make greater use of such statistics in the formulation of economic policies. Since 1971, the Committee on Fiscal Affairs of the OECD has been seeking to remedy this state of affairs by drawing up an agreed list of tax revenues and social security contributions to serve as a basis for the collection and classification of data in a standardised form […]. The aim is to provide a comprehensive coverage for data on tax revenues and social security and similar contributions and eventually, other revenues, in a standardised framework.*" (OECD, 1972).

Similarly, the 2011 edition of Revenue Statistics specifies that the particular role of the Working Party on Tax Policy Analysis and Tax Statistics is to re-examine periodically the presentation of Revenue Statistics with the international-comparability requirement in mind.

The data provided by national administrations are reclassified into a universally accepted tax classification. Comparison of tax revenue data across countries requires accurate definitions of revenue streams. For example, is a tax on the use of a motor vehicle a property tax? Are VAT revenues accounted for before or after refunds? Is the income of the professions reported as individual or business income? Is the same definition of year being used (fiscal year or calendar year)? Are the same levels of government being referred to in federal and highly centralised countries? National classifications are designed to meet a country's specific needs, which makes them different from one another. The secretariat and the officials providing the data from the participating countries (Ministries of Finance, national tax authorities or national statistics institutes) discuss the national tax revenue data and the international tax classification categories and agree on moving from local statistics categories to international statistics categories. This is called aligning the classifications. They then together assign the country's annually provided revenue data to these international categories.

The resulting universal framework makes it possible to describe the present by highlighting similarities and differences amongst the different countries' structures and volumes of public revenues. It provides a tool which enables effective comparisons of all countries regardless of their wealth. It also provides a neutral perspective over and above specific national issues and interests. The framework enables countries to focus on what they have in common assuming that this is sufficiently structured to justify a comparison: a state, an administration, an annual budget, public accounts, the same relationship between private wealth and collective wealth and the same desire for economic development. Once the data is on the same basis, the figures – which are inherently discrete in the mathematical sense of the term – will identify the constants and the differences.

The comparisons do not imply either a rating or a ranking of the participating countries. Countries differ in their regulatory structure, their political objectives and their administrative organisation depending on their history, their location and their environment. Tax systems should be designed to fit a country's individual situation – they are not comparable on a common scale. The revenue indicators used in this publication do not offer numerical thresholds to be reached or not to be exceeded in order to be positively or negatively judged; they should not be treated as performance indicators that imply specific tax objectives to be reached.

Why do we produce comparative statistics?

Comparable statistics are a tool to help governments in their decision making. The consideration of historical trends enables an evaluation and justification of previous policies. It also provides a basis for deciding on policies for the future.

Becoming part of world affairs

By voluntarily taking part in a global project, each country allows its tax system to be considered as comparable. It is part of the process of legitimising the tax system and the decisions on which it is based. The objective image offered by the presentation of the statistics encourages the country to conform to the ideas underlying the classification. The country allows itself to receive technical support in reference to international standards. Conversely, by joining the global debate on taxation, each country agrees to be scrutinised, sometimes criticised, and sometimes copied. These amount to both acknowledging that the tax system can be improved and to stating the political will to improve it.

Being integrated into an international publication contributes to improving the quality of national data and to acquiring new techniques being developed at the international level. As the data is processed, the project establishes strong individual links between the OECD experts and the national civil servants, as well as amongst the latter. The work requires the country's administrations that produce or provide the figures to co-operate. It exposes missing data and inconsistencies, which compel the administrations to go back to the data sources and make improvements for the following editions. The national officials benefit from an external technical drive enabling them to gain better understanding of international standards and to take advantage of them as they consider appropriate. The legitimacy of the officials is reinforced in the eyes of their political authority as a result of their co-operation with international organisations.

Considering the past and looking to the future

In order to adapt to the changing realities of the economic and political world, and to citizens' wishes, tax systems are a work in progress. Each tax policy decision, political or administrative, takes into consideration broader political objectives – increase revenues, reduce inequalities, correct external effects, etc. – by taking into account the impact of previous reforms, international constraints or foreign practices. The requirement for comparable revenue statistics became more pressing in the 2000s as the need to increase domestic revenues in African countries became more critical in the context of international dialogue on the future of development financing.[4]

Statistical comparison, within one country or with others over time, provides a framework for devising political solutions. By examining the policies and practices of other countries and historical trends in the data, countries can distinguish what is being done from what could be done. They can identify elements for possible and acceptable policies, and also where there is room to manoeuvre such as in VAT rates, environmental taxation, or taxation of labour or assets. Through correlation, modelling, etc., comparative data also provides a basis for simulating reforms, anticipating their impacts and informing decisions.

Statistical comparison, within one country or with others over time, reduces the uncertainty of change by attempting to anticipate it. Comparing one country with another can bring two types of opportunity. One is to follow the practice of a fellow country by bringing one's own tax structure closer to it. The second is to identify and evaluate reforms carried out in that country to draw conclusions for oneself. In this way, the provision of tax revenue data forms a basis for planning for the future.

To offer a state continuity over time is to offer it a means to compare the country as it is now with what it used to be. The measurement, analysis and comparison of data allows a country to account for changes over the long term. Revenue statistics can be a basis for econometric analyses that will allow a quantitative evaluation of the impacts of past reforms. The availability of historical data acts as an incentive to taking decisions.

The interpretation of internationally comparable data

Quality statistics aim to mirror reality but they can never really achieve this aim. A user derives great benefit from a statistic insofar as he or she knows how it was produced. The following paragraphs can be considered as an exercise in transparency forced upon themselves by the authors of these statistics in order to offer their users a mirror with conditions for appropriate use. The mirror metaphor helps to focus on the aims of reality and consistency of the project as well as the limits related to its construction: a single classification for varied situations and a regrouping of data with obvious individual shortcomings.

An analysis that is both simple and transparent is only seemingly compatible with a complex and varied world. Public opinion as well as international organisations, as users of the data, demand figures that are simple to understand and easy to use. The statistics are transparent in that they reflect the data provided by the participating countries in the format of the OECD tax classification. But the authors recognise that this can never represent a perfect reflection of taxation in each country. The presentation of the data involves translating information from a complex and varied world into a format that can easily be understood by the users. This can only be achieved by defining a classification of taxes and summarising the revenue data within this structure in the correct time periods. This process involves making choices in a conservative way on complicated issues that are opaque to the non-specialist. The search for total objectivity is thus a paradox.

In defining an indicator, it is necessary to equate heterogeneous data. The choice of a classification is fundamental to the presentation of the statistics. Countries define their national revenues in different ways which means that choices have to be made at every stage, which is the price to pay for producing a common statistical language. There are multiple dimensions to comparisons: geography, time and political regime. The data can only express in a condensed form the complex development work that made them possible.

The following paragraphs describe some limits to revenue statistics, and how understanding these limits can help statisticians improve both the amount of meaningful information that is collected, and make data interpretation more useful. These paragraphs aim to expose the limits and, through them, the variables in the exercise of producing data on public revenues. Figures are not able to speak for themselves, so the idea is to clarify what is implicit in their construction. This has been carried out with reference to the Latin American and Asian experiences, but primarily in a year of working in partnership with the statisticians of the eight African countries taking part in this first edition.

The impact of the classification and the methodologies

A classification can never be completely neutral. The OECD tax classification favours the perspective of the fiscal policy maker. When a painter produces a picture, the composition will vary according to the impression of the landscape that he/she wants to give to the viewer. This is why any indicator is constrained by its definition. In the OECD classification, the term "tax revenue" indicates compulsory, unrequited payments made to general government. This definition is used today as the reference for most of the national work on taxation. Even though it is clear and simple, it has to be complemented by the conventions set out in the OECD Interpretative Guide. For example, imputed social contributions are excluded and tax expenditures are not taken into account.

The classification of country revenue data is dependent on regulatory definitions and categories. Revenues are paid and collected in currency units and as such are directly quantifiable. The output is therefore, at the same time, both a currency and a statistical unit (unlike statistics on security, education or health, which require changing a qualitative element into a quantitative indicator). That being said, revenue statistics are mainly a compilation of pre-existing data (public, tax, direct, professional and local revenues, etc.), i.e. they are a by-product of the activity of administrative services. The records from which the data are extracted are designed for the purposes of collecting taxes. They reflect the rules, reporting and coding systems of national institutions rather than the tax category definitions used by the statisticians.

Tax reforms and methodological changes affect the interpretation of the data. In the area of taxes, as in others, statisticians face a time dilemma. They cannot revise statistical procedures too much or too often at the risk of harming the comparability of a time series. Nevertheless, they inevitably have to re-examine the statistical procedure when a national tax structure is reformed (for example – the introduction of a VAT) or when the statistical procedure shows deficiencies (for example – when moving from cash-based to accrual-based accounting). These issues are problematical in developing countries. Tax bases can be narrow and revenues volatile. The introduction of new software can affect the consistency of time series even though they are a sign of a country's political and administrative vitality.

In seeking clarification and transparency, all choices of classification are discussed in an Interpretative Guide, and the Report also includes footnotes. These notes record the micro-decisions made jointly by the country and the secretariat statisticians. In cases where some issues are unresolved, these notes make it possible to document them and make them visible to the users.

Limitations related to the nature of the data sources

National revenue statistics reflect the governments' perspective but they provide an incomplete picture of international taxation as information is missing on the taxation of multi-national enterprises and the informal economy. As a result, governments do not have a monopoly over tax information. However they can supplement the main data source, national accounts, with information from other sources.

The effective tax rate on the major multinational groups tends to be low. As taxpayers, they take advantage of the differences in the public policies of the countries with which they are negotiating, where those countries are competing with one another to have the lowest tax rate. And yet these companies are vital players within each country, and have influence on both major and politically sensitive economic indices (investment, employment, balance of payments and, of course, revenues). Multinationals have a different vision of wealth and its circulation. They are competing with one another and they stimulate competition between countries, including in the realm of taxation.

Revenue statistics only reflect the visible part of the economy. National accounts do not include any income hidden from the tax authorities, including in tax havens, nor the share of the informal sector, and yet these categories are prominent in African economies. Non-taxation is one of the criteria of informality and it results in simultaneous avoidance of various taxes. In addition, the informal economy has an impact on indicators unrelated to taxation such as the Gross Domestic Product (GDP). "The [differences in both amounts of tax evaded and the size of the underground economy are] not discussed because [this] necessarily involves consideration of numbers where true values are uncertain." (OECD, 1999, p. 28). The tax to GDP ratio measurement is therefore necessarily imprecise. The comparative data is unable to take into account this element, which actually varies in size between countries.

Conclusion: Future paths for progress

Countries joining the Revenue Statistics are considered to be full participants. The numbers of participating countries and their taxpayers is both substantial and rising. The aim is to establish a virtuous circle with an increasing number of participating countries; a classification necessarily adapted to their diversity; a growing interest in adapted statistics; and an interest in attracting new participating countries.

Expanding the geographical coverage

The number of participating countries is expected to increase gradually. The aim of the project is global knowledge of tax revenues and its scope is increasing over time. The new publications are produced on a continental basis with local partners. Beyond them is envisaged a global database with a unique classification. To ensure the quality of the data, extension of the number of countries covered is progressive: the work on Latin America and the Caribbean has moved from including 12 to 22 countries in 5 years; the one on Asia included 3 non-OECD countries in 2015 and the one on Africa is starting in 2016 with 8 countries.

Universalising the statistical machinery

Any classification is necessarily based on a particular perspective of the world as it is or as it should be. This means that it will not be entirely appropriate or politically neutral. It must therefore be shared under the principles underpinning it: usefulness for tax-policy decision makers, historicity and feasibility for all. Its publication in a collective framework based on partnership is at the hinge between the true (the present) and the fair (the hoped-for future), as in the British expression, "a true and fair view". The statistical machinery will be universalised in a spirit of parity, networking and mutual learning.

The heterogeneity of different forms of state has to be factored into the statistics. The development of government statistics is closely connected to the construction of a state through its roles in accountability, management, assessment and legislation. However, for some of these territories, the very concept of a sovereign and tax-collecting state is far from evident. These are states based on societies, empires and/or civilisations that are fundamentally different from this heritage and on which foreign legal and political systems were superimposed. Added to this diversity are: an upheaval in the global economic rankings; shifts in what falls under "national" and "international" because of the global division of labour and the movements of production factors; less standardised national accounts; lower potential for taxation; and relatively higher shares of non-tax revenues, including foreign aid.

The extension of the coverage of the project requires discussions on the indicators and their definitions. Already, each new participating country enters the project with a batch of questions. At the beginning of the collection process, each country sends technical questions to the secretariat's statistics team. Some are common (e.g. accounting of social contributions or of an annual charge) but others are more specific, such as the inclusion or not of data from the former "homelands" in South Africa and the status of the customs duties collected and distributed amongst the neighbouring countries under the Southern African Customs Union. Examples of the questions that are raised are those of refining the definitions of non-tax revenues, adding tax expenditure to the figures, earmarking tax revenues and the breakdown of revenues by sector.

The evolution of the project resulting from the entry of new participating countries is not only justified by equity or the positive effects for the latter, but also by the positive effects for all. The increase in diversity is both desirable and advantageous for all. Since the 1960s, developing countries have been places of true methodological inventiveness in statistical production in general (nomenclatures, coding conventions, collection methods, etc.). They have administrative and social structures less institutionalised than in longstanding developed countries. Therefore it has been possible in these countries to develop administrations that are able to carry out surveys and collect statistics. This will be beneficial for the revenue statistics.

Extending the debate made possible by comparable statistics

Transparency on the methodology is the foundation of the worldwide use of this statistical product by governments, citizens and researchers. The dissemination of comparative statistics provides transparency for the public debate and serves democracy. Publishing reliable and comparable figures reduces the information asymmetry between the public and decision makers, and even amongst decision makers themselves. Data compiled and published in a transparent way provide a basis for scientific research, administrative decisions and political dialogue in the countries in the region and at the international level.

Even though countries can learn much from each other, each must set its own course, in terms of its identity, its resources and its citizens' expectations. Copying "successful models" can never be a solution. We should be wary of the idea that there is a set of best practices whereby each country can at its convenience extract from a toolbox of available instruments that have been enhanced by the experience of others. Regardless of the effectiveness of certain instruments, this would be both an illusion and a denial of the political responsibility of decision makers.

Statistics alone cannot define what the correct policies should be. The statistics themselves are evidence of the outcome of past and current policies. But they do not say anything about the fairness of the policies that underlie them.

The publication of these statistics contributes to improving the information flow to citizens, to stimulating and informing the economic and policy debate, and accounting to constituents on performance and the impact of initiatives. They offer citizens information on the make-up of government revenues providing a tool to support decision making and oversight of public-policy issues. Their existence will extend the scope of the public debate – for instance by combining them with other statistics or by ordering them differently – and increase the spheres in which citizens can exercise political responsibility. Let us hope that individuals show interest in the information that they provide on themselves – with or without their knowledge – and can overcome the technical appearance that would keep tax issues within the exclusive reach of the specialists.

The publication of these statistics helps to meet the information needs of potential foreign investors and visitors (including the media and other intermediary organisations) to a country; to satisfy the accountability requirements of foreign governments and international institutions before and after any aid is granted; and to draft accurate reports to organisations that have been charged by the international community with keeping track of the worldwide performance on many economic, environmental, social and other issues.

Comparable tax statistics help countries to participate in a global debate on taxation. The statistics promote dialogue between countries and enable them to assert and justify their choices. These statistics represent another step towards transparency and also to greater influence.

Notes

1. www.sars.gov.za/About/SATaxSystem/Pages/Tax-Statistics.aspx.
2. Economic Commission for Africa, African Development Bank and Economic Commission for Africa (2010), Strategy for the Harmonization of Statistics in Africa (SHaSA), www.eastc.ac.tz/cms-v1/sites/default/files/SHaSA.pdf.
3. This chapter benefited from contributions of the article prepared by Thomas Cantens (WCO) and Jocelyn Pierre (OECD) for the international conference organised by Ferdi, ICTD and Cerdi-University of Auvergne in collaboration with the World Bank, the Centre Norbert Elias and the WCO on measuring the performance of tax and customs administrations in developing countries (12 and 13 June 2014, Clermont-Ferrand, France).
4. The Paris Declaration on Aid Effectiveness and the Accra Agenda for Action, 2005, www.oecd.org/development/effectiveness/34428351.pdf; Addis Ababa Action Agenda, 2015, www.un.org/ga/search/view_doc.asp?symbol=A/69/L.82&Lang=E.

ÉTUDE SPÉCIALE

Atouts et limites de la comparaison des statistiques des recettes publiques : quelles implications pour l'Afrique ?

Des statistiques disponibles et comparables sur les recettes publiques des pays d'Afrique

L'impôt est un instrument de justice sociale et de prospérité économique pour l'Afrique comme dans le reste du monde. L'éclatement de la crise économique et financière mondiale en 2008 a donné un nouvel élan aux initiatives et aux prises de position appelant à une fiscalité plus efficace, plus attractive pour les investissements, plus transparente, plus progressive, plus simple et plus stable afin de retrouver une croissance plus robuste et plus juste. Dans les pays d'Afrique, les enjeux sont d'autant plus importants. Sur le plan budgétaire d'une part, dans un contexte de croissance démographique rapide, États et collectivités locales peinent à fournir des services publics et des services sociaux de qualité à leurs citoyens. Les besoins de financement des infrastructures à même d'attirer les investisseurs et de libérer le potentiel productif des économies du continent sont colossaux. Sur le plan institutionnel d'autre part, la fiscalité est un instrument essentiel à la construction et la consolidation d'états modernes. En promouvant une circulation juste de la richesse dans une société, elle constitue un levier démocratique de « bonne gouvernance » et un moteur pour des réformes plus vastes.

Pour mettre en place une fiscalité efficace et équitable, et permettre aux gouvernements comme aux citoyens de se saisir de ces débats, encore faut-il que les informations sur les recettes publiques soient accessibles : quelques indicateurs simples, pertinents et disponibles de manière pérenne peuvent alors satisfaire les exigences de rigueur et d'objectivité des utilisateurs ; y faire référence peut devenir une pratique familière. Si de plus les méthodes de collecte et de classification de telles statistiques sont suffisamment détaillées et transparentes, les dirigeants, chercheurs et citoyens peuvent les utiliser aisément, se les approprier, s'y référer, les enrichir, les modéliser, les agréger... en un mot, faire de ces statistiques un bien public. Le continent africain recèle plusieurs exemples de bonnes pratiques en la matière, comme en Afrique du Sud[1]. Néanmoins, la majorité des économies ont encore de nombreuses étapes à franchir pour atteindre cet objectif.

L'ambition panafricaine d'une intégration économique et politique accrue, et donc l'adoption de politiques publiques communes, rend nécessaire la construction d'un outil statistique efficient et l'utilisation de méthodologies communes. Dans le domaine fiscal, une telle harmonisation est un objectif explicite de la Stratégie pour l'Harmonisation des Statistiques en Afrique (SHaSA) promue par la Commission de l'Union Africaine (CUA), la Banque africaine de développement (BAfD) et la Commission économique pour l'Afrique (CEA)[2]. Cette ambition est également considérée comme un instrument de coopération renforcée entre les administrations fiscales africaines activement encouragée par le Forum sur l'administration fiscale en Afrique (ATAF).

C'est à ces besoins, et notamment celui de la comparabilité, que tente de répondre cette première édition des *Statistiques des recettes publiques en Afrique*. L'ambition des partenaires de l'initiative est de publier régulièrement les données de recettes publiques des économies du continent sous un format comparable, afin d'apporter des informations notamment sur le niveau des recettes, leur évolution et le positionnement de ce niveau par rapport à celui d'autres pays. À cette fin, ils ont entrepris, à l'aide d'une méthodologie établie pour des besoins fiscaux par l'OCDE, d'inviter les pays qui le souhaitaient à partager leurs données sur une base volontaire, afin de les rendre comparables entre elles et avec les statistiques d'autres régions du monde. Ils posent ainsi les fondations d'une base de données dont la vocation est de couvrir le plus grand nombre d'économies du continent, et de permettre aux organisations nationales, régionales et internationales, gouvernementales ou non, de parler un même langage. Ils capitalisent sur 40 ans d'expérience auprès des pays membres de l'Organisation mais aussi sur celle d'un nombre croissant de pays d'Amérique latine et d'Asie, qui depuis plusieurs années se sont joints à des initiatives semblables.

Toutefois, « mesurer l'impôt », et a fortiori rendre cette mesure comparable, présente des difficultés particulières, que ce projet s'est efforcé de surmonter. La multiplication des échanges internationaux et le déploiement de systèmes d'information automatisés facilitent la production de chiffres et banalisent les comparaisons internationales dans tous les domaines de l'action collective. Ils font parfois oublier que chaque nouveau dispositif mérite qu'on s'arrête sur les postulats de sa construction. Ainsi, par exemple, pour mesurer les recettes à des fins de comparaison on peut s'appuyer sur plusieurs dimensions communes aux différentes administrations nationales (base fiscale, type de contribuable, niveau de gouvernement, etc.) mais on oblitère au passage certaines spécificités (niveau de richesse, propriété du capital, nature du gouvernement, etc.). Comme tout outil de mesure unique, cet instrument statistique a donc les vertus d'un langage commun en même temps que les limites de la « taille unique » (*One size fits all*).

Cette Étude spéciale[3] a vocation à mettre en lumière les enjeux de la priorité donnée à l'objectif de comparabilité des systèmes fiscaux, afin d'en clarifier les bénéfices attendus et réels et les limites. Sa conclusion repose sur les deux principes qui sous-tendent cette initiative Statistiques des recettes publiques en Afrique que sont la coopération et la transparence.

Les bénéfices de la comparaison

L'objectif premier de cette entreprise est de parler un même langage grâce au partage d'un tableau de bord contenant des chiffres comparables utiles à chaque pays comme aux organisations internationales, gouvernementales ou non.

Que signifie comparer ? Comment avons-nous procédé ?

Rendre le monde commensurable et ses éléments comparables constituent la principale valeur ajoutée du multilatéralisme. Ainsi, dès la première édition de l'ouvrage en 1972 l'OCDE revendique une comparaison dont la finalité est la comparaison elle-même :

> « *Les données disponibles sur les recettes publiques sont limitées en périmètre et en comparabilité. C'est un inconvénient croissant au moment où les gouvernements et les organisations internationales en ont besoin pour formuler des politiques économiques. Depuis 1971, le Comité des affaires fiscales de l'OCDE cherche à remédier à cette difficulté en établissant une liste commune (agreed) de recettes fiscales et sociales pour servir de base à la collecte et la classification standardisées (...). L'objectif est de procurer une couverture complète (comprehensive) des données portant sur les recettes fiscales (tax revenues), sociales et assimilées, d'une façon standardisée. (...)* » (OCDE, 1972).

De même, l'édition 2011 des Statistiques des recettes publiques précise que le Groupe de travail sur l'analyse des politiques et les statistiques fiscales [...] a notamment pour mission de réexaminer périodiquement la présentation des Statistiques des recettes publiques en gardant à l'esprit l'impératif de comparabilité internationale.

Les données fournies par les administrations nationales sont re-classifiées dans des catégories communes. Comparer c'est compter « des pommes avec des pommes ». Les taxes d'utilisation des véhicules à moteur sont-elles des taxes sur la propriété ? Les recettes de TVA sont-elles comptabilisées avant ou après remboursements ? Les revenus des professions libérales sont-ils présentés comme des revenus des professionnels ou des particuliers ? Parle-t-on des mêmes années (fiscales, civiles) ? S'agit-il des mêmes niveaux de gouvernement dans des pays fédéraux ou hyper-centralisés ? Les classifications nationales répondent aux besoins spécifiques des pays et diffèrent donc toutes entre elles. Les statisticiens du Secrétariat du projet et ceux des pays participants, correspondants des ministères des finances, des administrations fiscales nationales ou des instituts de statistiques nationaux, s'accordent sur le passage de catégories statistiques locales à des catégories statistiques internationales. On parle d'alignement des classifications. Puis, ensemble, ils affectent les données de recettes fiscales du pays fournies annuellement dans les catégories ainsi déterminées.

Le cadre universel de comparaison permet de décrire le présent en soulignant les similitudes et les différences entre les structures et les volumes des recettes publiques des différents pays, indépendamment de leur richesse. Il permet aussi de « départiculariser » les situations, en adoptant un point de vue neutre, au-dessus des contingences, des intérêts et des conflits locaux. On met ainsi de côté ce qui éloigne les pays pour se focaliser sur ce qui les rapproche, à partir de l'idée que ce qu'ils ont en commun est suffisamment structurant pour être comparé : un État, une administration, un budget annuel, une comptabilité publique, un même rapport entre richesses privée et richesse collective et une même volonté de développement économique. Une fois les données présentées sur une base commune, les constantes comme les différences peuvent être mises en exergue par les chiffres – dont c'est le propre d'être discrets au sens mathématique du terme.

La comparaison n'implique ni notation, ni ordonnancement des pays participants. Les pays diffèrent par leur structure réglementaire, leurs objectifs politiques, leur organisation administrative, en fonction de leur histoire, leur localisation, leur environnement. Les régimes fiscaux doivent être imaginés en fonction de la situation du pays – ils ne sont pas comparables sur une échelle commune. Les indicateurs de revenus utilisés dans cette publication ne proposent pas de seuils numériques à atteindre ou à ne pas dépasser afin d'être bien ou mal jugés, pas « d'indicateurs de performance » qui induisent l'hypothèse d'un objectif fiscal spécifique à atteindre.

À quoi sert d'être comparé ?

Les statistiques comparables sont un outil d'aide à la décision pour les gouvernements. La prise en compte des tendances historiques permet d'évaluer et de justifier les politiques passées. Elle fournit également une base pour décider des politiques pour l'avenir.

Prendre sa part dans le dialogue mondial

En participant volontairement à un projet mondial, chaque pays permet que son système fiscal soit qualifié de comparable. Il participe au processus de légitimation du système fiscal et des décisions sur lesquelles il repose. Il est incité à une certaine forme de convergence spontanée autour des idées qui sous-tendent cette classification. Le pays s'autorise à recevoir un appui technique apporté en référence à des standards internationaux. A contrario, en devenant un sujet du débat mondial sur la fiscalité, chaque pays accepte d'être scruté, tantôt critiqué, tantôt copié. Cela revient à la fois à admettre que le système fiscal peut être amélioré et à affirmer la volonté politique de l'améliorer.

S'intégrer à une publication internationale contribue à l'amélioration de la qualité des données nationales et à l'apprentissage de nouvelles techniques valorisées au niveau international. Au gré du traitement des données, le projet établit des liens privilégiés individuels entre les experts de l'OCDE et les fonctionnaires locaux ainsi qu'entre ces derniers. Le travail d'alignement des classifications oblige à une coopération entre les administrations du pays qui produisent ou fournissent les chiffres. Il met en lumière les données manquantes ou des incohérences qui obligent les pays à un retour aux sources de données et à opérer des améliorations pour les éditions suivantes. Les fonctionnaires des pays volontaires bénéficient d'une impulsion technique extérieure leur permettant de mieux comprendre les standards internationaux et de les utiliser s'ils leur semblent opportuns. Les fonctionnaires voient aussi leur légitimité renforcée auprès de leur autorité politique du fait de leur coopération avec les organisations internationales.

Analyser le passé et imaginer l'avenir

Pour s'adapter aux réalités changeantes du monde économique et politique, aux souhaits des citoyens, les systèmes fiscaux sont en perpétuelle évolution. Chaque décision, politique ou administrative, a vocation à mieux atteindre un objectif de politique fiscale – accroitre ou réduire les recettes ; enrayer les inégalités ; corriger des effets externes ; etc. – tout en tenant compte de l'impact des réformes antérieures, des contraintes internationales, des pratiques étrangères. Le besoin de statistiques comparables s'est fait plus pressant dans les années 2000 à mesure que le besoin d'accroitre les recettes intérieures dans les pays africains était souligné avec plus de force dans le contexte du dialogue international sur l'avenir du financement du développement[4].

La comparaison statistique, aux autres et à soi-même au cours du temps, induit la création d'un cadre pour l'élaboration de solutions politiques. Au regard des pratiques et des politiques menées par les autres pays, et au vu des chiffres du présent et du passé, les décideurs peuvent distinguer ce qui se fait de ce qui pourrait se faire. Ils peuvent identifier les éléments des politiques possibles et acceptables, et aussi les marges de manœuvre telles que les taux de TVA, la taxation environnementale, la taxation du travail ou des actifs. Par corrélation, modélisation, etc. les données comparables fournissent une base pour simuler des réformes, prévoir leurs effets et fonder les décisions.

La comparaison statistique, aux autres et à soi-même au cours du temps, réduit l'incertitude du changement en tentant de le prévoir. Comparer un pays à un autre peut apporter deux sortes d'opportunités. La première est de suivre les pratiques d'un autre pays pour rapprocher sa propre structure fiscale de la sienne. La seconde est d'identifier et d'évaluer les réformes mises en œuvre dans d'autres pays pour tirer des conclusions pour sa propre situation. De cette manière, la compilation de données de recettes fiscales constitue une base pour la planification de l'avenir.

Offrir à chaque état la continuité temporelle c'est lui offrir le moyen de comparer sa situation actuelle avec son état passé. La mesure, l'analyse et la comparaison des données permettent pour un même pays de rendre compte d'évolutions sur le temps long. Les statistiques des recettes fiscales alimentent les analyses économétriques qui permettent d'évaluer quantitativement les effets des réformes passées. La disponibilité de données historiques sert d'incitation à prendre des décisions.

L'interprétation des données comparables au niveau international

Les statistiques de qualité visent à refléter la réalité, mais ils ne peuvent jamais complètement atteindre cet objectif. L'utilisateur tire un grand bénéfice d'une donnée statistique pour autant que les modes de sa production lui soient connus. Les paragraphes qui suivent sont donc à considérer comme un exercice de transparence que les auteurs de ces statistiques s'imposent à eux-mêmes en vue d'offrir à leurs utilisateurs le miroir avec ses conditions de bon usage. Cette métaphore du miroir aide à privilégier les objectifs de réalité et de cohérence du projet tout comme les limites liées à sa construction : une classification unique pour des situations variées et un regroupement de données présentent évidemment des failles individuelles.

Le monde étant complexe et divers, la simplicité et la transparence de ses grilles d'analyse ne vont pas forcément de pair. Les utilisateurs de données, qu'il s'agisse du grand public ou des organisations internationales, veulent des données faciles à comprendre et simples à utiliser. Les statistiques sont transparentes dans la mesure où elles reflètent les données fournies par les pays et classifiées selon la classification OCDE. Les auteurs de cet article reconnaissent néanmoins que ces statistiques ne sont pas la représentation parfaite de la fiscalité d'un pays. En effet ces statistiques synthétisent dans un format simplifié qui peut être aisément compris par tout utilisateur, un monde complexe et mouvant. Ce résultat ne peut être atteint qu'à travers la mise en place de règles de classification, d'actualisation et de mesure elles-mêmes subjectives, opaques pour les non-initiés et forcément conservatrices (condition même de la comparabilité). La recherche d'objectivité totale est donc un paradoxe.

Donner une définition à un indicateur c'est donc mettre en équivalence des données hétérogènes. Le choix d'une classification est fondamental pour la présentation des statistiques. Chaque pays a sa propre définition de ce que constituent les recettes fiscales et non fiscales. Par expérimentation successive et négociations techniques, les statisticiens construisent « ce qui est comparable ». À chaque étape, des partis sont pris, prix à payer pour s'assurer d'un langage statistique commun. Les dimensions géographique, temporelle et politique de la comparaison des données ne font qu'exprimer en le condensant tout le travail d'élaboration qui les a rendues possibles.

Les paragraphes qui suivent décrivent certaines limites inhérentes à l'exercice de production des statistiques comparables des recettes publiques : comprendre ces limites permet d'améliorer la collecte de ces informations, et de les interpréter plus finement. Parce que les chiffres ne parlent pas d'eux-mêmes, l'idée est d'éclairer certains implicites de leur construction, à la lumière des expériences latino-américaine et asiatique, mais surtout d'un an de travail en commun avec les statisticiens des huit pays participant à cette première édition africaine.

L'impact de la classification et des méthodologies

Une classification n'est jamais neutre. Celle de l'OCDE privilégie le point de vue du décideur de politique fiscale. Même si un tableau respecte les lois de la perspective, sa composition différera selon le spectateur à qui l'on s'adresse et l'effet qu'on souhaite produire. C'est ainsi que tout indicateur est contraint par sa définition. Dans la classification de l'OCDE, le terme « recettes fiscales » par exemple désigne uniquement les versements obligatoires effectués sans contrepartie au profit des administrations publiques. Cette définition initiale sert aujourd'hui de référence pour la plupart des travaux nationaux sur la fiscalité. Même claire et simple, elle doit être complétée par des conventions pour être entièrement opérationnelle. Sous cette définition, on ne retient dans les prélèvements obligatoires que ceux versés au profit d'une administration publique ; en sont exclues les cotisations sociales fictives ; les « dépenses fiscales » ne sont pas considérées.

Les données des pays sont tributaires de définitions et de catégories réglementaires. Les recettes publiques sont libellées en unité monétaire et sont donc directement quantifiables, à la différence de statistiques sur la sécurité, l'éducation, la santé qui réclament le passage d'un élément qualitatif à un indicateur quantitatif. Il n'en reste pas moins que les statistiques des recettes fiscales sont principalement une compilation de données pré-existantes (recettes publiques, fiscales, directes, des professionnels, locales, etc.) c'est-à-dire un « produit dérivé » de l'activité de services administratifs. Or, les registres dont sont extraites les données sont conçus à des fins de fiscalisation et reflètent les institutions, les règles nationales, les circuits d'enregistrement et de codage et non les catégories fiscales utilisées par les statisticiens.

Les réformes fiscales et les changements méthodologiques affectent l'interprétation des données. En matière fiscale comme en d'autres, le statisticien fait face à un dilemme temporel. Il ne peut pas réviser trop et trop souvent les dispositifs statistiques sous peine de nuire à la comparabilité des séries chronologiques. Néanmoins, il lui faut inévitablement réexaminer le dispositif statistique lors d'une refonte d'une structure fiscale nationale (comme l'introduction de la TVA) ou lorsque se manifestent des déficiences du dispositif statistique (comme le passage de la comptabilité de caisse à la comptabilité d'exercice). En outre, dans les pays en développement, l'étroitesse et la volatilité des bases ou l'arrivée de nouveaux logiciels rendent encore plus difficiles les séries historicisées – même si elles sont autant de marques de la vitalité politique et administrative des pays.

Dans un souci permanent d'explicitations et de transparence, tous les choix de classification sont repris dans un guide d'interprétation auquel s'ajoutent les notes de bas de page dans le rapport. Ces notes prennent acte des microdécisions prises en commun entre les statisticiens du pays et ceux du Secrétariat. Faute de résoudre tous les écarts, elles permettent de les documenter et de les rendre visible aux utilisateurs.

Les limites relatives à la nature des sources

Les statistiques des recettes publiques n'offrent qu'une image partielle de la fiscalité : elles reflètent la vision des gouvernements mais laissent notamment dans l'ombre la fiscalisation des multinationales et des acteurs économiques informels. Ainsi les gouvernements n'ont pas le monopole de l'information fiscale. Ils peuvent toutefois compléter leur principale source d'information, la comptabilité nationale, avec des informations d'autres sources.

Le taux de fiscalisation effectif des grands groupes multinationaux par exemple est très faible. En tant que contribuables, ils tirent avantage des différences entre les politiques publiques des États, avec lesquels ils négocient et pour lesquels les États se concurrencent entre eux sur le plan fiscal. Ils sont pourtant des acteurs incontournables des pays, capables de peser sur les indices économiques majeurs et/ou politiquement sensibles (investissement, emploi, balance des paiements et, bien sûr, recettes publiques). Les multinationales ont une vision différente de la richesse et de sa circulation. Elles sont en compétition entre elles et elles stimulent la compétition, y compris fiscale, entre les États.

Les statistiques des recettes publiques reflètent seulement la partie visible de l'économie. Les comptabilités nationales ne prennent pas en compte les revenus dissimulés, y compris dans les paradis fiscaux, ni la part du secteur informel, pourtant essentiel dans les économies africaines. D'une part, la non-fiscalisation est l'un des critères de l'informalité et concerne généralement plusieurs impôts en cascade. D'autre part, l'économie informelle influe sur les indicateurs exogènes à la fiscalité par rapport à laquelle elle est analysée. « Les données relatives à la fraude fiscale et à l'économie souterraine ne sont pas prises en compte car cela nécessiterait la prise en compte de chiffres « gris » dont les valeurs sont très incertaines. » (OCDE, 1999, p. 53). La mesure du PIB, au dénominateur du « ratio fiscal », est donc forcément imprécise. La comparaison est donc contrainte de ne pas tenir compte de cet élément essentiel à une situation réelle car son imprécision varie entre pays et n'est donc pas comparable.

Quelques pistes de progrès en guise de conclusion

Les pays qui rejoignent le projet des Recettes publiques en sont des acteurs à part entière. Ils représentent un nombre d'États important et en augmentation. L'espoir est de voir se mettre en place un cercle vertueux incluant : un plus grand nombre de pays participants ; une classification forcément appropriée à leur diversité ; un intérêt croissant pour des statistiques adaptées ; un intérêt attirant de nouveaux pays participants.

L'expansion de la couverture géographique

Il est prévu que le nombre des pays participants s'accroisse progressivement. Bien qu'à vocation universelle de connaissance et d'analyse du monde fiscal, le projet a aujourd'hui une couverture territoriale en expansion. Les publications se déploient par continent grâce à des partenaires locaux. Au-delà des ouvrages, la vocation universelle est incarnée par une classification et une base de données uniques. Pour assurer la qualité des données, l'extension du nombre de pays couverts est progressive : l'ouvrage sur l'Amérique latine et des Caraïbes est passé de 12 à 22 pays en cinq ans ; celui sur l'Asie compte 3 pays non-OCDE en 2015 et l'Afrique démarre en 2016 avec 8 pays.

L'universalisation de l'appareil statistique

Toute classification repose sur une vision du monde tel qu'il est et une représentation du monde tel qu'il devrait être. Elle n'est pas une pure technique politiquement neutre. Elle doit donc être partagée dans le respect des principes qui la porte : utilité pour les décideurs de politique fiscale, historicité, faisabilité pour tous. La publication dans un cadre collectif et partenarial se situe à ce point d'articulation entre le vrai (le présent) et le juste (le futur espéré) – cf. l'expression britannique *True and fair view* qui exprime à la fois la vérité et la justice. L'universalisation de l'appareil statistique se fera dans un esprit de parité, de réseau et d'apprentissage mutuel.

L'hétérogénéité des formes étatiques doit être prise en compte dans les statistiques. L'essor de la statistique est en effet étroitement lié à la construction de l'État au travers du déploiement de leurs fonctions - rendre compte (*accountability*), administrer, juger, légiférer. Pourtant, pour certains de ces territoires, la notion même d'État, souverain et percepteur, n'a rien d'évident. Il s'agit d'États constitués à partir de sociétés, d'empires, de civilisation fondamentalement différents de cet héritage auxquels ont été surimposé des formes juridiques et politiques extérieures. À cette diversité, s'ajoutent un bouleversement des hiérarchies économique mondiales ; une inversion de ce qui relève du national et de l'international, du fait de la division planétaire du travail et des mouvements des facteurs de production ; une comptabilité nationale moins standardisée ; un potentiel contributif plus relatif ; une part supérieure des recettes budgétaires non-fiscales, y compris l'aide extérieure.

L'extension géographique du périmètre du projet entrainera des discussions sur les indicateurs et leurs définitions. Déjà, chaque nouvel entrant vient avec son lot de questions. Au début du processus de collecte, le pays fait parvenir des questions techniques à l'équipe statistique du Secrétariat. Certaines sont bien partagées (comptabilisation des contributions sociales, imputation annuelle) mais d'autres sont plus spécifiques comme, pour l'Afrique du Sud par exemple, l'inclusion ou non des données des anciens « homelands », le statut des droits de douane collectés et répartis pour les pays voisins dans le cadre de l'union douanière SACU, etc. Les requêtes les plus fréquentes portent sur le raffinement des définitions sur les recettes non-fiscales, l'ajout d'indicateurs sur les exonérations et la sectorialisation des recettes.

A mesure qu'entrent de nouveaux pays, le projet évolue au bénéfice de ces derniers, mais également au bénéfice de tous. L'accroissement de la diversité est à la fois souhaitable et bénéfique pour tous les pays participants. Depuis les années 1960, les pays en développement ont constitué des lieux de réelle inventivité méthodologique de la production statistique en général (nomenclatures, conventions de codage, méthodes de collecte, etc.). Ces pays avaient des structures administratives et sociales moins instituées que dans les pays anciennement développés. Il leur a été alors possible de développer des organisations aptes à réaliser des enquêtes et à mettre en place des systèmes nécessaires à la collection de statistiques, ce qui sera bénéfique pour les statistiques des recettes publiques.

L'extension du débat permis par des statistiques comparables

La transparence sur les méthodes est le début de l'utilisation large de cette production statistique par les gouvernants, les citoyens et les chercheurs. La diffusion de statistiques comparables favorise la transparence du débat public et sert ainsi la démocratie. En publiant des chiffres fiables et comparables, l'asymétrie d'information est réduite entre le public et les décideurs, voire entre les décideurs eux-mêmes. Des données compilées et publiées de façon transparente permettent de nourrir les recherches scientifiques, les décisions administratives et le dialogue politique dans les pays, dans la région comme au niveau international.

Bien que les pays puissent beaucoup apprendre les uns des autres, chacun doit fixer son propre cap en fonction de son identité, de ses moyens et des attentes de ses citoyens. Copier des « modèles de réussite » n'est jamais une solution. Il faut se méfier de l'idée qu'il existe une caisse de « bonnes pratiques » où chaque pays peut emprunter des outils forcément disponibles et enrichis de l'expérience des autres qui lui conviendraient. Malgré l'efficacité de certains instruments, c'est non seulement un leurre mais surtout un déni de la responsabilité politique des décideurs.

Le chiffre seul ne fait pas le droit. Les statistiques elles-mêmes reflètent les résultats des politiques publiques, passées et présentes, mais ne disent rien de leur caractère équitable.

La publication de ces statistiques contribue à améliorer la circulation de l'information aux citoyens, à stimuler et alimenter le débat démocratique, à rendre compte à l'électorat de ses performances et de l'impact de ses initiatives. Elles offrent aux citoyens des informations sur les ressources budgétaires et donc de nouveaux outils de décisions et de contrôle démocratique sur les questions de politique publique. Ces statistiques étendront le spectre du débat public – par exemple en présentant d'autres chiffres ou en ordonnant les mêmes de façon différente – et accroitront les sphères d'exercice de la responsabilité politique des citoyens. Parions que les individus s'intéressent aux informations qu'ils fournissent sur eux-mêmes – à leur insu ou non – et sachent s'abstraire des apparences technicistes qui réservent les questions fiscales aux seuls spécialistes.

La publication de ces statistiques aide à répondre aux besoins d'information des investisseurs et des visiteurs étrangers potentiels (y compris la presse et autres organismes intermédiaires) ; à satisfaire aux requêtes des gouvernements étrangers et des institutions internationales avant et après toute assistance ; à la rédaction des rapports précis aux organismes chargés par la communauté internationale de suivre les tendances mondiales sur de nombreuses questions économiques, environnementales, sociales et autres.

Les statistiques fiscales comparables aident les pays à prendre leur place dans le monde. Elles promeuvent un dialogue entre eux autant qu'elles leur permettent d'être présents dans le débat mondial sur la fiscalité pour faire valoir et justifier leurs choix. Ces statistiques sont un pas supplémentaire vers la transparence mais aussi vers plus d'influence.

Notes

1. www.sars.gov.za/About/SATaxSystem/Pages/Tax-Statistics.aspx.
2. Commission de l'Union Africaine, Banque africaine de développement et Commission économique pour l'Afrique (2010), Stratégie pour l'harmonisation des statistiques en Afrique (SHaSA). http://ea.au.int/fr/sites/default/files/SHaSA%20-FR.pdf.
3. Ce chapitre a bénéficié des apports de l'article préparé par Thomas Cantens (OMD) et Jocelyn Pierre (OCDE) pour la Conférence internationale organisée par la Ferdi, l'ICTD, et le Cerdi-Université d'Auvergne, en collaboration avec la Banque mondiale, le Centre Norbert Elias et l'OMD sur la mesure de la performance dans les administrations fiscales et douanières des pays en développement (12 et 13 juin 2014, Clermont-Ferrand, France).
4. Déclaration de Paris sur l'efficacité de l'aide au développement, 2005, www.oecd.org/fr/cad/efficacite/34579826.pdf ; Programme d'action d'Addis-Abeba, 2015 www.un.org/ga/search/view_doc.asp?symbol=A/69/L.82&Lang=F.

CHAPTER 3

TAX LEVELS AND TAX STRUCTURES, 1990-2014

CHAPITRE 3

NIVEAUX ET STRUCTURES DES IMPÔTS, 1990-2014

Chapter 3 / Chapitre 3

3.1. Comparative tables, 1990-2014

In all of the following tables a (..) indicates not available or not applicable. The main series in this volume cover the years 1990 to 2014.

Figures referring to 1991-95 in Table 3.1 and figures relating to 1990-96, 1998-99 and 2001-04 and 2006-07 in Tables 3.4 to 3.19 have been omitted because of lack of space. Complete series are, however, available on line at http://stats.oecd.org/.

3.1. Tableaux comparatifs, 1990-2014

Dans tous les tableaux suivants le symbole (..) signifie que l'information n'est pas disponible ou qu'elle n'est pas applicable. La principale série dans ce volume couvre les années 1990 à 2014.

Les années 1991 à 1995 dans le tableau 3.1 et les années 1990-96, 1998-99, 2001-04 et 2006-07 dans les tableaux 3.4 à 3.19 ont été omis en raison du manque d'espace. Les séries complètes sont cependant disponibles en ligne sur http://stats.oecd.org/.

Table 3.1. Total tax revenue as percentage of GDP, 1990-2014
Tableau 3.1. Total des recettes fiscales en pourcentage du PIB, 1990-2014

	1990	1996	1997	1998	1999	2000	2001	2002	2003	2004
Cameroon / Cameroun	..	10.7	10.9	11.7	11.9	12.8	14.0	13.2	13.7	13.1
Côte d'Ivoire[1]	21.7	17.6	17.1	16.0	16.0	15.4	15.6	15.9	14.6	15.9
Mauritius / Maurice	21.4	16.5	17.8	17.5	17.9	19.1	17.3	16.8	18.0	18.1
Morocco / Maroc[2]	..	..	..	..	..	23.6	23.5	23.5	23.1	23.2
Rwanda[3]	..	9.8	10.3	10.8	10.8	10.2	11.3	12.4	12.2	12.1
Senegal / Sénégal[4,5]	..	..	15.3	15.4	16.1	16.8	16.8	17.7	17.7	18.2
South Africa / Afrique du Sud	23.9	22.2	22.6	23.5	23.5	22.4	23.7	23.1	23.3	23.4
Tunisia / Tunisie[3]	..	..	..	..	..	24.6	24.9	25.0	24.4	24.2
LAC Average / Moyenne ALC[6,7]	**14.6**	**16.3**	**16.9**	**16.5**	**16.8**	**17.2**	**17.4**	**17.2**	**17.5**	**18.1**
OECD Average / Moyenne OCDE[7]	**32.1**	**33.9**	**33.9**	**33.9**	**34.2**	**34.2**	**33.8**	**33.5**	**33.5**	**33.4**

	2005	2006	2007	2008	2009	2010	2011	2012	2013	2014
Cameroon / Cameroun	13.5	14.0	14.8	14.8	15.0	14.0	14.8	15.3	15.8	16.1
Côte d'Ivoire[1]	15.7	16.7	18.2	18.4	17.2	16.8	16.1	18.4	18.3	17.8
Mauritius / Maurice	18.8	18.8	17.9	19.4	20.1	19.8	19.6	20.2	19.9	20.0
Morocco / Maroc[2]	24.8	25.6	28.5	30.5	27.3	27.1	28.7	29.7	28.5	28.5
Rwanda[3]	12.1	12.0	12.4	13.5	12.9	13.3	14.0	14.6	15.6	16.1
Senegal / Sénégal[4,5]	19.3	19.7	20.1	19.0	18.9	19.8	19.9	19.5	19.2	20.1
South Africa / Afrique du Sud	25.2	27.1	27.5	27.7	25.7	25.6	26.3	26.7	27.3	27.8
Tunisia / Tunisie[3]	24.4	24.5	25.3	27.0	26.9	27.3	29.2	29.2	30.1	31.3
LAC Average / Moyenne ALC[6,7]	**19.0**	**20.0**	**20.2**	**20.6**	**19.9**	**20.0**	**20.8**	**21.4**	**21.5**	**21.7**
OECD Average / Moyenne OCDE[7]	**33.9**	**34.1**	**34.1**	**33.6**	**32.7**	**32.8**	**33.3**	**33.8**	**34.2**	**34.4**

Note: The figures exclude local government tax revenues for Cameroon, Côte d'Ivoire, Rwanda, Senegal and Tunisia as the data are not available. Local and provincial data prior to 2003 are not available for South Africa.

1. The tax to GDP ratio contains rents and royalties and sales of public goods and services normally classified as non-tax revenues in the OECD classification. They are considered to be tax revenues in Côte d'Ivoire. The inclusion of these elements represents 0.5% of GDP in 2014 and between 0.1% and 1.5% in the period from 2000 to 2014.
2. Estimated figures for 2013 and 2014 and years prior to 2005.
3. Rwanda and Tunisia do not include social security contributions in their tax to GDP ratio as neither country considers them as taxes. They are included as tax revenue in this publication.
4. Estimated figures for years prior to 2006.
5. Figures include social security contributions from the Institution de prévoyance retraite du Sénégal (IPRES) and exclude the data from the Caisse de Sécurité Sociale (CSS) as they are not available.
6. Represents a group of 22 Latin American and Caribbean countries (LAC).
7. Represents the unweighted average for the LAC and OECD countries.

Note : Les chiffres excluent les recettes fiscales des collectivités locales pour le Cameroun, la Côte d'Ivoire, le Rwanda, le Sénégal et la Tunisie car les données ne sont pas disponibles. Les données des collectivités locales et provinciales ne sont pas disponibles pour l'Afrique du Sud avant 2003.

1. Le ratio des recettes fiscales au PIB comprend les loyers, les redevances et les ventes de biens et services publics normalement classés comme des recettes non fiscales dans la classification de l'OCDE. Ils sont considérés comme des recettes fiscales pour la Côte d'Ivoire. L'inclusion de ces éléments représente 0.5% du PIB en 2014 et varie entre 0.1% et 1.5% pour la période 2000 à 2014.
2. Les chiffres sont estimés pour 2013 et 2014 ainsi que pour les années antérieures à 2005.
3. Le Rwanda et la Tunisie n'incluent pas les cotisations de sécurité sociale dans le ratio de pression fiscale car ces deux pays ne les considèrent pas comme des impôts. Elles sont incluses dans les recettes fiscales de cette publication.
4. Les chiffres sont estimés pour les années antérieures à 2006.
5. Les chiffres comprennent les cotisations de sécurité sociale de l'Institution de prévoyance retraite du Sénégal (IPRES) et excluent les cotisations de sécurité sociale de la Caisse de Sécurité Sociale (CSS) qui ne sont pas disponibles.
6. Représente un groupe de 22 pays d'Amérique latine et des Caraïbes (ALC).
7. Représente la moyenne non pondérée des pays ALC et OCDE.

StatLink http://dx.doi.org/10.1787/888933344525

Table 3.2. Tax revenue of main headings as percentage of GDP, 2014
Tableau 3.2. Recettes fiscales sous les principales rubriques en pourcentage du PIB, 2014

	1000 Income & profits / Impôts & profits	2000 Social security / Sécurité sociale	3000 Payroll / Salaires	4000 Property / Patrimoine	5000 Goods and services / Biens et services	6000 Others / Autres
Cameroon / Cameroun	4.9	0.9	0.3	0.1	9.6	0.2
Côte d'Ivoire[1]	4.2	2.0	0.1	0.5	10.9	0.1
Mauritius / Maurice	4.8	1.0	0.1	1.2	12.9	0.1
Morocco / Maroc[2]	8.3	5.9	0.0	1.9	11.9	0.5
Rwanda[3]	6.0	1.0	0.0	0.0	9.0	0.0
Senegal / Sénégal[4]	5.1	1.0	0.2	0.5	13.1	0.2
South Africa / Afrique du Sud	14.3	0.4	0.3	1.4	11.4	0.0
Tunisia / Tunisie[3]	9.9	8.6	0.4	0.3	11.3	0.8
LAC Average / Moyenne ALC[5,6,7]	**5.9**	**3.7**	**0.1**	**0.8**	**10.4**	**0.6**
OECD Average / Moyenne OCDE[6,7]	**11.5**	**9.1**	**0.4**	**1.9**	**11.0**	**0.2**

Note: The figures exclude local government tax revenues for Cameroon, Côte d'Ivoire, Rwanda, Senegal and Tunisia as the data are not available. Local and provincial data prior to 2003 are not available for South Africa.

1. The ratio for heading 5000 contains rents and royalties and sales of public goods and services normally classified as non-tax revenues in the OECD classification. They are considered to be tax revenues in Côte d'Ivoire. The inclusion of these elements represents 0.5% of GDP in 2014 and between 0.1% and 1.5% in the period from 2000 to 2014.
2. Estimated figures for heading 2000.
3. Rwanda and Tunisia do not include social security contributions in their tax to GDP ratio as neither country considers them as taxes. They are included in this publication.
4. Figures include social security contributions from the Institution de prévoyance retraite du Sénégal (IPRES) and exclude the data from the Caisse de Sécurité Sociale (CSS) as they are not available.
5. Represents a group of 22 Latin American and Caribbean countries (LAC).
6. Represents the unweighted average for LAC and OECD countries.
7. Data for 2013.

Note : Les chiffres excluent les recettes fiscales des collectivités locales pour le Cameroun, la Côte d'Ivoire, le Rwanda, le Sénégal et la Tunisie car les données ne sont pas disponibles. Les données des collectivités locales et provinciales ne sont pas disponibles pour l'Afrique du Sud avant 2003.

1. Le ratio des recettes fiscales au PIB pour la catégorie 5000 comprend les loyers, les redevances et les ventes de biens et services publics normalement classés comme des recettes non fiscales dans la classification de l'OCDE. Ils sont considérés comme des recettes fiscales en Côte d'Ivoire. L'inclusion de ces éléments représente 0.5% du PIB en 2014 et varie entre 0.1% et 1.5% pour la période 2000 à 2014.
2. Les chiffres sont estimés pour la catégorie 2000.
3. Le Rwanda et la Tunisie n'incluent pas les cotisations de sécurité sociale dans le ratio de pression fiscale car ces deux pays ne les considèrent pas comme des impôts. Elles sont incluses dans cette publication.
4. Les chiffres comprennent les cotisations de sécurité sociale de l'Institution de prévoyance retraite du Sénégal (IPRES) et excluent les cotisations de sécurité sociale de la Caisse de Sécurité Sociale (CSS) qui ne sont pas disponibles.
5. Représente un groupe de 22 pays d'Amérique latine et des Caraïbes (ALC).
6. Représente la moyenne non pondérée pour les pays de l'ALC et de l'OCDE.
7. Données pour l'année 2013.

StatLink http://dx.doi.org/10.1787/888933344536

Table 3.3. Tax revenue of main headings as percentage of total taxation, 2014
Tableau 3.3. Recettes fiscales sous les principales rubriques en pourcentage du total des recettes fiscales, 2014

	1000 Income & profits / Impôts & profits	2000 Social security / Sécurité sociale	3000 Payroll / Salaires	4000 Property / Patrimoine	5000 Goods and services / Biens et services	6000 Others / Autres
Cameroon / Cameroun	30.8	5.9	1.8	0.8	59.4	1.3
Côte d'Ivoire[1]	23.6	11.3	0.4	2.6	61.6	0.6
Mauritius / Maurice	23.9	5.2	0.3	5.8	64.6	0.3
Morocco / Maroc[2]	29.0	20.8	0.0	6.8	41.7	1.7
Rwanda[3]	37.3	6.4	0.0	0.0	56.3	0.0
Senegal / Sénégal[4]	25.6	4.9	1.1	2.5	64.8	1.1
South Africa / Afrique du Sud	51.2	1.5	1.3	5.1	41.0	0.0
Tunisia / Tunisie[3]	31.5	27.6	1.1	1.1	36.0	2.7
LAC Average / Moyenne ALC[5,6,7]	**27.4**	**16.6**	**0.6**	**3.4**	**49.6**	**2.5**
OECD Average / Moyenne OCDE[6,7]	**33.7**	**26.1**	**1.1**	**5.6**	**32.7**	**0.6**

Note: The figures exclude local government tax revenues for Cameroon, Côte d'Ivoire, Rwanda, Senegal and Tunisia as the data are not available. Local and provincial data prior to 2003 are not available for South Africa.

1. The ratio for heading 5000 contains rents and royalties and sales of public goods and services normally classified as non-tax revenues in the OECD classification. They are considered to be tax revenues in Côte d'Ivoire. The inclusion of these elements represents 0.5% of GDP in 2014 and between 0.1% and 1.5% in the period from 2000 to 2014.
2. Estimated figures for heading 2000.
3. Rwanda and Tunisia do not include social security contributions in their tax to GDP ratio as neither country considers them as taxes. They are included in this publication.
4. Figures include social security contributions from the Institution de prévoyance retraite du Sénégal (IPRES) and exclude the data from the Caisse de Sécurité Sociale (CSS) as they are not available.
5. Represents a group of 22 Latin American and Caribbean countries (LAC).
6. Represents the unweighted average for LAC and OECD countries.
7. Data for 2013.

Note : Les chiffres excluent les recettes fiscales des collectivités locales pour le Cameroun, la Côte d'Ivoire, le Rwanda, le Sénégal et la Tunisie car les données ne sont pas disponibles. Les données des collectivités locales et provinciales ne sont pas disponibles pour l'Afrique du Sud avant 2003.

1. Le ratio des recettes fiscales au PIB pour la catégorie 5000 comprend les loyers, les redevances et les ventes de biens et services publics normalement classés comme des recettes non fiscales dans la classification de l'OCDE. Ils sont considérés comme des recettes fiscales en Côte d'Ivoire. L'inclusion de ces éléments représente 0.5% du PIB en 2014 et varie entre 0.1% et 1.5% pour la période 2000 à 2014.
2. Les chiffres sont estimés pour la catégorie 2000.
3. Le Rwanda et la Tunisie n'incluent pas les cotisations de sécurité sociale dans le ratio de pression fiscale car ces deux pays ne les considèrent pas comme des impôts. Elles sont incluses dans cette publication.
4. Les chiffres comprennent les cotisations de sécurité sociale de l'Institution de prévoyance retraite du Sénégal (IPRES) et excluent les cotisations de sécurité sociale de la Caisse de Sécurité Sociale (CSS) qui ne sont pas disponibles.
5. Représente un groupe de 22 pays d'Amérique latine et des Caraïbes (ALC).
6. Représente la moyenne non pondérée pour les pays de l'ALC et de l'OCDE.
7. Données pour l'année 2013.

StatLink http://dx.doi.org/10.1787/888933344546

Table 3.4. Taxes on income and profits (1000) as percentage of GDP
Tableau 3.4. Impôts sur le revenu et les bénéfices (1000) en pourcentage du PIB

	1997	2000	2005	2008	2009	2010	2011	2012	2013	2014
Cameroon / Cameroun	2.6	3.4	3.7	4.3	4.7	3.6	4.0	4.7	4.7	4.9
Côte d'Ivoire	4.6	4.2	3.7	4.7	4.1	3.7	4.3	5.0	4.8	4.2
Mauritius / Maurice	2.6	2.5	3.1	4.1	5.6	5.0	4.5	4.5	4.6	4.8
Morocco / Maroc	..	5.7	7.7	11.2	9.3	8.0	8.4	9.1	8.4	8.3
Rwanda	2.6	2.7	3.5	4.7	4.5	4.8	5.1	5.6	6.3	6.0
Senegal / Sénégal	3.2	3.7	4.5	4.4	4.6	5.1	4.9	5.3	5.1	5.1
South Africa / Afrique du Sud	12.8	12.7	13.4	15.7	14.3	13.4	13.6	13.7	13.9	14.3
Tunisia / Tunisie	..	5.5	7.0	8.3	8.0	8.1	9.2	8.4	9.2	9.9
LAC Average / Moyenne ALC[1,2]	**4.1**	**4.0**	**5.0**	**5.9**	**5.7**	**5.4**	**5.7**	**5.9**	**5.9**	**6.1**
OECD Average / Moyenne OCDE[2]	**11.8**	**12.2**	**11.9**	**11.9**	**11.0**	**10.9**	**11.1**	**11.4**	**11.5**	**11.7**

Note: The figures exclude local government tax revenues for Cameroon, Côte d'Ivoire, Rwanda, Senegal and Tunisia as the data are not available. Local and provincial data prior to 2003 are not available for South Africa.

1. Represents a group of 22 Latin American and Caribbean countries (LAC).
2. Represents the unweighted average for LAC and OECD countries.

Note : Les chiffres excluent les recettes fiscales des collectivités locales pour le Cameroun, la Côte d'Ivoire, le Rwanda, le Sénégal et la Tunisie car les données ne sont pas disponibles. Les données des collectivités locales et provinciales ne sont pas disponibles pour l'Afrique du Sud avant 2003.

1. Représente un groupe de 22 pays d'Amérique latine et des Caraïbes (ALC).
2. Représente la moyenne non pondérée pour les pays de l'ALC et de l'OCDE.

StatLink http://dx.doi.org/10.1787/888933344559

Table 3.5. Taxes on income and profits (1000) as percentage of total taxation
Tableau 3.5. Impôts sur le revenu et les bénéfices (1000) en pourcentage du total des recettes fiscales

	1997	2000	2005	2008	2009	2010	2011	2012	2013	2014
Cameroon / Cameroun	24.0	27.0	27.5	28.8	31.6	26.0	27.3	30.8	30.1	30.8
Côte d'Ivoire	27.2	27.5	23.7	25.5	23.6	22.1	26.7	27.5	26.1	23.6
Mauritius / Maurice	14.9	12.9	16.7	21.1	27.9	25.4	22.9	22.6	23.2	23.9
Morocco / Maroc	..	24.2	31.0	36.7	34.2	29.4	29.3	30.7	29.5	29.0
Rwanda	25.3	26.0	28.6	34.9	34.7	36.2	36.4	38.2	40.5	37.3
Senegal / Sénégal	21.0	22.1	23.1	23.1	24.2	25.9	24.7	27.1	26.4	25.6
South Africa / Afrique du Sud	56.6	56.7	53.4	56.6	55.5	52.4	51.9	51.4	50.7	51.2
Tunisia / Tunisie	..	22.4	28.6	30.9	29.8	29.5	31.6	28.8	30.5	31.5
LAC Average / Moyenne ALC[1,2]	**22.8**	**22.4**	**25.1**	**27.9**	**27.9**	**26.4**	**27.3**	**27.5**	**27.4**	**27.9**
OECD Average / Moyenne OCDE[2]	**34.3**	**35.1**	**34.5**	**35.4**	**33.5**	**33.2**	**33.5**	**33.6**	**33.7**	..

Note: The figures exclude local government tax revenues for Cameroon, Côte d'Ivoire, Rwanda, Senegal and Tunisia as the data are not available. Local and provincial data prior to 2003 are not available for South Africa.

1. Represents a group of 22 Latin American and Caribbean countries (LAC).
2. Represents the unweighted average for LAC and OECD countries.

Note : Les chiffres excluent les recettes fiscales des collectivités locales pour le Cameroun, la Côte d'Ivoire, le Rwanda, le Sénégal et la Tunisie car les données ne sont pas disponibles. Les données des collectivités locales et provinciales ne sont pas disponibles pour l'Afrique du Sud avant 2003.

1. Représente un groupe de 22 pays d'Amérique latine et des Caraïbes (ALC).
2. Représente la moyenne non pondérée pour les pays de l'ALC et de l'OCDE.

StatLink http://dx.doi.org/10.1787/888933344560

Table 3.6. Social security contributions (2000) as percentage of GDP
Tableau 3.6. Cotisations de sécurité sociale (2000) en pourcentage du PIB

	1997	2000	2005	2008	2009	2010	2011	2012	2013	2014
Cameroon / Cameroun	0.9	1.0	1.0	1.0	1.0	1.2	1.1	1.1	1.1	0.9
Côte d'Ivoire	1.2	1.3	1.3	1.3	1.3	1.3	1.1	1.7	2.0	2.0
Mauritius / Maurice	1.1	1.1	0.7	0.7	0.9	1.0	1.0	1.0	1.0	1.0
Morocco / Maroc[1]	..	3.9	4.0	3.7	4.0	4.0	5.3	5.4	5.5	5.9
Rwanda[2]	0.4	0.5	0.8	0.9	0.9	0.8	0.9	1.0	1.1	1.0
Senegal / Sénégal[3,4]	0.6	0.7	0.8	0.9	0.9	1.1	0.9	0.9	1.0	1.0
South Africa / Afrique du Sud	0.0	0.0	0.4	0.4	0.4	0.4	0.4	0.4	0.4	0.4
Tunisia / Tunisie[2]	..	5.3	5.5	6.5	7.0	7.3	8.1	8.3	8.7	8.6
LAC Average / Moyenne ALC[5,6]	**2.4**	**2.7**	**2.7**	**3.0**	**3.2**	**3.3**	**3.4**	**3.5**	**3.7**	**3.7**
OECD Average / Moyenne OCDE[6]	**8.7**	**8.6**	**8.6**	**8.6**	**8.9**	**8.8**	**8.9**	**9.0**	**9.1**	..

Note: The figures exclude local government tax revenues for Cameroon, Côte d'Ivoire, Rwanda, Senegal and Tunisia as the data are not available. Local and provincial data prior to 2003 are not available for South Africa.

1. Estimated figures for 2013 and 2014 and years prior to 2005.
2. Rwanda and Tunisia do not include social security contributions in their tax to GDP ratio as they don't consider them as taxes. They are included in this publication.
3. Estimated figures for years prior to 2006.
4. Figures include social security contributions from the Institution de prévoyance retraite du Sénégal (IPRES) and exclude the data from the Caisse de Sécurité Sociale (CSS) as they are not available.
5. Represents a group of 22 Latin American and Caribbean countries (LAC).
6. Represents the unweighted average for LAC and OECD countries.

Note : Les chiffres excluent les recettes fiscales des collectivités locales pour le Cameroun, la Côte d'Ivoire, le Rwanda, le Sénégal et la Tunisie car les données ne sont pas disponibles. Les données des collectivités locales et provinciales ne sont pas disponibles pour l'Afrique du Sud avant 2003.

1. Les chiffres sont estimés pour 2013 et 2014 ainsi que pour les années antérieures à 2005.
2. Le Rwanda et la Tunisie n'incluent pas les cotisations de sécurité sociale dans le ratio de pression fiscale car ils ne les considèrent pas comme des impôts. Elles sont incluses dans cette publication.
3. Les chiffres sont estimés pour les années antérieures à 2006.
4. Les chiffres comprennent les cotisations de sécurité sociale de l'Institution de prévoyance retraite du Sénégal (IPRES) et excluent les cotisations de sécurité sociale de la Caisse de Sécurité Sociale (CSS) qui ne sont pas disponibles.
5. Représente un groupe de 22 pays d'Amérique latine et des Caraïbes (ALC).
6. Représente la moyenne non pondérée pour les pays de l'ALC et de l'OCDE.

StatLink http://dx.doi.org/10.1787/888933344578

Table 3.7. Social security contributions (2000) as percentage of total taxation
Tableau 3.7. Cotisations de sécurité sociale (2000) en pourcentage du total des recettes fiscales

	1997	2000	2005	2008	2009	2010	2011	2012	2013	2014
Cameroon / Cameroun	7.8	7.8	7.1	6.5	6.6	8.3	7.7	7.1	6.9	5.9
Côte d'Ivoire	7.1	8.7	8.3	7.1	7.7	7.8	6.8	9.3	10.9	11.3
Mauritius / Maurice	6.2	5.5	4.0	3.5	4.7	4.9	4.9	4.8	5.0	5.2
Morocco / Maroc[1]	..	16.7	16.1	12.2	14.6	14.8	18.4	18.1	19.5	20.8
Rwanda[2]	3.4	5.0	6.9	6.6	6.6	6.4	6.6	6.6	7.0	6.4
Senegal / Sénégal[3,4]	3.9	4.0	4.1	4.6	4.7	5.8	4.4	4.8	5.1	4.9
South Africa / Afrique du Sud	0.0	0.0	1.6	1.5	1.6	1.5	1.5	1.6	1.4	1.5
Tunisia / Tunisie[2]	..	21.4	22.6	23.9	26.0	26.9	27.6	28.4	28.9	27.6
LAC Average / Moyenne ALC[5,6]	**14.1**	**15.2**	**14.4**	**14.4**	**15.8**	**15.8**	**15.6**	**15.9**	**16.6**	**16.4**
OECD Average / Moyenne OCDE[6]	**24.8**	**24.5**	**24.9**	**25.2**	**26.4**	**26.4**	**26.1**	**26.1**	**26.1**	..

Note: The figures exclude local government tax revenues for Cameroon, Côte d'Ivoire, Rwanda, Senegal and Tunisia as the data are not available. Local and provincial data prior to 2003 are not available for South Africa.

1. Estimated figures for 2013 and 2014 and years prior to 2005.
2. Rwanda and Tunisia do not include social security contributions in their tax to GDP ratio as they don't consider them as taxes. They are included in this publication.
3. Estimated figures for years prior to 2006.
4. Figures include social security contributions from the Institution de prévoyance retraite du Sénégal (IPRES) and exclude the data from the Caisse de Sécurité Sociale (CSS) as they are not available.
5. Represents a group of 22 Latin American and Caribbean countries (LAC).
6. Represents the unweighted average for LAC and OECD countries.

Note : Les chiffres excluent les recettes fiscales des collectivités locales pour le Cameroun, la Côte d'Ivoire, le Rwanda, le Sénégal et la Tunisie car les données ne sont pas disponibles. Les données des collectivités locales et provinciales ne sont pas disponibles pour l'Afrique du Sud avant 2003.

1. Les chiffres sont estimés pour 2013 et 2014 ainsi que pour les années antérieures à 2005.
2. Le Rwanda et la Tunisie n'incluent pas les cotisations de sécurité sociale dans le ratio de pression fiscale car ils ne les considèrent pas comme des impôts. Elles sont incluses dans cette publication.
3. Les chiffres sont estimés pour les années antérieures à 2006.
4. Les chiffres comprennent les cotisations de sécurité sociale de l'Institution de prévoyance retraite du Sénégal (IPRES) et excluent les cotisations de sécurité sociale de la Caisse de Sécurité Sociale (CSS) qui ne sont pas disponibles.
5. Représente un groupe de 22 pays d'Amérique latine et des Caraïbes (ALC).
6. Représente la moyenne non pondérée pour les pays de l'ALC et de l'OCDE.

StatLink http://dx.doi.org/10.1787/888933344586

Table 3.8. Taxes on property (4000) as percentage of GDP
Tableau 3.8. Impôts sur le patrimoine (4000) en pourcentage du PIB

	1997	2000	2005	2008	2009	2010	2011	2012	2013	2014
Cameroon / Cameroun	0.1	0.2	0.2	0.2	0.2	0.2	0.1	0.1	0.1	0.1
Côte d'Ivoire	0.4	0.4	0.5	0.4	0.4	0.4	0.3	0.4	0.5	0.5
Mauritius / Maurice	1.3	1.2	1.0	1.3	1.2	1.1	1.0	1.1	1.0	1.2
Morocco / Maroc	..	1.3	1.5	1.7	1.5	1.6	1.6	1.8	1.9	1.9
Rwanda	0.0	0.0	0.0	0.0	0.0	0.0	0.0	0.0	0.0	0.0
Senegal / Sénégal	0.4	0.3	0.5	0.5	0.6	0.6	0.6	0.5	0.5	0.5
South Africa / Afrique du Sud	0.4	0.4	1.2	1.2	1.3	1.3	1.3	1.3	1.4	1.4
Tunisia / Tunisie	..	0.3	0.2	0.3	0.3	0.3	0.3	0.3	0.3	0.3
LAC Average / Moyenne ALC[1,2]	**0.5**	**0.6**	**0.8**	**0.8**	**0.7**	**0.7**	**0.7**	**0.8**	**0.8**	**0.8**
OECD Average / Moyenne OCDE[2]	**1.7**	**1.8**	**1.8**	**1.7**	**1.7**	**1.7**	**1.8**	**1.8**	**1.9**	..

Note: The figures exclude local government tax revenues for Cameroon, Côte d'Ivoire, Rwanda, Senegal and Tunisia as the data are not available. Local and provincial data prior to 2003 are not available for South Africa.

1. Represents a group of 22 Latin American and Caribbean countries (LAC).
2. Represents the unweighted average for LAC and OECD countries.

Note : Les chiffres excluent les recettes fiscales des collectivités locales pour le Cameroun, la Côte d'Ivoire, le Rwanda, le Sénégal et la Tunisie car les données ne sont pas disponibles. Les données des collectivités locales et provinciales ne sont pas disponibles pour l'Afrique du Sud avant 2003.

1. Représente un groupe de 22 pays d'Amérique latine et des Caraïbes (ALC).
2. Représente la moyenne non pondérée pour les pays de l'ALC et de l'OCDE.

StatLink http://dx.doi.org/10.1787/888933344598

Table 3.9. Taxes on property (4000) as percentage of total taxation
Tableau 3.9. Impôts sur le patrimoine (4000) en pourcentage du total des recettes fiscales

	1997	2000	2005	2008	2009	2010	2011	2012	2013	2014
Cameroon / Cameroun	0.8	1.6	1.1	1.2	1.1	1.1	0.7	0.7	0.9	0.8
Côte d'Ivoire	2.6	2.8	3.1	2.3	2.4	2.4	2.0	2.4	2.9	2.6
Mauritius / Maurice	7.5	6.3	5.5	6.7	5.8	5.6	5.0	5.4	5.1	5.8
Morocco / Maroc	..	5.5	6.1	5.5	5.4	6.0	5.6	6.1	6.6	6.8
Rwanda	0.1	0.2	0.0	0.0	0.0	0.0	0.0	0.0	0.0	0.0
Senegal / Sénégal	2.4	2.0	2.6	2.8	2.9	3.1	2.8	2.6	2.6	2.5
South Africa / Afrique du Sud	1.6	1.8	4.6	4.4	4.9	5.2	4.9	4.8	5.0	5.1
Tunisia / Tunisie	..	1.1	1.0	1.1	1.1	1.0	1.2	1.1	1.1	1.1
LAC Average / Moyenne ALC[1,2]	**2.5**	**2.9**	**3.9**	**3.5**	**3.3**	**3.2**	**3.2**	**3.3**	**3.4**	**3.3**
OECD Average / Moyenne OCDE[2]	**5.3**	**5.5**	**5.6**	**5.4**	**5.6**	**5.5**	**5.5**	**5.5**	**5.6**	..

Note: The figures exclude local government tax revenues for Cameroon, Côte d'Ivoire, Rwanda, Senegal and Tunisia as the data are not available. Local and provincial data prior to 2003 are not available for South Africa.

1. Represents a group of 22 Latin American and Caribbean countries (LAC).
2. Represents the unweighted average for LAC and OECD countries.

Note : Les chiffres excluent les recettes fiscales des collectivités locales pour le Cameroun, la Côte d'Ivoire, le Rwanda, le Sénégal et la Tunisie car les données ne sont pas disponibles. Les données des collectivités locales et provinciales ne sont pas disponibles pour l'Afrique du Sud avant 2003.

1. Représente un groupe de 22 pays d'Amérique latine et des Caraïbes (ALC).
2. Représente la moyenne non pondérée pour les pays de l'ALC et de l'OCDE.

StatLink http://dx.doi.org/10.1787/888933344606

Table 3.10. Taxes on goods and services (5000) as percentage of GDP
Tableau 3.10. Impôts sur les biens et services (5000) en pourcentage du PIB

	1997	2000	2005	2008	2009	2010	2011	2012	2013	2014
Cameroon / Cameroun	7.4	8.1	8.4	9.0	8.7	8.7	9.0	8.9	9.2	9.6
Côte d'Ivoire	10.7	9.2	10.0	11.8	11.2	11.2	10.3	11.0	10.8	10.9
Mauritius / Maurice	12.6	14.3	13.8	13.2	12.3	12.6	13.1	13.5	13.2	12.9
Morocco / Maroc	..	12.3	11.2	13.4	11.9	12.9	12.9	12.9	12.1	11.9
Rwanda	7.3	7.0	7.8	7.9	7.6	7.6	8.0	8.0	8.2	9.0
Senegal / Sénégal	10.7	11.6	13.1	12.8	12.5	12.6	13.1	12.4	12.2	13.1
South Africa / Afrique du Sud	9.2	8.9	9.8	10.0	9.5	10.2	10.6	10.9	11.4	11.4
Tunisia / Tunisie	..	12.7	10.9	11.0	10.7	10.7	10.6	11.2	10.8	11.3
LAC Average / Moyenne ALC[1,2]	**9.3**	**9.3**	**9.7**	**10.2**	**9.4**	**9.9**	**10.2**	**10.5**	**10.4**	**10.6**
OECD Average / Moyenne OCDE[2]	**11.1**	**11.0**	**11.0**	**10.6**	**10.4**	**10.6**	**10.8**	**10.9**	**11.0**	..

Note: The figures exclude local government tax revenues for Cameroon, Côte d'Ivoire, Rwanda, Senegal and Tunisia as the data are not available. Local and provincial data prior to 2003 are not available for South Africa.

1. Represents a group of 22 Latin American and Caribbean countries (LAC).
2. Represents the unweighted average for LAC and OECD countries.

Note : Les chiffres excluent les recettes fiscales des collectivités locales pour le Cameroun, la Côte d'Ivoire, le Rwanda, le Sénégal et la Tunisie car les données ne sont pas disponibles. Les données des collectivités locales et provinciales ne sont pas disponibles pour l'Afrique du Sud avant 2003.

1. Représente un groupe de 22 pays d'Amérique latine et des Caraïbes (ALC).
2. Représente la moyenne non pondérée pour les pays de l'ALC et de l'OCDE.

StatLink http://dx.doi.org/10.1787/888933344612

Table 3.11. Taxes on goods and services (5000) as percentage of total taxation
Tableau 3.11. Impôts sur les biens et services (5000) en pourcentage du total des recettes fiscales

	1997	2000	2005	2008	2009	2010	2011	2012	2013	2014
Cameroon / Cameroun	67.4	63.6	62.1	61.1	57.9	61.8	61.1	57.9	58.2	59.4
Côte d'Ivoire	62.4	60.0	64.1	64.2	65.3	66.7	63.8	60.0	59.2	61.6
Mauritius / Maurice	70.8	74.7	73.2	67.7	60.9	63.6	66.6	66.7	66.1	64.6
Morocco / Maroc	..	51.9	45.2	43.9	43.8	47.6	45.0	43.4	42.6	41.7
Rwanda	71.3	68.8	64.5	58.6	58.7	57.4	57.0	55.2	52.5	56.3
Senegal / Sénégal	69.9	69.2	67.8	67.5	66.3	63.4	66.1	63.6	63.7	64.8
South Africa / Afrique du Sud	40.7	39.9	39.1	36.2	36.9	39.7	40.4	40.9	41.6	41.0
Tunisia / Tunisie	..	51.5	44.7	40.8	39.7	39.3	36.4	38.4	36.0	36.0
LAC Average / Moyenne ALC[1,2]	**56.9**	**56.1**	**52.9**	**50.8**	**49.1**	**51.1**	**50.4**	**50.1**	**49.6**	**49.5**
OECD Average / Moyenne OCDE[2]	**33.6**	**33.1**	**33.2**	**32.1**	**32.5**	**33.1**	**33.0**	**32.9**	**32.7**	..

Note: The figures exclude local government tax revenues for Cameroon, Côte d'Ivoire, Rwanda, Senegal and Tunisia as the data are not available. Local and provincial data prior to 2003 are not available for South Africa.

1. Represents a group of 22 Latin American and Caribbean countries (LAC).
2. Represents the unweighted average for LAC and OECD countries.

Note : Les chiffres excluent les recettes fiscales des collectivités locales pour le Cameroun, la Côte d'Ivoire, le Rwanda, le Sénégal et la Tunisie car les données ne sont pas disponibles. Les données des collectivités locales et provinciales ne sont pas disponibles pour l'Afrique du Sud avant 2003.

1. Représente un groupe de 22 pays d'Amérique latine et des Caraïbes (ALC).
2. Représente la moyenne non pondérée pour les pays de l'ALC et de l'OCDE.

StatLink http://dx.doi.org/10.1787/888933344623

Table 3.12. Taxes on general consumption (5110) as percentage of GDP
Tableau 3.12. Impôts généraux sur la consommation (5110) en pourcentage du PIB

	1997	2000	2005	2008	2009	2010	2011	2012	2013	2014
Cameroon / Cameroun	3.4	4.4	4.7	5.3	4.9	4.8	5.2	5.1	5.4	5.6
Côte d'Ivoire	3.7	3.3	3.2	3.9	3.7	4.0	3.2	3.7	3.7	3.6
Mauritius / Maurice	2.8	4.8	6.8	7.1	6.8	7.1	7.1	7.3	7.2	6.8
Morocco / Maroc	..	5.2	5.9	8.5	7.4	8.3	8.7	8.8	8.3	8.1
Rwanda	1.4	2.0	4.0	4.5	4.1	4.0	4.1	4.2	4.5	5.2
Senegal / Sénégal	5.4	6.6	7.7	7.3	7.2	7.5	7.7	7.2	6.9	7.3
South Africa / Afrique du Sud	5.6	5.5	6.6	6.4	5.9	6.2	6.4	6.4	6.6	6.8
Tunisia / Tunisie	..	6.2	5.6	6.1	5.9	6.1	6.1	6.3	6.1	6.5
LAC Average / Moyenne ALC[1,2]	**5.1**	**5.1**	**5.7**	**6.3**	**5.9**	**6.2**	**6.4**	**6.6**	**6.6**	**6.7**
OECD Average / Moyenne OCDE[2]	**6.6**	**6.7**	**6.8**	**6.6**	**6.5**	**6.6**	**6.8**	**6.8**	**6.8**	..

Note: The figures exclude local government tax revenues for Cameroon, Côte d'Ivoire, Rwanda, Senegal and Tunisia as the data are not available. Local and provincial data prior to 2003 are not available for South Africa.

1. Represents a group of 22 Latin American and Caribbean countries (LAC).
2. Represents the unweighted average for LAC and OECD countries.

Note : Les chiffres excluent les recettes fiscales des collectivités locales pour le Cameroun, la Côte d'Ivoire, le Rwanda, le Sénégal et la Tunisie car les données ne sont pas disponibles. Les données des collectivités locales et provinciales ne sont pas disponibles pour l'Afrique du Sud avant 2003.

1. Représente un groupe de 22 pays d'Amérique latine et des Caraïbes (ALC).
2. Représente la moyenne non pondérée pour les pays de l'ALC et de l'OCDE.

StatLink http://dx.doi.org/10.1787/888933344639

Table 3.13. Taxes on general consumption (5110) as percentage of total taxation
Tableau 3.13. Impôts généraux sur la consommation (5110) en pourcentage du total des recettes fiscales

	1997	2000	2005	2008	2009	2010	2011	2012	2013	2014
Cameroon / Cameroun	30.8	34.8	34.5	35.8	32.5	34.1	35.2	33.1	34.2	35.0
Côte d'Ivoire	21.5	21.7	20.4	21.2	21.5	23.6	19.7	20.3	20.2	20.2
Mauritius / Maurice	15.9	25.0	35.9	36.7	33.9	35.6	36.1	36.4	35.9	34.1
Morocco / Maroc	..	22.0	23.7	28.0	27.0	30.6	30.3	29.7	29.3	28.5
Rwanda	13.3	20.0	33.1	33.1	32.1	29.9	29.0	28.8	28.9	32.3
Senegal / Sénégal	35.0	39.6	40.0	38.2	38.0	37.7	38.5	36.8	36.2	36.0
South Africa / Afrique du Sud	24.9	24.6	26.1	23.2	23.1	24.3	24.5	23.8	24.0	24.3
Tunisia / Tunisie	..	25.1	23.0	22.6	22.0	22.2	20.8	21.7	20.3	20.9
LAC Average / Moyenne ALC[1,2]	**30.4**	**30.4**	**30.5**	**30.9**	**30.3**	**31.6**	**31.4**	**31.1**	**31.2**	**31.3**
OECD Average / Moyenne OCDE[2]	**19.8**	**19.7**	**20.2**	**19.8**	**19.9**	**20.3**	**20.3**	**20.2**	**20.2**	..

Note: The figures exclude local government tax revenues for Cameroon, Côte d'Ivoire, Rwanda, Senegal and Tunisia as the data are not available. Local and provincial data prior to 2003 are not available for South Africa.

1. Represents a group of 22 Latin American and Caribbean countries (LAC).
2. Represents the unweighted average for LAC and OECD countries.

Note : Les chiffres excluent les recettes fiscales des collectivités locales pour le Cameroun, la Côte d'Ivoire, le Rwanda, le Sénégal et la Tunisie car les données ne sont pas disponibles. Les données des collectivités locales et provinciales ne sont pas disponibles pour l'Afrique du Sud avant 2003.

1. Représente un groupe de 22 pays d'Amérique latine et des Caraïbes (ALC).
2. Représente la moyenne non pondérée pour les pays de l'ALC et de l'OCDE.

StatLink http://dx.doi.org/10.1787/888933344646

Table 3.14. Taxes on specific goods and services (5120) as percentage of GDP
Tableau 3.14. Impôts sur les biens et services déterminés (5120) en pourcentage du PIB

	1997	2000	2005	2008	2009	2010	2011	2012	2013	2014
Cameroon / Cameroun	4.0	3.6	3.6	3.7	3.7	3.8	3.8	3.8	3.7	3.9
Côte d'Ivoire	6.8	5.5	6.5	7.5	7.1	6.8	6.9	6.9	6.7	6.9
Mauritius / Maurice	8.3	8.4	6.3	5.0	4.4	4.6	5.0	5.2	5.0	4.9
Morocco / Maroc	..	6.8	5.1	4.6	4.2	4.3	4.0	3.8	3.4	3.5
Rwanda	5.9	4.9	3.8	3.4	3.4	3.6	3.8	3.8	3.7	3.8
Senegal / Sénégal	5.3	4.9	5.3	5.5	5.3	5.0	5.4	5.2	5.2	5.7
South Africa / Afrique du Sud	3.6	3.4	3.1	3.4	3.4	3.8	4.0	4.4	4.6	4.5
Tunisia / Tunisie	..	6.3	5.0	4.7	4.5	4.4	4.4	4.6	4.5	4.5
LAC Average / Moyenne ALC[1,2]	**4.1**	**4.1**	**4.0**	**3.9**	**3.5**	**3.7**	**3.8**	**3.9**	**3.8**	**3.7**
OECD Average / Moyenne OCDE[2]	**3.9**	**3.7**	**3.6**	**3.4**	**3.3**	**3.4**	**3.5**	**3.5**	**3.5**	..

Note: The figures exclude local government tax revenues for Cameroon, Côte d'Ivoire, Rwanda, Senegal and Tunisia as the data are not available. Local and provincial data prior to 2003 are not available for South Africa.

1. Represents a group of 22 Latin American and Caribbean countries (LAC).
2. Represents the unweighted average for LAC and OECD countries.

Note : Les chiffres excluent les recettes fiscales des collectivités locales pour le Cameroun, la Côte d'Ivoire, le Rwanda, le Sénégal et la Tunisie car les données ne sont pas disponibles. Les données des collectivités locales et provinciales ne sont pas disponibles pour l'Afrique du Sud avant 2003.

1. Représente un groupe de 22 pays d'Amérique latine et des Caraïbes (ALC).
2. Représente la moyenne non pondérée pour les pays de l'ALC et de l'OCDE.

StatLink http://dx.doi.org/10.1787/888933344659

Table 3.15. Taxes on specific goods and services (5120) as percentage of total taxation
Tableau 3.15. Impôts sur les biens et services déterminés (5120) en pourcentage du total des recettes fiscales

	1997	2000	2005	2008	2009	2010	2011	2012	2013	2014
Cameroon / Cameroun	36.3	28.5	27.0	24.8	24.9	27.2	25.5	24.5	23.6	24.0
Côte d'Ivoire	39.7	36.0	41.6	40.7	41.4	40.7	43.1	37.6	36.7	38.9
Mauritius / Maurice	47.0	44.0	33.4	25.8	21.9	23.1	25.2	25.6	25.1	24.8
Morocco / Maroc	..	28.8	20.5	15.0	15.6	15.9	13.8	12.8	12.1	12.2
Rwanda	57.2	47.9	31.0	25.1	26.3	26.9	27.5	25.8	23.4	23.9
Senegal / Sénégal	34.4	29.2	27.4	28.9	27.8	25.4	27.1	26.4	27.0	28.3
South Africa / Afrique du Sud	15.8	15.3	12.2	12.3	13.1	14.7	15.2	16.4	16.9	16.0
Tunisia / Tunisie	..	25.6	20.7	17.3	16.9	16.2	14.9	15.9	14.9	14.4
LAC Average / Moyenne ALC[1,2]	**26.3**	**25.5**	**22.4**	**20.0**	**18.7**	**19.5**	**19.1**	**18.9**	**18.3**	**17.8**
OECD Average / Moyenne OCDE[2]	**12.0**	**11.6**	**11.1**	**10.5**	**10.6**	**10.9**	**10.8**	**10.8**	**10.5**	..

Note: The figures exclude local government tax revenues for Cameroon, Côte d'Ivoire, Rwanda, Senegal and Tunisia as the data are not available. Local and provincial data prior to 2003 are not available for South Africa.

1. Represents a group of 22 Latin American and Caribbean countries (LAC).
2. Represents the unweighted average for LAC and OECD countries.

Note : Les chiffres excluent les recettes fiscales des collectivités locales pour le Cameroun, la Côte d'Ivoire, le Rwanda, le Sénégal et la Tunisie car les données ne sont pas disponibles. Les données des collectivités locales et provinciales ne sont pas disponibles pour l'Afrique du Sud avant 2003.

1. Représente un groupe de 22 pays d'Amérique latine et des Caraïbes (ALC).
2. Représente la moyenne non pondérée pour les pays de l'ALC et de l'OCDE.

StatLink http://dx.doi.org/10.1787/888933344669

Table 3.16. Gross domestic product for tax reporting years at market prices, in millions of national currency units
Tableau 3.16. Produit intérieur brut pour les années de déclaration fiscale au prix du marché, en millions de monnaie nationale

	1997	2000	2005	2008	2009	2010	2011	2012	2013	2014
Cameroon / Cameroun	5 324 762	6 612 385	8 749 566	10 443 829	11 040 255	11 699 673	12 545 651	13 514 702	14 607 530	15 846 400
Côte d'Ivoire	6 841 856	7 630 266	9 011 755	10 848 040	11 463 500	12 324 723	11 976 725	13 804 940	15 459 777	17 021 000
Mauritius / Maurice	86 561	116 995	185 312	260 175	278 290	298 784	323 011	343 813	366 195	386 068
Morocco / Maroc	318 000	412 897	552 671	716 959	748 483	784 624	820 077	847 881	901 366	924 769
Rwanda	546 526	676 000	1 440 000	2 623 000	3 017 000	3 323 000	3 846 000	4 435 000	4 864 000	5 389 000
Senegal / Sénégal	2 727 198	3 331 768	4 592 673	5 994 476	6 033 412	6 401 810	6 782 805	7 263 778	7 386 722	7 741 328
South Africa / Afrique du Sud	703 117	946 324	1 639 254	2 369 063	2 507 677	2 748 008	3 024 951	3 262 545	3 534 327	3 796 460
Tunisia / Tunisie	24 400	29 433	41 871	55 268	58 677	63 055	64 492	70 371	74 984	80 510

Source: OECD National Accounts data for South Africa and official National Accounts data for the other countries. The World Economic Outlook (IMF) data published in April 2015 was used for years up to 1998 for Rwanda and up to 1999 for Mauritius. GDP for Mauritius for years prior to 2010 are on a July(n-1)/June(n) fiscal year basis and on a calendar year basis from 2010 onwards.

Source : Données des comptes nationaux de l'OCDE pour l'Afrique du Sud et des comptes nationaux des pays. Les données des Perspectives de l'économie mondiale (FMI) publiées en avril 2015 ont été utilisées jusqu'en 1998 pour le Rwanda et jusqu'en 1999 pour l'île Maurice. Le PIB de l'île Maurice est basé sur l'année fiscale juillet(n-1)/juin(n) avant 2010 et sur l'année civile à partir de 2010.

StatLink http://dx.doi.org/10.1787/888933344670

Table 3.17. Gross domestic product for tax reporting years at market prices, in millions of US Dollars at market exchange rates
Tableau 3.17. Produit intérieur brut pour les années de déclaration fiscale au prix du marché, en millions de dollars US aux taux de change du marché

	1997	2000	2005	2008	2009	2010	2011	2012	2013	2014
Cameroon / Cameroun	9 841	9 272	16 617	23 432	23 442	23 667	25 612	26 487	29 577	32 109
Côte d'Ivoire	11 831	10 748	17 115	24 339	24 341	24 931	25 405	27 056	31 302	34 489
Mauritius / Maurice	4 532	4 457	6 052	8 107	9 500	9 783	11 035	11 218	11 928	13 178
Morocco / Maroc	33 378	38 859	62 343	92 507	92 897	93 217	101 371	98 266	107 235	110 085
Rwanda	1 808	1 718	2 590	4 799	5 309	5 699	5 407	7 220	7 522	7 924
Senegal / Sénégal	4 672	4 693	8 722	13 449	12 811	12 950	14 388	14 236	14 956	15 686
South Africa / Afrique du Sud	152 609	136 453	257 667	287 095	297 221	375 304	417 057	397 391	366 236	350 082
Tunisia / Tunisie	22 063	21 473	32 272	44 855	43 456	44 051	45 811	45 055	46 154	47 346

Note: The figures are derived by multiplying the data from Table 3.16 (in millions of national currency) by the exchange rates from Table 3.19.

Note : Ce tableau est obtenu en multipliant les données du tableau 3.16 (en millions de monnaie nationale) par les taux de change du tableau 3.19.

StatLink http://dx.doi.org/10.1787/888933344689

Table 3.18. Total tax revenue in millions of US Dollars at market exchange rates
Tableau 3.18. Total des recettes fiscales en millions de dollars US aux taux de change du marché

	1997	2000	2005	2008	2009	2010	2011	2012	2013	2014
Cameroon / Cameroun	1 076	1 183	2 248	3 469	3 508	3 318	3 934	4 061	4 666	5 162
Côte d'Ivoire	2 023	1 654	2 683	4 469	4 189	4 196	4 082	4 970	5 721	6 126
Mauritius / Maurice	805	853	1 140	1 574	1 913	1 938	2 168	2 262	2 377	2 631
Morocco / Maroc	..	9 182	15 487	28 179	25 322	25 304	29 137	29 207	30 518	31 375
Rwanda	186	175	314	646	686	756	895	1 051	1 176	1 273
Senegal / Sénégal	715	788	1 685	2 556	2 417	2 565	2 856	2 782	2 864	3 158
South Africa / Afrique du Sud	34 414	30 506	64 832	79 409	76 346	95 917	109 518	106 234	100 157	97 456
Tunisia / Tunisie	..	5 280	7 878	12 095	11 691	12 040	13 385	13 150	13 874	14 836

Note: The figures are derived by multiplying the total tax revenue data in the tables from Chapter 4 by the exchange rate data in Table 3.19.
Note : Ce tableau est obtenu en multipliant les données du chapitre 4 par les taux de change du tableau 3.19.

StatLink http://dx.doi.org/10.1787/888933344696

Table 3.19. Exchange rates used, national currency per US dollar
Tableau 3.19. Taux de change utilisés, unités de monnaie nationale par dollar des ÉU

	1997	2000	2005	2008	2009	2010	2011	2012	2013	2014
Cameroon / Cameroun	0.0018	0.0014	0.0019	0.0022	0.0021	0.0020	0.0021	0.0020	0.0020	0.0020
Côte d'Ivoire	0.0017	0.0014	0.0019	0.0022	0.0021	0.0020	0.0021	0.0020	0.0020	0.0020
Mauritius / Maurice	0.0524	0.0381	0.0327	0.0312	0.0341	0.0327	0.0342	0.0326	0.0326	0.0341
Morocco / Maroc	0.1050	0.0941	0.1128	0.1290	0.1241	0.1188	0.1236	0.1159	0.1190	0.1190
Rwanda	0.0033	0.0025	0.0018	0.0018	0.0018	0.0017	0.0017	0.0016	0.0015	0.0015
Senegal / Sénégal	0.0017	0.0014	0.0019	0.0022	0.0021	0.0020	0.0021	0.0020	0.0020	0.0020
South Africa / Afrique du Sud	0.2170	0.1442	0.1572	0.1212	0.1185	0.1366	0.1379	0.1218	0.1036	0.0922
Tunisia / Tunisie	0.9042	0.7296	0.7708	0.8116	0.7406	0.6986	0.7103	0.6402	0.6155	0.5881

Source: OECD financial indicators data.
Source : Indicateurs financiers de l'OCDE.

StatLink http://dx.doi.org/10.1787/888933344707

3.2. Comparative figures / 3.2. Graphiques comparatifs

Figure 3.1. Tax revenue of main headings as percentage of total tax revenue, 2014
Graphique 3.1. Recettes fiscales sous les principales rubriques en pourcentage du total des recettes fiscales, 2014

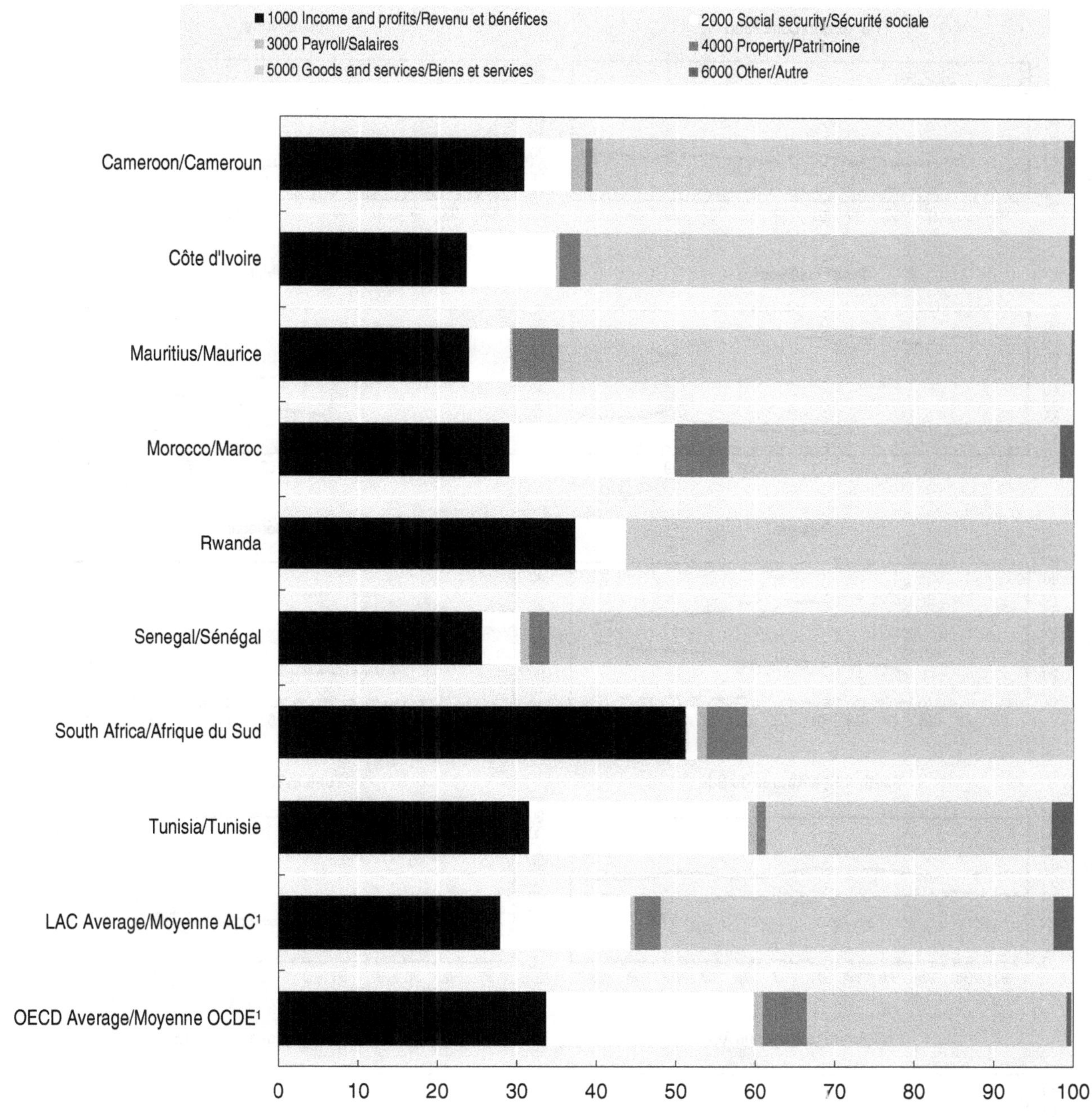

1. Represents the unweighted average for LAC and OECD member countries. 2013 data for the OECD average.
1. Représente la moyenne non pondérée des pays ALC et de l'OCDE. Données 2013 pour la moyenne OCDE.
Source: Table 1.2 / Tableau 1.2.

StatLink http://dx.doi.org/10.1787/888933343976

Figure 3.2. **Tax structures by country, 1990-2014**

Receipts as percentage of total tax revenues

Graphique 3.2. **Structures des impôts par pays, 1990-2014**

Recettes en pourcentage du total des recettes fiscales

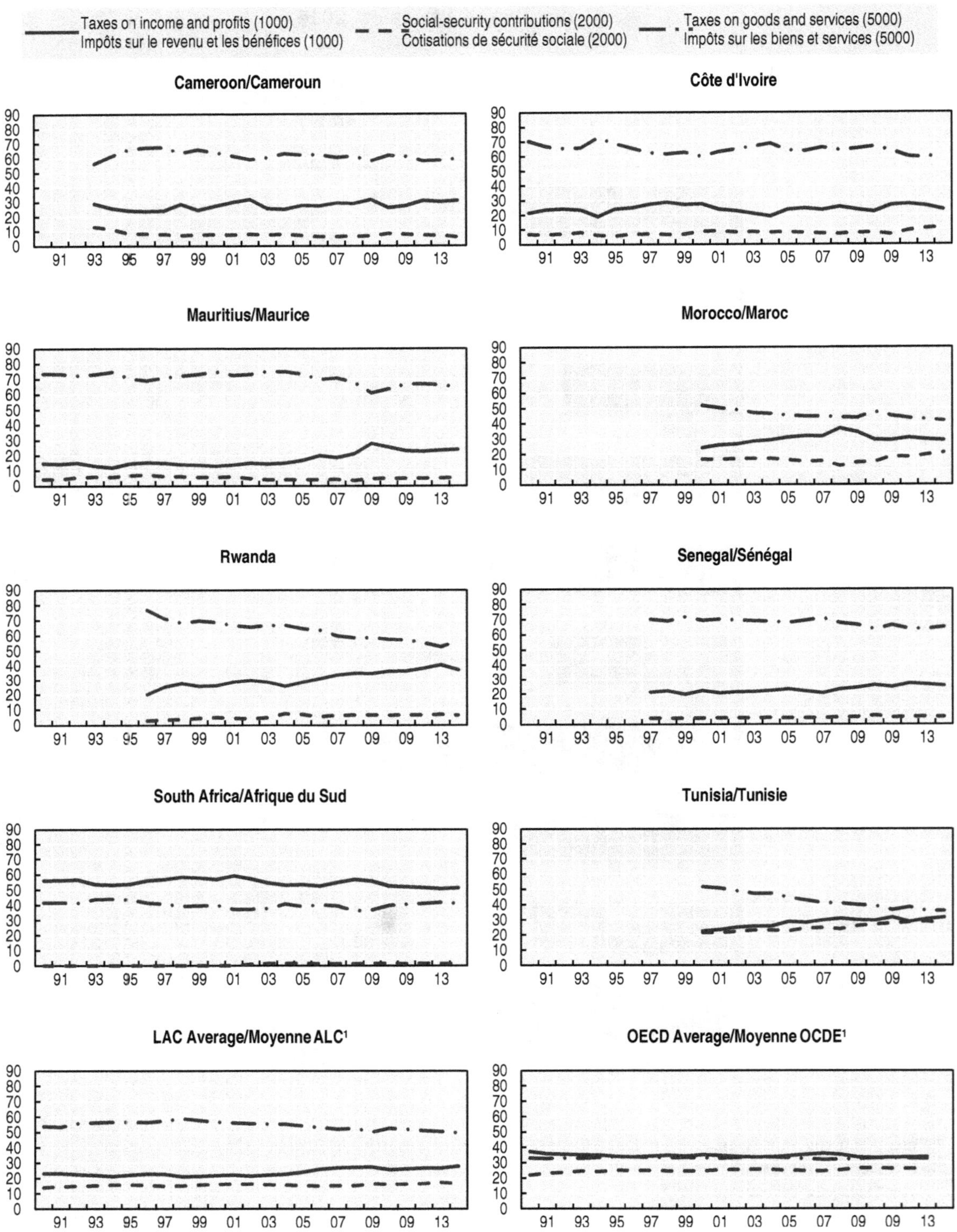

1. Represents the unweighted average for LAC and OECD countries. / 1. Représente la moyenne sans pondération des pays ALC et de l'OCDE.

Source: Tables 3.5, 3.7 and 3.11. / Tableaux 3.5, 3.7 et 3.11.

StatLink http://dx.doi.org/10.1787/888933343987

CHAPTER 4

COUNTRY TABLES 1990-2014 – TAX REVENUES

CHAPITRE 4

TABLEAUX PAYS, 1990-2014 – RECETTES FISCALES

Table 4.1. Cameroon / Cameroun
Details of tax revenue / Recettes fiscales détaillées

Million XAF

	1997	2000	2007	2008	2009	2010	2011	2012	2013	2014
Recettes fiscales totales	**582 398**	**843 400**	**1 445 182**	**1 546 259**	**1 652 112**	**1 640 028**	**1 854 735**	**2 072 275**	**2 304 490**	**2 547 477**
1000 Impôts sur revenu, bénéfices et gains en capital	**140 000**	**228 100**	**422 080**	**444 902**	**522 719**	**425 741**	**505 594**	**637 416**	**693 317**	**784 122**
1100 Des personnes physiques	66 400	87 100	72 819	86 602	97 774	102 793	116 950	130 516	158 622	175 021
1110 Sur le revenu et les bénéfices	66 400	87 100	72 813	86 592	97 743	102 728	116 928	130 483	158 338	174 190
Traitements, salaires, pensions et rentes viagères	40 100	60 800	61 193	74 082	80 469	86 440	96 097	101 245	120 908	127 331
Revenus fonciers	0	0	2 321	2 231	2 715	2 402	4 487	5 346	6 135	13 247
Bénéfices artisanaux, industriels et commerciaux	0	0	5 364	4 722	6 116	5 342	6 609	11 648	16 267	13 648
Bénéfices agricoles	0	0	45	52	29	47	7	14	22	27
Bénéfices des professions non commerciales	0	0	230	263	462	295	397	577	612	592
Autres impôts sur le revenu	26 300	26 300	3 661	5 243	7 952	8 202	9 331	11 653	14 394	19 345
1120 Sur les gains en capital	0	0	6	10	31	65	22	33	284	831
Impôts sur plus-values sur cession immobilière	..	..	5	6	29	46	8	17	263	830
Impôts sur les autres gains en capital	..	..	1	4	2	19	14	16	21	1
1200 Des sociétés	57 100	119 400	285 929	292 488	362 677	256 404	311 102	421 796	428 360	460 571
1210 Sur les bénéfices	57 100	119 400	285 929	292 488	362 677	256 404	311 102	421 796	428 360	460 571
Bénéfices des sociétés pétrolières	19 000	39 000	126 581	124 379	188 766	83 764	96 729	160 589	169 689	161 724
Bénéfices des sociétés non pétrolières	38 100	80 400	159 348	168 109	173 911	172 639	214 373	261 207	258 671	298 847
1220 Sur les gains en capital	0	0	0	0	0	0	0	0	0	0
1300 Non-ventilables entre 1100 et 1200	16 500	21 600	63 332	65 812	62 268	66 544	77 542	85 105	106 335	148 530
Taxe spéciale sur les revenus payés à l'étranger	11 000	12 400	31 504	37 301	34 250	38 877	42 626	43 572	61 708	97 511
Impôts sur les revenus des capitaux mobiliers	5 500	9 200	31 302	27 780	27 218	27 629	32 441	38 313	40 177	44 489
Centimes additionnels communaux sur l'impôt sur le revenu	0	0	526	731	800	39	2 475	3 219	4 450	6 530
2000 Cotisations de sécurité sociale	**45 598**	**65 500**	**89 640**	**99 828**	**109 161**	**135 747**	**143 734**	**147 543**	**160 134**	**150 201**
2100 A la charge des salariés	11 998	19 747	27 459	28 944	31 477	33 297	34 741	34 414	42 212	40 917
2110 Sur la base du salaire	11 998	19 747	27 459	28 944	31 477	33 297	34 741	34 414	42 212	40 917
2120 Sur la base de l'impôt sur le revenu	0	0	0	0	0	0	0	0	0	0
2200 A la charge des employeurs	..	..	..	..	..	..	..	..	..	..
2210 Sur la base du salaire	..	..	..	..	..	..	..	..	..	..
2220 Sur la base de l'impôt sur le revenu	..	..	..	..	..	..	..	..	..	..
2300 A charge des travailleurs indép. ou sans emploi	..	..	..	..	..	..	..	..	..	..
2310 Sur la base du salaire	..	..	..	..	..	..	..	..	..	..
2320 Sur la base de l'impôt sur le revenu	..	..	..	..	..	..	..	..	..	..
2400 Non-ventilables entre 2100, 2200 et 2300	33 600	45 753	62 181	70 884	77 684	102 450	108 993	113 129	117 922	109 284
2410 Sur la base du salaire	33 600	45 753	62 181	70 884	77 684	102 450	108 993	113 129	117 922	109 284
2420 Sur la base de l'impôt sur le revenu	0	0	0	0	0	0	0	0	0	0
3000 Sur salaires ou main d'oeuvre	**0**	**0**	**10 190**	**12 656**	**18 063**	**17 860**	**30 792**	**40 427**	**39 817**	**46 902**
4000 Impôts sur le patrimoine	**4 500**	**13 100**	**17 411**	**18 379**	**17 897**	**18 003**	**12 973**	**15 087**	**20 816**	**21 024**
4100 Impôts périodiques sur la propriété immobilière	100	500	1 762	1 728	1 716	1 552	386	59	1 714	1 692
4110 Ménages	..	..	..	..	..	..	..	..	..	..
4120 Autres agents	..	..	..	..	..	..	..	..	..	..
4200 Impôts périodiques sur l'actif net	0	0	0	0	0	0	0	0	0	0
4210 Personnes physiques	..	..	..	..	..	..	..	..	..	..
4220 Sociétés	..	..	..	..	..	..	..	..	..	..
4300 Impôts sur mut. par décès, succ. et donations	0	0	14	10	25	39	176	176	157	214
4310 Impôts sur mut. par décès et successions	..	..	14	10	25	39	176	176	157	214
4320 Impôts sur les donations	..	..	0	0	0	0	0	0	0	0
4400 Impôts sur transact. mobilières et immob.	4 400	12 600	15 635	16 641	16 156	16 412	12 411	14 853	18 945	19 117
Droits d'enregistrement sur les mutations entre vifs	..	..	30	32	50	32	96	96	287	586
Droits d'enregistrement sur les mutations immobilières	..	..	1 084	1 704	2 052	2 747	411	3 650	3 343	3 250
Droits de bail	..	..	4 420	5 224	4 147	4 602	3 373	2 575	2 337	2 725
Droits autres mutations et transactions	..	..	10 101	9 680	9 907	9 031	8 532	8 532	12 978	12 556
4500 Impôts non-périodiques	0	0	0	0	0	0	0	0	0	0
4510 Sur l'actif net	..	..	..	..	..	..	..	..	..	..
4520 Autres non-périodiques	..	..	..	..	..	..	..	..	..	..
4600 Autres impôts périodiques sur patrimoine	0	0	0	0	0	0	0	0	0	0
5000 Impôts sur les biens et services	**392 300**	**536 700**	**874 785**	**944 540**	**956 328**	**1 012 746**	**1 132 350**	**1 199 972**	**1 341 989**	**1 513 344**
5100 Impôts sur production, vente, transfert, etc.	390 600	534 000	868 249	938 075	948 886	1 004 898	1 124 800	1 192 226	1 333 576	1 503 461
5110 Impôts généraux	179 100	293 800	505 394	553 992	537 431	558 854	652 187	684 934	788 850	891 189
5111 Taxes sur la valeur ajoutée	179 100	293 800	505 394	553 991	537 428	558 847	652 164	684 924	788 830	891 164
Valeur ajoutée intérieure	87 000	186 500	311 002	329 785	303 271	299 504	373 531	373 917	472 885	532 980
Valeur ajoutée à la porte	92 100	107 300	194 392	224 207	234 157	259 343	278 633	311 008	315 945	358 184
5112 Impôts sur les ventes	0	0	0	0	0	0	0	0	0	0
5113 Autres impôts	0	0	0	1	4	8	23	10	21	25
5120 Impôts sur biens et services déterminés	211 500	240 200	362 855	384 083	411 455	446 043	472 613	507 292	544 726	612 272

Table 4.1. Cameroon / Cameroun (*cont.*)
Details of tax revenue / Recettes fiscales détaillées

Million XAF

	1997	2000	2007	2008	2009	2010	2011	2012	2013	2014
5121 Accises	77 400	84 000	138 017	147 182	158 910	164 943	182 730	198 030	220 643	240 269
Droits d'accises intérieure	19 300	26 500	57 303	65 410	80 572	68 414	81 616	84 068	95 553	98 327
Droits d'accises à la porte	1 100	1 900	7 358	10 320	317	12 936	15 861	15 867	14 817	14 762
Taxe spéciale sur les produits pétroliers	57 000	55 600	73 355	71 451	78 019	82 962	84 580	97 423	109 598	118 515
Vignette sur tabac et produits manufacturés	0	0	2	2	2	632	672	672	675	8 665
5122 Bénéfices des monopoles fiscaux	0	0	0	0	0	0	0	0	0	0
5123 Droits de douane et droits à l'importation	85 700	119 900	207 423	219 745	240 690	261 731	268 898	289 838	299 976	345 511
5124 Taxes à l'exportation	45 900	24 300	4 843	5 289	6 174	8 793	8 082	7 482	13 054	15 089
5125 Impôts sur biens d'équipement	0	0	0	0	0	0	0	0	0	0
5126 Impôts sur services déterminés	1 200	1 100	3 086	3 223	107	3 600	4 392	4 603	4 930	5 238
5127 Autres impôts sur commerce et transact. internat.	0	0	0	0	0	0	0	0	0	0
5128 Autres impôts	1 300	10 900	9 487	8 644	5 574	6 977	8 512	7 340	6 123	6 165
5130 Non-ventilables entre 5110 et 5120	0	0	0	0	0	0	0	0	0	0
5200 Impôts sur utilisation des biens et exerc. activités	1 700	2 700	6 537	6 465	7 442	7 848	7 550	7 746	8 413	9 883
5210 Impôts périodiques	1 700	2 700	6 537	6 465	7 442	7 848	7 550	7 746	8 413	9 883
5211 A la charge des ménages: véhicules à moteur	1 300	1 600	4 552	4 735	5 622	6 111	5 803	6 138	6 640	7 819
5212 A la charge autres agents: véhicules à moteur	400	1 100	1 719	1 652	1 669	1 663	1 676	1 530	1 707	1 985
5213 Autres impôts périodiques	0	0	266	78	151	74	71	78	67	79
5220 Impôts non-périodiques	0	0	0	0	0	0	0	0	0	0
5300 Non-ventilables entre 5100 et 5200	0	0	0	0	0	0	0	0	0	0
6000 Autres impôts	**0**	**0**	**31 077**	**25 953**	**27 946**	**29 932**	**29 292**	**31 829**	**48 416**	**31 885**
6100 A la charge exclusive des entreprises	..	..	..	..	..	..	..	..	..	..
6200 A la charge d'autres agents	..	..	..	..	..	..	..	..	..	..

Note: Année civile se terminant le 31 décembre.

Les données sont sur la base des encaissements.

Les chiffres n'incluent pas les données des collectivités locales car elles ne sont pas disponibles.

Les taxes domaniales, la taxe à l'extraction des carrières et la redevance à la production des eaux sont incluses dans les recettes non fiscales comme le préconise la classification OCDE. Elles sont considérées comme des recettes fiscales au Cameroun.

Source: Ministère des Finances du Cameroun.

StatLink http://dx.doi.org/10.1787/888933344713

Table 4.2. Côte d'Ivoire
Details of tax revenue / Recettes fiscales détaillées

Million XOF

	1997	2000	2007	2008	2009	2010	2011	2012	2013	2014
Recettes fiscales totales	**1 170 063**	**1 173 811**	**1 776 380**	**1 992 059**	**1 972 863**	**2 074 546**	**1 924 497**	**2 535 916**	**2 825 507**	**3 023 456**
1000 Impôts sur revenu, bénéfices et gains en capital	**317 831**	**323 315**	**416 774**	**507 383**	**466 138**	**458 266**	**513 142**	**696 372**	**737 518**	**712 140**
1100 Des personnes physiques	..	..	..	..	..	..	..	..	..	..
1110 Sur le revenu et les bénéfices	..	..	..	..	..	..	..	..	..	..
1120 Sur les gains en capital	..	..	..	..	..	..	..	..	..	..
1200 Des sociétés	..	..	97 261	150 351	76 872	63 649	128 537	201 519	141 732	92 389
1210 Sur les bénéfices	..	..	97 261	150 351	76 872	63 649	128 537	201 519	141 732	92 389
1220 Sur les gains en capitals	..	..	0	0	0	0	0	0	0	0
1300 Non-ventilables entre 1100 et 1200	317 831	323 315	319 513	357 032	389 266	394 617	384 604	494 854	595 786	619 751
Acompte d'impôt sur le revenu du secteur informel	52 369	33 983	8 228	6 464	6 713	7 624	6 850	9 128	12 286	12 509
Impôt général sur le revenu	0	0	51	203	336	1 420	115	761	995	635
Impôt BIC hors pétrole-gaz	141 899	132 755	122 032	146 251	151 002	142 932	144 851	169 053	210 965	226 590
Impôt synthétique	3 816	4 291	4 413	5 093	5 512	5 437	3 136	5 858	7 150	7 980
Impôt sur le revenu des capitaux	7 350	5 313	8 020	9 762	8 336	11 069	8 876	12 891	12 086	13 996
Impôt sur le revenu des valeurs mobilières	13 505	15 940	24 702	29 814	29 895	28 669	29 941	38 415	51 392	47 642
Impôt sur traitements et salaires (ITS), solde	98 893	131 033	152 067	159 445	187 473	197 467	190 837	258 748	300 912	310 400
2000 Cotisations de sécurité sociale	**83 054**	**102 700**	**129 600**	**141 400**	**151 180**	**162 754**	**131 021**	**235 903**	**307 259**	**340 667**
2100 A la charge des salariés	..	..	..	..	..	..	..	..	..	..
2110 Sur la base du salaire	..	..	..	..	..	..	..	..	..	..
2120 Sur la base de l'impôt sur les revenus	..	..	..	..	..	..	..	..	..	..
2200 A la charge des employeurs	..	..	..	..	..	..	..	..	..	..
2210 Sur la base du salaire	..	..	..	..	..	..	..	..	..	..
2220 Sur la base de l'impôt sur le revenu	..	..	..	..	..	..	..	..	..	..
2300 A charge des travailleurs indép. ou sans emploi	..	..	..	..	..	..	..	..	..	..
2310 Sur la base du salaire	..	..	..	..	..	..	..	..	..	..
2320 Sur la base de l'impôt sur le revenu	..	..	..	..	..	..	..	..	..	..
2400 Non-ventilables entre 2100, 2200 et 2300	..	..	..	..	..	..	..	..	..	..
2410 Sur la base du salaire	..	..	..	..	..	..	..	..	..	..
2420 Sur la base de l'impôt sur le revenu	..	..	..	..	..	..	..	..	..	..
3000 Sur salaires ou main d'oeuvre	**6 089**	**6 990**	**8 524**	**8 460**	**8 702**	**9 776**	**8 012**	**10 754**	**12 783**	**12 484**
Fonds de formation professionnelle	6 089	6 990	8 524	8 460	8 702	9 776	8 012	10 754	12 783	12 484
4000 Impôts sur le patrimoine	**30 581**	**32 732**	**42 260**	**45 753**	**48 123**	**49 706**	**38 442**	**61 144**	**82 326**	**79 839**
4100 Impôts périodiques sur la propriété immobilière	21 824	24 664	31 033	32 471	37 316	38 009	30 278	49 013	61 322	64 645
4110 Ménages	..	..	..	..	..	..	..	..	..	..
4120 Autres agents	..	..	..	..	..	..	..	..	..	..
4200 Impôts périodiques sur l'actif net	0	0	0	0	0	0	0	0	0	0
4210 Personnes physiques	..	..	..	..	..	..	..	..	..	..
4220 Sociétés	..	..	..	..	..	..	..	..	..	..
4300 Impôts sur mut. par décès, succ. et donations	0	0	0	0	0	0	0	0	0	0
4310 Impôts sur mut. par décès et successions	..	..	..	..	..	..	..	..	..	..
4320 Impôts sur les donations	..	..	..	..	..	..	..	..	..	..
4400 Impôts sur transact. mobilières et immob.	8 757	8 068	11 227	13 282	10 807	11 697	8 164	12 131	21 004	15 194
4500 Impôts non-périodiques	0	0	0	0	0	0	0	0	0	0
4510 Sur l'actif net	..	..	..	..	..	..	..	..	..	..
4520 Autres non-périodiques	..	..	..	..	..	..	..	..	..	..
4600 Autres impôts périodiques sur patrimoine	0	0	0	0	0	0	0	0	0	0
5000 Impôts sur les biens et services	**729 949**	**703 722**	**1 173 116**	**1 279 042**	**1 288 000**	**1 383 279**	**1 227 772**	**1 520 912**	**1 671 857**	**1 861 244**
5100 Impôts sur production, vente, transfert, etc.	715 376	678 410	1 133 606	1 234 636	1 240 935	1 333 913	1 207 497	1 468 732	1 606 691	1 787 593
5110 Impôts généraux	251 446	255 297	388 045	423 172	424 587	490 521	378 695	515 586	571 079	610 340
5111 Taxes sur la valeur ajoutée	251 446	255 297	361 503	393 439	401 132	473 711	369 742	514 898	570 444	610 020
Taxes sur la valeur ajoutée (DGI)	82 346	106 797	136 484	140 639	173 249	178 761	145 883	195 936	228 450	255 464
Taxes sur la valeur ajoutée (DGD)	169 100	148 500	225 019	252 800	227 883	294 950	223 860	318 962	341 994	354 556
5112 Impôts sur les ventes	0	0	0	0	0	0	0	0	0	0
5113 Autres impôts	0	0	26 542	29 733	23 455	16 810	8 953	688	635	320
Contribution à la reconstitution nationale	..	..	26 542	29 733	23 455	1 567	296	436	123	63
Taxe de solidarité pour la sortie de crise	..	..	0	0	0	15 243	8 656	251	511	257
5120 Impôts sur biens et services déterminés	463 930	423 113	745 562	811 464	816 348	843 393	828 802	953 146	1 035 612	1 177 253
5121 Accises	75 919	74 908	66 381	72 172	120 478	128 698	73 865	97 017	122 689	130 450
Taxe SIDA	0	0	0	0	385	740	767	845	832	908
Taxe sur le caoutchouc	0	0	0	0	0	0	0	16 828	17 780	3 124
Taxe sur le tabac pour le dévelopment du sport	0	0	0	1 385	1 505	1 708	1 568	1 954	1 946	2 158
Taxe sur les sacs et sachets en matière plastique	0	0	0	0	0	0	0	4	179	172
Taxe sur les boissons	1 779	3 642	3 658	3 043	4 014	5 050	4 885	6 100	7 609	14 563
Taxes sur le carburant	242	290	74	90	91	81	61	80	81	95
Taxes sur le tabac	12 898	15 518	10 272	11 461	10 877	12 040	12 096	13 307	13 191	19 817
Taxes sur les produits pétroliers	61 000	50 300	42 907	47 501	95 347	96 560	43 842	44 381	64 166	72 567

Table 4.2. Côte d'Ivoire *(cont.)*
Details of tax revenue / Recettes fiscales détaillées

Million XOF

	1997	2000	2007	2008	2009	2010	2011	2012	2013	2014
5123 Droits de douane et droits à l'importation	178 700	126 512	231 011	223 447	213 444	288 039	256 698	344 173	383 583	459 675
5124 Taxes à l'exportation	173 200	185 114	312 741	310 685	377 133	331 261	374 771	304 216	326 539	363 222
Droits d'enregistrement du café et cacao	0	21 114	56 481	79 773	150 610	103 669	95 775	74 308	27 389	38 033
Taxe sur le cacao et café (DGD)	165 900	156 700	246 066	220 807	217 587	221 180	273 686	222 760	291 819	316 371
Taxe sur le bois et autres produits (DGD)	7 300	7 300	10 194	10 105	8 936	6 412	5 310	7 149	7 331	8 819
5125 Impôts sur biens d'équipement	0	0	0	0	0	0	0	0	0	0
5126 Impôts sur services déterminés	33 217	32 375	30 954	50 789	64 438	60 423	54 650	89 434	96 670	143 813
Contribution de solidarité sur les billets d'avion	0	0	0	211	234	216	249	279	709	1 274
Taxe d'embarquement sur les titres de transport aérien affecté à l'Office ivoirien du tourisme et de l'hôtellerie (OITH)	0	0	0	178	718	799	608	1 332	1 680	2 054
Taxe pour la promotion de la culture	0	0	0	1 089	1 613	1 598	1 172	1 610	1 874	2 279
Taxe pour le développement des nouvelles technologies de l'information et de la communication (NTIC) en zone rurale	0	0	0	9 194	17 538	11 486	10 088	14 150	14 938	16 528
Taxe sur les télécommunications	0	0	0	0	0	0	0	17 925	22 177	43 080
Taxes sur les transports urbains	0	0	0	23	868	1 019	412	613	394	174
Prélèvement aux jeux de casino	449	168	304	323	286	378	13	230	245	273
Taxe d'abattage	2 522	2 434	1 699	1 573	937	1 125	716	1 349	1 335	1 280
Taxe sur la publicité	19	137	197	176	251	300	328	408	508	411
Taxe pour le développement touristique	0	0	0	0	0	0	0	1 085	972	1 001
Taxe spécifique sur les communications téléphoniques	0	0	0	0	0	0	0	0	0	16 667
Taxe sur les assurances	8 238	6 942	6 571	6 727	8 757	7 739	7 500	11 512	11 466	12 214
Taxe sur les encours bancaires	1 966	2 002	2 428	2 813	2 992	3 627	3 739	1 106	2	3
Taxe sur les opérations bancaires	20 023	20 692	19 755	25 129	26 066	28 028	27 487	32 273	34 805	40 554
Redevance RTI (radiodiffusion télévision ivoirienne)	0	0	0	3 281	4 173	4 107	2 340	5 564	5 568	6 021
Taxe audiovisuelle	0	0	0	72	6	0	0	0	0	0
5127 Autres impôts sur commerce et transact. internat.	0	0	0	0	0	0	0	0	0	0
5128 Autres impôts	2 895	4 204	104 474	154 371	40 856	34 971	68 818	118 306	106 131	80 092
Taxe d'exploitation pétrolière	0	0	97 262	150 351	32 945	27 275	60 966	87 080	60 764	39 595
Taxes domaniales	2 895	4 204	7 212	4 020	7 911	7 696	7 852	31 226	45 367	40 497
5130 Non-ventilables entre 5110 et 5120	0	0	0	0	0	0	0	0	0	0
5200 Impôts sur utilisation des biens et exerc. activites	14 573	25 312	39 510	44 406	47 065	49 366	20 275	52 180	65 167	73 651
5210 Impôts périodiques	14 573	25 312	39 510	44 406	47 065	49 366	20 275	52 180	65 167	73 651
5211 A la charge des ménages: véhicules à moteur	2 354	4 176	6 159	7 361	7 928	9 171	283	10 197	12 183	13 403
5212 A la charge autres agents: véhicules à moteur	0	0	0	0	0	0	0	0	0	0
5213 Autres impôts périodiques	12 219	21 136	33 351	37 044	39 137	40 195	19 991	41 983	52 984	60 248
5220 Impôts non-périodiques	0	0	0	0	0	0	0	0	0	0
5300 Non-ventilables entre 5100 et 5200	0	0	0	0	0	0	0	0	0	0
6000 Autres impôts	**2 560**	**4 352**	**6 106**	**10 021**	**10 719**	**10 765**	**6 109**	**10 831**	**13 764**	**17 082**
6100 A la charge exclusive des entreprises	0	0	0	3 374	3 823	3 732	4 005	5 822	5 428	5 622
Fonds de soutien à l'habitat	..	..	..	307	266	45	0	0	0	0
Fonds interprofessionnel pour la recherche et le conseil agricole	..	..	..	3 067	3 557	3 687	4 005	5 822	5 428	5 622
6200 A la charge d'autres agents	2 560	4 352	6 106	6 647	6 896	7 033	2 104	5 008	8 336	11 460

Note: Année civile se terminant le 31 décembre.

Les données sont sur la base des encaissements.

Les chiffres n'incluent pas les données des collectivités locales car elles ne sont pas disponibles.

La rubrique 5113 comprend la Contribution à la reconstruction nationale (CRN) instituée en 2004 pour cinq ans et est arrivée à expiration en 2009. Elle a été remplacée par la Contribution pour la sortie de crise. Celle-ci était basée sur les charges d'exploitation des entreprises réalisant un chiffre d'affaire annuel supérieur ou égal à 1 milliard de francs, au titre de l'exercice clos au 31 décembre 2009.

La rubrique 5126 comprend la taxe audiovisuelle et la redevance radiodiffusion télévision ivoirienne (RTI). Ces recettes – normalement considérées comme des recettes non fiscales selon la classification OCDE – sont des recettes fiscales en Côte d'Ivoire.

La rubrique 5128 comprend les taxes domaniales et la taxe d'exploitation pétrolière. Ces recettes – normalement considérées comme des recettes non-fiscales selon la classification OCDE – sont des recettes fiscales en Côte d'Ivoire.

La rubrique 6100 comprend le Fonds de Soutien à l'habitat alimenté par des recettes fiscales affectées (contribution patronale sur la masse salariale, taxes sur services déterminés et taxe sur le carburant). Il n'est pas possible de distinguer ces différents éléments d'où sa classification dans la catégorie 6100. Cette taxe a été supprimée en 2010.

Source: Ministère de l'Économie et des Finances.

StatLink http://dx.doi.org/10.1787/888933344723

Table 4.3. Mauritius / Maurice
Details of tax revenue / Recettes fiscales détaillées

Million MUR

	1997	2000	2007	2008	2009	2010	2011	2012	2013	2014
Total tax revenue	**15 367**	**22 390**	**40 717**	**50 509**	**56 048**	**59 179**	**63 469**	**69 313**	**72 966**	**77 065**
1000 Taxes on income, profits and capital gains	**2 287**	**2 881**	**7 608**	**10 669**	**15 629**	**15 005**	**14 560**	**15 642**	**16 956**	**18 385**
1100 Of individuals	1 220	1 540	2 332	3 524	4 175	4 583	4 913	5 331	6 214	7 049
1110 On income and profits	..	..	..	..	..	..	..	..	..	..
1120 On capital gains	..	..	..	..	..	..	..	..	..	..
1200 Corporate	1 067	1 341	5 275	6 347	10 592	9 457	8 788	9 380	9 763	10 268
1210 On profits	1 067	1 341	5 275	6 347	10 592	9 457	8 788	9 380	9 763	10 268
Income Tax - companies & bodies corporate	..	..	5 275	6 236	10 259	8 428	7 847	8 372	8 727	8 972
Special levy on banks	..	..	0	68	333	455	448	482	473	772
Solidarity levy on telecommunication companies	..	..	0	0	0	424	376	397	438	358
Corporate social responsibility	..	..	0	0	0	150	116	130	125	167
Special contribution from hotels	..	..	0	43	0	0	0	0	0	0
1220 On capital gains	..	..	0	0	0	0	0	0	0	0
1300 Unallocable between 1100 and 1200	..	..	0	797	862	965	859	931	979	1 068
Tax deduction at source	..	..	..	797	862	965	859	931	979	1 068
2000 Social security contributions	**948**	**1 230**	**1 668**	**1 783**	**2 616**	**2 888**	**3 111**	**3 316**	**3 670**	**4 016**
2100 Employees	..	..	556	594	640	713	782	840	904	1 004
2110 On a payroll basis	..	..	..	..	..	..	..	..	..	..
2120 On an income tax basis	..	..	..	..	..	..	..	..	..	..
2200 Employers	..	..	1 112	1 188	1 280	1 426	1 564	1 680	1 807	2 009
2210 On a payroll basis	..	..	..	..	..	..	..	..	..	..
2220 On an income tax basis	..	..	..	..	..	..	..	..	..	..
2300 Self-employed or non-employed	..	..	0	0	0	1	1	1	1	1
2310 On a payroll basis	..	..	..	..	..	..	..	..	..	..
2320 On an income tax basis	..	..	..	..	..	..	..	..	..	..
2400 Unallocable between 2100, 2200 and 2300[1]	..	..	0	0	696	748	764	795	959	1 002
2410 On a payroll basis	..	..	..	..	..	..	..	..	..	..
2420 On an income tax basis	..	..	..	..	..	..	..	..	..	..
3000 Taxes on payroll and workforce	**101**	**140**	**253**	**272**	**263**	**176**	**187**	**201**	**214**	**226**
Extra-budgetary taxes on payroll and workforce[1]	101	140	253	272	263	176	187	201	214	226
4000 Taxes on property	**1 147**	**1 411**	**2 271**	**3 402**	**3 245**	**3 328**	**3 184**	**3 719**	**3 708**	**4 446**
4100 Recurrent taxes on immovable property	171	205	348	357	347	417	417	238	407	426
Local government recurrent taxes on immovable property[1]	171	205	288	306	337	410	410	235	400	422
4110 Households	..	..	..	..	..	..	..	..	..	..
4120 Others	..	..	..	..	..	..	..	..	..	..
4200 Recurrent taxes on net wealth	..	..	0	0	0	0	0	0	0	0
4210 Individual	..	..	..	..	..	..	..	..	..	..
4220 Corporate	..	..	..	..	..	..	..	..	..	..
4300 Estate, inheritance and gift taxes	..	..	0	0	0	0	0	0	0	0
4310 Estate and inheritance taxes	..	..	..	..	..	..	..	..	..	..
4320 Gift taxes	..	..	..	..	..	..	..	..	..	..
4400 Taxes on financial and capital transactions	976	1 206	1 923	3 045	2 891	2 902	2 747	3 471	3 277	4 000
Land transfer tax	..	..	762	1 349	1 348	1 190	1 243	1 618	1 496	1 652
Registration duty on transfer of immovable property	..	..	875	1 212	1 053	1 180	959	1 382	1 239	1 522
Tax on transfer of leasehold rights in state lands	..	..	39	105	161	175	119	187	272	374
Registration duty on transfer of shares	..	..	27	142	79	84	121	32	24	182
Registration duty on fixed and floating charges	..	..	111	126	161	180	213	168	169	162
Stamp duties	..	..	77	79	71	75	81	85	78	109
Registration duty on loans	..	..	13	13	7	9	4	0	0	0
Mortgages, inscriptions and transcriptions	..	..	18	20	12	11	8	0	0	0
4500 Non-recurrent taxes	..	..	0	0	6	10	20	9	24	20
4510 On net wealth	..	..	..	..	0	0	0	0	0	0
4520 Other non-recurrent taxes	..	..	..	..	6	10	20	9	24	20
4600 Other recurrent taxes on property	..	..	0	0	0	0	0	0	0	0
5000 Taxes on goods and services	**10 873**	**16 717**	**28 771**	**34 214**	**34 146**	**37 618**	**42 244**	**46 247**	**48 235**	**49 784**
5100 Taxes on production, sale, transfer, etc	9 665	15 446	26 472	31 699	31 396	34 853	38 949	42 934	44 526	45 393
5110 General taxes	2 442	5 604	15 468	18 542	18 980	21 095	22 921	25 204	26 210	26 281
5111 Value added taxes	0	5 604	15 463	18 541	18 980	21 095	22 714	24 958	26 000	26 060
5112 Sales tax	2 442	0	5	2	0	0	0	0	0	0
5113 Other	0	0	0	0	0	0	207	245	210	221
Extra-budgetary general taxes on goods and services[1]	..	..	..	..	..	..	136	148	108	114
Local government general taxes on goods and services[1]	..	..	..	..	..	..	72	97	102	108
5120 Taxes on specific goods and services	7 224	9 842	10 893	13 031	12 282	13 660	16 014	17 716	18 301	19 097

Table 4.3. Mauritius / Maurice *(cont.)*
Details of tax revenue / Recettes fiscales détaillées

Million MUR

	1997	2000	2007	2008	2009	2010	2011	2012	2013	2014
5121 Excises	..	..	7 143	8 198	8 506	9 331	11 502	13 052	13 570	14 438
Spirits, liquors and alcoholic beverages	..	..	1 801	2 118	2 124	2 351	3 097	3 705	4 122	4 170
Tobacco products	..	..	2 035	2 479	2 098	2 371	3 039	3 420	3 697	3 823
Motor vehicles and motor cycle	..	..	1 291	1 527	1 852	1 928	1 942	2 340	2 054	2 400
Petroleum products (including MID levy)	..	..	1 939	1 962	2 213	2 421	3 018	3 099	3 069	3 219
PET bottles and other plastic products	..	..	74	112	124	159	205	255	223	242
Sugar content of soft drinks	..	..	0	0	0	0	0	0	177	330
Energy inefficient products	..	..	0	0	0	0	0	0	1	5
Sugar brokerage	..	..	2	0	0	0	0	0	0	0
Extra-budgetary excise taxes[1]	..	..	0	0	0	0	15	13	14	14
Other excises	..	..	0	0	96	101	186	220	214	233
5122 Profits of fiscal monopolies	..	..	0	0	0	0	0	0	0	0
5123 Customs and import duties	..	..	2 158	2 646	1 501	1 525	1 560	1 506	1 390	1 239
5124 Taxes on exports	..	..	0	0	0	0	0	0	0	0
5125 Taxes on investment goods	..	..	0	0	0	0	0	0	0	0
5126 Taxes on specific services	..	..	1 447	1 985	2 137	2 731	2 945	3 152	3 334	3 413
Taxes on the national lottery and other lotteries	..	..	18	14	16	694	623	588	682	652
Betting taxes on horse racing, football, etc.	..	..	402	445	569	658	786	773	793	934
Gaming taxes on casinos and gaming houses	..	..	665	982	962	818	744	495	541	529
Passenger fee on air tickets	..	..	360	543	591	561	793	1 204	1 219	1 213
Levy on messaging services	..	..	0	0	0	0	0	92	99	85
Hotel and restaurant tax	..	..	1	1	0	0	0	0	0	0
5127 Other taxes on internat. trade and transactions	..	..	0	0	0	0	0	0	0	0
5128 Other taxes	..	..	145	201	138	73	7	7	7	7
Temporary solidarity tax on hotels	..	..	145	201	102	0	0	0	0	0
Local government taxes on goods and services	..	..	0	0	37	73	7	7	7	7
5130 Unallocable between 5110 and 5120	..	..	112	127	134	98	14	15	15	16
Extra-budgetary taxes on goods and services[1]	..	..	112	127	134	98	14	15	15	16
5200 Taxes on use of goods and perform activities	1 208	1 271	2 298	2 515	2 749	2 765	3 295	3 313	3 709	4 391
5210 Recurrent taxes	146	203	1 560	1 709	1 861	1 934	2 292	2 368	2 638	2 674
5211 Paid by households: motor vehicles	..	..	732	810	1 023	1 117	1 155	1 211	1 291	1 345
5212 Paid by others: motor vehicles	..	..	0	0	0	0	0	0	0	0
5213 Paid in respect of other goods	146	203	828	899	838	816	1 137	1 157	1 347	1 329
Company licences	0	0	127	136	154	148	156	160	236	235
Incorporation & lodging fees, search duty, etc.	0	0	8	11	9	9	10	9	18	18
Tourist enterprise licences	0	0	47	61	69	74	81	81	85	85
Gambling licences	0	0	47	69	89	100	224	349	352	317
Liquor licences	0	0	10	10	11	10	25	21	24	23
Freeport licences	0	0	1	5	5	0	0	2	8	7
Pharmacy licences	0	0	1	1	5	1	1	1	1	1
Fishing vessel licences	0	0	49	30	33	52	39	43	64	54
Registration of factories	0	0	2	2	2	2	3	3	3	3
Registration of associations	0	0	1	2	2	2	2	2	1	1
Recruitment licences	0	0	0	0	0	2	0	0	0	0
Environment protection fee	0	0	186	209	159	141	302	145	130	160
Advertising structure fee	0	0	0	0	0	0	0	62	68	67
Regional government taxes on use of goods and permission to use goods[1]	0	0	11	16	19	20	21	27	62	45
Local government taxes on use of goods and permission to use goods[1]	0	0	2	3	2	2	3	2	3	3
Other recurrent taxes on goods and activities	146	203	336	346	281	255	271	251	295	311
5220 Non-recurrent taxes	..	..	738	806	888	832	1 003	944	1 071	1 716
Processing fee on application for acquisition of Integrated Resort Scheme (IRS), Real Estate Scheme (RES) and Invest-Hotel Scheme (IHS)	..	..	0	0	0	0	0	0	2	3
Registration duty on transfer of motor vehicles	..	..	657	764	792	794	818	895	972	1 196
Land conversion tax	..	..	82	43	96	38	185	49	96	518
5300 Unallocable between 5100 and 5200	..	..	0	0	0	0	0	0	0	0
6000 Other taxes	**11**	**12**	**147**	**169**	**150**	**164**	**183**	**189**	**184**	**209**
Mauritius Revenue Authority penalties	..	..	..	..	..	..	..	34	34	59
Unidentified local government taxes[1]	..	..	..	..	..	..	..	18	19	20
Unidentified taxes	11	12	147	169	150	164	183	137	131	130
6100 Paid solely by business	..	..	..	..	..	..	..	..	..	..
6200 Other	..	..	..	..	..	..	..	..	..	..

Note: Year ending 31st December. Data are on a July(n-1)/June(n) fiscal year basis for years prior to 2010 and are on a calendar year basis from 2010 onwards. For example, the data for 2009 represent July 2008 to June 2009.

Data for the central government budgetary tax prior to 2007 and all extra-budgetary, regional and local data were classified according to the IMF Government Finance Statistics Manual. The 1986 manual was used for data up to 2009 and the 2001 manual for data up to 2009 onwards. Data from 2007 onwards are classified according to OECD classification.

Heading 1210: the Solidarity Levy on Telecommunications Companies, the Corporate Social Responsibility Tax and the Special Contribution from Hotels are classified as "other taxes" by the Mauritius Revenue Authority.

Heading 2000: Social Security contributions collected by the central government are taken from the IMF GFS 2001 dataset.

Heading 5213: the Environment Protection Fee and Advertising Structure Fee are classified as other taxes by the Mauritius Revenue Authority.

Heading 5220: includes the Registration Duty on Transfer of Motor Vehicles and the Land Conversion Tax that are classified as taxes on property by the Mauritius Revenue Authority.

1. Values for 2013 and 2014 are estimated.

Source: Mauritius Revenue Authority for the central government budgetary tax data from 2007 to 2014; Statistics Mauritius for extra-budgetary, local and regional government tax revenues from 1990 to 2014; Statistics Mauritius for budgetary central government tax revenues up to 2006.

StatLink http://dx.doi.org/10.1787/888933344738

Table 4.4. Morocco / Maroc
Details of tax revenue / Recettes fiscales détaillées

Million MAR

	1997	2000	2007	2008	2009	2010	2011	2012	2013	2014
Recettes fiscales totales	..	**97 565**	**184 758**	**218 394**	**204 025**	**212 990**	**235 716**	**252 008**	**256 522**	**263 566**
1000 Impôts sur revenu, bénéfices et gains en capital	..	**23 656**	**58 515**	**80 204**	**69 769**	**62 646**	**69 071**	**77 317**	**75 636**	**76 342**
1100 Des personnes physiques	..	14 540	28 262	33 614	27 116	26 598	29 405	33 717	34 846	34 573
1110 Sur le revenu et les bénéfices	..	12 473	22 864	26 118	23 324	22 391	24 727	28 492	30 046	30 651
Salaires	..	10 829	20 236	22 421	19 396	19 409	21 769	25 052	25 815	26 452
Revenus professionnels	..	1 645	2 628	3 698	3 928	2 982	2 958	3 440	4 232	4 199
1120 Sur les gains en capital	..	2 067	5 398	7 496	3 793	4 207	4 678	5 225	4 799	3 922
1200 Des sociétés	..	9 116	30 253	46 590	42 653	36 049	39 667	43 600	40 790	41 769
1210 Sur les bénéfices	..	8 330	26 062	41 606	38 808	31 164	34 277	37 936	33 579	34 327
Bénéfices	..	8 084	24 968	40 253	36 943	29 381	32 409	34 896	31 580	31 017
Produits bruts versés aux sociétés étrangères	..	246	1 094	1 353	1 865	1 783	1 868	3 039	1 999	3 310
1220 Sur les gains en capitals	..	786	4 191	4 984	3 845	4 884	5 390	5 665	7 211	7 442
1300 Non-ventilables entre 1100 et 1200	..	0	0	0	0	0	0	0	0	0
2000 Cotisations de sécurité sociale	..	**16 309**	**28 601**	**26 617**	**29 768**	**31 495**	**43 330**	**45 568**	**50 017**	**54 900**
2100 A la charge des salariés	..	..	..	..	..	..	..	..	..	..
2110 Sur la base du salaire	..	..	..	..	..	..	..	..	..	..
2120 Sur la base de l'impôt sur les revenus	..	..	..	..	..	..	..	..	..	..
2200 A la charge des employeurs	..	..	..	..	..	..	..	..	..	..
2210 Sur la base du salaire	..	..	..	..	..	..	..	..	..	..
2220 Sur la base de l'impôt sur le revenu	..	..	..	..	..	..	..	..	..	..
2300 A charge des travailleurs indép. ou sans emploi	..	..	..	..	..	..	..	..	..	..
2310 Sur la base du salaire	..	..	..	..	..	..	..	..	..	..
2320 Sur la base de l'impôt sur le revenu	..	..	..	..	..	..	..	..	..	..
2400 Non-ventilables entre 2100, 2200 et 2300	..	..	..	..	..	..	..	..	..	..
2410 Sur la base du salaire	..	..	..	..	..	..	..	..	..	..
2420 Sur la base de l'impôt sur le revenu	..	..	..	..	..	..	..	..	..	..
3000 Sur salaires ou main d'oeuvre	..	**0**	**0**	**0**	**0**	**0**	**0**	**0**	**0**	**0**
4000 Impôts sur le patrimoine	..	**5 405**	**11 423**	**11 930**	**10 988**	**12 702**	**13 137**	**15 456**	**17 002**	**17 906**
4100 Impôts périodiques sur la propriété immobilière	..	3 340	4 935	4 592	4 983	5 740	5 485	5 770	7 397	6 081
4110 Ménages	..	1 989	3 337	2 977	3 282	3 898	3 564	3 770	4 878	3 857
Taxe d'habitation	..	517	771	317	295	382	297	290	430	271
Taxe sur les terrains non bâtis	..	135	497	602	717	839	627	831	1 121	901
Taxe sur les services communaux	..	1 337	2 069	2 058	2 270	2 677	2 640	2 649	3 327	2 685
4120 Autres agents	..	1 351	1 598	1 615	1 701	1 842	1 920	2 000	2 519	2 224
4200 Impôts périodiques sur l'actif net	..	0	0	0	0	0	0	0	0	0
4210 Personnes physiques	..	..	..	..	..	..	..	..	..	..
4220 Sociétés	..	..	..	..	..	..	..	..	..	..
4300 Impôts sur mut. par décès, succ. et donations	..	0	0	0	0	0	0	0	0	0
4310 Impôts sur mut. par décès et successions	..	..	..	..	..	..	..	..	..	..
4320 Impôts sur les donations	..	..	..	..	..	..	..	..	..	..
4400 Impôts sur transact. mobilières et immob.	..	2 065	6 488	7 338	6 005	6 962	7 652	9 686	9 605	11 825
4500 Impôts non-périodiques	..	0	0	0	0	0	0	0	0	0
4510 Sur l'actif net	..	..	..	..	..	..	..	..	..	..
4520 Autres non-périodiques	..	..	..	..	..	..	..	..	..	..
4600 Autres impôts périodiques sur patrimoine	..	0	0	0	0	0	0	0	0	0
5000 Impôts sur les biens et services	..	**50 655**	**82 569**	**95 959**	**89 282**	**101 384**	**106 168**	**109 460**	**109 215**	**110 024**
5100 Impôts sur production, vente, transfert, etc.	..	49 539	80 675	93 911	86 882	99 056	103 842	106 929	106 303	107 068
5110 Impôts généraux	..	21 476	49 695	61 228	55 077	65 247	71 321	74 772	75 260	74 995
5111 Taxes sur la valeur ajoutée	..	21 476	49 695	61 228	55 077	65 247	71 321	74 772	75 260	74 995
5112 Impôts sur les ventes	..	0	0	0	0	0	0	0	0	0
5113 Autres impôts	..	0	0	0	0	0	0	0	0	0
5120 Impôts sur biens et services déterminés	..	28 063	30 980	32 683	31 805	33 809	32 521	32 157	31 043	32 073
5121 Accises	..	15 223	17 489	18 872	19 843	21 382	22 086	22 983	23 150	24 119
Taxes intérieures de consommation	..	15 183	17 341	18 693	19 629	21 132	21 861	22 731	22 873	23 849
Taxe sur la vente de produits forestiers	..	4	15	19	22	26	24	24	31	20
Taxe sur les débits de boissons	..	23	85	102	122	143	131	138	161	156
Taxe sur les eaux minerales et de table	..	13	48	58	70	81	70	90	85	94
5122 Bénéfices des monopoles fiscaux	..	0	0	0	0	0	0	0	0	0
5123 Droits de douane et droits à l'importation	..	12 810	13 382	13 679	11 805	12 242	10 262	9 003	7 681	7 738
5124 Taxes à l'exportation	..	0	0	0	0	0	0	0	0	0
5125 Impôts sur biens d'équipement	..	0	0	0	0	0	0	0	0	0
5126 Impôts sur services déterminés	..	30	109	132	157	184	174	170	212	216
Taxe de séjour	..	26	95	115	137	160	155	149	178	191
Taxe sur le transport public de voyageurs	..	4	14	17	20	24	19	21	34	25
5127 Autres impôts sur commerce et transact. internat.	..	0	0	0	0	0	0	0	0	0
5128 Autres impôts	..	0	0	0	0	0	0	0	0	0

Table 4.4. Morocco / Maroc *(cont.)*
Details of tax revenue / Recettes fiscales détaillées

Million MAR

	1997	2000	2007	2008	2009	2010	2011	2012	2013	2014
5210 Impôts périodiques	..	964	1 334	1 372	1 594	1 385	1 448	1 560	1 933	1 973
5211 A la charge des ménages: véhicules à moteur	..	959	1 315	1 348	1 566	1 351	1 418	1 525	1 898	1 937
5212 A la charge autres agents: véhicules à moteur	..	0	0	0	0	0	0	0	0	0
5213 Autres impôts périodiques	..	5	20	24	28	33	30	35	35	36
Taxe sur les permis de chasse	..	5	20	24	28	33	30	35	35	36
5220 Impôts non-périodiques	..	152	559	676	805	943	878	971	980	983
Taxe sur les opérations de construction	..	113	416	504	600	703	664	722	720	718
Taxe sur les opérations de lotissement	..	39	142	172	205	240	214	249	260	265
5300 Non-ventilables entre 5100 et 5200	..	0	0	0	0	0	0	0	0	0
6000 Autres impôts	..	**1 540**	**3 650**	**3 684**	**4 218**	**4 762**	**4 010**	**4 207**	**4 651**	**4 394**
Droits de timbres	..	1 132	1 531	1 492	1 537	1 683	1 601	1 853	2 061	2 010
Majorations et pénalités	..	339	1 865	1 885	2 315	2 650	2 055	1 986	1 994	1 740
Taxes locales	..	69	254	307	366	429	354	368	596	644
6100 A la charge exclusive des entreprises	..	..	..	..	..	..	..	..	..	..
6200 A la charge d'autres agents	..	..	..	..	..	..	..	..	..	..

Note: Année civile se terminant le 31 décembre.

Les données autres que les cotisations de sécurité sociale sont sur la base des encaissements.

Les impôts affectés pour les Fonds Spéciaux du Trésor sont compris dans les données pour la période 2000-14.

Les données de cotisations de sécurité sociales sont issues de la base de données des statistiques de finances publiques 2001 (SFP 2001) du FMI. Ces données sont estimées pour les années antérieures à 2005 et pour 2013 et 2014.

Source: Ministère de l'Économie et des Finances.

StatLink http://dx.doi.org/10.1787/888933344742

Table 4.5. Rwanda / Rwanda
Details of tax revenue / Recettes fiscales détaillées

Million RWF

	1997	2000	2007	2008	2009	2010	2011	2012	2013	2014
Total tax revenue	**56 249**	**68 909**	**255 835**	**352 997**	**389 940**	**440 724**	**537 439**	**645 448**	**760 158**	**865 554**
1000 Taxes on income, profits and capital gains	**14 205**	**17 943**	**86 032**	**123 024**	**135 218**	**159 567**	**195 395**	**246 467**	**308 107**	**322 827**
1100 Of individuals	4 313	6 622	48 079	63 400	81 595	102 037	124 133	157 814	182 996	193 212
1110 On income and profits	4 313	6 622	48 079	63 400	81 595	102 037	124 133	157 814	182 996	193 212
1120 On capital gains	0	0	0	0	0	0	0	0	0	0
1200 Corporate	9 893	11 322	37 953	59 624	53 623	57 530	71 262	88 653	125 111	129 615
1210 On profits	9 893	11 322	37 953	59 624	53 623	57 530	71 262	88 653	125 111	129 615
Corporate income taxes	7 245	3 603	9 721	27 788	27 881	26 459	30 756	32 815	48 962	39 157
Withholding Tax	545	59	3 549	5 294	6 932	10 764	16 227	32 383	42 363	49 948
Personal Income Tax	1 045	868	11 526	5 569	6 558	7 316	7 264	7 530	7 828	6 950
Other taxes on profits	0	0	0	0	0	0	0	0	0	0
1300 Unallocable between 1100 and 1200	0	0	0	0	0	0	0	0	0	0
2000 Social security contributions	**1 915**	**3 423**	**16 611**	**23 248**	**25 741**	**28 235**	**35 636**	**42 890**	**53 123**	**55 530**
2100 Employees	717	1 283	6 227	8 717	9 652	10 586	13 361	16 081	19 918	20 821
2110 On a payroll basis	717	1 283	6 227	8 717	9 652	10 586	13 361	16 081	19 918	20 821
2120 On an income tax basis	0	0	0	0	0	0	0	0	0	0
2200 Employers	1 196	2 138	10 378	14 528	16 086	17 644	22 269	26 802	33 197	34 701
2210 On a payroll basis	1 196	2 138	10 378	14 528	16 086	17 644	22 269	26 802	33 197	34 701
2220 On an income tax basis	0	0	0	0	0	0	0	0	0	0
2300 Self-employed or non-employed	2	3	6	4	4	4	6	7	8	9
2310 On a payroll basis	2	3	6	4	4	4	6	7	8	9
2320 On an income tax basis	0	0	0	0	0	0	0	0	0	0
2400 Unallocable between 2100, 2200 and 2300	0	0	0	0	0	0	0	0	0	0
2410 On a payroll basis	..	..	..	..	..	..	..	..	..	..
2420 On an income tax basis	..	..	..	..	..	..	..	..	..	..
3000 Taxes on payroll and workforce	**0**	**0**	**0**	**0**	**0**	**0**	**0**	**0**	**0**	**0**
4000 Taxes on property	**48**	**130**	**28**	**26**	**79**	**97**	**69**	**28**	**18**	**19**
4100 Recurrent taxes on immovable property	48	130	27	25	78	96	69	28	18	19
4110 Households	48	130	27	25	78	96	69	28	18	19
4120 Others	0	0	0	0	0	0	0	0	0	0
4200 Recurrent taxes on net wealth	0	0	0	0	0	0	0	0	0	0
4210 Individual	..	..	..	..	..	..	..	..	..	..
4220 Corporate	..	..	..	..	..	..	..	..	..	..
4300 Estate, inheritance and gift taxes	0	0	0	0	0	0	0	0	0	0
4310 Estate and inheritance taxes	..	..	..	..	..	..	..	..	..	..
4320 Gift taxes	..	..	..	..	..	..	..	..	..	..
4400 Taxes on financial and capital transactions	0	0	0	0	0	0	0	0	0	0
4500 Non-recurrent taxes	0	0	0	0	0	0	0	0	0	0
4510 On net wealth	..	..	..	..	..	..	..	..	..	..
4520 Other non-recurrent taxes	..	..	..	..	..	..	..	..	..	..
4600 Other recurrent taxes on property	0	0	1	2	1	0	0	0	0	0
5000 Taxes on goods and services	**40 081**	**47 413**	**153 164**	**206 698**	**228 901**	**252 826**	**306 339**	**356 062**	**398 910**	**487 178**
5100 Taxes on production, sale, transfer, etc	39 683	46 777	152 158	205 614	227 785	250 214	304 131	352 857	397 084	485 735
5110 General taxes	7 485	13 777	85 286	116 862	125 055	131 665	156 082	186 016	219 501	279 275
5111 Value added taxes	7 485	13 777	85 286	116 862	125 055	131 665	156 082	186 016	219 501	279 275
5112 Sales tax	0	0	0	0	0	0	0	0	0	0
5113 Other	0	0	0	0	0	0	0	0	0	0
5120 Taxes on specific goods and services	32 198	32 999	66 872	88 752	102 730	118 548	148 049	166 842	177 583	206 461
5121 Excises	11 637	18 849	31 928	39 184	55 078	75 236	98 005	99 071	105 304	121 220
Beers	8 109	7 146	13 895	17 937	19 311	22 548	28 760	33 372	34 319	36 872
Petroleum	540	7 857	5 062	6 558	16 605	30 941	40 346	33 489	35 982	37 283
Other Excises	2 988	3 846	12 972	14 689	19 162	21 746	28 900	32 210	35 003	47 065
5122 Profits of fiscal monopolies	0	0	0	0	0	0	0	0	0	0
5123 Customs and import duties	16 299	14 151	34 944	49 568	47 620	43 313	50 044	67 770	72 280	85 241
Import duties	12 447	9 260	26 953	40 054	35 303	26 215	31 413	45 891	46 448	55 106
Road fund	2 077	2 531	6 276	7 378	9 833	14 843	17 219	20 588	23 865	25 167
Other Customs and import duties	1 776	2 360	1 714	2 137	2 484	2 254	1 412	1 292	1 967	4 968
5124 Taxes on exports	4 262	0	0	0	33	0	0	0	0	0
5125 Taxes on investment goods	0	0	0	0	0	0	0	0	0	0
5126 Taxes on specific services	0	0	0	0	0	0	0	0	0	0
5127 Other taxes on internat. trade and transactions	0	0	0	0	0	0	0	0	0	0
5128 Other taxes	0	0	0	0	0	0	0	0	0	0
5130 Unallocable between 5110 and 5120	0	0	0	0	0	0	0	0	0	0
5200 Taxes on use of goods and perform activities	398	636	1 005	1 084	1 116	2 612	2 208	3 205	1 825	1 442
5210 Recurrent taxes	398	636	1 005	1 084	1 116	2 612	2 208	3 205	1 825	1 442
5211 Paid by households: motor vehicles	398	636	1 005	1 084	1 116	2 612	2 208	3 205	1 825	1 442

Table 4.5. Rwanda / Rwanda (cont.)
Details of tax revenue / Recettes fiscales détaillées

Million RWF

	1997	2000	2007	2008	2009	2010	2011	2012	2013	2014
5220 Non-recurrent taxes	0	0	0	0	0	0	0	0	0	0
5300 Unallocable between 5100 and 5200	0	0	0	0	0	0	0	0	0	0
6000 Other taxes	**0**	**0**	**0**	**0**	**0**	**0**	**0**	**0**	**0**	**0**
6100 Paid solely by business	..	..	..	..	..	..	..	..	..	..
6200 Other	..	..	..	..	..	..	..	..	..	..

Note: Year ending 31st December. From 2008, the figures for social security contributions are on a fiscal year basis beginning 1st July. For example, data for 2010 represent July 2009 to June 2010.

The data are on a cash basis.

Figures exclude local government tax revenues as the data are not available.

Heading 2000: Rwanda does not include social security contributions in their tax revenue data as the Rwandan authorities do not consider them as taxes.

Source: Rwanda Revenue Authority.

StatLink http://dx.doi.org/10.1787/888933344750

Table 4.6. Senegal / Sénégal
Details of tax revenue / Recettes fiscales détaillées

Million XOF

	1997	2000	2007	2008	2009	2010	2011	2012	2013	2014
Recettes fiscales totales	**417 544**	**559 295**	**1 085 663**	**1 139 131**	**1 138 498**	**1 267 799**	**1 346 487**	**1 419 281**	**1 414 720**	**1 558 565**
1000 Impôts sur revenu, bénéfices et gains en capital	**87 500**	**123 771**	**221 880**	**262 980**	**275 078**	**328 200**	**333 200**	**384 040**	**373 800**	**398 500**
1100 Des personnes physiques	53 600	64 021	122 840	152 880	175 378	192 900	213 700	240 640	217 300	238 200
1110 Sur le revenu et les bénéfices	53 000	63 370	120 640	151 300	173 578	191 000	211 400	238 140	214 400	234 700
1120 Sur les gains en capital	600	651	2 200	1 580	1 800	1 900	2 300	2 500	2 900	3 500
1200 Des sociétés	29 000	49 418	78 740	86 700	78 000	106 100	98 000	113 900	135 700	133 800
1210 Sur les bénéfices	29 000	49 418	78 740	86 700	78 000	106 100	98 000	113 900	135 700	133 800
1220 Sur les gains en capitals	..	..	..	..	..	..	..	..	..	..
1300 Non-ventilables entre 1100 et 1200	4 900	10 332	20 300	23 400	21 700	29 200	21 500	29 500	20 800	26 500
2000 Cotisations de sécurité sociale	**16 474**	**22 215**	**44 233**	**51 943**	**53 889**	**72 999**	**59 627**	**67 611**	**72 000**	**76 065**
2100 A la charge des salariés	..	..	..	..	..	..	..	..	..	..
2110 Sur la base du salaire	..	..	..	..	..	..	..	..	..	..
2120 Sur la base de l'impôt sur les revenus	..	..	..	..	..	..	..	..	..	..
2200 A la charge des employeurs	..	..	..	..	..	..	..	..	..	..
2210 Sur la base du salaire	..	..	..	..	..	..	..	..	..	..
2220 Sur la base de l'impôt sur le revenu	..	..	..	..	..	..	..	..	..	..
2300 A charge des travailleurs indép. ou sans emploi	..	..	..	..	..	..	..	..	..	..
2310 Sur la base du salaire	..	..	..	..	..	..	..	..	..	..
2320 Sur la base de l'impôt sur le revenu	..	..	..	..	..	..	..	..	..	..
2400 Non-ventilables entre 2100, 2200 et 2300	..	..	..	..	..	..	..	..	..	..
2410 Sur la base du salaire	..	..	..	..	..	..	..	..	..	..
2420 Sur la base de l'impôt sur le revenu	..	..	..	..	..	..	..	..	..	..
3000 Sur salaires ou main d'oeuvre	**5 650**	**6 668**	**9 700**	**9 600**	**10 000**	**10 800**	**12 400**	**15 100**	**16 100**	**16 900**
4000 Impôts sur le patrimoine	**9 900**	**11 200**	**27 800**	**32 200**	**33 200**	**39 100**	**38 200**	**37 200**	**36 600**	**39 600**
4100 Impôts périodiques sur la propriété immobilière	0	0	0	0	0	0	0	0	0	0
4110 Ménages	..	..	..	..	..	..	..	..	..	..
4120 Autres agents	..	..	..	..	..	..	..	..	..	..
4200 Impôts périodiques sur l'actif net	0	0	0	0	0	0	0	0	0	0
4210 Personnes physiques	..	..	..	..	..	..	..	..	..	..
4220 Sociétés	..	..	..	..	..	..	..	..	..	..
4300 Impôts sur mut. par décès, succ. et donations	2 178	2 464	6 116	6 620	5 481	12 445	9 669	7 651	7 809	8 086
4310 Impôts sur mut. par décès et successions	..	..	..	..	..	..	..	..	..	..
4320 Impôts sur les donations	..	..	..	..	..	..	..	..	..	..
4400 Impôts sur transact. mobilières et immob.	7 722	8 736	21 684	25 580	27 719	26 655	28 531	29 549	28 791	31 514
Droits de mutation sur vente ou échanges d'immeubles	..	..	..	13 939	16 388	15 418	15 710	19 398	15 713	18 352
Droits d'enregistrement autre que patrimoine	..	..	..	11 640	11 331	11 237	12 821	10 151	13 078	13 162
4500 Impôts non-périodiques	0	0	0	0	0	0	0	0	0	0
4510 Sur l'actif net	..	..	..	..	..	..	..	..	..	..
4520 Autres non-périodiques	..	..	..	..	..	..	..	..	..	..
4600 Autres impôts périodiques sur patrimoine	0	0	0	0	0	0	0	0	0	0
5000 Impôts sur les biens et services	**291 820**	**386 940**	**769 050**	**769 408**	**754 431**	**804 400**	**890 060**	**902 830**	**900 820**	**1 010 700**
5100 Impôts sur production, vente, transfert, etc.	289 920	384 590	765 050	764 508	749 731	799 400	884 060	896 830	894 420	1 002 700
5110 Impôts généraux	146 240	221 410	436 700	435 001	432 821	478 000	518 930	522 090	512 200	561 400
5111 Taxes sur la valeur ajoutée	146 240	221 410	436 700	435 001	432 821	478 000	518 930	522 090	512 200	561 400
5112 Impôts sur les ventes	0	0	0	0	0	0	0	0	0	0
5113 Autres impôts	0	0	0	0	0	0	0	0	0	0
5120 Impôts sur biens et services déterminés	143 680	163 180	328 350	329 507	316 910	321 400	365 130	374 740	382 220	441 300
5121 Accises	6 140	61 100	87 300	78 940	83 600	82 600	77 800	79 800	76 095	84 100
Taxe spécifique sur les prod. pétroliers	..	..	71 900	64 040	59 300	63 900	55 600	53 800	53 740	59 600
Taxes sur les tabacs	..	..	8 212	7 661	9 016	9 647	9 931	13 116	13 205	13 289
Taxes sur les corps gras	..	..	1 093	962	1 745	978	993	1 375	2 648	1 447
Taxes sur les alcools	..	..	3 985	4 224	5 987	5 297	5 278	4 975	5 498	5 382
Taxe sur la cola	..	..	429	247	439	273	203	183	48	26
Taxe sur les thés	..	..	140	162	334	154	95	102	125	124
Taxe sur le café	..	..	160	160	502	175	216	153	285	367
Taxe sur les produits comestiques	..	..	0	0	0	0	0	0	500	1 400
Autres accises non classées ailleurs	..	..	1 381	1 485	6 277	2 176	5 484	6 096	45	2 466
5122 Bénéfices des monopoles fiscaux	0	0	0	0	0	0	0	0	0	0
5123 Droits de douane et droits à l'importation	129 500	90 340	185 300	190 067	163 810	181 600	203 800	195 200	218 000	221 100
5124 Taxes à l'exportation	0	0	0	0	0	0	0	0	0	0
5125 Impôts sur biens d'équipement	0	0	0	0	0	0	0	0	0	0
5126 Impôts sur services déterminés	8 040	11 740	30 000	27 100	37 600	45 000	55 900	62 500	63 825	69 500
Taxe sur les activités financières (TAF)	6 400	9 340	25 200	23 100	28 500	30 600	34 300	39 100	40 340	45 800
Redevance d'utilisation des télécommunications	0	0	0	0	5 100	10 000	16 700	18 600	18 645	18 700
Taxe sur les contrats d'assurances	1 640	2 400	4 800	4 000	4 000	4 400	4 900	4 800	4 840	5 000

Table 4.6. Senegal / Sénégal *(cont.)*
Details of tax revenue / Recettes fiscales détaillées

Million XOF

	1997	2000	2007	2008	2009	2010	2011	2012	2013	2014
5128 Autres impôts	0	0	25 750	33 400	31 900	12 200	27 630	37 240	24 300	66 600
Fonds de sécurisation des importations de produits pétroliers	..	..	25 750	33 400	31 900	12 200	27 630	32 240	19 400	62 600
Contribution spéciale des produits des mines et carrières	..	..	0	0	0	0	0	5 000	4 900	4 000
5130 Non-ventilables entre 5110 et 5120	0	0	0	0	0	0	0	0	0	0
5200 Impôts sur utilisation des biens et exerc. activites	1 900	2 350	4 000	4 900	4 700	5 000	6 000	6 000	6 400	8 000
5210 Impôts périodiques	1 900	2 350	4 000	4 900	4 700	5 000	6 000	6 000	6 400	8 000
5211 A la charge des ménages: véhicules à moteur	..	..	..	..	..	..	..	..	..	..
5212 A la charge autres agents: véhicules à moteur	..	..	..	..	..	..	..	..	..	..
5213 Autres impôts périodiques	..	..	..	..	..	..	..	..	..	..
5220 Impôts non-périodiques	0	0	0	0	0	0	0	0	0	0
5300 Non-ventilables entre 5100 et 5200	0	0	0	0	0	0	0	0	0	0
6000 Autres impôts	**6 200**	**8 500**	**13 000**	**13 000**	**11 900**	**12 300**	**13 000**	**12 500**	**15 400**	**16 800**
6100 A la charge exclusive des entreprises	..	..	..	..	..	..	..	..	..	..
6200 A la charge d'autres agents	..	..	..	..	..	..	..	..	..	..

Note: Année civile se terminant le 31 décembre.

Les données sont sur la base des encaissements.

Les chiffres n'incluent pas les données des collectivités locales car elles ne sont pas disponibles.

Les chiffres ne comprennent pas les taxes parafiscales car elles ne sont pas disponibles. Les taxes parafiscales pourraient s'élever à un montant d'environ 70 milliards, objectif programmé du gouvernement dans la loi de finances 2015.

La rubrique 2000 comprend les cotisations de sécurité sociale de l'Institution de prévoyance retraite du Sénégal (IPRES) à partir de 2006. Les données antérieures sont estimées et les données 2014 sont provisoires. Ces données sont intégrées dans le tableau d'ensemble de manière statistique, car elles ne proviennent pas encore d'une comptabilité déposée auprès du Trésor. Les données des cotisations de sécurité sociale de la Caisse de sécurité sociale (CSS) ne sont pas disponibles.

La rubrique 5126 comprend la Redevance sur l'accès ou l'utilisation du réseau des télécommunications publiques (RUTEL) classifiée comme accise au Sénégal.

Source: Ministère de l'Économie, des Finances et du Plan.

StatLink http://dx.doi.org/10.1787/888933344765

Table 4.7. South Africa / Afrique du Sud
Details of tax revenue / Recettes fiscales détaillées

Million ZAR

	1997	2000	2007	2008	2009	2010	2011	2012	2013	2014
Total tax revenue	**158 556**	**211 566**	**580 869**	**655 266**	**644 142**	**702 316**	**794 345**	**872 171**	**966 559**	**1 056 866**
1000 Taxes on income, profits and capital gains	**89 772**	**119 979**	**317 850**	**370 816**	**357 740**	**368 118**	**412 135**	**447 924**	**490 305**	**541 543**
1100 Of individuals	65 681	87 105	160 814	189 698	198 117	219 886	243 056	267 952	300 559	338 974
1110 On income and profits	65 681	87 105	160 814	189 698	198 117	219 886	243 056	267 952	300 559	338 974
1120 On capital gains	0	0	0	0	0	0	0	0	0	0
1200 Corporate	19 409	23 987	137 885	160 235	142 319	132 275	149 777	155 751	173 738	182 083
1210 On profits	19 409	23 987	137 885	160 235	142 319	132 275	149 777	155 751	173 738	182 083
1220 On capital gains	0	0	0	0	0	0	0	0	0	0
1300 Unallocable between 1100 and 1200	4 682	8 887	19 151	20 884	17 303	15 957	19 303	24 220	16 008	20 486
2000 Social security contributions	**0**	**0**	**8 648**	**9 867**	**10 455**	**10 754**	**11 947**	**13 788**	**13 909**	**15 337**
2100 Employees	..	..	4 324	4 934	5 227	5 377	5 974	6 894	6 955	7 669
2110 On a payroll basis	..	..	0	0	0	0	0	0	0	0
2120 On an income tax basis	..	..	4 324	4 934	5 227	5 377	5 974	6 894	6 955	7 669
2200 Employers	..	..	4 324	4 934	5 227	5 377	5 974	6 894	6 955	7 669
2210 On a payroll basis	..	..	0	0	0	0	0	0	0	0
2220 On an income tax basis	..	..	4 324	4 934	5 227	5 377	5 974	6 894	6 955	7 669
2300 Self-employed or non-employed	..	..	0	0	0	0	0	0	0	0
2310 On a payroll basis	..	..	..	..	..	..	..	..	..	..
2320 On an income tax basis	..	..	..	..	..	..	..	..	..	..
2400 Unallocable between 2100, 2200 and 2300	..	..	0	0	0	0	0	0	0	0
2410 On a payroll basis	..	..	..	..	..	..	..	..	..	..
2420 On an income tax basis	..	..	..	..	..	..	..	..	..	..
3000 Taxes on payroll and workforce	**0**	**870**	**6 177**	**7 024**	**7 737**	**8 240**	**9 885**	**11 334**	**11 900**	**13 264**
4000 Taxes on property	**2 592**	**3 829**	**18 491**	**28 980**	**31 700**	**36 257**	**39 296**	**42 129**	**48 182**	**53 513**
4100 Recurrent taxes on immovable property	0	0	6 588	18 789	23 159	27 190	31 041	33 984	38 150	41 502
4110 Households	..	..	6 387	18 437	22 566	26 694	30 533	33 502	37 659	40 950
4120 Others	..	..	200	351	593	496	509	482	491	551
4200 Recurrent taxes on net wealth	0	0	0	0	0	0	0	0	0	0
4210 Individual	..	..	..	..	..	..	..	..	..	..
4220 Corporate	..	..	..	..	..	..	..	..	..	..
4300 Estate, inheritance and gift taxes	304	436	761	783	888	855	1 065	887	1 266	1 519
4310 Estate and inheritance taxes	287	417	727	672	815	794	1 013	820	1 163	1 349
4320 Gift taxes	17	19	34	111	73	61	53	67	103	170
4400 Taxes on financial and capital transactions	439	1 094	3 564	3 863	3 294	2 912	2 919	3 147	3 617	4 098
4500 Non-recurrent taxes	1 850	2 299	7 577	5 546	4 359	5 300	4 270	4 112	5 149	6 394
4510 On net wealth	0	0	0	0	0	0	0	0	0	0
4520 Other non-recurrent taxes	1 850	2 299	7 577	5 546	4 359	5 300	4 270	4 112	5 149	6 394
4600 Other recurrent taxes on property	0	0	0	0	0	0	0	0	0	0
5000 Taxes on goods and services	**64 471**	**84 467**	**228 744**	**236 908**	**237 451**	**278 924**	**321 102**	**356 967**	**402 257**	**433 237**
5100 Taxes on production, sale, transfer, etc	64 471	84 467	224 552	232 555	233 027	273 602	315 028	350 226	394 896	425 654
5110 General taxes	39 461	52 059	146 062	151 905	148 721	170 548	194 296	207 480	231 545	256 482
5111 Value added taxes	39 461	52 059	146 062	151 905	148 708	170 552	194 295	207 472	231 528	256 464
5112 Sales tax	0	0	0	0	14	-5	1	9	16	17
5113 Other	0	0	0	0	0	0	0	0	0	0
5120 Taxes on specific goods and services	25 010	32 408	78 490	80 650	84 306	103 054	120 732	142 746	163 352	169 172
5121 Excises	19 091	24 341	50 441	53 981	63 158	76 240	87 407	96 044	103 156	112 446
5122 Profits of fiscal monopolies	0	0	0	0	0	0	0	0	0	0
5123 Customs and import duties	6 273	7 714	25 423	24 216	19 134	25 196	30 930	43 584	54 881	54 631
Import duties	..	..	25 423	24 216	19 134	25 196	30 930	37 470	42 794	44 390
Ad valorem Imported	..	..	0	0	0	0	0	4 251	8 011	7 573
Excise Imported	..	..	0	0	0	0	0	1 862	4 076	2 668
5124 Taxes on exports	0	0	0	0	19	61	65	60	72	118
5125 Taxes on investment goods	0	0	0	0	0	0	0	0	0	0
5126 Taxes on specific services	0	0	1 907	2 026	1 922	2 252	2 405	2 792	2 967	2 992
5127 Other taxes on internat. trade and transactions	-353	353	720	427	73	-695	-74	266	2 276	-1 015
5128 Other taxes	0	0	0	0	0	0	0	0	0	0
5130 Unallocable between 5110 and 5120	0	0	0	0	0	0	0	0	0	0
5200 Taxes on use of goods and perform activities	0	0	4 192	4 354	4 424	5 322	6 073	6 741	7 361	7 583
5210 Recurrent taxes	0	0	4 192	4 354	4 424	5 322	6 073	6 741	7 361	7 583
5211 Paid by households: motor vehicles	..	..	3 190	3 303	3 321	4 046	4 762	5 224	5 742	5 879
5212 Paid by others: motor vehicles	..	..	798	826	830	1 012	1 191	1 306	1 436	1 470
5213 Paid in respect of other goods	..	..	204	225	273	264	120	210	184	234
5220 Non-recurrent taxes	0	0	0	0	0	0	0	0	0	0
5300 Unallocable between 5100 and 5200	0	0	0	0	0	0	0	0	0	0
6000 Other taxes	**1 721**	**2 421**	**959**	**1 671**	**-941**	**23**	**-20**	**29**	**5**	**-29**
6100 Paid solely by business	0	0	0	0	0	0	0	0	0	0

Note: Year ending 31st December. Some fiscal years data have been adjusted to align to calendar years. Social security contributions and taxes at provincial and local level are reported on a fiscal year basis beginning 1st April. For example, the data for 2006 data represent April 2006 to March 2007.

Data prior to 1995/96 were restated retrospectively to aggregate the revenues from TBVC States and Self-Governing Territories. With the adoption of the interim Constitution in 1994, these were abolished.

- TBVC States: Transkei, Bophuthatswana, Venda and Ciskei.
- Self-Governing Territories: Gazankulu, Kangwane, Kwandebele, Kwazulu, Lebowa and Qwaqwa.

Tax revenues on national and provincial government level in South Africa are on a cash basis, while local authorities and public entities are on an accrual basis.

Tax revenues at the local and provincial levels are only available from 2003 (representing fiscal year 2003/04).

Headings 1110 and 1120: Capital Gains Tax (CGT) cannot been listed separately under 1120 and 1220 because the data that South African Revenue Service (SARS) collated for CGT are for liability raised and not actual CGT collections received. The CGT is included under 1110. The figures exclude interest and fines from 1994 onwards.

Heading 2000: the social security contributions in South Africa consist of contributions to the Unemployment Insurance Fund (UIF). Standard practice in South Africa is to classify UIF under non-tax revenue. The methodology applied in the compilation of the data was to allocate 50% of the total social security contributions (UIF) to each of employees and employers.

Heading 4120: the figures refer to penalties and collection charges on property rates.

Heading 5111: includes interests and fines.

Heading 5121: following the OECD classification, the Road accident fund (RAF) is classified as an excise tax as opposed to a social security contribution.

Headings 5121 and 5123: The data for customs duties and excise include revenue for Botswana, Lesotho, Namibia and Swaziland (BLNS) on import duties plus specific and ad valorem excise duties.

Heading 5123: SARS only started separately reporting ordinary custom duties on imported goods, specific excise duties on imported goods and ad valorem duties on imported goods from April 2012. From April 2014 onwards, the Customs Duty amounts for the specific tariff headings under chapter 27 (Mineral Fuels) were treated as fuel levies (5121 Excises).

Headings 5127 and 6200: include negative figures due to refund accounting adjustments.

Heading 5211: an 80:20 ratio was used to split provincial recurrent motor vehicle taxes based on research about South Africa's commercial and private household motor vehicle fleet.

Heading 6200: includes stamp duties and fees plus unallocated tax revenue.

Taxes that were discontinued and introduced (causing breaks in the data) include the following:

a. Ordinary levy discontinued in March 2003 (heading 5121).
b. Demutualisation charge has been included in heading 4400. There were two collections in March 1999 and August 1999.
c. Secondary Tax on Companies (STC) in heading 4400 effective from July 1993 and changed to Dividends Tax (DT) in April 2012.
d. Small business tax amnesty (heading 1300) effective from March 2007.
e. VAT (heading 5111) effective from September 1991 at a rate of 10% and increased to 14% in 1993. Prior to that, sales tax data was restated to VAT.
f. Levy on financial services (heading 4400) effective from January 1992.
g. Skills development levy (heading 3000) effective from May 2000.
h. Excises (5121)
 - Plastic bags effective from June 2005.
 - Electricity levy effective from August 2009.
 - Incandescent light bulbs effective from March 2010.
 - CO2 tax effective from September 2010.
i. Air departure tax (heading 5126) effective from December 2000.
j. Universal services fund (heading 5213) effective from March 2006.

Source: Data on national government taxation from the South African Revenue Service (SARS); data on social security contributions, and taxes levied at the provincial and local level from the National Treasury of South Africa.

StatLink http://dx.doi.org/10.1787/888933344778

Table 4.8. Tunisia / Tunisie

Details of tax revenue / Recettes fiscales détaillées

Million TND

	1997	2000	2007	2008	2009	2010	2011	2012	2013	2014
Recettes fiscales totales	..	**7 237**	**12 628**	**14 903**	**15 786**	**17 235**	**18 843**	**20 539**	**22 540**	**25 228**
1000 Impôts sur revenu, bénéfices et gains en capital	..	**1 624**	**3 744**	**4 611**	**4 701**	**5 091**	**5 959**	**5 921**	**6 878**	**7 959**
1100 Des personnes physiques	..	1 049	1 995	2 195	2 435	2 657	2 918	3 188	3 711	4 096
1110 Sur le revenu et les bénéfices	..	1 037	1 987	2 187	2 423	2 644	2 905	3 173	3 686	4 057
Traitements et salaires	..	742	1 473	1 606	1 843	2 006	2 326	2 640	3 068	3 261
Honoraires, commissions, courtage et loyers	..	20	124	143	158	184	177	180	205	236
Intérêts des dépôts des comptes spéciaux d'épargne	..	65	58	66	61	68	90	82	102	125
Revenus des capitaux mobiliers	..	32	67	82	79	75	62	57	69	87
Avances sur les marchés	..	27	42	47	48	50	45	41	46	57
Bénéfices industriels et commerciaux	..	43	71	75	89	94	78	76	95	98
Bénéfices non commerciaux	..	17	28	28	39	49	44	41	46	71
Impôt forfaitaire	..	14	20	23	23	25	13	23	22	31
Revenus agricoles	..	5	6	6	8	8	5	9	11	15
Revenus fonciers et autres	..	5	5	7	6	8	7	9	10	12
Autres impôts sur le revenu et bénéfices	..	66	93	102	69	78	59	15	13	65
1120 Sur les gains en capital	..	12	8	9	12	13	12	15	24	38
1200 Des sociétés	..	575	1 747	2 414	2 264	2 432	3 041	2 730	3 165	3 859
1210 Sur les bénéfices	..	575	1 742	2 413	2 253	2 424	3 035	2 722	3 159	3 852
Sociétés pétrolières	..	96	884	1 150	647	813	999	1 117	1 438	1 582
Sociétés non-pétrolières	..	359	439	706	926	864	1 258	822	779	1 137
Avances sur les marchés	..	33	192	277	309	356	346	331	389	476
Avance au titre des importations	..	7	35	42	97	111	124	156	166	184
Revenus des capitaux mobiliers	..	58	94	115	114	113	144	141	174	214
Honoraires, commissions, courtage et loyers	..	16	75	102	128	125	125	127	169	183
Redevances servies aux non résidents	..	3	20	17	30	39	35	26	36	53
Autres impôts sur les bénéfices	..	3	3	3	2	3	3	2	8	22
1220 Sur les gains en capitals	..	0	5	1	12	7	6	7	6	7
1300 Non-ventilables entre 1100 et 1200	..	0	2	1	2	2	1	3	3	4
2000 Cotisations de sécurité sociale	..	**1 551**	**3 116**	**3 568**	**4 098**	**4 629**	**5 210**	**5 839**	**6 504**	**6 950**
2100 A la charge des salariés	..	..	..	..	..	..	..	..	..	..
2110 Sur la base du salaire	..	..	..	..	..	..	..	..	..	..
2120 Sur la base de l'impôt sur les revenus	..	..	..	..	..	..	..	..	..	..
2200 A la charge des employeurs	..	..	..	..	..	..	..	..	..	..
2210 Sur la base du salaire	..	..	..	..	..	..	..	..	..	..
2220 Sur la base de l'impôt sur le revenu	..	..	..	..	..	..	..	..	..	..
2300 A charge des travailleurs indép. ou sans emploi	..	..	..	..	..	..	..	..	..	..
2310 Sur la base du salaire	..	..	..	..	..	..	..	..	..	..
2320 Sur la base de l'impôt sur le revenu	..	..	..	..	..	..	..	..	..	..
2400 Non-ventilables entre 2100, 2200 et 2300	..	..	..	..	..	..	..	..	..	..
2410 Sur la base du salaire	..	..	..	..	..	..	..	..	..	..
2420 Sur la base de l'impôt sur le revenu	..	..	..	..	..	..	..	..	..	..
3000 Sur salaires ou main d'oeuvre	..	**107**	**149**	**143**	**171**	**199**	**212**	**224**	**242**	**285**
Fonds de promotion des logements	..	71	97	87	115	124	136	143	147	177
Taxe de formation professionnelle	..	35	52	56	56	75	76	81	95	107
4000 Impôts sur le patrimoine	..	**81**	**142**	**157**	**172**	**177**	**218**	**228**	**244**	**278**
4100 Impôts périodiques sur la propriété immobilière	..	7	9	11	9	10	4	8	8	8
4110 Ménages	..	7	9	11	9	10	4	8	8	8
4120 Autres agents	..	0	0	0	0	0	0	0	0	0
4200 Impôts périodiques sur l'actif net	..	0	0	0	0	0	0	0	0	0
4210 Personnes physiques	..	..	..	..	..	..	..	..	..	..
4220 Sociétés	..	..	..	..	..	..	..	..	..	..
4300 Impôts sur mut. par décès, succ. et donations	..	0	0	0	0	0	0	0	0	0
4310 Impôts sur mut. par décès et successions	..	..	..	..	..	..	..	..	..	..
4320 Impôts sur les donations	..	..	..	..	..	..	..	..	..	..
4400 Impôts sur transact. mobilières et immob.	..	74	134	146	164	168	213	220	236	270
4500 Impôts non-périodiques	..	0	0	0	0	0	0	0	0	0
4510 Sur l'actif net	..	..	..	..	..	..	..	..	..	..
4520 Autres non-périodiques	..	..	..	..	..	..	..	..	..	..
4600 Autres impôts périodiques sur patrimoine	..	0	0	0	0	0	0	0	0	0
5000 Impôts sur les biens et services	..	**3 729**	**5 178**	**6 076**	**6 266**	**6 768**	**6 866**	**7 892**	**8 116**	**9 084**
5100 Impôts sur production, vente, transfert, etc.	..	3 665	5 060	5 949	6 131	6 612	6 724	7 726	7 948	8 899
5110 Impôts généraux	..	1 814	2 722	3 373	3 468	3 819	3 918	4 465	4 581	5 267
5111 Taxes sur la valeur ajoutée	..	1 792	2 660	3 309	3 400	3 750	3 850	4 383	4 460	5 116
5112 Impôts sur les ventes	..	0	0	0	0	0	0	0	0	0
5113 Autres impôts	..	21	62	64	69	69	69	82	121	151

Table 4.8. Tunisia / Tunisie (cont.)

Details of tax revenue / Recettes fiscales détaillées

Million TND

	1997	2000	2007	2008	2009	2010	2011	2012	2013	2014
5121 Accises	..	1 023	1 515	1 631	1 781	1 814	1 801	2 109	2 143	2 311
Tabac	..	371	679	736	826	799	893	1 033	1 014	1 081
Boissons alcoolisées	..	147	158	164	154	174	164	218	267	305
Essences et huiles	..	260	271	262	257	268	266	263	258	279
Voitures	..	86	132	161	180	242	167	241	251	251
Produits alimentaires	..	19	34	32	34	31	31	32	35	45
Ciment	..	11	15	15	15	17	17	16	18	20
Autres accises	..	131	225	261	314	282	262	306	299	330
5122 Bénéfices des monopoles fiscaux	..	0	0	0	0	0	0	0	0	0
5123 Droits de douane et droits à l'importation	..	654	534	619	578	620	617	763	796	882
Hors tabac	..	565	405	466	401	428	432	562	570	605
Redevances sur prestations douanières à l'importation	..	68	99	123	115	142	138	157	166	182
Taxe conjoncturelle sur ventes du ciment importé	..	0	0	0	0	0	0	0	18	41
Tabac	..	9	15	13	21	23	22	28	27	31
Autres droits de douane	..	0	5	3	3	4	2	2	2	2
Prèlevements à l'importation	..	12	8	11	34	20	19	11	11	18
Autres taxes et prélèvements à l'importation	..	1	2	2	4	3	4	3	3	3
5124 Taxes à l'exportation	..	11	27	29	19	27	36	43	38	38
5125 Impôts sur biens d'équipement	..	0	0	0	0	0	0	0	0	0
5126 Impôts sur services déterminés	..	162	261	297	283	330	352	346	389	400
Taxe sur les télécommunications	..	72	98	126	103	136	150	139	160	150
Taxe de compensation sur les transports	..	55	88	93	97	105	102	113	119	123
Taxe sur les assurances	..	33	71	76	79	86	97	92	109	120
Autres impôts sur services déterminés	..	2	3	2	3	3	3	2	2	8
5127 Autres impôts sur commerce et transact. internat.	..	0	0	0	0	0	0	0	0	0
5128 Autres impôts	..	0	1	1	1	1	1	1	1	1
5130 Non-ventilables entre 5110 et 5120	..	0	0	0	0	0	0	0	0	0
5200 Impôts sur utilisation des biens et exerc. activites	..	64	118	127	135	156	142	166	168	185
5210 Impôts périodiques	..	55	83	89	94	103	97	111	116	124
5211 A la charge des ménages: véhicules à moteur	..	35	49	51	55	60	56	64	69	74
5212 A la charge autres agents: véhicules à moteur	..	18	32	35	39	43	41	47	46	49
5213 Autres impôts périodiques	..	1	2	2	0	0	0	0	0	0
5220 Impôts non-périodiques	..	9	35	38	41	53	44	56	52	61
5300 Non-ventilables entre 5100 et 5200	..	0	0	0	0	0	0	0	0	0
6000 Autres impôts	**..**	**145**	**299**	**348**	**377**	**371**	**379**	**434**	**556**	**673**
Droits de timbres	..	25	132	165	157	133	215	208	256	289
Droits d'enregistrements	..	40	77	83	95	107	85	103	124	145
Amendes et condamnations	..	40	58	70	86	92	50	61	133	153
Droits sur les voyages à l'étranger	..	12	19	19	18	21	19	24	26	30
Divers	..	28	14	12	21	17	9	39	17	57
6100 A la charge exclusive des entreprises	..	..	..	..	..	..	..	..	..	..
6200 A la charge d'autres agents	..	..	..	..	..	..	..	..	..	..

Note: Année civile se terminant le 31 décembre.

Les données sont sur la base des encaissements.

Les chiffres n'incluent pas les données des collectivités locales car elles ne sont pas disponibles.

Les impôts affectés pour les Fonds spéciaux du Trésor et les Fonds de concours sont compris dans les données pour la période 2000-14.

La rubrique 1210 exclut les redevances des compagnies pétrolières. En Tunisie, elles sont considérées comme un complément de l'impôt sur les sociétés depuis avril 2012.

Les cotisations de sécurité sociale sous la rubrique 2000 ne sont pas considérées comme des recettes fiscales en Tunisie.

Source: Ministère des Finances pour toutes les données des recettes fiscales. Ministère des Affaires Sociales pour les données de cotisations de sécurité sociale.

StatLink http://dx.doi.org/10.1787/888933344780

CHAPTER 5

NON-TAX REVENUES, 1997-2014

CHAPITRE 5

RECETTES NON FISCALES, 1997-2014

Table 5.1. Total non-tax revenue as % of GDP, 1997-2014
Tableau 5.1. Total des recettes non fiscales en % du PIB, 1997-2014

	1997	2000	2007	2008	2009	2010	2011	2012	2013	2014
Cameroon / Cameroun	5.3	8.0	8.4	9.2	4.6	4.8	6.2	5.0	4.9	4.2
Côte d'Ivoire[1]	1.3	1.1	2.8	2.3	3.2	1.3	1.0	1.0	1.8	2.2
Mauritius / Maurice[2]	4.4	3.3	2.5	3.0	4.3	3.8	3.5	3.1	3.2	2.4
Morocco / Maroc	..	2.2	3.2	3.0	3.4	3.2	3.6	3.4	3.9	3.5
Rwanda	7.5	11.8	10.8	12.7	12.1	12.5	12.5	9.0	11.3	9.5
Senegal / Sénégal	2.4	2.7	3.5	3.4	3.6	3.2	2.9	3.8	4.1	5.7
South Africa / Afrique du Sud	0.3	0.5	0.5	0.6	0.4	0.6	0.7	0.7	0.7	0.6
Tunisia / Tunisie	..	2.3	2.6	3.5	3.1	2.7	3.9	3.4	3.4	2.2

Note: The figures exclude local government tax revenues for Cameroon, Côte d'Ivoire, Rwanda, Senegal and Tunisia as the data are not available. Local and provincial data for South Africa are not available prior to 2003.

1. The non-tax revenues as a percentage of GDP excludes rents, royalties and fees for public services as these are considered to be tax revenues in Côte d'Ivoire. These elements represent 0.5% of GDP in 2014 and range from 0.1% to 1.5% in the period between 2000 and 2014.
2. Estimated figures for 2013 and 2014.

Note : Les chiffres excluent les recettes fiscales des collectivités locales pour le Cameroun, la Côte d'Ivoire, le Rwanda, le Sénégal et la Tunisie car les données ne sont pas disponibles. Les données des collectivités locales et provinciales ne sont pas disponibles pour l'Afrique du Sud avant 2003.

1. Le ratio des recettes non-fiscales au PIB ne comprend pas les loyers, les redevances et les frais d'usage des services publics car ils sont considérés comme des recettes fiscales en Côte d'Ivoire. Ces éléments représentent 0.5% du PIB en 2014 et varient entre 0.1% et 1.5% pour la période 2000 à 2014.
2. Les chiffres sont estimés pour 2013 et 2014.

StatLink http://dx.doi.org/10.1787/888933344790

Table 5.2. Non-tax revenue of main headings as percentage of GDP, 2014
Tableau 5.2. Recettes non fiscales sous les principales rubriques en % du PIB, 2014

	Grants / Dons	Property income / Revenus de la propriété	Sales of goods and services / Ventes de biens et de services	Fines, penalties and forfeits / Amendes, pénalités et confiscations	Miscellaneous and unidentified revenue / Recettes diverses et non identifiées[5]
Cameroon / Cameroun	0.2	3.7	0.3	0.0	0.0
Côte d'Ivoire[1]	1.8	0.1	0.2	0.0	0.1
Mauritius / Maurice[2]	0.1	1.4	0.7	0.1	0.1
Morocco / Maroc[3]	0.0	1.4	1.6	0.1	0.8
Rwanda[4]	7.8	..	..	..	1.7
Senegal / Sénégal	3.3	1.7	0.0	0.6	0.1
South Africa / Afrique du Sud	0.1	0.5	0.0	0.0	0.0
Tunisia / Tunisie	0.5	1.2	0.0	0.2	0.2

Note: The figures exclude local government tax revenues for Cameroon, Côte d'Ivoire, Rwanda, Senegal and Tunisia as the data are not available. Local and provincial data for South Africa are not available prior to 2003.

1. The "Property income" heading excludes rents and royalties and the "Sales of goods and services" heading excludes fees for user goods and services. These are considered as tax revenues in Côte d'Ivoire.
2. Estimated figures for the headings "Property income" and "Sales of goods and services".
3. Data for 2013.
4. Data for property income, sales of goods and services and fines, penalties and forfeits are included in miscellaneous and unidentified revenue.
5. Including capital transfers not elsewhere classified and voluntary transfers other than grants.

Note : Les chiffres excluent les recettes fiscales des collectivités locales pour le Cameroun, la Côte d'Ivoire, le Rwanda, le Sénégal et la Tunisie car les données ne sont pas disponibles. Les données des collectivités locales et provinciales ne sont pas disponibles pour l'Afrique du Sud avant 2003.

1. La catégorie "Revenus de la propriété" ne comprend pas les loyers et les redevances et la catégorie "ventes de biens et de services" ne comprend pas les frais pour l'utilisation des biens et services. Ceux-ci sont classés comme des recettes fiscales en Côte d'Ivoire.
2. Les chiffres sont estimés pour les catégories "Revenus de la propriété" et "ventes de biens et de services".
3. Données pour 2013.
4. Les données des revenus de la propriété, ventes de biens et de services, pénalités et confiscations sont incluses dans la catégorie "Recettes diverses et non identifiées".
5. Y compris transferts de capitaux non compris ailleurs et transferts volontaires autres que les dons des gouvernements et institutions étrangers.

StatLink http://dx.doi.org/10.1787/888933344804

Table 5.3. Non-tax revenue of main headings as percentage of total non-tax revenues, 2014
Tableau 5.3. Recettes non fiscales sous les principales rubriques en % du total des recettes non fiscales, 2014

	Grants / Dons	Property income / Revenus de la propriété	Sales of goods and services / Ventes de biens et de services	Fines, penalties and forfeits / Amendes, pénalités et confiscations	Miscellaneous and unidentified revenue / Recettes diverses et non identifiées[5]
Cameroon / Cameroun	3.6	87.1	7.9	0.6	0.8
Côte d'Ivoire[1]	82.2	5.5	6.9	0.1	5.2
Mauritius / Maurice[2]	4.3	57.1	29.5	3.5	5.6
Morocco / Maroc[3]	0.0	37.3	40.6	1.5	20.5
Rwanda[4]	82.0	..	..	..	18.0
Senegal / Sénégal	57.1	29.4	0.0	11.0	2.5
South Africa / Afrique du Sud	9.1	81.6	3.6	5.4	0.3
Tunisia / Tunisie	21.2	55.8	1.4	11.0	10.6

Note: The figures exclude local government tax revenues for Cameroon, Côte d'Ivoire, Rwanda, Senegal and Tunisia as the data are not available. Local and provincial data for South Africa are not available prior to 2003.

1. The "Property income" heading excludes rents and royalties and the "Sales of goods and services" heading excludes fees for user goods and services. These are considered as tax revenues in Côte d'Ivoire.
2. Estimated figures for the headings "Property income" and "Sales of goods and services".
3. Data for 2013.
4. Data for property income, sales of goods and services and fines, penalties and forfeits are included in miscellaneous and unidentified revenue.
5. Including capital transfers not elsewhere classified and voluntary transfers other than grants.

Note : Les chiffres excluent les recettes fiscales des collectivités locales pour le Cameroun, la Côte d'Ivoire, le Rwanda, le Sénégal et la Tunisie car les données ne sont pas disponibles. Les données des collectivités locales et provinciales ne sont pas disponibles pour l'Afrique du Sud avant 2003.

1. La catégorie "Revenus de la propriété" ne comprend pas les loyers et les redevances et la catégorie "ventes de biens et de services" ne comprend pas les frais pour l'utilisation des biens et services. Ceux-ci sont classés comme des recettes fiscales en Côte d'Ivoire.
2. Les chiffres sont estimés pour les catégories "Revenus de la propriété" et "ventes de biens et de services".
3. Données pour 2013.
4. Les données des revenus de la propriété, ventes de biens et de services, pénalités et confiscations sont incluses dans la catégorie "Recettes diverses et non identifiées".
5. Y compris transferts de capitaux non compris ailleurs et transferts volontaires autres que les dons des gouvernements et institutions étrangers.

StatLink http://dx.doi.org/10.1787/888933344804

Table 5.4. Total non-tax revenue in millions of US Dollars at market exchange rates
Tableau 5.4. Totale des recettes non fiscales en millions de dollars américains au taux de change du marché

	1997	2000	2007	2008	2009	2010	2011	2012	2013	2014
Cameroon / Cameroun	523.9	739.1	1 723.4	2 153.8	1 070.0	1 134.2	1 660.8	1 336.5	1 461.9	1 351.2
Côte d'Ivoire	159.4	115.2	572.1	559.4	787.3	335.8	242.8	273.8	560.9	749.1
Mauritius / Maurice	200.6	146.6	197.3	246.8	407.2	375.1	385.2	348.1	381.1	321.8
Morocco / Maroc	..	841.2	2 558.0	2 811.6	3 142.4	3 008.1	3 694.8	3 376.7	4 169.3	3 850.3
Rwanda	135.1	203.1	406.6	607.5	640.4	712.5	799.3	647.2	852.8	756.6
Senegal / Sénégal	112.4	125.5	396.9	459.0	467.3	411.7	423.2	544.4	617.4	899.1
South Africa / Afrique du Sud	399.0	627.2	1 620.2	1 657.9	1 154.3	2 291.6	2 980.8	2 604.9	2 549.2	1 979.3
Tunisia / Tunisie	..	499.9	1 006.4	1 560.3	1 340.6	1 192.3	1 800.0	1 530.7	1 582.9	1 021.7

Note: This table is derived by multiplying total non-tax revenue figures for each country (in millions of national currency) by the exchange rate figures shown in table 3.19.

Note : Ce tableau est obtenu en multipliant les chiffres des recettes non fiscales en millions de monnaie nationale pour chaque pays par les taux de change du tableau 3.19.

StatLink http://dx.doi.org/10.1787/888933344822

Table 5.5. Cameroon / Cameroun

Details of non-tax revenue / Recettes non-fiscales détaillées

Million XAF

	1997	2000	2007	2008	2009	2010	2011	2012	2013	2014
Total des recettes non fiscales	**283 502**	**527 053**	**824 783**	**959 970**	**503 912**	**560 690**	**782 963**	**681 934**	**722 010**	**666 820**
Dons	..	6 900	193 941	193 393	118 472	78 805	62 084	56 049	75 879	23 813
Revenus de la propriété	221 100	404 500	566 417	721 834	343 193	442 296	668 984	566 680	577 877	580 497
Loyers et redevances	221 100	404 500	549 918	711 058	337 442	437 650	662 428	556 891	568 962	570 574
Redevance pétrolière	219 000	399 300	504 706	685 925	318 528	418 971	541 153	532 375	538 733	517 040
Droits de passage du pipeline	0	0	10 382	8 749	8 344	9 080	8 248	7 747	8 802	24 675
Autres loyers et redevances	2 100	5 200	34 831	16 384	10 570	9 599	113 027	16 769	21 428	28 860
Intérêts et dividendes	0	0	16 499	10 776	5 751	4 646	6 557	9 789	8 915	9 922
Autres revenus de la propriété	0	0	0	0	0	0	0	0	0	0
Ventes de biens et de services	30 400	33 500	49 781	32 588	37 810	37 732	41 027	47 664	62 682	52 990
Amendes, pénalités et confiscations	0	0	4 113	2 580	2 401	1 858	1 664	2 498	5 362	3 975
Recettes diverses et non identifiées[1]	32 002	82 153	10 531	9 576	2 037	0	9 204	9 043	211	5 546
Total des recettes fiscales et non fiscales	865 900	1 370 453	2 269 965	2 506 228	2 156 024	2 200 718	2 637 698	2 754 209	3 026 500	3 214 297

Note: Année civile se terminant le 31 décembre.
Les données sont sur la base des encaissements.
Les chiffres n'incluent pas les données des collectivités locales car elles ne sont pas disponibles.
Les taxes domaniales, la taxe à l'extraction des carrières et la redevance à la production des eaux sont inclues dans les recettes non fiscales. Elles sont considérées comme des recettes fiscales au Cameroun.
1. Y compris transferts de capitaux non compris ailleurs et transferts volontaires autres que les dons.
Source: Ministère des Finances du Cameroun.

StatLink http://dx.doi.org/10.1787/888933344839

Table 5.6. Côte d'Ivoire

Details of non-tax revenue / Recettes non-fiscales détaillées

Million XOF

	1997	2000	2007	2008	2009	2010	2011	2012	2013	2014
Total des recettes non fiscales	**92 153**	**81 800**	**273 814**	**249 336**	**370 796**	**165 995**	**114 454**	**139 688**	**277 008**	**369 693**
Dons	..	..	..	183 300	310 928	106 540	81 208	81 208	201 460	303 989
Revenus de la propriété	..	..	..	41 606	40 004	41 337	20 056	39 426	51 074	20 496
Loyers et redevances	..	..	..	12 637	11 014	9 930	5 802	28 116	20 856	10 714
Revenus du domaine	..	..	..	689	186	283	172	396	941	1 363
Autres loyers et redevances	..	..	..	11 947	10 827	9 647	5 631	27 720	19 915	9 351
Intérêts et dividendes	..	..	..	28 932	28 969	27 981	13 678	11 230	29 973	9 693
Autres revenus de la propriété	..	..	..	38	21	3 426	576	80	245	89
Ventes de biens et de services	..	..	..	13 162	14 766	17 592	12 837	18 742	22 529	25 535
Amendes, pénalités et confiscations	..	..	..	208	200	173	99	99	219	291
Recettes diverses et non identifiées[1]	..	..	..	11 061	4 898	353	253	213	1 727	19 382
Total des recettes fiscales et non fiscales	1 262 216	1 255 611	2 050 194	2 241 395	2 343 658	2 240 541	2 038 951	2 675 604	3 102 516	3 393 149

Note: Année civile se terminant le 31 décembre.
Les données sont sur la base des encaissements.
Les chiffres n'incluent pas les données des collectivités locales car elles ne sont pas disponibles.
Les recettes non fiscales ne contiennent pas les taxes domaniales et la taxe d'exploitation pétrolière normalement classées dans la catégorie "Loyers et Redevances" selon la classification OCDE. Elles sont considérées comme des recettes fiscales en Côte d'Ivoire.
Les recettes non fiscales ne contiennent pas non plus la taxe audiovisuelle et la redevance radiodiffusion télévision ivoirienne (RTI) normalement classée dans la catégorie "Vente de biens et services" selon la classification OCDE. Elles sont considérées comme des recettes fiscales en Côte d'Ivoire.
1. Y compris transferts de capitaux non compris ailleurs et transferts volontaires autres que les dons.
Source: Ministère de l'Économie et des Finances.

StatLink http://dx.doi.org/10.1787/888933344846

Table 5.7. Mauritius / Maurice
Details of non-tax revenue / Recettes non-fiscales détaillées

Million MUR

	1997	2000	2007	2008	2009	2010	2011	2012	2013	2014
Total non-tax revenue	**3 831**	**3 847**	**5 729**	**7 920**	**11 930**	**11 458**	**11 275**	**10 668**	**11 701**	**9 427**
Grants	63	161	322	454	2 781	1 991	2 345	2 398	1 403	406
Property income	3 104	2 914	3 372	5 119	6 627	5 020	4 328	4 846	5 567	5 379
Rents and royalties	..	..	184	358	962	1 284	1 167	1 068	1 219	1 087
Interest and dividends	..	..	1 140	1 861	1 344	979	1 018	1 074	1 827	1 408
Interest	..	..	376	362	415	392	376	589	408	465
Dividends	..	..	764	1 500	929	587	643	484	1 418	943
Other property income	581	620	2 049	2 900	4 320	2 756	2 142	2 705	2 521	2 883
Budgetary	0	0	1 040	1 458	2 406	1 549	1 127	1 167	1 066	1 437
Extra-budgetary[1]	0	0	158	162	504	349	341	325	393	390
Social security funds[1]	527	544	775	1 172	1 313	777	598	1 131	970	964
Regional government[1]	0	0	7	7	10	11	11	10	12	12
Local government[1]	54	76	69	102	87	71	64	73	80	80
Sales of goods and services	542	646	1 589	1 952	1 825	2 028	2 427	2 576	2 670	2 784
Work/occupational permits	0	0	60	60	66	95	112	125	163	206
Extra-budgetary fees, charges, and non-industrial sales[1]	185	177	439	704	586	543	621	779	752	747
Fees, charges, and non-industrial sales by social security funds[1]	22	20	31	80	0	51	145	126	125	124
Regional government sales of goods and services[1]	0	0	8	7	4	5	7	8	7	7
Local government sales of goods and services[1]	32	60	106	123	98	113	127	101	132	132
Other sales of goods and services	304	390	946	979	1 071	1 222	1 415	1 436	1 490	1 569
Fines, penalties and forfeits	44	65	166	178	219	272	306	282	313	331
Budgetary fines, penalties and forfeits	44	65	164	176	198	269	302	276	308	326
Extra-budgetary fines, penalties and forfeits[1]	0	0	0	0	0	0	0	1	0	0
Fines, penalties and forfeits for social security funds[1]	0	0	0	0	19	0	0	0	0	0
Regional government fines, penalties and forfeits[1]	0	0	2	1	2	3	4	6	5	5
Local government fines, penalties and forfeits	0	0	0	0	0	0	0	0	0	0
Miscellaneous and unidentified revenue[2]	79	61	280	217	479	2 147	1 870	566	1 749	527
Budgetary miscellaneous and unidentified revenue	0	0	10	0	46	1 803	1 468	187	1 360	140
Extra-budgetary miscellaneous and unidentified revenue[1]	75	44	265	215	367	293	223	315	322	320
Miscellaneous and unidentified revenue for social security funds[1]	0	4	0	0	0	3	117	0	0	0
Regional government miscellaneous and unidentified revenue[1]	0	0	0	0	3	1	1	1	1	1
Local government miscellaneous and unidentified revenue[1]	4	13	5	2	63	47	61	64	67	66
Total tax and non-tax revenue	19 199	26 238	46 446	58 429	67 978	70 637	74 743	79 982	84 668	86 491

Note: Year ending 31st December. Prior to 2010 the data are on a fiscal year basis beginning 1st July. For example, the data for 2007 represent July 2006 to June 2007.

The data are on a cash basis, except for revenue from grants, which is reported on an accrual basis.

1. Values for 2013 and 2014 are estimated.
2. No capital transfers or voluntary transfers other than grants were reported for Mauritius within this category.

Source: Mauritius Revenue Authority for central government budgetary non-tax revenue data from 2007 to 2014; Statistics Mauritius for extra-budgetary, local and regional government non-tax revenues from 1990 to 2014; Statistics Mauritius for budgetary central government non-tax revenues up to 2006.

StatLink http://dx.doi.org/10.1787/888933344857

Table 5.8. Morocco / Maroc
Details of non-tax revenue / Recettes non-fiscales détaillées

Million MAR

	1997	2000	2007	2008	2009	2010	2011	2012	2013	2014
Total des recettes non fiscales	..	**8 939**	**20 956**	**21 791**	**25 319**	**25 320**	**29 890**	**29 135**	**35 045**	**32 345**
Dons	..	2	1 112	2	1	199	9	8	7	0
Revenus de la propriété	..	3 125	5 861	6 563	9 470	9 786	12 181	12 257	13 063	10 356
Loyers et redevances	..	1 507	3 249	3 674	3 813	3 868	5 279	4 577	5 360	4 776
Redevance gazoduc	..	298	1 379	1 748	1 695	1 442	2 151	2 146	2 327	..
Redevances et contribution pour licence de pêche en haute mer	..	94	456	412	399	329	635	3	177	..
Redevances pour l'occupation du domaine public	..	132	225	192	233	331	325	289	566	..
Autres redevances reçues par l'administration centrale	..	7	13	13	54	63	3	3	9	..
Loyers et redevances reçues par les collectivités locales	..	977	1 176	1 310	1 432	1 703	2 165	2 136	2 281	2 128
Intérêts et dividendes	..	1 618	2 612	2 888	5 657	5 918	6 902	7 680	7 702	5 580
Dividendes des monopole	..	1 008	2 324	2 615	5 422	5 584	6 510	7 376	7 378	..
Intérêts sur placements et avances	..	419	85	57	20	96	158	74	73	..
Interêts et dividendes reçus par les collectivités locales	..	191	203	216	215	239	234	230	251	259
Autres revenus de la propriété	..	0	0	0	0	0	0	0	0	0
Ventes de biens et de services	..	4 573	9 703	11 125	11 352	10 286	11 745	11 796	14 244	15 511
Carte, passeport et documents divers	..	453	560	471	483	567	555	515	489	..
Produits de certains établissements publics	..	1 544	4 532	4 940	4 949	2 990	3 684	3 855	5 410	..
Revenus des immeubles domaniaux (loyers, charges locatives ...)	..	137	229	238	226	250	184	287	239	..
Autres produits de l'administration centrale	..	175	674	1 354	663	646	1 494	649	801	..
Ventes de biens et de services par les collectivités locales	..	2 265	3 709	4 123	5 031	5 832	5 828	6 490	7 304	8 566
Amendes, pénalités et confiscations	..	59	117	117	180	152	207	378	532	0
Amendes et condamnations pécuniaires	..	17	25	27	30	21	23	32	46	..
Amendes transactionnelles	..	36	75	89	149	130	183	345	485	..
Autres (produits des confiscations, pénalités et amendes autres que fiscales)	..	6	17	1	1	1	1	1	1	..
Recettes diverses et non identifiées	..	1 180	4 162	3 984	4 315	4 897	5 748	4 696	7 200	6 477
Fonds de concours	..	147	2 254	3 310	3 191	3 597	3 624	2 246	4 441	..
Recettes en atténuation des dépenses de la dette	..	801	1 246	68	230	480	1 044	725	1 024	..
Reversements sur traitements et salaires	..	55	209	122	249	99	106	155	96	..
Créances sur le Trésor prescrites	..	30	72	50	54	39	56	186	112	..
Autres (divers remboursements à l'État) reçues par l'administration centrale	..	7	6	108	6	6	133	198	281	..
Recettes diverses et non identifiées des collectivités locales	..	139	374	327	587	677	785	1 186	1 246	1 536
Total des recettes fiscales et non fiscales	..	48 904	108 072	128 612	124 856	119 461	142 291	152 021	160 698	151 098

Note: Année civile se terminant le 31 décembre.

Les données sont sur la base des encaissements.

Les données de 2014 sont provisoires.

Les recettes non fiscales reçues par les collectivités locales désagrégées ne sont pas disponibles pour les années 2000 à 2014. De même, les recettes non fiscales reçues par l'Administration centrale désagrégées ne sont pas disponibles pour 2014.

Source: Ministère de l'Économie et des Finances.

StatLink http://dx.doi.org/10.1787/888933344864

Table 5.9. Rwanda / Rwanda
Details of non-tax revenue / Recettes non-fiscales détaillées

Million RWF

	1997	2000	2007	2008	2009	2010	2011	2012	2013	2014
Total non-tax revenue	**40 858**	**79 888**	**222 421**	**332 060**	**363 942**	**415 465**	**479 815**	**397 600**	**551 411**	**514 565**
Grants	37 731	76 710	207 293	279 775	347 397	397 352	443 150	345 510	459 200	421 821
Property income	..	..	..	..	..	..	..	..	..	..
Rents and royalties	..	..	..	..	..	..	..	..	..	..
Interest and dividends	..	..	..	..	..	..	..	..	..	..
Other property income	..	..	..	..	..	..	..	..	..	..
Sales of goods and services	..	..	..	..	..	..	..	..	..	..
Fines, penalties and forfeits	..	..	..	..	..	..	..	..	..	..
Miscellaneous and unidentified revenue[1]	3 127	3 178	15 128	52 284	16 545	18 113	36 665	52 090	92 211	92 745
Total tax and non-tax revenue	97 107	148 797	478 256	685 056	753 881	856 189	1 017 253	1 043 048	1 311 569	1 380 119

Note: Year ending 31st December.
The data are on a cash basis.
Figures exclude local government non-tax revenues as the data are not available.
1. This category includes non-tax fines, administrative fees and revenue from public property and public assets for Rwanda. These data could not be disaggregated to allocate revenue to the relevant non-tax revenue categories.

Source: Rwanda Revenue Authority.

StatLink http://dx.doi.org/10.1787/888933344879

Table 5.10. Senegal / Sénégal
Details of non-tax revenue / Recettes non-fiscales détaillées

Million XOF

	1997	2000	2007	2008	2009	2010	2011	2012	2013	2014
Total des recettes non fiscales	**65 600**	**89 100**	**189 939**	**204 600**	**220 100**	**203 550**	**199 500**	**277 800**	**304 935**	**443 700**
Dons	65 600	64 000	131 339	139 700	182 800	161 850	150 000	206 300	187 540	253 500
Revenus de la propriété	0	21 100	53 100	58 500	34 900	39 600	34 100	68 500	88 795	130 300
Loyers et redevances	..	..	19 700	5 800	6 500	20 300	15 800	38 000	18 320	25 200
Intérêts et dividendes	..	..	33 400	52 700	28 400	19 300	18 300	30 500	43 375	56 100
Autres revenus de la propriété	..	..	0	0	0	0	0	0	0	0
Ventes de biens et de services	0	0	0	0	0	0	0	0	0	0
Amendes, pénalités et confiscations	0	0	0	0	0	0	0	0	27 100	49 000
Recettes diverses et non identifiées[1]	0	4 000	5 500	6 400	2 400	2 100	15 400	3 000	1 500	10 900
Total des recettes fiscales et non fiscales	483 144	648 395	1 275 602	1 343 731	1 358 598	1 471 349	1 545 987	1 697 081	1 719 655	2 002 265

Note: Année civile se terminant le 31 décembre.
Les données sont sur la base des encaissements.
Les chiffres n'incluent pas les données des collectivités locales car elles ne sont pas disponibles.
Les données de 2014 sont provisoires.
La nomenclature actuelle des recettes budgétaires du Sénégal ne considère pas les dons comme une recette non-fiscale.
1. Y compris transferts de capitaux non compris ailleurs et transferts volontaires autres que les dons des gouvernements et institutions étrangers.

Source: Ministère de l'Économie, des Finances et du Plan.

StatLink http://dx.doi.org/10.1787/888933344881

Table 5.11. South Africa / Afrique du Sud
Details of non-tax revenue / Recettes non-fiscales détaillées

Million ZAR

	1997	2000	2007	2008	2009	2010	2011	2012	2013	2014
Total non-tax revenue	**1 838**	**4 350**	**11 430**	**13 681**	**9 739**	**16 779**	**21 620**	**21 386**	**24 601**	**21 464**
Grants	265	637	1 285	1 993	1 844	1 012	1 480	1 966	2 335	1 960
Property income	1 222	1 593	6 851	7 525	3 652	11 725	15 952	15 236	17 511	17 512
Rents and royalties	0	0	0	0	0	3 555	5 612	5 015	6 439	5 413
Interest and dividends	1 222	1 378	6 539	6 547	2 798	3 721	4 554	5 098	4 524	6 602
Other property income	0	215	312	978	854	4 449	5 787	5 123	6 548	5 497
Sales of goods and services	218	2 006	2 841	3 393	2 314	2 335	2 894	2 620	2 866	767
Fines, penalties and forfeits	134	114	448	479	1 698	1 457	934	993	1 466	1 162
Miscellaneous and unidentified revenue	0	0	4	292	232	251	360	572	423	63
Total tax and non-tax revenue	158 821	212 203	582 154	657 259	645 986	703 328	795 825	874 136	968 894	1 058 826

Note: Data are reported on a fiscal year basis beginning 1st April. For example, the data for 2006 data represent April 2006 to March 2007.
The data are on a cash basis.
Unaudited estimates for grants data for the years 2013 and 2014 (representing 2013/14 and 2014/15). The data represents total grants and donations received mainly from foreign governments and multilateral institutions. Moreover, this flow does not go through the Government Revenue fund, it is earmarked for specific projects implemented across government (by line departments).

Source: National Treasury of South Africa. Data for grants are from the financial statements of the Reconstruction and Development Fund Programme (RDP) Fund administered by the office of Accountant General.

StatLink http://dx.doi.org/10.1787/888933344905

Table 5.12. Tunisia / Tunisie
Details of non-tax revenue / Recettes non-fiscales détaillées

Million TND

	1997	2000	2007	2008	2009	2010	2011	2012	2013	2014
Total des recettes non fiscales	..	**685**	**1 290**	**1 923**	**1 810**	**1 707**	**2 534**	**2 391**	**2 572**	**1 737**
Dons[1]	..	7	38	192	178	54	207	633	225	368
Revenus de la propriété	..	525	979	1 442	1 327	1 299	2 044	1 267	1 514	970
Loyers et redevances	..	185	305	387	444	435	419	394	372	352
Redevances pétrolières et du gaz	..	177	290	370	423	415	410	379	353	332
Loyers	..	8	14	17	21	19	10	15	18	20
Intérêts et dividendes	..	341	674	1 055	883	864	1 625	872	1 143	618
Intérêts	..	56	88	71	59	56	49	66	31	42
Transferts des entreprises publiques et bénéfices de la Banque Centrale	..	274	581	977	789	796	1 567	757	1 070	503
Remises sur crédit	..	3	3	3	2	2	2	2	2	3
Autres intérêts et dividendes non compris ailleurs	..	9	3	4	33	10	8	46	39	70
Autres revenus de la propriété	..	0	0	0	0	0	0	0	0	0
Ventes de biens et de services	..	22	33	42	33	40	20	54	26	25
Ventes de produits divers	..	21	32	41	31	38	19	53	25	23
Frais administratifs	..	1	1	1	2	2	1	1	2	2
Amendes, pénalités et confiscations	..	47	51	73	83	94	48	294	598	190
Recettes diverses et non identifiées[2]	..	85	189	174	190	220	214	143	208	184
Total des recettes fiscales et non fiscales	..	7 922	13 918	16 826	17 596	18 941	21 377	22 929	25 112	26 965

Note: Année civile se terminant le 31 décembre.
Les données sont sur la base des encaissements.

1. Les dons affectés pour les Fonds spéciaux du Trésor et les Fonds de concours sont compris dans les données des dons des gouvernements et institutions étrangers.
2. Les recettes diverses et non identifiées incluent entre autres des recettes accidentelles à divers titres et des recettes non fiscales des Fonds spéciaux du Trésor et des Fonds de concours.

Source: Ministère des Finances.

StatLink http://dx.doi.org/10.1787/888933344894

ANNEX A

The OECD Interpretative Guide

Table of contents

A.1. The OECD classification of taxes

1000 *Taxes on income, profits and capital gains*

- 1100 Individuals
  - 1110 Income and profits
  - 1120 Capital gains
- 1200 Corporates
  - 1210 Income and profits
  - 1220 Capital gains
- 1300 Unallocable as between 1100 and 1200

2000 *Social security contributions*

- 2100 Employees
  - 2110 On a payroll basis
  - 2120 On an income tax bas
- 2200 Employers
  - 2210 On a payroll basis
  - 2220 On an income tax basis
- 2300 Self-employed, non-employed
  - 2310 On a payroll basis
  - 2320 On an income tax basis
- 2400 Unallocable as between 2100, 2200 and 2300
  - 2410 On a payroll basis
  - 2420 On an income tax basis

3000 *Taxes on payroll and workforce*

4000 *Taxes on property*

- 4100 Recurrent taxes on immovable property
  - 4110 Households
  - 4120 Other
- 4200 Recurrent net wealth taxes
  - 4210 Individuals
  - 4220 Corporates
- 4300 Estate, inheritance and gift taxes
  - 4310 Estate and inheritance taxes
  - 4320 Gift taxes
- 4400 Taxes on financial and capital transactions

4500 Other non-recurrent taxes on property

4510 On net wealth

4520 Other non-recurrent taxes

4600 Other recurrent taxes on property

5000 *Taxes on goods and services*

5100 Taxes on production, sale and transfer of goods and services

5110 General sales taxes

5111 Value-added taxes

5112 Sales taxes

5113 Other general taxes

5120 Taxes on specific goods and services

5121 Excises

5122 Profits of fiscal monopolies

5123 Customs and import duties

5124 On exports

5125 On investment goods

5126 On specific services

5127 Other taxes on international trade and transactions

5128 Other taxes on specific goods and services

5130 Unallocable as between 5110 and 5120

5200 Taxes on use of goods, or on permission to use goods or perform activities

5210 Recurrent taxes

5211 Motor vehicles taxes households

5212 Motor vehicles taxes others

5213 Other recurrent taxes

5220 Non-recurrent taxes

5300 Unallocable as between 5100 and 5200

6000 *Other taxes*

6100 Paid solely by business

6200 Paid by other than business, or unidentifiable

The OECD Interpretative Guide[1]

A.2. Coverage

General criteria

1. In the OECD classification the term "taxes" is confined to compulsory unrequited payments to general government. Taxes are unrequited in the sense that benefits provided by government to taxpayers are not normally in proportion to their payments.

2. The term 'tax' does not include fines unrelated to tax offences and compulsory loans paid to government. Borderline cases between tax and non-tax revenues in relation to certain fees and charges are discussed in §9–13.

3. General government consists of the central administration, agencies whose operations are under its effective control, state and local governments and their administrations, certain social security schemes and autonomous governmental entities, excluding public enterprises. This definition of government follows that of the 2008 System of National Accounts (SNA).[2] In that publication, the general government sector and its sub-sectors are defined in chapter 4, section F, pages 80-84.

4. Compulsory payments to supra-national bodies and their agencies are no longer included as taxes as from 1998, with some exceptions. However, custom duties collected by EU member states on behalf of the European Union are still identified as memorandum items and included in overall tax revenue amounts in the country tables (Part III) of the country in which they are collected. (See §95). In countries where the church forms part of general government church taxes are included, provided they meet the criteria set out in §1 above. As the data refer to receipts of general government, levies paid to non-government bodies, welfare agencies or social insurance schemes outside general government, trade unions or trade associations, even where such levies are compulsory, are excluded. Compulsory payments to general government earmarked for such bodies are, however, included, provided that the government is not simply acting in an agency capacity.[3] Profits from fiscal monopolies are distinguished from those of other public enterprises and are treated as taxes because they reflect the exercise of the taxing power of the state by the use of monopoly powers (see §62–64), as are profits received by the government from the purchase and sale of foreign exchange at different rates (see §70).

5. Taxes paid by governments (e.g. social security contributions and payroll taxes paid by governments in their capacity as an employer, consumption taxes on their purchases or taxes on their property) are not excluded from the data provided. However, where it is possible to identify the amounts of revenue involved,[4] they are shown in section III.C of this Report.

6. The relationship between this classification and that of the System of National Accounts (SNA) is set out in Sections H and J below. Because of the differences between the two classifications, the data shown in national accounts are sometimes calculated or classified differently from the practice set out in this guide. These and other differences are mentioned where appropriate (e.g. in §13 and §26 below) but it is not possible to refer to all of them. There may also be some differences between this classification and that employed domestically by certain national administrations (e.g. see §10 below), so that OECD and national statistics data may not always be consistent: any such differences, however, are likely to be very slight in terms of amounts of revenues involved.

Social security contributions

7. Compulsory social security contributions, as defined in §35 below, paid to general government, are treated here as tax revenues. Being compulsory payments to general government they clearly resemble taxes. They may, however, differ from other taxes in that the receipt of social security benefits depends, in most countries, upon appropriate contributions having been made, although the size of the benefits is not necessarily related to the amount of the contributions. Better comparability between countries is obtained by treating social security contributions as taxes, but they are listed under a separate heading so that they can be distinguished in any analysis.

8. Social security contributions which are either voluntary or not payable to general government (see §1) are not treated as taxes, though in some countries, as indicated in the country footnotes, there are difficulties in eliminating voluntary contributions and certain compulsory payments to the private sector.

Fees, user charges and licence fees

9. Apart from vehicle licence fees, which are universally regarded as taxes, it is not easy to distinguish between those fees and user charges which are to be treated as taxes and those which are not, since, whilst a fee or charge is levied in connection with a specific service or activity, the strength of the link between the fee and the service provided may vary considerably, as may the relation between the amount of the fee and the cost of providing the service. Where the recipient of a service pays a fee clearly related to the cost of providing the service, the levy may be regarded as requited and under the definition of §1 would not be considered as a tax. In the following cases, however, a levy could be considered as 'unrequited':

a) where the charge greatly exceeds the cost of providing the service;

b) where the payer of the levy is not the receiver of the benefit (e.g. a fee collected from slaughterhouses to finance a service which is provided to farmers);

c) where government is not providing a specific service in return for the levy which it receives even though a licence may be issued to the payer (e.g. where the government grants a hunting, fishing or shooting licence which is not accompanied by the right to use a specific area of government land);

d) where benefits are received only by those paying the levy but the benefits received by each individual are not necessarily in proportion to his payments (e.g. a milk marketing levy paid by dairy farmers and used to promote the consumption of milk).

10. In marginal cases, however, the application of the criteria set out in §1 can be particularly difficult. The solution adopted – given the desirability of international uniformity and the relatively small amounts of revenue usually involved – is to follow the predominant practice among tax administrations rather than to allow each country to adopt its own view as to whether such levies are regarded as taxes or as non-tax revenue.[5]

11. A list of the main fees and charges in question and their normal[6] treatment in this publication is as follows:

Non-tax revenues:	court fees; driving licence fees; harbour fees; passport fees; radio and television licence fees where public authorities provide the service.
Taxes within heading 5200:	permission to perform such activities as distributing films; hunting, fishing and shooting; providing entertainment or gambling facilities; selling alcohol or tobacco; permission to own dogs or to use or own motor vehicles or guns; severance taxes.

12. In practice it may not always be possible to isolate tax receipts from non-tax revenue receipts when they are recorded together. If it is estimated that the bulk of the receipts derive from non-tax revenues, the whole amount involved is treated as a non-tax revenue; otherwise, such government receipts are included and classified according to the rules provided in §28 below.

13. Two differences between the OECD classification and SNA regarding the borderline between tax and non-tax revenues are:

a) SNA classifies a number of levies as indirect taxes if paid by enterprises, but as non-tax revenues if paid by households, a distinction which is regarded as irrelevant in this classification for distinguishing between tax and non-tax revenues.[7]

b) Predominant practice among most OECD tax administrations, which is occasionally used in this classification for distinguishing between tax and non-tax revenues, is not a relevant criterion for SNA purposes.

Royalties

14. Royalty payments for the right to extract oil and gas or to exploit other mineral resources are normally regarded as non-tax revenues since they are property income from government-owned land or resources.

Fines and penalties

15. Receipts from fines and penalties paid for infringement of regulations identified as relating to a particular tax and interest on payments overdue in respect of a particular tax are recorded together with receipts from that tax. Other kinds of fines identifiable as relating to tax offences are classified in the residual heading 6000. Fines not relating to tax offences (e.g. for parking offences), or not identifiable as relating to tax offences, are not treated as taxes.

A.3. Basis of reporting

Accrual reporting

16. The data reported in this publication for recent years are predominantly recorded on an accrual basis, i.e. recorded at the time that the tax liability was created. Further information is provided in the footnotes to the country table in Part III of the Report.

17. However, data for earlier years are still predominantly recorded on a cash basis, i.e. at the time at which the payment was received by government. Thus, for example, taxes withheld by employers in one year but paid to the government in the following year and taxes due in one year but actually paid in the following year are both included in the receipts of the second year. Corrective transactions, such as refunds, repayments and drawbacks, are deducted from gross revenues of the period in which they are made.

18. Data on tax revenues are recorded without offsets for the administrative expenses connected with tax collection. Similarly, where the proceeds of tax are used to subsidise particular members of the community, the subsidy is not deducted from the yield of the tax, though the tax may be shown net of subsidies in the national records of some countries.

19. As regards fiscal monopolies (heading 5122), only the amount actually transferred to the government is included in government revenues. However, if any expenditures of fiscal monopolies are considered to be government expenditures (e.g. social expenditures undertaken by fiscal monopolies at the direction of the government) they are added back for the purpose of arriving at tax revenue figures (see §62 below).

The distinction between tax and expenditure provisions[8]

20. Because this publication is concerned only with the revenue side of government operations, no account being taken of the expenditure side, a distinction has to be made between tax and expenditure provisions. Normally there is no difficulty in making this distinction as expenditures are made outside the tax system and the tax accounts and under legislation separate from the tax legislation. In borderline cases, cash flow is used to distinguish between tax provisions and expenditure provisions. Insofar as a provision affects the flow of tax payments from the taxpayer to the government, it is regarded as a tax provision and is taken into account in the data shown in this publication. A provision which does not affect this flow is seen as an expenditure provision and is disregarded in the data recorded in this publication.

21. Tax allowances, exemptions and deductions against the tax base clearly affect the amount of tax paid to the government and are therefore considered as tax provisions. At the other extreme, those subsidies which cannot be offset against tax liability and which are clearly not connected with the assessment process, do not reduce tax revenues as recorded in this publication. Tax credits are amounts deductible from tax payable (as distinct from deductions from the tax base). Two types of tax credits are distinguished, those (referred to here as wastable tax credits) which are limited to the amount of the tax liability and therefore cannot give rise to a payment by the authorities to the taxpayer, and those (referred to as non-wastable tax credits) which are not so limited, so that the excess of the credit over the tax liability can be paid to the taxpayer.[9] A wastable tax credit, like a tax allowance, clearly affects the amount of tax paid to the government, and is therefore considered as a tax provision. The practice followed for non-wastable tax credits[10] is to distinguish between the "tax expenditure component",[11] which is that portion of the credit that is used to reduce or eliminate a taxpayer's liability, and the 'transfer component', which is the portion that exceeds the taxpayer's liability and is paid to that taxpayer. Reported tax revenues should be reduced by the amount of the tax expenditure component but not by the amount of the transfer component. In addition, the amounts of the tax expenditure and transfer components should be reported as memorandum items in the country tables. Countries that are unable to distinguish between the tax expenditure and transfer components should indicate whether or not the tax revenues have been reduced by the total of these components, and provide any available estimates of the amounts of the two components. Further information is given in section C of Part I of the Report, which illustrates the effect of alternative treatments of non-wastable tax credits on Tax to GDP.

Calendar and fiscal years

22. National authorities whose fiscal years do not correspond to the calendar year show data, where possible, on a calendar year basis to permit maximum comparability with the data of other countries. There remain a few countries where data refer to fiscal years. For these the GDP data used in the comparative tables also correspond to the fiscal years.

A.4. General classification criteria

The main classification criteria

23. The classification of receipts among the main headings (1000, 2000, 3000, 4000, 5000 and 6000) is generally governed by the base on which the tax is levied: 1000 income, profits and capital gains; 2000 and 3000 earnings, payroll or number of employees; 4000 property; 5000 goods and services; 6000 multiple bases, other bases or unidentifiable bases. Where a tax is calculated on more than one base, the receipts are, where possible, split among the various headings (see §28 and §78). The headings 4000 and 5000 cover

not only taxes where the tax base is the property, goods or services themselves but also certain related taxes. Thus, taxes on the transfer of property are included in 4400[12] and taxes on the use of goods or on permission to perform activities in 5200. In headings 4000 and 5000 a distinction is made in certain sub-headings between recurrent and non-recurrent taxes: recurrent taxes are defined as those levied at regular intervals (usually annually) and non-recurrent taxes are levied once and for all (see also §43 to §46, §49, §50 and §76 for particular applications of this distinction).

24. Earmarking of a tax for specific purposes does not affect the classification of tax receipts. However, as explained in §35 on the classification of social security contributions, the conferment of an entitlement to social benefits is crucial to the definition of the 2000 main heading.

25. The way that a tax is levied or collected (e.g. by use of stamps) does not affect classification.

Classification of taxpayers

26. In certain sub-headings distinctions are made between different categories of taxpayers. These distinctions vary from tax to tax:

a) Between individuals and corporations in relation to income and net wealth taxes

The basic distinction is that corporation income taxes, as distinct from individual income taxes, are levied on the corporation as an entity, not on the individuals who own it, and without regard to the personal circumstances of these individuals. The same distinction applies to net wealth taxes on corporations and those on individuals. Taxes paid on the profits of partnerships and the income of institutions, such as life insurance or pension funds, are classified according to the same rule. They are classified as corporate taxes (1200) if they are charged on the partnership or institution as an entity without regard to the personal circumstances of the owners. Otherwise, they are treated as individual taxes (1100). Usually, there is different legislation for the corporation taxes and for the individual taxes.[13] The distinction made here between individuals and corporations does not follow the sector classification between households, enterprises, and so on of the System of National Accounts for income and outlay accounts. The SNA classification requires certain unincorporated businesses[14] to be excluded from the household sector and included with non-financial enterprises and financial institutions. The tax on the profits of these businesses, however, cannot always be separated from the tax on the other income of their owners, or can be separated only on an arbitrary basis. No attempt at this separation is made here and the whole of the individual income tax is shown together without regard to the nature of the income chargeable.

b) Between households and others in relation to taxes on immovable property

Here the distinction is that adopted by the SNA for the production and consumption expenditure accounts. The distinction is between households as consumers (i.e. excluding non-incorporated business) on the one hand and producers on the other hand. However, taxes on dwellings occupied by households, whether paid by owner-occupiers, tenants or landlords, are classified under households. This follows the common distinction made between taxes on domestic property versus taxes on business property. Some countries are not, however, in a position to make this distinction.

c) Between households and others in relation to motor vehicle licences

Here the distinction is between households as consumers on the one hand and producers on the other, as in the production and consumption expenditure accounts of the SNA.

d) Between business and others in relation to the residual taxes (6000)

The distinction is the same as in c) above between producers on the one hand and households as consumers on the other hand. Taxes which are included under the heading 6000 because they involve more than one tax base or because the tax base does not fall within any of the previous categories but which are identifiable as levyable only on producers and not on households are included under "business". The rest of the taxes which are included under the heading 6000 are shown as "other" or non-identified.

Surcharges

27. Receipts from surcharges in respect of particular taxes are usually classified with the receipts from the relevant tax whether or not the surcharge is temporary. If, however, the surcharge has a characteristic which would render it classifiable in a different heading of the OECD list, receipts from the surcharge are classified under that heading separately from the relevant tax.

Unidentifiable tax receipts and residual sub-headings

28. A number of cases arise where taxes cannot be identified as belonging entirely to a heading or sub-heading of the OECD classification and the following practices are applied in such cases:

a) The heading is known, but it is not known how receipts should be allocated between sub-headings: receipts are classified in the appropriate residual sub-heading (1300, 2400, 4520, 4600, 5130, 5300 or 6200).

b) It is known that the bulk of receipts from a group of taxes (usually local taxes) is derived from taxes within a particular heading or sub-heading, but some of the taxes in the group whose amount cannot be precisely ascertained may be classifiable in other headings or sub-headings: receipts are shown in the heading or sub-heading under which most of the receipts fall.

c) Neither the heading nor sub-heading of a tax (usually local) can be identified: the tax is classified in 6200 unless it is known that it is a tax on business in which case it is classified in 6100.

A.5. Commentaries on items of the list

1000 – *Taxes on income, profits and capital gains*

29. This heading covers taxes levied on the net income or profits (i.e. gross income minus allowable tax reliefs) of individuals and enterprises. Also covered are taxes levied on the capital gains of individuals and enterprises, and gains from gambling.

30. Included in the heading are:

a) taxes levied predominantly on income or profits, though partially on other bases. Taxes on various bases which are not predominantly income or profits are classified according to the principles laid down in §28 and §78;

b) taxes on property, which are levied on a presumed or estimated income as part of an income tax (see also §43(a), (c) and (d));

c) compulsory payments to social security fund contributions that are levied on income but do not confer an entitlement to social benefits. When such contributions do confer an entitlement to social benefits, they are included in heading 2000 (see §35);

d) receipts from integrated scheduler income tax systems are classified as a whole in this heading, even though certain of the scheduler taxes may be based upon gross income and may not take into account the personal circumstances of the taxpayer.

31. The main subdivision of this heading is between levies on individuals (1100) and those on corporate enterprises (1200). Under each subdivision a distinction is made between taxes on income and profits (1110 and 1210), and taxes on capital gains (1120 and 1220). If certain receipts cannot be identified as appropriate to either 1100 or 1200, or if in practice this distinction cannot be made (e.g., because there are no reliable data on the recipients of payments from which withholding taxes are deducted) they are classified in 1300 as not-allocable.

Treatment of credits under imputation systems

32. Under imputation systems of corporate income tax, a company's shareholders are wholly or partly relieved of their liability to income tax on dividends paid by the company out of income or profits liable to corporate income tax. In countries with such systems,[15] part of the tax on the company's profits is available to provide relief against the shareholders' own tax liability. The relief to the shareholder takes the form of a tax credit, the amount of which may be less than, equal to, or more than the shareholder's overall tax liability. If the tax credit exceeds this tax liability the excess may be payable to the shareholder. As this type of tax credit is an integral part of the imputation system of corporate income tax, any payment to the shareholders is treated as a repayment of tax and not as expenditure (compare the treatment of other tax credits described in §21).

33. As the tax credit under imputation systems (even when exceeding tax liability) is to be regarded as a tax provision, the question arises whether it should be deducted from individual income tax receipts (1110) or corporate income tax receipts (1210). In this Report, the full amount of corporate income tax paid is shown under 1210 and no imputed tax is included under 1110. Thus, the full amount of the credit reduces the amount of 1110 whether the credit results in a reduction of personal income tax liability or whether an actual refund is made because the credit exceeds the income tax liability. (Where, however, such tax credits are deducted from corporation tax in respect of dividends paid to corporations the amounts are deducted from the receipts of 1210.)

1120 and 1220 – *Taxes on capital gains*

34. These sub-headings comprise taxes imposed on capital gains, 1120 covering those levied on the gains of individuals and 1220 those levied on the gains of corporate enterprises, where receipts from such taxes can be separately identified. In many countries this is not the case and the receipts from such taxes are then classified with those from the income tax. Heading 1120 also includes taxes on gains from gambling.

2000 – *Social security contributions*

35. Classified here are all compulsory payments that confer an entitlement to receive a (contingent) future social benefit. Such payments are usually earmarked to finance social benefits and are often paid to institutions of general government that provide such benefits. However, such earmarking is not part of the definition of social security contributions and is not required for a tax to be classified here. However, conferment of an entitlement is required for a tax to be classified under this heading. So, levies on income or payroll that are earmarked for social security funds but do not confer an entitlement to benefit are excluded from this heading and shown under personal income taxes (1100) or taxes on payroll and workforce (3000). Taxes on other bases, such as goods and services, which are earmarked for social security benefits are not shown

here but are classified according to their respective bases because they generally confer no entitlement to social security benefits.

36. Contributions for the following types of social security benefits would, *inter alia*, be included: unemployment insurance benefits and supplements, accident, injury and sickness benefits, old-age, disability and survivors' pensions, family allowances, reimbursements for medical and hospital expenses or provision of hospital or medical services. Contributions may be levied on both employees and employers.

37. Contributions may be based on earnings or payroll ("on a payroll basis") or on net income after deductions and exemptions for personal circumstances ("on an income tax basis"), and the revenues from the two bases should be separately identified if possible. However, where contributions to a general social security scheme are on a payroll basis, but the contributions of particular groups (such as the self-employed) cannot be assessed on this basis and net income is used as a proxy for gross earnings, the receipts may still be classified as being on a payroll basis. In principle, this heading excludes voluntary contributions paid to social security schemes. When separately identifiable these are shown in the memorandum item on the financing of social security benefits. In practice, however, they cannot always be separately identified from compulsory contributions, in which case they are included in this heading.

38. Contributions to social insurance schemes which are not institutions of general government and to other types of insurance schemes, provident funds, pension funds, friendly societies or other saving schemes are not considered as social security contributions. Provident funds are arrangements under which the contributions of each employee and of the corresponding employer on his/her behalf are kept in a separate account earning interest and withdrawable under specific circumstances. Pension funds are separately organised schemes negotiated between employees and employers and carry provisions for different contributions and benefits, sometimes more directly tied to salary levels and length of service than under social security schemes. When contributions to these schemes are compulsory or quasi-compulsory (e.g. by virtue of agreement with professional and union organisations) they are shown in the memorandum item (refer to Section III.B of the Report).

39. Contributions by government employees and by governments in respect of their employees, to social security schemes classified within general government are included in this heading. Contributions to separate schemes for government employees, which can be regarded as replacing general social security schemes, are also regarded as taxes.[16] Where, however, a separate scheme is not seen as replacing a general scheme and has been negotiated between the government, in its role as an employer, and its employees, it is not regarded as social security and contributions to it are not regarded as taxes, even though the scheme may have been established by legislation.

40. This heading excludes 'imputed' contributions, which correspond to social benefits paid directly by employers to their employees or former employees or to their representatives (e.g. when employers are legally obliged to pay sickness benefits for a certain period).

41. Contributions are divided into those of employees (2100), employers (2200), and self-employed or non-employed (2300), and then further sub-divided according to the basis on which they are levied. Employees are defined for this purpose as all persons engaged in activities of business units, government bodies, private non-profit institutions, or other paid employment, except the proprietors and their unpaid family members in the case of unincorporated businesses. Members of the armed forces are included, irrespective of the duration and type of their service, if they contribute to social security schemes. The

contributions of employers are defined as their payments on account of their employees to social security schemes. Where employees or employers are required to continue the payment of social security contributions when the employee becomes unemployed these contributions, data permitting, are shown in 2100 and 2200 respectively. Accordingly, the sub-heading 2300 is confined to contributions paid by the self-employed and by those outside of the labour force (e.g. disabled or retired individuals).

3000 – *Taxes on payroll and workforce*

42. This heading covers taxes paid by employers, employees or the self-employed either as a proportion of payroll or as a fixed amount per person, and which do not confer entitlement to social benefits. Examples of taxes classified here are the United Kingdom national insurance surcharge (introduced in 1977), the Swedish payroll tax (1969–1979), and the Austrian Contribution to the Family Burden Equalisation Fund and Community Tax.

4000 – *Taxes on property*

43. This heading covers recurrent and non-recurrent taxes on the use, ownership or transfer of property. These include taxes on immovable property or net wealth, taxes on the change of ownership of property through inheritance or gift and taxes on financial and capital transactions. The following kinds of tax are excluded from this heading:

a) taxes on capital gains resulting from the sale of a property (1120 or 1220);

b) taxes on the use of goods or on permission to use goods or perform activities (5200); see §73;

c) taxes on immovable property levied on the basis of a presumed net income which take into account the personal circumstances of the taxpayer. They are classified as income taxes along with taxes on income and capital gains derived from property (1100);

d) taxes on the use of property for residence, where the tax is payable by either proprietor or tenant and the amount payable is a function of the user's personal circumstances (pay, dependants, and so on). They are classified as taxes on income (1100);

e) taxes on building in excess of permitted maximum density, taxes on the enlargement, construction or alteration of certain buildings beyond a permitted value and taxes on building construction. They are classified as taxes on permission to perform activities (5200);

f) taxes on the use of one's own property for special trading purposes like selling alcohol, tobacco, meat or for exploitation of land resources (e.g. United States severance taxes). They are classified as taxes on permission to perform activities (5200).

4100 – *Recurrent taxes on immovable property*

44. This sub-heading covers taxes levied regularly in respect of the use or ownership of immovable property.

- these taxes are levied on land and buildings;
- they can be in the form of a percentage of an assessed property value based on a national rental income, sales price, or capitalised yield; or in terms of other characteristics of real property, (for example size or location) from which a presumed rent or capital value can be derived.

- such taxes can be levied on proprietors, tenants, or both. They can also be paid by one level of government to another level of government in respect of property under the jurisdiction of the latter.
- debts are not taken into account in the assessment of these taxes, and they differ from taxes on net wealth in this respect.

45. Taxes on immovable property are further sub-divided into those paid by households (4110) and those paid by other entities (4120), according to the criteria set out in §26(b) above.

4200 – *Recurrent taxes on net wealth*

46. This sub-heading covers taxes levied regularly (in most cases annually) on net wealth, i.e. taxes on a wide range of movable and immovable property, net of debt. It is sub-divided into taxes paid by individuals (4210) and taxes paid by corporate enterprises (4220) according to the criteria set out in §26(a) above. If separate figures exist for receipts paid by institutions, the tax payments involved are added to those paid by corporations.

4300 – *Estate, inheritance and gift taxes*

47. This sub-heading is divided into taxes on estates and inheritances (4310) and taxes on gifts (4320).[17] Estate taxes are charged on the amount of the total estate whereas inheritance taxes are charged on the shares of the individual recipients; in addition the latter may take into account the relationship of the individual recipients to the deceased.

4400 – *Taxes on financial and capital transactions*

48. This sub-heading comprises, inter alia, taxes on the issue, transfer, purchase and sale of securities, taxes on cheques, and taxes levied on specific legal transactions such as validation of contracts and the sale of immovable property. The heading does not include:

a) taxes on the use of goods or property or permission to perform certain activities (5200);

b) fees paid to cover court charges, charges for birth, marriage or death certificates, which are normally regarded as non-tax revenues (see §9);

c) taxes on capital gains (1000);

d) recurrent taxes on immovable property (4100);

e) recurrent taxes on net wealth (4200);

f) once-and-for-all levies on property or wealth (4500).

4500 – *Other non-recurrent taxes on property*[17]

49. This sub-heading covers once-and-for-all, as distinct from recurrent, levies on property. It is divided into taxes on net wealth (4510) and other non-recurrent taxes on property (4520). Heading 4510 would include taxes levied to meet emergency expenditures, or for redistribution purposes. Heading 4520 would cover taxes levied to take account of increases in land value due to permission given to develop or provision of additional local facilities by general government, any taxes on the revaluation of capital and once-and-for-all taxes on particular items of property.

4600 – *Other recurrent taxes on property*

50. These rarely exist in OECD member countries, but the heading would include taxes on goods such as cattle, jewellery, windows, and other external signs of wealth.

5000 – *Taxes on goods and services*

51. All taxes and duties levied on the production, extraction, sale, transfer, leasing or delivery of goods, and the rendering of services (5100), or in respect of the use of goods or permission to use goods or to perform activities (5200) are included here. The heading thus covers:

a) multi-stage cumulative taxes;

b) general sales taxes – whether levied at manufacture/production, wholesale or retail level;

c) value-added taxes;

d) excises;

e) taxes levied on the import and export of goods;

f) taxes levied in respect of the use of goods and taxes on permission to use goods, or perform certain activities;

g) taxes on the extraction, processing or production of minerals and other products.

52. Borderline cases between this heading and heading 4000 (taxes on property) and 6100 (other taxes on business) are referred to in §43, §48 and §75. Residual sub-headings (5300) and (5130) cover tax receipts which cannot be allocated between 5100 and 5200 and between 5110 and 5120, respectively; see §28.

5100 – *Taxes on the production, sale, transfer, leasing and delivery of goods and rendering of services*

53. This sub-heading consists of all taxes, levied on transactions in goods and services on the basis of their intrinsic characteristics (e.g. value, weight of tobacco, strength of alcohol, and so on) as distinct from taxes imposed on the use of goods, or permission to use goods or perform activities, which fall under 5200.

5110 – *General taxes on goods and services*

54. This sub-heading includes all taxes, other than import and export duties (5123 and 5124), levied on the production, leasing, transfer, delivery or sales of a wide range of goods and/or the rendering of a wide range of services, irrespective of whether they are domestically produced or imported and irrespective of the stage of production or distribution at which they are levied. It thus covers value-added taxes, sales taxes and multi-stage cumulative taxes. Receipts from border adjustments in respect of such taxes when goods are imported are added to gross receipts for this category, and repayments of such taxes when goods are exported are deducted. These taxes are subdivided into 5111 value-added taxes, 5112 sales taxes, 5113 other general taxes on goods and services.

55. Borderline cases arise between this heading and taxes on specific goods (5120) when taxes are levied on a large number of goods, for example, the United Kingdom purchase tax (repealed in 1973) and the Japanese commodity tax (repealed in 1988). In conformity with national views, the former United Kingdom purchase tax is classified as a general tax (5112) and the former Japanese commodity tax as excises (5121).

5111 – *Value-added taxes*

56. All general consumption taxes charged on value-added are classified in this sub-heading, irrespective of the method of deduction and the stages at which the taxes are levied. In practice, all OECD countries with value-added taxes normally allow immediate deduction of taxes on purchases by all but the final consumer and impose

tax at all stages. In some countries the heading may include certain taxes, such as those on financial and insurance activities, either because receipts from them cannot be identified separately from those from the value-added tax, or because they are regarded as an integral part of the value-added tax, even though similar taxes in other countries might be classified elsewhere (e.g. 5126 as taxes on services or 4400 as taxes on financial and capital transactions).

5112 – *Sales taxes*

57. All general taxes levied at one stage only, whether at manufacturing or production, wholesale or retail stage are classified here.

5113 – *Other general taxes on goods and services*

58. This sub-heading covers multi-stage cumulative taxes (also know as 'cascade taxes') where tax is levied each time a transaction takes place without deduction for tax paid on inputs, and also those general consumption taxes where elements of value-added, sales or cascade taxes are combined.

5120 – *Taxes on specific goods and services*

59. Excises, profits generated and transferred from fiscal monopolies, and customs and imports duties as well as taxes on exports, foreign exchange transactions, investment goods and betting stakes and special taxes on services, which do not form part of a general tax of 5110, are included in this category.

5121 – *Excises*

60. Excises are taxes levied on particular products, or on a limited range of products, which are not classifiable under 5110 (general taxes), 5123 (import duties) and 5124 (export duties). They may be imposed at any stage of production or distribution and are usually assessed by reference to the weight or strength or quantity of the product, but sometimes by reference to value. Thus, special taxes on, for example, sugar, beetroot, matches, chocolates, and taxes at varying rates on a certain range of goods, as well as those levied in most countries on tobacco goods, alcoholic drinks and hydrocarbon oils and other energy sources, are included in this sub-heading.

61. Excises are distinguished from:

a) 5110 (general taxes). This is discussed in §54-55;

b) 5123 (import duties). If a tax collected principally on imported goods also applies, or would apply, under the law by which the tax is imposed to comparable home-produced goods, the receipts there from would be classified as excises (5121). This principle applies even if there is no comparable home production or no possibility of it (see also §65);

c) 5126 (taxes on services). The problem here arises in respect of taxes on electricity, gas and energy. All of these are regarded as taxes on goods and are included under 5121.

5122 – *Profits of fiscal monopolies*

62. This sub-heading covers that part of the profits of fiscal monopolies which is transferred to general government or which is used to finance any expenditures considered to be government expenditures (see §19). Amounts are shown when they are transferred to general government or used to make expenditures considered to be government expenditures

63. Fiscal monopolies reflect the exercise of the taxing power of government by the use of monopoly powers. Fiscal monopolies are non-financial public enterprises exercising a monopoly in most cases over the production or distribution of tobacco,

alcoholic beverages, salt, matches, playing cards and petroleum or agricultural products (i.e. on the kind of products which are likely to be, alternatively or additionally, subject to the excises of 5121), to raise the government revenues which in other countries are gathered through taxes on dealings in such commodities by private business units. The government monopoly may be at the production stage or, as in the case of government-owned and controlled liquor stores, at the distribution stage.

64. Fiscal monopolies are distinguished from public utilities such as rail transport, electricity, post offices, and other communications, which may enjoy a monopoly or quasi-monopoly position but where the primary purpose is normally to provide basic services rather than to raise revenue for government. Transfers from such other public enterprises to the government are considered as non-tax revenues. The traditional concept of fiscal monopoly has not been extended to include state lotteries, the profits of which are accordingly regarded as non-tax revenues. Fiscal monopoly profits are distinguished from export and import monopoly profits (5127) transferred from marketing boards or other enterprises dealing with international trade.

5123 – *Customs and other import duties*

65. Taxes, stamp duties and surcharges restricted by law to imported products are included here. Also included are levies on imported agricultural products which are imposed in member countries of the European Union and amounts paid by certain of these countries under the Monetary Compensation Accounts (MCA) system.[18] Starting from 1998, customs duties collected by European Union member states on behalf of the European Union are no longer reported under this heading in the country tables (in Part III of the Report). Excluded here are taxes collected on imports as part of a general tax on goods and services, or an excise applicable to both imported and domestically produced goods.

5124 – *Taxes on exports*

66. In the 1970s, export duties were levied in Australia, Canada and Portugal as a regular measure and they have been used in Finland for counter-cyclical purposes. Some member countries of the European Union pay, as part of the MCA system, a levy on exports (see note 18 to §65). Where these amounts are identifiable, they are shown in this heading. This heading does not include repayments of general consumption taxes or excises or customs duties on exported goods, which should be deducted from the gross receipts under 5110, 5121 or 5123, as appropriate.

5125 – *Taxes on investment goods*

67. This sub-heading covers taxes on investment goods, such as machinery. These taxes may be imposed for a number of years or temporarily for counter-cyclical purposes. Taxes on industrial inputs which are also levied on consumers [e.g., the Swedish energy tax which is classified under (5121)] are not included here.

5126 – *Taxes on specific services*

68. All taxes assessed on the payment for specific services, such as taxes on insurance premiums, banking services, gambling and betting stakes (e.g., from horse races, football pools, lottery tickets), transport, entertainment, restaurant and advertising charges, fall into this category. Taxes levied on the gross income of companies providing the service (e.g. gross insurance premiums or gambling stakes received by the company) are also classified under this heading. Tax revenues from bank levies and payments to deposit insurance and financial stability schemes are provisionally included here for the 2012 edition. The detailed classification is set out in paragraph 105.

69. Excluded from this sub-heading are:

a) taxes on services forming part of a general tax on goods and services (5110);

b) taxes on electricity, gas and energy (5121 as excises);

c) taxes on individual gains from gambling (1120 as taxes on capital gains of individuals and non-corporate enterprises) and lump-sum taxes on the transfer of private lotteries or on the permission to set up lotteries (5200);[19]

d) taxes on cheques and on the issue, transfer or redemption of securities (4400 as taxes on financial and capital transactions).

5127 – *Other taxes on international trade and transactions*

70. This sub-heading covers revenue received by the government from the purchase and sale of foreign exchange at different rates. When the government exercises monopoly powers to extract a margin between the purchase and sales price of foreign exchange, other than to cover administrative costs, the revenue derived constitutes a compulsory levy exacted in indeterminate proportions from both purchaser and seller of foreign exchange. It is the common equivalent of an import duty and export duty levied in a single exchange rate system or of a tax on the sale or purchase of foreign exchange. Like the profits of fiscal monopolies and import or export monopolies transferred to government, it represents the exercise of monopoly powers for tax purposes and is included in tax revenues.

71. The sub-heading covers also the profits of export or import monopolies, which do not however exist in OECD countries, taxes on purchase or sale of foreign exchange, and any other taxes levied specifically on international trade or transactions.

5128 – *Other taxes on specific goods and services*

72. This item includes taxes on the extraction of minerals, fossil fuels and other exhaustible resources from deposits owned privately or by another government together with any other unidentifiable receipts from taxes on specific goods and services. Taxes on the extraction of exhaustible resources are usually a fixed amount per unit of quality or weight, but can be a percentage of value. The taxes are recorded when the resources are extracted. Payments from the extraction of exhaustible resources from deposits owned by the government unit receiving the payment are classified as rent.

5200 – *Taxes on use of goods or on permission to use goods or perform activities*

73. This sub-heading covers taxes which are levied in respect of the use of goods as distinct from taxes on the goods themselves. Unlike the latter taxes – reported under 5100 –, they are not assessed on the value of the goods but usually as fixed amounts. Taxes on permission to use goods or to perform activities are also included here, as are pollution taxes not based upon the value of particular goods. It is sometimes difficult to distinguish between compulsory user charges and licence fees which are regarded as taxes and those which are excluded as non-tax revenues. The criteria which are employed are noted in §9–10.

74. Although the sub-heading refers to the 'use' of goods, registration of ownership rather than use may be what generates liability to tax, so that the taxes of this heading may apply to the ownership of animals or goods rather than their use (e.g. race horses, dogs and motor vehicles) and may apply even to unusable goods (e.g. unusable motor vehicles or guns).

75. Borderline cases arise with:

a) taxes on the permission to perform business activities which are levied on a combined income, payroll or turnover base and, accordingly, are classified following the rules in §78;

b) taxes on the ownership or use of property of headings 4100, 4200 and 4600. The heading 4100 is confined to taxes on the ownership or tenancy of immovable property and – unlike the taxes of 5200 – they are related to the value of the property. The net wealth taxes and taxes on chattels of 4200 and 4600 respectively are confined to the ownership rather than the use of assets, apply to groups of assets rather than particular goods and again are related to the value of the assets.

5210 – *Recurrent taxes on use of goods and on permission to use goods or perform activities*

76. The principal characteristic of taxes classified here is that they are levied at regular intervals and that they are usually fixed amounts. The most important item in terms of revenue receipts is vehicle licence taxes. This sub-heading also covers taxes on permission to hunt, shoot, fish or to sell certain products and taxes on the ownership of dogs and on the performance of certain services, provided that they meet the criteria set out in §9–10. The sub-divisions of 5210 are user taxes on motor vehicles paid by households (5211) and those paid by others (5212).[20] Sub-heading 5213 covers dog licences and user charges for permission to perform activities such as selling meat or liquor when the levies are on a recurring basis. It also covers recurrent general licences for hunting, shooting and fishing where the right to carry out these activities is not granted as part of a normal commercial transaction (e.g. the granting of the licence is not accompanied by the right to use a specific area which is owned by government).

5220 – *Non-recurrent taxes on use of goods and on permission to use goods or perform activities*

77. This section covers non-recurrent taxes levied on the use of goods or on permission to use goods or perform activities and taxes levied each time goods are used. It includes taxes levied on the emission or discharge into the environment of noxious gases, liquids or other harmful substances.

- Payments for tradable emission permits issued by governments under cap and trade schemes should be recorded here at the time the emissions occur. No revenue should be recorded for permits that governments issue free of charge. The accrual basis of recording means that there can be a timing difference between the cash being received by government for the permits and the time the emission occurs. In the national accounts, this timing gives rise to a financial liability for government during the period.
- Payments made for the collection and disposal of waste or noxious substances by public authorities should be excluded as they constitute a sale of services to enterprises.

78. Other taxes falling under heading 5200 that are not levied recurrently are also included here. Thus, once-and-for-all payments for permission to sell liquor or tobacco or to set up betting shops are included provided they meet the criteria set out in §9–10.

6000 – *Other taxes*

79. Taxes levied on a base, or bases, other than those described under headings 1000, 3000, 4000 and 5000, or on bases of which none could be regarded as being predominantly the same as that of any one of these headings, are covered here. As regards taxes levied on a multiple base, if it is possible to estimate receipts related to each base (e.g. the Austrian and German 'Gewerbesteuer') this is done and the separate amounts included under the appropriate headings. If the separate amounts cannot be estimated, but it is known that most of the receipts are derived from one base, the whole of the receipts are classified according to that base. If neither of these procedures can be followed, they are classified here. The sub-headings may also include receipts from taxes which

governments are unable to identify or isolate (see §28). Included here also are fines and penalties paid for infringement of regulations relating to taxes but not identifiable as relating to a particular category of taxes (see §15). A subdivision is made between taxes levied wholly or predominantly on business (6100) and those levied on others (6200).

A.6. Conciliation with National Accounts

80. This section of the tables provides a re-conciliation between the OECD calculation of total tax revenues and the total of all taxes and social contributions paid to general government as recorded in the country's National Accounts. Where the country is a member of the European Union (EU), the comparison is between the OECD calculation of total tax revenues and the sum of tax revenues and social contributions recorded in the combination of the general government and the institutions of the EU sectors of the National Accounts.

A.7. Memorandum item on the financing of social security benefits

81. In view of the varying relationship between taxation and social security contributions and the cases referred to in §35 to §41, a memorandum item collects together all payments earmarked for social security-type benefits, other than voluntary payments to the private sector. Data are presented as follows (refer section III.B of the Report):

a) Taxes of 2000 series.

b) Taxes earmarked for social security benefits.

c) Voluntary contributions to the government.

d) Compulsory contributions to the private sector.

Guidance on the breakdown of (a) to (d) above is provided in §35 to §41.

A.8. Memorandum item on identifiable taxes paid by government

82. Identifiable taxes actually paid by government are presented in a memorandum item classified by the main headings of the OECD classification of taxes. In the vast majority of countries, only social security contributions and payroll taxes paid by government can be identified. These are, however, usually the most important taxes paid by governments (refer section III.C of the Report).

A.9. Relation of OECD classification of taxes to national accounting systems

83. A system of national accounts (SNA) seeks to provide a coherent framework for recording and presenting the main flows relating respectively to production, consumption, accumulation and external transactions of a given economic area, usually a country or a major region within a country. Government revenues are an important part of the transactions recorded in SNA. The final version of the 2008 SNA was jointly published by five international organisations: the United Nations, the International Monetary Fund, the European Union, the Organisation for Economic Co-operation and Development, and the World Bank in August 2009. The System is a comprehensive, consistent and flexible set of macroeconomic accounts. It is designed for use in countries with market economies, whatever their stage of economic development, and also in countries in transition to market economies. The important parts of the SNA's conceptual framework and its definitions of the various sectors of the economy have been reflected in the OECD's classification of taxes.

84. There are, however, some differences between the OECD classification of taxes and SNA concepts that are listed below. They arise because the aim of the former is to provide the maximum disaggregation of statistical data on what are generally regarded as taxes by tax administrations.

a) OECD includes social security contributions in total tax revenues (§7 and §8 above);

b) there are different points of view on whether or not some levies and fees are classified as taxes (§9 and §10 above);

c) OECD excludes imputed taxes or subsidies resulting from the operation of official multiple exchange rates;

d) there are differences in the treatment of non-wastable tax credits

85. As noted in §1 and §2, headings 1000 to 6000 of the OECD list of taxes cover all unrequited payments to general government, other than compulsory loans and fines. Such unrequited payments including fines, but excluding compulsory loans can be obtained from adding together the following figures in the 2008 SNA

- value-added type taxes (D.211);
- taxes and duties on imports, excluding VAT (D.212);
- export taxes (D.213);
- taxes on products, excluding VAT, import and export taxes (D.214);
- other taxes on production (D.29);
- taxes on income (D.51);
- other current taxes (D.59);
- social contributions (D.61), excluding voluntary contributions;
- capital taxes (D.91).

A.10. The OECD classification of taxes and the International Monetary Fund (GFS) system

86. The coverage and valuation of tax revenues in the GFS system and the 2008 SNA are very similar. Therefore, with the exception of the treatment of non-wastable tax credits, the differences between the OECD classification and that of the 2008 SNA (see §84 above) also apply to the GFS. In addition the International Monetary Fund subdivides the OECD 5000 heading into section IV (Domestic Taxes on Goods and Services) and section V (Taxes on International Trade and Transactions). This reflects the fact that while the latter usually yield insignificant amounts of revenue in OECD countries, this is not the case in many non-OECD countries.

A.11. Comparison of the OECD classification of taxes with other international classifications

87. The table below describes an item by item comparison of the OECD classification of taxes and the classifications used in the following:

i) System of National Accounts (2008 SNA);

ii) European System of Accounts (1995 ESA);

iii) IMF *Government Finance Statistics Manual* (GFSM2001).

88. These comparisons represent those that would be expected to apply in the majority of cases. However in practice some flexibility should be used in their application. This is because in particular cases, countries can adopt varying approaches to the classification of revenues in National Accounts.

OECD Classification		2008 SNA	1995 ESA	GFSM2001
1000	Taxes on income, profits and capital gains			
	1100 Individuals			
	1110 Income/profits	D51-8.61a	D51A	1111
	1120 Capital gains	D51-8.61c,d	D51C,D	1111
	1200 Corporations			
	1210 Income/profits	D51-8.61b	D51B	1112
	1220 Capital gains	D51-8.61c	D51C	1112
	1300 Unallocable as between 1100 and 1200			1113
2000	Social security contributions			
	2100 Employees	D613-8.85	D611[illegible]1	1211
	2200 Employers	D611-8.83	D61121	1212
	2300 Self-employed, non-employed	D613-8.85	D61131	1213
	2400 Unallocable as between 2100, 2200 and 2300			1214
3000	Taxes on payroll and workforce	D29-7.97a	D29C	112
4000	Taxes on property			
	4100 Recurrent taxes on immovable property			
	4110 Households	D59-8.63a	D59A	1131
	4120 Other	D29-7.97b	D29A	1131
	4200 Recurrent net wealth taxes			
	4210 Individual	D59-8.63b	D59A	1132
	4220 Corporations	D59-8.63b	D59A	1132
	4300 Estate, inheritance and gift taxes			
	4310 Estate and inheritance taxes	D91-10.207b	D91A	1133
	4320 Gift taxes	D91-10.207b	D91A	1133
	4400 Taxes on financial and capital transactions	D59-7.96d; D29-7.97e	D2143,C	1134:1161
	4500 Other non-recurrent taxes on property	D91-10.207a	D91B	1135
	4600 Other recurrent taxes on property	D59-8.63c	D59A	1136
5000	Taxes on goods and services			
	5100 Taxes on production, sale and transfer of goods and services			
	5110 General sales taxes			
	5111 Value-added taxes	D211-7.89	D211; D29G	11411
	5112 Sales taxes	D2122-7.94a; D214-7.96a	D2122D; D214I	11412
	5113 Other general taxes	D214-7.96a	D214I	11413
	5120 Taxes on specific goods and services			
	5121 Excises	D2122-7.94b; D214-7.96b	D2122C; D214A,B,D	1142
	5122 Profits of fiscal monopolies	D214-7.96e	D214J	1143
	5123 Customs/import duties	D2121-7.93	D2121; D2122A,B	1151
	5124 On exports	D213-7.95a	D214K	1152-4
	5125 On investment goods			
	5126 On specific services	D2122-7.94c; D214-7.96c	D2122E; D214E,F,G; D29F	1144; 1156
	5127 Other taxes on international trade and transactions	D2122-7.94d D29-7.95b D29-7.97g D59-8.64d	D2122F; D29D; D59E	1153 1155-6
	5128 Other taxes on specific goods and services			1146
	5130 Unallocable as between 5110 and 5120			
	5200 Taxes on use of goods			
	5210 Recurrent taxes			
	5211 Motor vehicle taxes households	D59-8.64c	D59D	11451
	5212 Motor vehicles taxes others	D29-7.97d	D214D; D29B	11451
	5213 Other recurrent taxes	D29-7.97c,d,f D59-8.64c	D29B,E,F; D59D	11452
	5220 Non-recurrent taxes			
	5300 Unallocable as between 5100 and 5200			
6000	Other taxes			
	6100 Paid solely by business			
	6200 Paid by other than business, or unidentifiable	D59-8.64a,b	D59B,C	1162

A.12. Attribution of tax revenues by sub-sectors of general government

89. The OECD classification requires a breakdown of tax revenues by sub-sectors of government. The definition of each sub-sector and the criteria to be used to attribute tax revenues between these sub-sectors are set out below. They follow the guidance of the 2008 SNA and GFSM2001.

Sub-sectors of general government to be identified

a) Central government

90. The central government sub-sector includes all governmental departments, offices, establishments and other bodies which are agencies or instruments of the central authority whose competence extends over the whole territory, with the exception of the administration of social security funds.Central government therefore has the authority to impose taxes on all resident and non-resident units engaged in economic activities within the country.

b) State, provincial or regional government

91. This sub-sector consists of intermediate units of government exercising a competence at a level below that of central government. It includes all such units operating independently of central government in a part of a country's territory encompassing a number of smaller localities, with the exception of the administration of social security funds. In unitary countries, regional governments may be considered to have a separate existence where they have substantial autonomy to raise a significant proportion of their revenues from sources within their control and their officers are independent of external administrative control in the actual operation of the unit's activities.

92. At present, federal countries comprise the majority of cases where revenues attributed to intermediate units of government are identified separately. Spain is the only unitary country in this position. In the remaining unitary countries, regional revenues are included with those of local governments.

c) Local government

93. This sub-sector includes all other units of government exercising an independent competence in part of the territory of a country, with the exception of the administration of social security funds. It encompasses various urban and/or rural jurisdictions (e.g. local authorities, municipalities, cities, boroughs, districts).

d) Social security funds

94. Social security funds form a separate sub-sector of general government. The social security sub-sector is defined in the 2008 SNA by the following extracts from paragraphs 4.124 to 4.126 and 4.147:

"Social security schemes are social insurance schemes covering the community as a whole or large section of the community that are imposed and controlled by government units. The schemes cover a wide variety of programmes, providing benefits in cash or in kind for old age, invalidity or death, survivors, sickness and maternity, work injury, unemployment, family allowance, health care, etc. There is not necessarily a direct link between the amount of the contribution paid by an individual and the benefits he or she may receive." (Paragraph 4.124).

"When social security schemes are separately organised from the other activities of government units and hold their assets and liabilities separately from the latter and engage in financial transactions on their own account they qualify as institutional units that are described as social security funds." (Paragraph 4.125).

"The amounts raised, and paid out, in social security contributions and benefits may be deliberately varied in order to achieve objectives of government policy that have no direct connection with the concept of social security as a scheme to provide social benefits to members of the community. They may be raised or lowered in order to influence the level of aggregate demand in the economy, for example. Nevertheless, so long as they remain separately constituted funds, they must be treated as separate institutional units in the SNA." (Paragraph 4.126).

"The social security funds sub-sector (of general government) consists of the social security funds operating at all levels of government. Such funds are social insurance schemes covering the community as a whole or large section of the community that are imposed by government units." (Paragraph 4.147).

95. This definition of social security funds is followed in the OECD classification with the two following exceptions which are excluded:

- Schemes imposed by government and operated by bodies outside the general government sector, as defined in §3 of this manual; and
- Schemes to which all contributions are voluntary.

Supra-national authorities

96. This sub-sector covers the revenue-raising operations of supra-national authorities within a country. In practice, the only relevant supra-national authority in the OECD area is that of the institutions of the European Union (EU). As from 1998, supra-national authorities are no longer included in the *Revenue Statistics*, to achieve consistency with the SNA definition of general government which excludes them. For example, income taxes and social security contributions collected by European Institutions and paid by European civil servants who are resident of EU member countries should not be included. However the specific levies paid by the member states of the EU continue to be included in total tax revenues and they are shown under this heading.

Criteria to be used for the attribution of tax revenues

97. When a government collects taxes and pays them over in whole or in part to other governments, it is necessary to determine whether the revenues should be considered to be those of the collecting government which it distributes to others as grants, or those of the beneficiary governments which the collecting government receives and passes on only as their agent. The criteria to be used in the attribution of revenues are set out in §98 to §101 which replicate paragraphs 3.70 to 3.73 from the 2008 SNA.

98. In general, a tax is attributed to the government unit that:

a) exercises the authority to impose the tax (either as a principal or through the delegated authority of the principal);

b) has final discretion to set and vary the rate of the tax.

99. Where an amount is collected by one government for and on behalf of another government, and the latter government has the authority to impose the tax, and set and vary its rate, then the former is acting as an agent for the latter and the tax is reassigned. Any amount retained by the collecting government as a collection charge should be treated as a payment for a service. Any other amount retained by the collecting

government, such as under a tax-sharing arrangement, should be treated as a current grant. If the collecting government was delegated the authority to set and vary the rate, then the amount collected should be treated as tax revenue of this government.

100. Where different governments jointly and equally set the rate of a tax and jointly and equally decide on the distribution of the proceeds, with no individual government having ultimate overriding authority, then the tax revenues are attributed to each government according to its respective share of the proceeds. If an arrangement allows one government unit to exercise ultimate overriding authority, then all of the tax revenue is attributed to that unit.

101. There may also be the circumstance where a tax is imposed under the constitutional or other authority of one government, but other governments individually set the tax rate in their jurisdictions. The proceeds of the tax generated in each respective government's jurisdiction are attributed as tax revenues of that government.

Levies paid by member states of the European Union

102. The levies paid by the member states of the EU take the form:

- VAT own resources; and
- Specific levies which include:

a) custom duties and levies on agricultural goods (5123);

b) gross monetary compensation accounts (5123 if relating to imports and 5124 if relating to exports); and

c) Steel, coal, sugar and milk levies (5128).

103. The custom duties collected by member states on behalf of the EU are recorded:

- on a gross of collection fee basis;
- using figures adjusted so that duties are shown on a 'final destination' as opposed to a 'country of first entry' basis where such adjustments can be made. These adjustments concern in particular duties collected at important (sea) ports. Although the EU duties are collected by the authorities of the country of first entry, when possible these duties should be excluded from the revenue of the collecting country and be included in the revenue of the country of final destination.

104. This is the specific EU levy that most clearly conforms to the attribution criterion described in §96 above. Consequently as from 1998, these amounts are footnoted as a memorandum item to the EU member state country tables (in Part III) and no longer shown under heading 5123. However the figures are included in the total tax revenue figures on the top line for all the relevant years shown in the tables.

105. The VAT own resources, which are determined by applying a rate not exceeding 1% to an assessment basis specified in the Sixth Directive,[21] are more of a borderline case. They have some of the characteristics of a transfer (they are not derived from a clearly identifiable source of funds that are actually collected) and some of a tax (the amount of the transfer is determined by the receiving sub-sector of government). In this publication they are not shown as a tax of the European Union (but as a tax of the EU member states), though the amounts involved are footnoted in the tables contained in Part IV.

A.13. Provisional classification of revenues from bank levies and payments to deposit insurance and financial stability schemes

106. The OECD have adopted the following interim approach to reporting revenue from bank levies plus deposit insurance and stability fees for the 2012 edition of *OECD Revenue Statistics*; The amounts should be recorded under category 5126.

- Compulsory payments of stability fees, bank levies and deposit insurance should generally be treated as tax revenues where the payments are made to General Government and allocated to the governments' consolidated or general funds so that the Government is free to make immediate use of the money for the purposes that it chooses. This principle would apply regardless of whether the Government is promising to make payments to guarantee the banks' customer deposits in some future contingency.
- If the compulsory payments are made to general government and placed in funds that are earmarked to be entirely channelled back to the sector of the economy that comprises the companies that are subject to the payment, they would still generally be treated as tax revenues on the grounds that the funds would be available for the government and would reduce its budget deficit, the fee is unrequited for an individual entity and the amounts raised could be unrelated to any eventual pay out to depositors or expenditure on wider support for the financial sector.
- Payments to made to the smaller long-standing schemes for insuring 'retail' deposits, where the payment levels are consistent with the costs of insurance should be classified as fee for service.
- Any payments which involve governments realising the assets of a failed institution or receiving a priority claim on its assets in liquidation in order to fund payments of compensation to customers for their lost deposits would be treated as a fee for a service as opposed to tax revenues.
- Compulsory payments that are made to funds operated outside the government sector and non-state institutions backed by the deposit takers and all payments to voluntary schemes should not be treated as tax revenues.

Notes

1. References in this annex to Sections or Parts of "this Report" refer to OECD (2015), *Revenue Statistics* 1965-2014, OECD Publishing, Paris.
2. All references to SNA are to the 2008 edition.
3. See section A.12 of this guide for a discussion of the concept of agency capacity.
4. It is usually possible to identify amounts of social security contributions and payroll taxes, but not other taxes paid by government.
5. If, however, a levy which is considered as non-tax revenue by most countries is regarded as a tax – or raises substantial revenue – in one or more countries, the amounts collected are footnoted at the end of the relevant country tables, even though the amounts are not included in total tax revenues.
6. Names, however, can frequently be misleading. For example, though a passport fee would normally be considered a non-tax revenue, if a supplementary levy on passports (as is the case in Portugal) were imposed in order to raise substantial amounts of revenue relative to the cost of providing the passport, the levy would be regarded as a tax under 5200.
7. There are practical difficulties in operating the distinction made by 1993 SNA.
8. A more detailed explanation of this distinction can be found in the special feature, "Current issues in reporting tax revenues", in the 2001 edition of the *Revenue Statistics*.
9. Sometimes the terms "non-refundable" and "refundable" are used, but it may be considered illogical to talk of "refundable" when nothing has been paid.
10. A different treatment, however, is accorded to non-wastable tax credits under imputation systems of corporate income tax (§32–34).
11. This is not strictly a true tax expenditure in the formal sense. Such tax expenditures require identification of a benchmark tax system for each country or, preferably, a common international benchmark. In practice it has not been possible to reach agreement on a common international benchmark.
12. Unless based on the profit made on a sale, in which case they would be classified as capital gains taxes under 1120 or 1220.
13. In some countries the same legislation applies to both individual and corporate enterprises for particular taxes on income. However, the receipts from such taxes are usually allocable between individuals and enterprises and can therefore be shown in the appropriate sub-heading.
14. For example, "...sufficiently self-contained and independent that they behave in the same way as corporations.......(including) keeping a complete set of accounts" (2008SNA, section 4.44).
15. In Canada – a country also referred to as having an imputation system – the (wastable) tax credit for the shareholder is in respect of domestic corporation tax deemed to have been paid whether or not a corporation tax liability has arisen. As there is no integral connection between the corporation tax liability and the credit given against income tax under such systems, these credits for dividends are treated, along with other tax credits, on the lines described in §21.
16. This may also apply where a scheme for government employees existed prior to the introduction of a general social security scheme.
17. In the 2008 SNA these are regarded as capital transfers and not as taxes (see section G).
18. This is the system by which the European Union adjusts for differences between the exchange rates used to determine prices under the Common Market Agricultural Policy and actual exchange rates. Payments under the system may relate to imports or exports and where these amounts are separately identifiable they are shown under the appropriate heading (5123 or 5124). In this Report, these amounts are shown gross (i.e. without deducting any subsidies paid out under the MCA system).
19. Transfers of profits of State lotteries are regarded as non-tax revenues (see also §64).
20. See §26(c) as regards this distinction.
21. At the Edinburgh Summit (1992) EU Member countries have decided to gradually reduce this percentage from 1.4 to 1, and to effectuate this reduction between years 1995 and 1999. During the period 1970–1983 this percentage also amounted to 1.

ANNEXE A

Guide d'interprétation de l'OCDE

Table des matières

A.1. Classification d'impôts de l'OCDE

1000 *Impôts sur le revenu, les bénéfices et les gains en capital*

1100 Impôts sur le revenu, les bénéfices et les gains en capital des personnes physiques

1110 Sur le revenu et les bénéfices

1120 Sur les gains en capital

1200 Impôts sur le revenu, les bénéfices et les gains en capital des sociétés

1210 Sur le revenu et les bénéfices

1220 Sur les gains en capital

1300 Non ventilable entres les rubriques 1100 et 1200

2000 *Cotisations de sécurité sociale*

2100 A la charge des salariés

2110 Sur la base du salaire

2120 Sur la base de l'impôt sur le revenu

2200 A la charge des employeurs

2210 Sur la base du salaire

2220 Sur la base de l'impôt sur le revenu

2300 A la charge des travailleurs indépendants ou des personnes n'occupant pas d'emploi

2310 Sur la base du salaire

2320 Sur la base de l'impôt sur le revenu

2400 Non ventilables entre les rubriques 2100, 2200 et 2300

2410 Sur la base du salaire

2420 Sur la base de l'impôt sur le revenu

3000 *Impôts sur les salaires et la main-d'œuvre*

4000 *Impôts sur le patrimoine*

4100 Impôts périodiques sur la propriété immobilière

4110 Ménages

4120 Autres agents

4200 Impôts périodiques sur l'actif net

4210 Personnes physiques

4220 Sociétés

4300 Impôts sur les mutations par décès, les successions et les donations

4310 Impôts sur les mutations par décès et les successions

4320 Impôts sur les donations

4400 Impôts sur les transactions mobilières et immobilières

4500 Autres impôts non périodiques sur le patrimoine

4510 Impôts sur l'actif net

4520 Autres impôts non périodiques

4600 Autres impôts périodiques sur le patrimoine

5000 *Impôts sur les biens et services*

5100 Impôts sur la production, la vente, le transfert, la location et la livraison des biens et la prestation de services

5110 Impôts généraux

5111 Taxes sur la valeur ajoutée

5112 Impôts sur les ventes

5113 Autres impôts généraux sur les biens et services

5120 Impôts sur des biens et des services déterminés

5121 Accises

5122 Bénéfices des monopoles fiscaux

5123 Droits de douane et droits à l'importation

5124 Taxes à l'exportation

5125 Impôts sur les biens d'équipement

5126 Impôts sur des services déterminés

5127 Autres impôts sur les transactions et les échanges internationaux

5128 Autres impôts sur des biens et services déterminés

5130 Non ventilables entre les rubriques 5110 et 5120

5200 Impôts sur l'utilisation des biens ou l'autorisation d'utiliser des biens ou d'exercer des activités

5210 Impôts périodiques

5211 A la charge des ménages au titre de véhicules à moteur

5212 A la charge d'autres agents au titre de véhicules à moteur

5213 Autres impôts périodiques

5220 Impôts non périodiques

5300 Non ventilables entre les rubriques 5100 et 5200

6000 *Autres impôts*

6100 A la charge exclusive des entreprises

6200 A la charge d'autre agents que les entreprises ou non identifiables

Le Guide d'interprétation de l'OCDE[1]

A.2. Champ couvert

Principes généraux

1. Dans la classification de l'OCDE, le terme "impôts" désigne uniquement les versements obligatoires effectués sans contrepartie au profit des administrations publiques. Les impôts n'ont pas de contrepartie en ce sens que, normalement, les prestations fournies par les administrations au contribuable ne sont pas proportionnelles à ses versements.

2. Le terme "impôts" ne couvre pas les amendes sans lien avec une infraction fiscale ni les prêts obligatoires aux administrations. Les cas dans lesquels la délimitation entre recettes fiscales et non fiscales est délicate à tracer, pour certains droits et taxes d'utilisation, sont examinés dans les § 9 à § 13.

3. Les administrations publiques comprennent l'administration centrale et les organismes dont les opérations sont sous son contrôle effectif, les administrations régionales et locales et leurs services, les organismes de sécurité sociale et les entités publiques autonomes, à l'exception des entreprises publiques. Cette définition des administrations est calquée sur celle du Système de comptabilité nationale 2008 (SCN)[2]. Dans cette publication, les administrations publiques et leurs sous-secteurs sont décrits dans le chapitre 4, section F, pages 80-84.

4. Les paiements obligatoires à des organismes supranationaux et aux organismes qui en dépendent ne sont plus compris depuis 1998 parmi les impôts sauf quelques exceptions. En effet, les droits de douane collectés par les États membres de l'Union européenne pour le compte de celle-ci sont toujours présentés à titre de rubrique "Pour mémoire" et compris dans le total des recettes fiscales, à la Partie III, tableaux par pays. (Voir § 95.) Dans les pays où les églises font partie des administrations publiques, les impôts sur les cultes sont inclus dans ces paiements, à condition qu'ils répondent aux critères énoncés au § 1 ci-dessus. Comme les données se réfèrent aux montants encaissés par les administrations publiques, les contributions versées à des organismes privés, aux organismes sociaux ou régimes de sécurité sociale extérieurs aux administrations publiques, aux syndicats ou aux associations professionnelles sont exclues, même si elles sont obligatoires. Sont toutefois inclus les versements obligatoires aux administrations publiques dont le montant est affecté à ces organismes, à condition que l'administration ne fasse pas simplement office d'agent collecteur[3]. On a distingué les bénéfices des monopoles fiscaux de ceux d'autres entreprises publiques et on les a considérés comme des impôts parce qu'ils reflètent l'exercice du pouvoir d'imposition de l'État par l'intermédiaire du monopole (voir § 62 à § 64), comme le sont les bénéfices de l'État provenant de l'achat et de la vente de monnaies étrangères à des taux différents (voir § 70).

5. Les impôts payés par les administrations à elles-mêmes (tels que les cotisations de sécurité sociale et les impôts sur les salaires payés par les administrations en tant qu'employeurs (2200 et 3000), les impôts sur la consommation qu'elles acquittent à l'occasion de leurs achats ou les impôts sur leur patrimoine) sont inclus dans les données présentées. Toutefois, lorsqu'il est possible de les isoler, les montants provenant de ces impôts[4] sont indiqués dans section III.C de cette publication.

6. Les rapports entre cette classification et celle du Système de comptabilité nationale (SCN) sont indiquées dans les sections H et J. À cause des différences qui existent entre les deux classifications, les statistiques de la comptabilité nationale ne sont pas toujours

établies ou classées suivant la pratique adoptée dans le présent guide. Ces différences et d'autres encore sont mentionnées dans les cas appropriés (voir par exemple § 13 et § 26), mais il est impossible de toutes les signaler. Il peut y avoir aussi certaines différences entre cette classification et celle utilisée par certaines administrations nationales (voir par exemple § 10), aussi les statistiques nationales et celles de l'OCDE ne peuvent pas toujours être compatibles ; ces différences, cependant, sont vraisemblablement très insignifiantes dans les montants des recettes en cause.

Cotisations de sécurité sociale

7. Les cotisations de sécurité sociale, définies au § 35, qui sont versées aux administrations publiques, font partie des recettes fiscales. Elles sont évidemment assimilables à des impôts puisqu'il s'agit de versements obligatoires à des administrations publiques. Mais elles peuvent différer toutefois des autres impôts du fait que le paiement des prestations de sécurité sociale dépend dans la plupart des pays du versement des cotisations appropriées, encore qu'il n'y ait pas forcément un lien entre l'importance des prestations et le montant des cotisations. La comparabilité entre les pays sera meilleure si on considère les cotisations de sécurité sociale comme des impôts ; elles figurent cependant sous une rubrique distincte de façon à permettre un traitement séparé pour n'importe quelle analyse.

8. Les cotisations de sécurité sociale qui sont volontaires ou qui ne sont pas versées à des administrations publiques (voir § 1) ne sont pas considérées comme des impôts, bien que dans certains pays (comme il est indiqué dans les notes correspondantes) il soit difficile d'éliminer les cotisations volontaires et certains versements obligatoires au secteur privé.

Droits, taxes d'utilisation et droits de licence

9. Si l'on excepte les droits perçus sur les permis de circulation des véhicules à moteur, qui sont universellement considérés comme des impôts, il n'est pas facile de distinguer les droits et taxes d'utilisation qui doivent être traitées comme des impôts de celles qui ne doivent pas l'être. Si, en effet, un droit ou une taxe est perçu au titre d'un service ou d'une activité déterminée, le lien entre ce prélèvement et la prestation fournie peut être plus ou moins important, de même que la relation entre le montant du prélèvement et le coût de la prestation. Lorsque le bénéficiaire d'une prestation acquitte un droit dont le montant est clairement lié au coût de la prestation fournie, on peut considérer que le prélèvement comporte une contrepartie, et d'après la définition donnée au § 1, il ne sera pas traité comme un impôt. Toutefois, dans les cas suivants, les prélèvements seraient 'sans contrepartie':

a) lorsque le prélèvement est très supérieur au coût de la prestation fournie ;

b) lorsque le redevable de la contribution n'est pas le bénéficiaire de la prestation correspondante (par exemple, un droit perçu sur l'abattage du bétail pour financer un service qui est fourni aux agriculteurs) ;

c) lorsque l'État ne fournit pas un service déterminé en contrepartie du droit qu'il perçoit, même si un permis est délivré à celui qui acquitte le droit (par exemple, lorsque l'État délivre des permis de chasse, de pêche ou de port d'armes qui ne sont pas assortis du droit d'utiliser une parcelle déterminée de terres appartenant à l'État) ;

d) lorsque les bénéficiaires de la prestation sont les personnes qui ont acquitté le droit, mais que la prestation dont chacun bénéficie n'est pas nécessairement en rapport avec le montant de ses propres versements (par exemple, le droit de commercialisation du lait acquitté par les fermiers qui sert à promouvoir la consommation de lait.

10. Dans des cas limites, cependant, l'application des critères énoncés au § 1 peut être particulièrement difficile. La solution adoptée, dans un souci d'uniformité entre les pays et eu égard aux montants relativement faibles des recettes en cause, consiste à s'en tenir à la pratique prépondérante des administrations fiscales plutôt que de laisser chaque pays décider si ces prélèvements sont des impôts ou des recettes non fiscales[5].

11. On trouvera ci-après la liste des principaux droits et taxes en question et leur traitement normal[6] dans la présente publication :

Recettes non fiscales :	frais de justice ; droits de délivrance de permis de conduire ; droits portuaires ; redevances de passeport ; redevances de radio et de télévision lorsque le service est assuré par les pouvoirs publics.
Impôts du sous-groupe 5200:	autorisation d'exercer certaines activités telles que : distribution de films ; chasse, pêche et utilisation d'armes à feu ; organisation de spectacles ou de jeux et paris ; vente de boissons alcoolisées ou de tabacs ; autorisation de posséder des chiens et d'utiliser ou posséder des véhicules à moteur ou des armes à feu ; droit de lotissement.

12. Dans la pratique, il se peut qu'il ne soit pas toujours possible d'isoler les recettes fiscales des recettes non fiscales quant elles sont enregistrées ensemble. Si l'on estime qu'il s'agit surtout de recettes non fiscales, l'ensemble sera traité comme tel ; dans le cas contraire, les recettes seront comptabilisées et classées conformément aux règles énoncées au § 28.

13. La classification de l'OCDE et celle du SCN présentent deux différences concernant la définition entre recettes fiscales et non fiscales :

- Le SCN traite un certain nombre de prélèvements comme des impôts indirects quand ils sont à la charge des entreprises et comme des recettes non fiscales quand ils sont à la charge des ménages, distinction dont il n'est pas tenu compte dans la présente classification pour séparer les recettes fiscales des recettes non fiscales[7].
- La solution qui consiste à s'en tenir à la pratique la plus courante des administrations fiscales dans la zone de l'OCDE et qui est parfois utilisée dans la présente classification pour distinguer les recettes fiscales des recettes non fiscales n'est pas un critère retenu aux fins du SCN.

Redevances

14. Les redevances versées pour obtenir le droit d'extraire du pétrole et du gaz ou de mettre en valeur d'autres ressources minérales sont considérées normalement comme des recettes non fiscales, car il s'agit de revenus immobiliers procurés par des terres ou des ressources appartenant à l'État.

Amendes et pénalités

15. Les recettes provenant d'amendes et pénalités acquittées pour infraction aux réglementations relatives à un impôt particulier et les intérêts de retard afférents au dit impôt sont enregistrés avec les recettes procurées par cet impôt. Mais les autres catégories d'amendes identifiables comme se rapportant à des infractions fiscales sont classées au poste résiduel 6000. Les amendes qui ne concernent pas des infractions fiscales (comme les infractions au stationnement), ou qui ne sont pas identifiables en tant que telles, ne sont pas considérées comme des impôts.

A.3. Bases de comptabilisation

Droits constatés

16. Les données enregistrées dans cette publication pour les années récentes sont essentiellement indiquées en droits constatés, c'est-à-dire qu'elles sont enregistrées au moment du fait générateur de l'impôt. D'autres informations sont fournies dans les notes des tableaux par pays de la Partie III de ce rapport.

17. Toutefois, les données des années antérieures sont encore principalement comptabilisées sur la base des décaissements, c'est-à-dire au moment où l'administration reçoit le versement. Ainsi, les impôts retenus à la source par les employeurs au cours d'un exercice, mais versés à l'administration au cours de l'exercice suivant, et les impôts dus au titre d'une année mais effectivement versés l'année suivante, figurent les uns et les autres dans les recettes du second exercice. Les restitutions, remboursements et retraits résultant d'opérations rectificatives sont déduits des recettes brutes de la période au cours de laquelle ces opérations sont effectuées.

18. Les données relatives aux recettes fiscales sont comptabilisées, sans déduction compensatoire des dépenses administratives liées au recouvrement de l'impôt. De même, lorsque le produit d'un impôt sert à subventionner certains membres de la collectivité, la subvention n'est pas déduite du rendement de l'impôt, encore que certains pays fassent figurer dans leurs données l'impôt après déduction des subventions.

19. Pour les monopoles fiscaux (sous-groupe 5122), seul le montant effectivement transféré à l'État est inclus dans les recettes publiques. Toutefois, les dépenses des monopoles fiscaux qui sont considérées comme des dépenses publiques (par exemple, des dépenses de caractère social engagées par les monopoles fiscaux à l'instigation de l'État) sont ajoutées après coup pour calculer le montant des recettes fiscales (voir § 62).

La distinction entre dispositions fiscales et dépenses directes[8]

20. Étant donné que la présente publication ne vise que les recettes publiques en faisant abstraction des dépenses, il convient de distinguer entre les dispositions fiscales et les dépenses directes. Normalement, cette distinction ne soulève aucune difficulté, car les dépenses directes sont effectuées en dehors du système fiscal et des comptes fiscaux et en vertu de dispositions législatives distinctes. Dans les cas limites, on recourt, pour établir la distinction, au principe de la comptabilisation sur la base des paiements. Dans la mesure où une disposition affecte le montant des paiements du contribuable à l'État, elle est considérée comme une disposition fiscale dont il est tenu compte dans les données figurant dans cette publication. Une disposition qui n'affecte pas ce montant est considérée comme une dépense directe dont il n'est pas tenu compte dans les données reproduites dans cette publication.

21. Il est clair que les abattements fiscaux, exonérations et déductions de l'assiette de l'impôt modifient le montant de l'impôt acquitté à l'État ; il s'agit donc de dispositions fiscales. Inversement, les formes d'aides qui ne sont pas imputables sur l'impôt et n'ont donc aucun lien avec le processus d'imposition, ne réduisent pas les recettes publiques qui sont consignées dans ce volume. Les crédits d'impôt sont des montants déductibles de l'impôt à acquitter (par opposition aux déductions, qui sont opérées sur l'assiette de l'impôt). On distingue deux catégories de crédits d'impôt : ceux (que l'on qualifiera ici de 'non récupérables') qui sont limités au montant de l'impôt à acquitter et ne peuvent donc donner lieu à un versement de l'administration au contribuable, et ceux (qualifiés ici de 'récupérables') qui n'ont pas cette limite, de sorte que l'excédent du crédit sur l'impôt peut être versé au contribuable[9]. Le crédit d'impôt non récupérable, comme un

abattement fiscal, affecte évidemment le montant de l'impôt acquitté à l'État ; aussi est-il considéré comme une disposition fiscale. La solution adoptée pour les crédits d'impôts récupérables[10] consiste à distinguer l'élément de « dépense fiscale »[11], qui est la part du crédit utilisée pour réduire ou supprimer l'impôt dû par le contribuable, et l'« élément de transfert », qui correspond à la part excédant l'impôt dû par le contribuable et qui lui est reversée. Les recettes fiscales rapportées doivent être diminuées du montant de l'élément de dépense, mais non de l'élément de transfert. En outre, les montants de l'élément de dépense fiscale et de l'élément de transfert doivent être indiqués pour mémoire dans les tableaux par pays. Les pays qui ne sont pas en mesure de faire la distinction entre l'élément de dépense fiscale et l'élément de transfert doivent indiquer si leurs recettes fiscales ont été ou non diminuées du montant total de ces éléments, et fournir toutes les estimations dont ils disposent concernant les montants de ces deux éléments. Des informations complémentaires figurent à la section C de la Partie I de ce Rapport, qui fait apparaître les effets des différents traitements possibles des crédits d'impôts récupérables sur les ratios impôt rapportant les impôts au PIB.

Année civile et année fiscale (exercice budgétaire)

22. Les autorités nationales dont l'exercice budgétaire ne correspond pas à l'année civile fournissent, autant que possible, leurs données sur la base de l'année civile afin de faciliter au maximum la comparaison avec les données des autres pays. Les données d'un petit nombre de pays se réfèrent à l'exercice budgétaire. Pour ceux-ci, les statistiques de PIB utilisées dans les tableaux comparatifs portent aussi sur les exercices budgétaires.

A.4. Principes généraux de classification

Les fondements essentiels de la classification

23. Les recettes sont classées par groupes principaux (1000, 2000, 3000, 4000, 5000, 6000) suivant l'assiette de l'impôt : 1000 revenus, bénéfices et gains en capital ; 2000 et 3000 salaires et nombre d'employés ; 4000 patrimoine ; 5000 biens et services ; 6000 assiettes diverses, autres ou non identifiables. Lorsqu'un impôt est calculé en fonction de plusieurs assiettes, les recettes sont, chaque fois que c'est possible, réparties entre les divers groupes (voir § 28 et § 78). Les groupes 4000 et 5000 ne comprennent pas seulement les impôts ayant pour assiette le patrimoine, les biens ou les services eux-mêmes, mais aussi certains impôts connexes. Ainsi, les impôts sur les mutations du patrimoine sont classés dans le groupe 4400[12] et les impôts sur l'utilisation des biens, ou l'autorisation d'exercer une activité, dans le groupe 5200. Dans les groupes 4000 et 5000, une distinction est faite dans certains sous-groupes entre impôts périodiques et impôts non périodiques : on entend par impôts périodiques ceux qui sont perçus à intervalles réguliers (ordinairement tous les ans) et par impôts non périodiques ceux qui ne sont perçus qu'une seule fois (voir aussi les § 43 à § 46, § 49, § 50, § 76 et § 77 pour une application particulière de cette distinction).

24. L'affectation spéciale de certaines recettes fiscales n'influe pas sur leur classification. Toutefois comme explicité au § 35 sur la classification des cotisations de sécurité sociale, l'octroi d'un droit aux prestations sociales est crucial dans la définition de la rubrique principale 2000.

25. La manière selon laquelle un impôt est perçu ou recouvré (par exemple, au moyen de timbres) n'affecte pas sa classification.

Classification des contribuables

26. Dans certains sous-groupes, des distinctions sont faites entre les différentes catégories de contribuables. Ces distinctions varient d'un impôt à l'autre :

a) Ventilation des impôts sur le revenu et sur l'actif net entre personnes physiques et sociétés

La distinction fondamentale entre les impôts sur le revenu des sociétés et les impôts sur le revenu des personnes physiques est que les premiers sont perçus sur la société en tant qu'entité et non sur les personnes physiques qui en sont propriétaires, donc sans tenir compte de la situation personnelle de celles-ci. La même distinction est applicable aux impôts sur l'actif net des sociétés et des personnes physiques. Les impôts perçus sur les bénéfices des sociétés de personnes et sur le revenu de certaines institutions comme les caisses d'assurance-vie ou de retraite, sont classés selon le même principe. Ils sont compris dans les impôts sur les sociétés (1200) lorsqu'ils sont perçus sur la société de personnes ou l'institution en tant qu'entité sans que la situation personnelle des propriétaires entre en ligne de compte ; dans les autres cas, ils sont considérés comme des impôts sur les personnes physiques (1100). Ordinairement, les impôts sur les sociétés et les impôts sur les personnes physiques sont régis par des dispositions législatives différentes[13]. La distinction qui est faite ici entre personnes physiques et sociétés ne reprend pas la classification par secteur (ménages, entreprises, etc.) adoptée dans les comptes de revenus et de dépenses du SCN. Cette dernière classification exclut du secteur des ménages certaines entreprises non constituées en sociétés[14] et les fait figurer parmi les entreprises non financières et les institutions financières. Toutefois, l'impôt sur les bénéfices de ces entreprises ne peut pas toujours être isolé de l'impôt sur les autres revenus des propriétaires de ces entreprises, ou ne peut l'être que d'une façon arbitraire. On n'a pas cherché ici à faire la distinction et l'impôt sur le revenu des personnes physiques figure globalement, quelle que soit la nature du revenu imposable.

b) Ventilation des impôts sur les biens immobiliers entre ménages et autres agents

En l'occurrence, la distinction est celle qui a été adoptée par le SCN dans les comptes de production et de consommation. On distingue, en effet, les ménages en tant que consommateurs d'une part (c'est-à-dire à l'exclusion des entreprises individuelles), et les producteurs d'autre part. Cependant, les impôts sur les logements occupés par les ménages, qu'ils soient à la charge des propriétaires qui les occupent, du locataire ou du propriétaire, sont classés comme étant à la charge des ménages. C'est la distinction faite habituellement entre les impôts sur les biens des personnes et les impôts sur les biens des entreprises. Toutefois, certains pays ne sont pas en mesure d'établir cette distinction.

c) Ventilation des permis de circuler des véhicules à moteur entre taxes à la charge des ménages et à la charge d'autres agents

On distingue ici les ménages en tant que consommateurs d'une part, et producteurs d'autre part, comme dans les comptes de production et de consommation du SCN.

d) Ventilation des autres impôts (6000) entre les entreprises et les autres agents

Il est fait la même distinction qu'au point (c) ci-dessus entre les producteurs, d'une part, et les ménages consommateurs d'autre part. Les impôts qui figurent dans le groupe 6000 parce qu'ils ne comportent pas une assiette unique ou parce que leur assiette ne relève d'aucune des catégories précédentes, mais qui ne sont manifestement perçus que sur les producteurs et non sur les ménages, sont classés comme étant 'à la charge des entreprises'. Les autres impôts du groupe 6000 figurent sous la rubrique 'à la charge d'autres agents' ou 'non identifiés'.

Surtaxes

27. Les recettes des surtaxes relatives à des impôts particuliers sont classées ordinairement avec les recettes de l'impôt correspondant, que la surtaxe ait ou non un caractère temporaire. Toutefois, si l'une des caractéristiques de la surtaxe permet de la classer sous une rubrique différente de la classification de l'OCDE, les recettes de cette surtaxe sont classées sous cette rubrique et non pas avec les recettes de l'impôt correspondant

Recettes fiscales non identifiables et sous-groupes résiduels

28. Il arrive parfois qu'on ne puisse déterminer si des impôts relèvent entièrement d'un groupe ou d'un sous-groupe de la classification de l'OCDE ; dans ces cas on applique les méthodes suivantes :

a) le groupe est connu, mais on ne sait pas comment répartir les recettes entre les sous-groupes ; les recettes sont alors classées dans le sous-groupe résiduel approprié (1300, 2400, 4520, 4600, 5130, 5300 ou 6200) ;

b) on sait que l'ensemble des recettes d'un groupe d'impôts (ordinairement des impôts locaux) provient d'impôts relevant d'un groupe ou sous-groupe particulier, mais certains impôts du groupe, dont le montant ne peut être déterminé avec précision, peuvent être classés dans d'autres groupes ou sous-groupes ; dans ce cas les recettes sont comptabilisées dans le groupe ou sous-groupe dont relève l'essentiel des recettes ;

c) il est impossible d'identifier le groupe ou le sous-groupe d'un impôt (ordinairement un impôt local) ; l'impôt est alors classé dans le groupe 6200, à moins qu'il ne s'agisse d'un impôt manifestement à la charge des entreprises, auquel cas il est classé dans le sous-groupe 6100.

A.5. Commentaires sur les postes de la liste

1000 – *Impôts sur le revenu, les bénéfices et les gains en capital*

29. Ce groupe couvre les impôts prélevés sur le revenu ou le bénéfice net (c'est-à-dire le revenu brut déduction faite des abattements autorisés) des personnes physiques et des entreprises. Sont aussi couverts les impôts prélevés sur les gains en capital des personnes physiques et des entreprises et sur les gains provenant de jeux.

30. Ce groupe comprend :

a) les impôts perçus principalement sur les revenus ou les bénéfices, bien qu'ils puissent l'être partiellement sur d'autres bases. Les impôts qui ont une autre assiette principale que le revenu ou les bénéfices sont classés selon les principes énoncés au § 28 et § 78 ;

b) les impôts sur la propriété immobilière, qui sont perçus sur la base d'un revenu présumé ou estimé faisant partie de l'assiette de l'impôt sur le revenu (voir aussi § 43 (a), (c) et (d)) ;

c) les versements obligatoires aux caisses de sécurité sociale qui sont prélevés sur les revenus mais ne donnent pas droit à des prestations sociales. Lorsque ces contributions donnent droit à des prestations sociales, elles figurent à la rubrique 2000 (voir § 35) ;

d) les recettes provenant d'impôts cédulaires sur le revenu intégrés dans le régime général qui sont globalement classés dans ce groupe, bien que certains de ces impôts soient sur le revenu brut et ne tiennent pas toujours compte de la situation personnelle du contribuable.

31. Les impôts figurant dans ce groupe sont subdivisés en deux grands sous-groupes, les impôts sur le revenu des personnes physiques (1100) et les impôts sur le revenu des sociétés (1200), une ventilation étant faite dans chacun d'eux entre les impôts sur le revenu et les bénéfices (1110 et 1210) et les impôts sur les gains en capital (1120 et 1220). Si certaines recettes ne peuvent être identifiées comme relevant soit du sous-groupe 1100, soit du sous-groupe 1200, ou si cette distinction ne peut être faite dans la pratique (parce qu'il n'y a pas de données fiables sur les bénéficiaires des paiements sur lesquels la retenue à la source est faite), elles sont classées dans le sous-groupe 1300 (non ventilables).

Traitement des crédits d'impôt dans les systèmes d'imputation

32. Dans les régimes d'imputation de l'impôt sur les bénéfices des sociétés, les actionnaires bénéficient d'une compensation totale ou partielle d'imposition sur les dividendes que la société leur a versés et pour lesquels elle a acquitté l'impôt sur le revenu des sociétés. Dans les pays[15] qui appliquent un tel régime, une fraction de l'impôt sur les bénéfices des sociétés sert à alléger l'impôt dû par l'actionnaire. Cet allégement prend la forme d'un crédit d'impôt, dont le montant peut être inférieur, égal ou supérieur au montant total de l'impôt dont il est redevable. Si le crédit d'impôt dépasse ce montant, l'excédent peut être versé à l'actionnaire. Comme ce type de crédit d'impôt fait partie intégrante des systèmes d'imputation de l'impôt sur le revenu des sociétés, tout paiement à l'actionnaire est considéré comme un remboursement d'impôt et non comme une dépense (se référer au traitement des autres crédits d'impôt exposé au § 21).

33. Puisque, dans les systèmes d'imputation, le crédit d'impôt (même lorsqu'il dépasse l'impôt dû) est censé être une disposition fiscale, on peut se demander s'il doit être déduit des recettes de l'impôt sur le revenu des personnes physiques (1110) ou de celles de l'impôt sur les bénéfices de sociétés (1210). Dans ce Rapport le montant intégral de l'impôt acquitté sur les bénéfices des sociétés figure sous le poste 1210 et aucun impôt imputé n'est inclus dans le poste 1110. Le montant total du crédit d'impôt réduit donc le montant des recettes du poste 1110, que ce crédit se traduise par une réduction de l'impôt dû sur le revenu des personnes physiques ou par un remboursement réel du fait que le crédit dépasse le montant de l'impôt. (Cependant, lorsque ces crédits sont déduits de l'impôt sur les sociétés au titre de dividendes versés à des sociétés, le montant est déduit des recettes du poste 1210).

1120 et 1220 – *Impôts sur les gains en capital*

34. Ces postes comprennent les impôts perçus sur les gains en capital, le sous-groupe 1120 comptabilisant les impôts prélevés sur les gains des personnes physiques et le sous-groupe 1220 ceux qui sont perçus sur les gains des entreprises constituées sous forme de sociétés, lorsque ces recettes peuvent être ventilées. Ce n'est pas le cas dans de nombreux pays et les recettes de ces impôts sont alors classées avec celles de l'impôt sur le revenu. Les impôts sur les gains provenant de jeux sont aussi classés sous le poste 1120.

2000 – *Cotisations de sécurité sociale*

35. Figurent dans ce groupe tous les versements obligatoires qui donnent le droit de bénéficier d'une prestation sociale future (éventuelle). Ces versements sont généralement affectés au financement de prestations sociales et souvent effectués au profit d'institutions ou d'administrations publiques qui fournissent de telles prestations. Cependant, cette affectation n'entre pas dans la définition des cotisations de sécurité sociale et n'est pas nécessaire pour qu'un impôt soit classé dans cette rubrique. Cependant, il faut qu'un impôt confère un droit pour être classé dans cette rubrique. Par

conséquent, les prélèvements sur les revenus ou la masse salariale qui sont affectés aux caisses de sécurité sociale mais ne donnent aucun droit à des prestations sont exclus de cette rubrique et figurent à celle des impôts sur le revenu des personnes physiques (1100) ou des impôts sur les salaires et la main d'œuvre (3000). Les impôts assis sur d'autres bases, telles que les biens et services, qui sont affectés à des prestations de sécurité sociale, ne sont pas indiqués ici, mais sont classés en fonction de leurs bases respectives parce qu'en général ils ne donnent pas droit à des prestations de sécurité sociale.

36. Seraient entre autres incluses les cotisations au titre des catégories suivantes de prestations de sécurité sociale : les allocations d'assurance-chômage et les compléments, les allocations pour accidents, blessures et maladie, les pensions de retraite, d'invalidité et de survivant, les allocations familiales, les remboursements de dépenses médicales et d'hospitalisation ou la fourniture de services médicaux ou hospitaliers. Les cotisations peuvent être collectées à la fois auprès des employés et des employeurs.

37. Les cotisations peuvent être assises sur les gains ou la masse salariale (« sur la base du salaire ») ou sur le revenu net après déductions et exemptions en fonction de la situation personnelle (« sur la base de l'impôt sur le revenu ») et les recettes correspondant à ces deux bases doivent être identifiées séparément si possible. Cependant, lorsque les cotisations à un régime général de sécurité sociale sont assises sur la masse salariale, mais que les cotisations de groupes particuliers (tels que les travailleurs indépendants) ne peuvent être évaluées sur cette base et que le revenu net est utilisé comme valeur rapprochée des gains bruts, les recettes peuvent encore être considérées comme assises sur la masse salariale. En principe, cette rubrique exclut les contributions volontaires à des régimes de sécurité sociale. Lorsqu'elles peuvent être identifiées séparément, elles figurent pour mémoire dans le tableau indiquant le financement des prestations de sécurité sociale. Toutefois, en pratique, elles ne peuvent pas toujours être distinguées des cotisations volontaires, et dans ce cas elles figurent à cette rubrique.

38. Les cotisations à des régimes d'assurance sociale qui ne relèvent pas des pouvoirs publics et à d'autres régimes d'assurance ou de prévoyance, aux caisses de retraite, sociétés de secours mutuel ou autres systèmes d'épargne, ne sont pas considérées comme des cotisations de sécurité sociale. Les caisses de prévoyance résultant d'arrangements aux termes desquels les cotisations de chaque salarié et celles que l'employeur verse en son nom sont comptabilisées séparément dans un compte productif d'intérêts d'où elles peuvent être retirées dans des conditions biens déterminées. Les caisses de retraite sont des régimes autonomes organisés par négociations entre salariés et employeurs, qui comportent diverses contributions et prestations, parfois liées plus directement au salaire et à la durée d'activité que dans les régimes de sécurité sociale. Lorsque les cotisations à ces régimes sont obligatoires ou quasi obligatoires (par exemple en vertu d'un accord entre organisations professionnelles et syndicales), elles sont comptabilisées dans le poste pour mémoire (voir Section B dans la partie III du rapport).

39. Les cotisations versées par les agents des administrations et par les administrations au titre de leurs agents à des régimes de sécurité sociale relevant des pouvoirs publics sont incluses dans ce groupe. Sont aussi assimilées à des impôts les cotisations à des régimes particuliers réservés aux agents des administrations qui sont censés remplacer un régime général de la sécurité sociale[16]. Par contre, lorsqu'un régime distinct n'est pas censé remplacer un régime général et résulte de négociations entre l'administration, agissant en qualité d'employeur, et ses agents, il n'est pas considéré comme un régime de sécurité sociale et les cotisations à ce titre ne sont pas assimilées à des impôts, même si le régime a été institué par des dispositions législatives.

40. Cette rubrique ne comprend pas les cotisations 'imputées', qui correspondent aux prestations sociales versées directement par les employeurs à leurs salariés, ou anciens salariés, ou à leurs représentants (par exemple, lorsque des employeurs sont légalement tenus de verser des prestations maladies pendant une certaine période).

41. Le groupe comprend les cotisations à la charge des salariés (2100), à la charge des employeurs (2200), et à la charge des travailleurs indépendants ou des personnes n'occupant pas d'emploi (2300). À cet effet, on entend par salariés toutes les personnes qui exercent une activité dans des entreprises, des administrations, des institutions privées sans but lucratif, ou qui occupent d'autres emplois rémunérés, à l'exception des propriétaires et des membres de leur famille non rémunérés dans le cas d'entreprises individuelles. Sont également compris les membres des forces armées, quelle que soit la durée et la nature de leurs services, s'ils cotisent à un régime de sécurité sociale. Par cotisations à la charge des employeurs, on entend les versements qu'ils effectuent au régime de sécurité sociale pour le compte de leurs salariés. Si, en cas de chômage, les salariés ou employeurs sont tenus de continuer à effectuer ces versements, ces derniers doivent figurer respectivement dans les sous-groupes 2100 et 2200. En conséquence, le sous-groupe 2300 est réservé aux cotisations versées par les travailleurs indépendants et par ceux qui n'appartiennent pas à la population active (comme les handicapés ou les retraités).

3000 – *Impôts sur les salaires et la main-d'œuvre*

42. Ce groupe couvre les impôts acquittés par les employeurs, les salariés et les travailleurs indépendants, en pourcentage du salaire ou d'après un montant forfaitaire par personne, qui ne sont pas affectés aux dépenses de sécurité sociale. Parmi les impôts classés ici, on peut citer l'impôt complémentaire d'assurance nationale sans affectation (institué en 1977) au Royaume-Uni, l'impôt sur la masse salariale en Suède (1969–1979), la fraction du 'Gewerbesteuer' autrichien et allemand qui reposait sur la masse salariale (1965–1978).

4000 – *Impôts sur le patrimoine*

43. Ce groupe couvre les impôts périodiques et non périodiques sur l'utilisation, la propriété ou la mutation des biens. Sont comptabilisés ici les impôts sur la propriété immobilière et sur l'actif net, les impôts sur les mutations par décès, les successions et les donations, et les impôts sur les transactions mobilières et immobilières. Sont exclus de ce groupe :

a) les impôts sur les gains en capital provenant de la vente d'un bien (1120 ou 1220) ;

b) les impôts sur l'utilisation des biens ou l'autorisation d'utiliser des biens ou d'exercer des activités (5200) [voir § 73] ;

c) les impôts immobiliers perçus sur la base d'un revenu net présumé qui tiennent compte de la situation personnelle du contribuable. Ces impôts sont classés dans le groupe 1100 en tant qu'impôts sur le revenu, avec les impôts sur le revenu et les gains en capital provenant des biens immobiliers ;

d) les impôts sur l'utilisation de biens immobiliers aux fins d'habitation qui sont à la charge du propriétaire ou du locataire et dont le montant est fonction de la situation personnelle de l'utilisateur (salaire, personnes à charge, etc.). Ils sont classés dans le groupe 1100 en tant qu'impôts sur le revenu ;

e) les impôts sur les constructions dépassant la densité autorisée, les impôts sur l'extension, la construction ou la modification de certains immeubles au-delà d'une valeur autorisée et les impôts sur la construction d'immeubles. Ces impôts sont classés dans le poste 5200 en tant qu'impôts sur l'autorisation d'exercer certaines activités ;

f) les impôts sur l'utilisation de biens immobiliers par le propriétaire à des fins commerciales particulières, comme la vente de boissons alcoolisées, de tabac, de viande, ou pour l'exploitation de sols ou terrains (par exemple aux États-Unis, les taxes de lotissement). Ils sont classés dans le poste 5200 en tant qu'impôts sur l'autorisation d'exercer certaines activités.

4100 – *Impôts périodiques sur la propriété immobilière*

44. Ce sous-groupe comprend les impôts prélevés régulièrement au titre de l'utilisation ou de la propriété de biens immobiliers.

- ces impôts sont prélevés sur les terrains et les bâtiments ;
- ces impôts sont calculés en pourcentage de la valeur du bien évalué d'après un revenu locatif fictif, le prix de vente ou le rendement capitalisé, ou en fonction d'autres caractéristiques du bien, comme sa dimension ou son emplacement, d'où l'on peut déduire une valeur locative présumée ou la valeur du capital.
- ces impôts sont à la charge du propriétaire, du locataire ou des deux. Ils peuvent également être payés par une administration à une autre administration au titre d'un bien relevant de la compétence de cette dernière.
- il n'est pas tenu compte des dettes pour la détermination de l'assiette de ces impôts, contrairement aux impôts sur l'actif net.

45. Les impôts sur la propriété immobilière sont en outre subdivisés en impôts acquittés par les ménages (4110) et impôts acquittés par d'autres agents (4120), suivant les critères exposés au § 26(b) ci-dessus.

4200 – *Impôts périodiques sur l'actif net*

46. Ce sous-groupe comprend les impôts prélevés régulièrement (dans la plupart des cas annuellement) sur l'actif net, c'est-à-dire les impôts perçus sur un large éventail de biens mobiliers et immobiliers, endettement déduit. Il est subdivisé en impôts acquittés par des personnes physiques (4210), et en impôts acquittés par des sociétés (4220) selon les critères exposés plus haut au § 26(a). Si les recettes provenant des institutions sont comptabilisées à part, elles doivent être ajoutées aux impôts des entreprises.

4300 – *Impôts sur les mutations par décès, les successions et les donations*

47. Ce sous-groupe comprend les impôts sur les mutations par décès et les successions (4310) et les impôts sur les donations (4320)[17]. Les impôts sur les mutations par décès sont calculés soit sur l'ensemble de la masse successorale, soit en fonction de la part de chacun des bénéficiaires ("part héréditaire") ; en outre, ces derniers impôts peuvent tenir compte du degré de parenté entre chacun des bénéficiaires et le défunt.

4400 – *Impôts sur les transactions mobilières et immobilières*

48. Sont compris, entre autres, dans ce sous-groupe les impôts sur l'émission, le transfert, l'achat et la vente de valeurs mobilières, les impôts sur les chèques, ainsi que les droits perçus à l'occasion d'actes juridiques déterminés, comme la validation de contrats et la vente de biens immobiliers. Sont exclus :

a) les impôts sur l'utilisation de biens, mobiliers ou immobiliers, ou l'autorisation d'exercer certaines activités (5200) ;

b) les droits acquittés au titre de frais de justice, ou pour la délivrance de certificats de naissance, de mariage ou de décès, car ces droits sont considérés comme des recettes non fiscales (voir § 9) ;

c) les impôts sur les gains en capital (1000) ;

d) les impôts périodiques sur la propriété immobilière (4100) ;

e) les impôts périodiques sur l'actif net (4200) ;

f) les prélèvements sur le patrimoine ou sur l'actif net effectués une fois pour toutes (4500) ;

4500 – *Autres impôts non périodiques sur le patrimoine*[17]

49. Ce sous-groupe comprend les prélèvements sur le patrimoine effectués une fois pour toutes (par opposition aux prélèvements périodiques). Il est subdivisé en impôts sur l'actif net (4510) et en autres impôts non périodiques sur le patrimoine (4520). Le poste 4510 inclurait les impôts perçus pour couvrir des dépenses exceptionnelles ou à des fins de redistribution. Le poste 4520 comprendrait les impôts prélevés pour tenir compte d'une plus-value prise par les terrains du fait que les administrations publiques ont autorisé l'extension ou l'aménagement d'installations locales, ainsi que les impôts sur la réévaluation du capital ou les impôts perçus une seule fois sur certains biens déterminés.

4600 – *Autres impôts périodiques sur le patrimoine*

50. Ils sont rares dans des pays Membres de l'OCDE ; ce sous-groupe comprendrait les impôts sur des biens tels que le cheptel, les bijoux, les fenêtres et les signes extérieurs de richesse.

5000 – *Impôts sur les biens et services*

51. Ce poste couvre tous les impôts et droits perçus sur la production, l'extraction, la vente, le transfert, la location ou la livraison de biens et la prestation de services (5100), ou sur l'utilisation ou l'autorisation d'utiliser des biens ou d'exercer des activités (5200). Ce groupe comprend donc :

a) les taxes cumulatives en cascade ;

b) les taxes générales sur les ventes — perçues au stade de la production ou de la fabrication, du gros ou du détail ;

c) les taxes sur la valeur ajoutée ;

d) les accises ;

e) les taxes perçues à l'importation et à l'exportation de biens ;

f) les impôts perçus sur l'utilisation de biens et sur l'autorisation d'utiliser des biens ou d'exercer certaines activités ;

g) les impôts sur l'extraction, le traitement ou la production de minéraux et autres produits.

52. Les cas douteux de délimitation entre ce groupe et le groupe 4000 (impôts sur le patrimoine) et le sous-groupe 6100 (autres impôts à la charge des entreprises) sont examinés au § 43, § 48 et § 75. Des postes résiduels (5300 et 5130) ont été prévus pour comptabiliser les recettes fiscales qui ne peuvent être ventilées respectivement entre les postes 5100 et 5200 et entre les postes 5110 et 5120 (voir § 28).

5100 – *Impôts sur la production, la vente, le transfert, la location et la livraison de biens et la prestation de services*

53. Ce sous-groupe comprend tous les impôts perçus sur les transactions afférentes à des biens ou services, en fonction de leurs caractéristiques propres (comme la valeur, le poids du tabac, le degré d'alcool, etc.), à la différence des impôts perçus au titre de

l'utilisation ou de l'autorisation d'utiliser des biens ou d'exercer des activités, qui entrent dans le sous-groupe 5200.

5110 – *Impôts généraux sur les biens et services*

54. Ce sous-groupe comprend tous les impôts, autres que les droits à l'importation et à l'exportation (5123 et 5124), perçus sur la production, la location, le transfert, la livraison ou la vente d'une gamme de biens ou la prestation d'une gamme de services, qu'ils soient produits dans le pays ou importés, et quel que soit le stade de la production ou de la distribution aux quel ils sont perçus. Il couvre ainsi les taxes sur la valeur ajoutée, les taxes sur les ventes et les taxes de caractère cumulatif en cascade. On a ajouté aux recettes brutes de cette catégorie les recettes provenant de la compensation à la frontière de ces impôts lorsque les biens sont importés, et déduit les remboursements d'impôts effectués lorsque les marchandises sont exportées. Ces impôts sont ventilés en : taxes sur la valeur ajoutée (5111), impôts sur les ventes (5112), autres impôts généraux sur les biens et services (5113).

55. Certains cas se trouvent à la limite entre ce sous-groupe et celui des impôts sur des biens et services déterminés (5120) lorsque ces impôts sont perçus sur un grand nombre de biens, comme dans le cas de la "purchase tax" au Royaume-Uni (abrogée en 1973) et l'impôt japonais sur les biens marchands (abrogé en 1988). Conformément aux options nationales, la "purchase tax" britannique est classée impôt général (5112) et l'impôt japonais dans les accises (5121).

5111 – *Taxes sur la valeur ajoutée*

56. Sont classés dans ce sous-groupe tous les impôts généraux sur la consommation prélevés sur la valeur ajoutée, quels que soient le mode de déduction et les stades auxquels ils sont perçus. En pratique, tous les pays de l'OCDE où existe une taxe sur la valeur ajoutée autorisent normalement la déduction immédiate des taxes sur les achats par tous les redevables, à l'exception du consommateur final, et imposent la taxe à tous les stades. Dans certains pays, le poste peut inclure aussi certains impôts, comme les taxes sur les activités financières et les assurances, soit parce que les recettes correspondantes ne peuvent être dissociées de celles de la taxe sur la valeur ajoutée, soit parce qu'elles sont considérées comme faisant partie intégrante de la taxe sur la valeur ajoutée, même si les taxes similaires qui existent dans d'autres pays peuvent être classées autrement (par exemple, sous le poste 5126 comme impôts sur les services ou sous le poste 4400 comme impôts sur les transactions mobilières et immobilières).

5112 – *Impôts sur les ventes*

57. Sont classés ici tous les impôts perçus à un stade unique, que ce soit celui de la fabrication, de la production, du gros ou du détail.

5113 – *Autres impôts généraux sur les biens et services*

58. Ce sous-groupe comprend les impôts cumulatifs, connus également sous le nom d'impôt en cascade, qui sont perçus sans déduction de l'impôt sur les moyens de production chaque fois qu'une opération a lieu, ainsi que les impôts généraux sur la consommation lorsqu'il s'y ajoute des éléments qui les font assimiler à la taxe sur la valeur ajoutée, à la taxe sur les ventes ou à des taxes en cascade.

5120 – *Impôts sur des biens et des services déterminés*

59. Ce sous-groupe couvre les accises, les bénéfices engendrés et transférés par les monopoles fiscaux, et les droits de douane et à l'importation, ainsi que les taxes à l'exportation, les opérations de change, les biens d'équipement et les paris, et aussi

les impôts spéciaux sur les services qui ne font pas partie d'un impôt général du sous-groupe 5110.

5121 – *Accises*

60. Les accises sont perçues sur des produits particuliers, ou sur une gamme limitée de produits, qui ne peuvent être classés sous le poste 5110 (impôts généraux), 5123 (droits à l'importation) ou 5124 (droits à l'exportation). Elles peuvent être perçues à un stade quelconque de la production ou de la distribution et sont calculées ordinairement par référence au poids, au degré ou au volume du produit, mais parfois aussi à sa valeur. Cette subdivision couvre ainsi les impôts spéciaux, qui frappent notamment le sucre, la betterave, les allumettes, les chocolats, et les impôts auxquels sont soumis à des taux divers certains produits, comme ceux perçus dans la plupart des pays sur les tabacs, boissons alcoolisées, hydrocarbures et autres sources d'énergie.

61. Les accises sont à distinguer de :

a) 5110 (impôts généraux) ; ce cas est examiné aux § 54 et § 55 ;

b) 5123 (droits à l'importation) ; lorsqu'un impôt perçu principalement sur des biens importés s'applique, ou s'appliquerait, aussi légalement à un bien comparable produit dans le pays, les recettes procurées par cet impôt seront classées avec les accises (5121) ; ce principe s'applique même lorsqu'il n'y a pas de production locale, réelle ou potentielle, comparable (voir aussi § 65) ;

c) 5126 (impôts sur les services) ; le problème ici concerne les impôts sur l'électricité, le gaz et l'énergie ; ils sont tous considérés comme des impôts sur les biens et inclus dans le poste 5121.

5122 – *Bénéfices des monopoles fiscaux*

62. Ce sous-groupe couvre la fraction des bénéfices des monopoles fiscaux qui est transférée aux administrations publiques ou qui sert à financer des dépenses considérées comme dépenses publiques (voir § 19). Les montants sont comptabilisés lorsqu'ils sont transférés aux administrations publiques ou utilisés pour effectuer des dépenses considérées comme des dépenses publiques.

63. Les monopoles fiscaux reflètent l'exercice du pouvoir d'imposition de l'État par l'intermédiaire du monopole. Les monopoles fiscaux sont des entreprises publiques non financières, qui exercent dans la plupart des cas un monopole sur la production ou la distribution du tabac, des boissons alcoolisées, du sel, des allumettes, des cartes à jouer et des produits pétroliers ou agricoles (c'est-à-dire, sur le genre de produits qui peuvent être soumis, principalement ou accessoirement, aux accises du poste 5121), pour procurer des recettes publiques qui, dans d'autres pays, sont obtenues par le biais d'impôts frappant les transactions sur ces produits d'entreprises privées. Le monopole d'État peut être exercé au stade de la production, ou au stade de la distribution comme dans le cas des magasins de vente de boissons alcoolisées qui appartiennent à l'État et sont contrôlés par lui.

64. Les monopoles fiscaux sont différents des services publics, comme les chemins de fer, l'électricité, les postes et autres moyens de communication, qui peuvent avoir une position de monopole ou de quasi-monopole, mais dont l'objet principal est, normalement, de fournir des services essentiels et non pas de procurer des recettes à l'État. Les transferts à l'administration de ces autres entreprises publiques sont considérés comme des recettes non fiscales. La notion traditionnelle de monopole fiscal n'a pas été élargie pour inclure les loteries nationales, dont les bénéfices sont donc considérés comme des recettes non fiscales. On distingue les bénéfices des monopoles fiscaux des bénéfices

des monopoles d'exportation et d'importation (5127), qui sont transférés des offices de commercialisation ou d'autres entreprises s'occupant du commerce international.

5123 – *Droits de douane et autres droits à l'importation*

65. Figurent ici les taxes, droits de timbre et surtaxes qui, selon la loi sont perçus exclusivement sur des produits importés. Sont aussi inclus dans ce poste les droits perçus sur l'importation de denrées agricoles dans les pays Membres de l'Union Européenne et les montants acquittés par certains de ces pays en vertu du Système de Montants Compensatoires[18]. À partir de 1998 les droits de douane collectés par les États membres de l'Union européenne pour le compte de l'Union européenne ne sont plus reportés sous cette rubrique dans les tableaux par pays (Partie III de ce rapport). Sont exclues ici les taxes perçues sur les importations au titre d'un impôt général sur les biens et les services ou d'une accise applicable aussi bien aux produits importés qu'aux produits fabriqués dans le pays.

5124 – *Taxes à l'exportation*

66. Pendant les années 70, les droits à l'exportation étaient perçus normalement en Australie, au Canada et au Portugal, et ils étaient utilisés en Finlande à des fins conjoncturelles. Certains pays Membres de l'Union Européenne acquittent, dans le cadre du système des montants compensatoires, une taxe sur les exportations (voir la note 18 du § 65). Lorsque ces montants sont identifiables, ils sont inclus dans ce poste. Ce dernier ne comprend pas les remboursements effectués au titre d'impôts généraux sur la consommation d'accises ou de droits de douane sur des biens exportés, qui doivent être déduits des recettes brutes comptabilisées, selon le cas, sous le poste 5110, 5121 ou 5123.

5125 – *Impôts sur les biens d'équipement*

67. Ce sous-groupe comprend les impôts perçus sur les biens d'équipement, comme les machines. Ils peuvent exister depuis un certain nombre d'années ou avoir un caractère temporaire et être prélevés à des fins conjoncturelles. Ne sont pas inclus les impôts sur les 'inputs' industriels qui frappent aussi les consommateurs (comme l'impôt suédois sur l'énergie qui est classé sous le poste 5121).

5126 – *Impôts sur des services déterminés*

68. Sous ce poste figurent tous les impôts calculés sur la rémunération de services spécifiques, comme les taxes sur les primes d'assurance, les taxes sur les services bancaires, sur les jeux et paris (par exemple : courses de chevaux, pronostics de football, billets de loterie nationale), les transports, les spectacles, les restaurants et la publicité. Les impôts prélevés sur le revenu brut des sociétés prestataires d'un service (exemple : primes d'assurance brutes, mises de jeux encaissées par les sociétés) sont classés sous ce poste. Les recettes fiscales provenant des prélèvements sur les banques et des contributions aux mécanismes de garantie des dépôts et de stabilité financière sont provisoirement classés ici pour l'édition 2012. La classification détaillée est présentée dans le § 105.

69. Ne figurent pas sous ce poste :

a) les impôts sur les services qui font partie d'un impôt général sur les biens et services et sont classés sous le poste 5110 ;

b) les taxes sur l'électricité, le gaz et l'énergie (classées sous le poste 5121 en tant qu'accises) ;

c) les taxes sur les gains personnels tirés de jeux et paris (qui sont classées sous le poste 1120, en tant qu'impôts sur les gains en capital des personnes physiques et entreprises individuelles) et les montants forfaitaires perçus sur le transfert de loteries privées ou sur l'autorisation de créer des loteries (5200)[19] ;

d) les impôts sur les chèques et sur l'émission, le transfert ou le remboursement de valeurs mobilières, (qui sont classés sous le poste 4400, en tant qu'impôts sur les transactions mobilières et immobilières).

5127 – ***Autres impôts sur les transactions et les échanges internationaux***

70. Ce sous-groupe couvre les recettes perçues par l'État sur l'achat et la vente de monnaies étrangères à des taux différents. Lorsque l'État exerce le privilège exclusif dont il dispose pour s'assurer une marge entre le prix d'achat et le prix de vente de devises qui ne se réduit pas à la simple couverture des frais administratifs, ce bénéfice représente un prélèvement obligatoire imposé dans des proportions indéterminées à l'acheteur et au vendeur des monnaies étrangères. Il équivaut normalement au droit à l'importation et au droit à l'exportation perçus dans un système de taux de change unique, ou à une taxe sur la vente ou l'achat de monnaies étrangères. Comme les bénéfices des monopoles fiscaux et des monopoles d'importation ou d'exportation transférés à l'État, il représente l'exercice d'un monopole aux fins d'imposition et est inclus dans les recettes fiscales.

71. Ce sous-groupe comprend aussi les bénéfices des monopoles d'exportation ou d'importation, bien qu'il n'en existe pas dans les pays de l'OCDE, les impôts sur l'achat ou la vente de devises et tous les autres impôts perçus spécifiquement sur les opérations ou les échanges internationaux.

5128 – ***Autres impôts sur des biens et services déterminés***

72. Cette rubrique comprend les impôts sur l'extraction de minéraux, combustibles fossiles et autres ressources non renouvelables provenant de gisements privés ou détenus par une autre administration, ainsi que toute autre recette non ventilable provenant des impôts sur des biens et services déterminés. Les impôts sur l'extraction de ressources non renouvelables correspondent généralement à un montant forfaitaire par unité de qualité ou de poids, mais peuvent être calculés ad valorem. Les impôts sont comptabilisés à la date d'extraction des ressources. Les versements tirés de l'extraction de ressources non renouvelables issues de gisements appartenant à l'administration publique qui perçoit ces versements sont classés en tant que loyers.

5200 – ***Impôts sur l'utilisation des biens ou l'autorisation d'utiliser des biens ou d'exercer des activités***

73. Ce sous-groupe comprend les taxes prélevées en raison de l'utilisation de biens, indépendamment des impôts frappant les biens eux-mêmes. Contrairement à ceux-ci (5100), les impôts du sous-groupe 5200 ne sont pas calculés d'après la valeur des biens, mais ordinairement d'après un montant forfaitaire. Sont aussi couverts les impôts perçus au titre du droit d'utiliser des biens ou d'exercer des activités, comme les taxes sur la pollution qui ne reposent pas sur la valeur de biens déterminés. Il est parfois difficile de distinguer les taxes d'utilisation et droits de licence obligatoires, qui sont considérés comme des impôts, de ceux qui ne le sont pas parce qu'ils sont assimilés à des recettes non fiscales ; les critères appliqués sont ceux indiqués aux § 9 et § 10.

74. Bien que le sous-groupe se réfère à l'utilisation des biens, le fait générateur de l'impôt peut être aussi bien l'enregistrement de la propriété, de sorte que les impôts relevant de ce sous-groupe peuvent viser la possession d'animaux ou de biens plutôt que leur utilisation (par exemple, les chevaux de course, les chiens, les véhicules à moteur) et même s'appliquer à des biens inutilisables (comme les véhicules à moteur ou les fusils inutilisables).

75. Les cas limites concernent :

a) les impôts sur l'autorisation d'exercer des activités commerciales, qui sont classés selon les règles exposées au § 78 lorsqu'ils ont une assiette mixte associant le revenu, les salaires versés ou le chiffre d'affaires ;

b) les impôts sur la propriété ou l'utilisation de la propriété de biens visés par les postes 4100, 4200 et 4600. Le poste 4100 ne vise que les impôts sur la propriété ou la location de biens immobiliers et, contrairement aux impôts du sous-groupe 5200, ils sont fonction de la valeur du bien. Les impôts sur l'actif net et les impôts sur les biens meubles des sous-groupes 4200 et 4600 visent la propriété et non pas l'utilisation des biens, couvrent un groupe d'actifs et non pas de biens particuliers et sont aussi fonction de la valeur du bien.

5210 – *Impôts périodiques sur l'utilisation de biens ou sur l'autorisation d'utiliser des biens ou d'exercer certaines activités*

76. Ces impôts ont pour principale caractéristique d'être perçus à intervalles réguliers et de représenter ordinairement des montants forfaitaires. Le poste le plus important, du point de vue du volume des recettes, est constitué par les permis de circulation des véhicules. Ce sous-groupe inclut aussi les taxes perçues lors de la délivrance de permis de chasse, de tir ou de pêche, ou l'autorisation de vendre certains produits, ainsi que les taxes sur la possession de chiens et sur la prestation de certains services à condition qu'elles répondent aux critères définis aux § 9 et § 10. Les subdivisions du poste 5210 comprennent les taxes d'utilisation de véhicules à moteur à la charge des ménages (5211) et à la charge d'autres agents (5212)[20]. Le poste 5213 couvre les plaques de chiens et les taxes perçues pour l'autorisation d'exercer certaines activités, comme la vente de viande et d'alcool, lorsque les prélèvements ont un caractère périodique. Il couvre aussi les permis généraux de chasse, de port d'armes et de pêche, lorsque le droit d'exercer ces activités n'est pas accordé au titre d'une opération commerciale normale (par exemple, la délivrance du permis ne comporte pas le droit d'utiliser une parcelle déterminée de terrain appartenant à l'État).

5220 – *Impôts non périodiques sur l'utilisation de biens ou sur l'autorisation d'utiliser des biens ou d'exercer certaines activités*

77. Cette rubrique recouvre les taxes non périodiques perçues sur l'utilisation de biens ou sur l'autorisation d'utiliser des biens ou d'exercer certaines activités et celles qui sont prélevées chaque fois que des biens sont utilisés. Les impôts prélevés sur l'émission ou le rejet dans l'environnement de gaz toxiques, liquides nocifs ou autres substances dangereuses figurent ici.

- Les paiements au titre des permis d'émission négociables délivrés par les administrations publiques dans le cadre des dispositifs de plafonnement et d'échange doivent également être comptabilisés sous cette rubrique au moment où les émissions sont produites. Les permis délivrés gratuitement par les administrations ne donnent lieu à aucun enregistrement comptable de recettes. La comptabilisation en droits constatés implique un éventuel délai entre la date à laquelle l'administration perçoit le règlement des permis et la date à laquelle les émissions sont produites. Dans les comptes nationaux, ce délai se traduit pour l'administration par un engagement financier sur la période.
- Il convient d'exclure les paiements effectués au titre de la collecte et de l'élimination de déchets ou de substances nocives par les autorités publiques, étant donné qu'il s'agit là de vente de services aux entreprises.

78. D'autres impôts non périodiques qui relèvent du poste 5200 sont aussi classés dans cette rubrique. Ainsi figurent les paiements uniques effectués au titre de l'autorisation

de vendre des boissons alcoolisées ou des tabacs ou d'ouvrir des guichets de « paris mutuels », à condition qu'ils répondent aux critères définis aux § 9 et § 10.

6000 – *Autres impôts*

79. Ce groupe couvre les impôts prélevés sur une ou plusieurs bases différentes de celles qui sont indiquées pour les groupes 1000, 3000, 4000 et 5000, ou sur des bases dont aucune ne pourrait être considérée comme étant essentiellement la même que l'une de celles afférentes à ces groupes. Quant aux impôts perçus sur plusieurs bases différentes, il convient si possible d'évaluer les recettes liées à chaque base de perception (par exemple, pour l'impôt allemand 'Gewerbesteuer') et d'inclure les montants séparés dans le groupe approprié. S'il est impossible d'évaluer les montants séparés, mais si l'on sait que la plus grande partie des recettes provient de l'impôt perçu sur une même base, la totalité des recettes sont classées en fonction de cette base. Si aucune de ces procédures ne peut être appliquée, les impôts sont classés dans le présent groupe. Les sous-groupes peuvent comprendre également les recettes provenant d'impôts que les administrations ne sont pas en mesure d'identifier ou d'isoler (voir § 28). Figurent aussi dans ce groupe les recettes provenant d'amendes et de pénalités acquittées pour infraction aux réglementations fiscales, mais qui ne peuvent être identifiées comme se rapportant à une catégorie particulière d'impôts (voir § 15). Ce poste est divisé en impôts exclusivement ou principalement à la charge des entreprises (6100) et en impôts à la charge d'autres contribuables (6200).

A.6. Conciliation avec les comptes nationaux

80. Cette section des tableaux permet de concilier les calculs des recettes fiscales totales de l'OCDE et l'ensemble des impôts et cotisations sociales versés aux administrations publiques qui sont enregistrés dans les comptes nationaux par pays. Lorsque le pays en question est membre de l'Union européenne (UE) la comparaison est effectuée entre les calculs des recettes fiscales totales des pays de l'OCDE et la somme des recettes fiscales et cotisations de sécurité sociale perçues par les administrations publiques et les institutions des secteurs de l'Union européenne des comptes nationaux.

A.7. Poste pour mémoire relatif au financement des prestations de sécurité sociale

81. Le rapport entre les impôts et les cotisations de sécurité sociale étant variable, et en raison des problèmes évoqués aux § 35 et § 41, on a réuni dans un poste pour mémoire l'ensemble des versements affectés à des prestations du type sécurité sociale, en dehors des versements volontaires au secteur privé. Les données sont présentées de la façon suivante (voir Partie III.B)

a) impôts du groupe 2000 ;

b) impôts affectés aux prestations de sécurité sociale ;

c) cotisations volontaires à l'administration ;

d) cotisations obligatoires au secteur privé.

Les § 35 et § 41 ci-dessus contiennent des directives pour la ventilation entre ces quatre catégories.

A.8. Poste pour mémoire relatif aux impôts identifiables payés par les administrations

82. Les impôts effectivement payés par les administrations elles-mêmes et que l'on peut identifier sont indiqués dans un poste pour mémoire et classés suivant les grandes

rubriques de la classification des impôts de l'OCDE. Dans la très grande majorité des pays, seuls peuvent être identifiées en l'occurrence les cotisations de sécurité sociale et les impôts sur les salaires, mais il s'agit là en général des impôts les plus importants acquittés par les administrations (voir Partie III.C de cette publication).

A.9. Rapport de la classification des impôts de l'OCDE avec les systèmes nationaux de comptabilité nationale

83. Un système de comptabilité nationale (SCN) tend à fournir un cadre cohérent pour enregistrer et présenter les principaux flux relatifs à la production, à la consommation, à l'accumulation et aux transactions extérieures d'une zone économique donnée, d'ordinaire un pays ou une grande région d'un pays. Les recettes publiques sont une partie importante des transactions enregistrées dans le SCN. La version finale du SCN 2008 a été diffusée conjointement par cinq organisations internationales : les Nations Unies, le Fonds Monétaire International, l'Union européenne, l'Organisation de Coopération et de Développement Économiques et la Banque Mondiale, en août 2009. Le Système est un ensemble complet, cohérent et souple de comptes macro-économiques. Il est élaboré pour être utilisé dans les pays à économie de marché quel que soit leur niveau de développement économique ainsi que dans les pays en transition vers l'économie de marché. De larges extraits du cadre théorique ainsi que les définitions des divers secteurs de l'économie du SCN figurent dans la classification des impôts de l'OCDE.

84. Il existe cependant un certain nombre de différences entre la classification des impôts de l'OCDE et les concepts du SCN qui sont indiqués ci-dessous. Ils proviennent du fait que l'objectif de cette classification est de permettre une ventilation aussi large que possible des données statistiques pour ce que les administrations fiscales conviennent de considérer de manière générale comme des impôts.

a) l'OCDE inclut les cotisations de sécurité sociale dans les recettes fiscales totales (§ 7 et § 8 ci-dessus) ;

b) les avis diffèrent sur la question de savoir s'il y a lieu de classer certains prélèvements et redevances dans les impôts (§ 9 et §10 ci-dessus) ;

c) l'OCDE exclut les impôts imputés ou les subventions résultant d'opérations de taux de change officiels multiples ;

d) il existe des différences dans le traitement des crédits d'impôt récupérables.

85. Comme on l'a noté aux § 1 et § 2, les groupes 1000 à 6000 de la classification de l'OCDE comprennent tous les versements sans contrepartie aux administrations publiques, à l'exclusion des prêts obligatoires et des amendes. On peut obtenir le total de ces versements sans contrepartie, amendes incluses, mais prêts obligatoires exclus, en additionnant les postes suivants du SCN 2008 :

- impôts du type valeur ajoutée (D.211) ;
- droits et taxes sur les importations à l'exclusion de la TVA (D.212) ;
- droits sur les exportations (D.213) ;
- taxes sur les produits, à l'exclusion de la TVA, des droits sur les importations et les exportations (D.214) ;
- autres impôts sur la production (D.29) ;
- impôts sur le revenu (D.51) ;
- autres impôts périodiques (D.59) ;
- cotisations de sécurité sociale (D.61) à l'exclusion des cotisations volontaires ;
- impôts sur le capital (D.91).

A.10. La classification des impôts de l'OCDE et le système du Fonds monétaire international (GFS)

86. Le champ d'application et l'évaluation des recettes fiscales dans le système GFS et dans le système SCN 2008 sont très proches. Par conséquent, à l'exception du traitement des crédits d'impôt récupérables, les différences entre la classification de l'OCDE et celle du SCN 2008 (voir § 84 ci dessus) sont également valables pour le GFS. En outre, le Fonds monétaire international subdivise le groupe 5000 de la classification de l'OCDE en une section iv (Taxes intérieures sur les biens et services) et une section v (Taxes sur les transactions et les échanges internationaux). Cela tient à ce que le rendement de ces dernières taxes représente généralement des sommes infimes dans les pays de l'OCDE ce qui n'est pas le cas dans beaucoup de pays non membres.

A.11. Comparaison de la classification des impôts de l'OCDE et des autres classifications internationales des recettes publiques

87. Le tableau ci dessous décrit point par point la comparaison entre la classification des impôts de l'OCDE et les classifications suivantes :

i) Système des comptes nationaux (SCN 2008) ;

ii) Système européen des comptes (SEC 1995) ;

iii) Manuel de statistiques des finances publiques du Fonds monétaire international (MSFP 2001).

88. Ces comparaisons correspondent à celles qui devraient s'appliquer dans la majorité des cas. Toutefois, en pratique il faut faire preuve d'une certaine souplesse dans leur application. En effet, dans certains cas, les pays peuvent adopter des méthodes diverses de classification des recettes dans les comptes nationaux.

A.12. Répartition des recettes fiscales par sous-secteurs d'administration publique

89. La classification de l'OCDE appelle une ventilation des recettes fiscales par sous-secteurs d'administration. On trouvera ci-après la définition de chaque sous-secteur et les critères à utiliser pour répartir entre eux les recettes fiscales. Ces définitions et critères suivent les orientations qui figurent dans le SCN 2008 et le MSFP 2001.

Sous-secteurs des administrations publiques à identifier

a) Administration centrale

90. Le sous-secteur des administrations centrales groupe tous les ministères, bureaux, établissements et autres organismes qui sont des services ou des moyens d'action du pouvoir central et dont la compétence s'étend à la totalité du territoire, à l'exception de l'administration des caisses de sécurité sociale. L'administration centrale a donc le pouvoir de prélever des impôts sur toutes les unités résidentes et non résidentes exerçant des activités économiques à l'intérieur du pays.

b) Administration d'un État fédéré, d'une province ou d'une région

91. Ce sous-secteur comprend les unités administratives intermédiaires et inclut toutes les unités administratives dont la compétence s'exerce indépendamment de l'Administration centrale sur une partie du territoire englobant un certain nombre de petites localités, à l'exception des caisses de sécurité sociale. Dans les pays unitaires, les administrations régionales peuvent être considérées comme dotées d'une existence distincte lorsqu'elles disposent d'une autonomie substantielle pour percevoir une part importante de leurs recettes de sources placées sous leur contrôle et lorsque leurs agents ne sont pas soumis à un contrôle administratif externe dans l'exercice des activités de l'unité.

Classification de l'OCDE		SCN 2008	SEC 1995	MEFP 2001
1000	Impôts sur le revenu, les bénéfices et les gains en capital			
	1100 Personnes physiques			
	1110 Sur le revenu et les bénéfices	D51-8.61a	D51A	1111
	1120 Sur les gains en capital	D51-8.61c,d	D51C,D	1111
	1200 Sociétés			
	1210 Sur le revenu et les bénéfices	D51-8.61b	D51B	1112
	1220 Sur les gains en capital	D51-8.61c	D51C	1112
	1300 Non ventilables entre les rubriques 1100 et 1200			1113
2000	Cotisations de sécurité sociale			
	2100 Salariés	D613-8.85	D61111	1211
	2200 Employeurs	D611-8.83	D61121	1212
	2300 À la charge des travailleurs indépendants ou des personnes sans occupation	D613-8.85	D61131	1213
	2400 Non ventilables entre les rubriques 2100, 2200 et 2300			1214
3000	Impôts sur les salaires et la main-d'oeuvre	D29-7.97a	D29C	112
4000	Impôts sur le patrimoine			
	4100 Impôts périodiques sur la propriété immobilière			
	4110 Ménages	D59-8.63a	D59A	1131
	4120 Autres agents	D29-7.97b	D29A	1131
	4200 Impôts périodiques sur l'actif net			
	4210 Personnes physiques	D59-8.63b	D59A	1132
	4220 Sociétés	D59-8.63b	D59A	1132
	4300 Impôts sur les mutations par décès, les successions et les donations			
	4310 Impôts sur les mutations par décès et les successions	D91-10.207b	D91A	1133
	4320 Impôts sur les donations	D91-10.207b	D91A	1133
	4400 Impôts sur les transactions mobilières et immobilières	D59-7.96d; D29-7.97e	D214B,C	1134:1161
	4500 Autres impôts non périodiques sur le patrimoine	D91-10.207a	D91B	1135
	4600 Autres impôts périodiques sur le patrimoine	D59-8.63c	D59A	1136
5000	Impôts sur les biens et services			
	5100 Impôts sur les biens et services			
	5110 Impôts généraux sur les biens et services			
	5111 Taxes sur la valeur ajoutée	D211-7.89	D211; D29G	11411
	5112 Impôts sur les ventes	D2122-7.94a; D214-7.96a	D2122D; D214I	11412
	5113 Autres impôts généraux sur les biens et services	D214-7.96a	D214I	11413
	5120 Impôts sur des biens et services déterminés			
	5121 Accises	D2122-7.94b; D214-7.96b	D2122C; D214A,B,D	1142
	5122 Bénéfices des monopoles fiscaux	D214-7.65e	D214J	1143
	5123 Droits de douane et autres droits à l'importation	D2121-7.93	D2121; D2122A,B	1151
	5124 Taxes à l'exportation	D213-7.95a	D214K	1152-4
	5125 Impôts sur les biens d'équipements			
	5126 Impôts sur les services déterminés	D2122-7.94c; D214-7.96c	D2122E; D214E,F,G; D29F	1144; 1156
	5127 Autres impôts sur les transactions et les échanges internationaux	D2122-7.94d D29-7.95b D29-7.97g D59-8.64d	D2122F; D29D D59E	1153 1155-6
	5128 Autres impôts sur des et services déterminés			1146
	5130 Non ventilable entre les rubriques 5110 et 5120			
	5200 Impôts sur l'utilisation des biens ou l'autorisation d'utiliser des biens ou d'exercer des activités			
	5210 Impôts périodiques sur l'utilisation des biens ou l'autorisation d'utiliser des biens ou d'exercer des activités			
	5211 À la charge des ménages au titre de véhicules à moteurs	D59-8.64c	D59D	11451
	5212 À la charge d'autres agents au titre de véhicules à moteurs	D29-7.97d	D214D; D29B	11451
	5213 Autres impôts périodiques sur l'utilisation des biens ou l'autorisation d'utiliser des biens ou d'exercer des activités	D29-7.97c,d,f D59-8.64c	D29B,E,F; D59D	11452
	5220 Impôts non périodiques			
	5300 Non ventilable entre les rubriques 5100 et 5200			
6000	Autres impôts			
	6100 À la charge exclusive des entreprises			
	6200 À la charge d'autres agents que les entreprises ou non identifiables	D59-8.64a,b	D59B,C	1162

92. Actuellement, les pays à structure fédérale représentent la majorité des cas dans lesquels les recettes attribuées aux unités administratives intermédiaires sont identifiées séparément. L'Espagne est le seul pays à structure unitaire qui se trouve dans cette situation. Dans les autres pays unitaires, les recettes des administrations régionales sont incluses dans celles des administrations locales.

c) Collectivités locales

93. Ce sous-secteur comprend toutes les autres unités administratives exerçant une compétence indépendante sur une partie du territoire d'un pays, à l'exception des administrations des caisses de sécurité sociale. Il englobe les diverses circonscriptions urbaines et/ou rurales (par exemple les collectivités locales, les municipalités, les villes, les bourgs ou les districts).

d) Caisses de sécurité sociale

94. Les caisses de sécurité sociale constituent un sous-secteur distinct des administrations publiques. Le sous secteur de la sécurité sociale est défini dans le SCN de 2008 par les extraits suivants des paragraphes 4.124 à 4.126 et 4.147 :

« Les systèmes de sécurité sociale sont des systèmes d'assurance sociale qui couvrent l'ensemble de la collectivité ou d'importants sous ensembles de la collectivité : ces systèmes sont imposés et contrôlés par les administrations publiques. Ces systèmes couvrent une grande variété de programmes qui consistent à fournir des prestations, en espèces ou en nature, au titre des circonstances suivantes : vieillesse, invalidité ou décès, survie, maladie et maternité, accident du travail, chômage, allocations familiales, soins de santé etc. Il n'existe pas nécessairement de lien direct entre le montant de la cotisation versée par un particulier et les prestations qu'il est susceptible de recevoir » (paragraphe 4.124).

« Lorsque les systèmes de sécurité sociale ont une organisation distincte des autres activités des administrations publiques et détiennent des actifs et des engagements indépendamment de ces dernières et effectuent des opérations financières pour leur propre compte, ils peuvent être considérés comme des unités institutionnelles désignées sous le nom de caisses de sécurité sociale » (paragraphe 4.125).

« Il est possible de faire varier de façon discrétionnaire les montants prélevés et versés sous forme de cotisations de sécurité sociale et de prestations afin d'atteindre des objectifs de politique publique qui n'ont pas de lien direct avec la notion de sécurité sociale en tant que système visant à fournir des prestations à des membres de la collectivité. Ainsi, ces cotisations ou prestations peuvent être augmentées ou diminuées afin d'influer sur le niveau de la demande globale au sein de l'économie. Néanmoins, tant que ces caisses restent indépendantes, elles doivent être traitées comme des unités institutionnelles distinctes dans le SCN ». (paragraphe 4.126).

« Le sous-secteur des administrations de sécurité sociale comprend les administrations de sécurité sociale opérant à tous les niveaux des administrations publiques. Les administrations de sécurité sociale sont des systèmes couvrant l'ensemble de la collectivité ou d'importants sous ensembles de la collectivité qui sont rendus obligatoires et contrôlés par des administrations publiques » (paragraphe 4.147).

95. Cette définition des administrations de sécurité sociale est suivie dans la classification de l'OCDE à l'exception des régimes suivants :

- Les régimes imposés par l'administration et exploités par des organismes extérieurs au secteur des administrations publiques, tel qu'il est défini au § 3 de ce manuel et
- Les régimes qui perçoivent des cotisations volontaires.

Autorités supranationales

96. Ce sous-secteur s'applique aux activités de collecte de recettes publiques des autorités supranationales sur le territoire d'un pays. En pratique, le seul cas d'autorité supranationale de la zone de l'OCDE est celui des institutions de l'Union européenne (UE). Depuis 1998, les autorités supranationales ne figurent plus dans les Statistiques des recettes publiques dans un souci de cohérence avec la définition du SCN des administrations publiques qui les exclut. Par exemple, les impôts sur le revenu et des contributions de sécurité sociale rassemblées par des Institutions européennes et payé par les fonctionnaires européens qui sont résidents de pays membres de l'Union européenne ne devraient pas être inclus. Toutefois, les prélèvements spécifiques versés par les États membres à l'Union européenne continuent à être inclus dans les recettes fiscales totales et ils sont indiqués sous cette rubrique.

Critères à utiliser pour l'attribution des recettes fiscales

97. Lorsqu'une administration collecte l'impôt et le reverse, en totalité ou en partie, à d'autres administrations, il est nécessaire de déterminer si ces recettes doivent être considérées comme étant celles de l'administration qui les perçoit et les répartit entre d'autres administrations ou celles des administrations bénéficiaires auxquelles l'administration qui les a perçues les a transférées en simple qualité d'agent. Les critères à utiliser dans l'attribution des recettes sont indiqués aux § 98 à § 101, qui reprennent les § 3.70 à § 3.73 du SCN 2008.

98. En général, un impôt est attribué à l'Unité administrative qui

a) exerce le pouvoir de percevoir l'impôt (soit en tant que détenteur de ce pouvoir soit par délégation de l'autorité qui le détient),

b) dispose du pouvoir discrétionnaire final de fixer et de faire varier le taux de l'impôt.

99. Lorsqu'une somme est collectée par une administration au profit d'une autre administration et en son nom, et que cette dernière a le pouvoir de percevoir l'impôt et de fixer et de faire varier son taux, la première intervient comme agent pour le compte de la dernière et l'impôt est réaffecté. Toute somme retenue par l'administration collectrice au titre des frais de recouvrement doit être considérée comme la rémunération d'un service rendu. Toute autre somme conservée par l'administration collectrice, notamment dans le cadre d'un accord de partage d'impôt, doit être considérée comme une subvention courante. Si l'administration collectrice s'est vu déléguer le pouvoir de fixer et de faire varier le taux, le montant recouvré doit être considéré comme une recette fiscale de cette administration.

100. Lorsque des administrations différentes fixent conjointement et sur un pied d'égalité la répartition du produit de cet impôt, aucune administration ne disposant d'un pouvoir prépondérant en dernier ressort, les recettes fiscales sont attribuées à chaque administration en fonction de sa part respective du produit de l'impôt. Si un accord permet à une unité administrative d'exercer un pouvoir prépondérant en dernier ressort, la totalité des recettes fiscales est attribuée à cette unité.

101. Dans certains cas aussi, un impôt est perçu dans le cadre des compétences d'une administration qui résulte de la constitution ou d'autres dispositions mais d'autres administrations fixent individuellement le taux d'imposition sur leurs territoires. Le produit de l'impôt généré sur les territoires respectifs de chaque administration est attribué à l'administration en question comme constituant ses recettes fiscales.

Versements effectués par les États membres de l'Union européenne

102. Les versements effectués par les États membres de l'Union européenne prennent la forme :

- Ressources TVA, et
- Prélèvements spécifiques qui comprennent :

a) les droits de douane et les prélèvements agricoles (5123),

b) les montants compensatoires monétaires bruts (5123 si relatifs aux importations et 5124 si relatifs aux exportations), et

c) les prélèvements de la CECA, les cotisations sucre et les taxes de co-responsabilité sur le lait (5128).

103. Les droits de douane collectés par les États membres pour le compte de l'Union européenne sont comptabilisés :

- sur une base qui ne tient pas compte des droits d'encaissement,
- en utilisant des chiffres corrigés de manière à exprimer les droits sur la base de la « destination finale » et non du « pays de première entrée » lorsque de telles corrections sont possibles. Ces corrections concernent en particulier les droits prélevés dans des ports (maritimes) importants. Bien que les droits de l'UE soient prélevés par les autorités du pays de première entrée, ces droits doivent être dans la mesure du possible déduits des recettes du pays qui les recouvre et inclus dans les recettes du pays de destination finale.

104. Ces droits de l'UE sont le plus clairement conformes au critère d'attribution décrit au § 96 ci dessus. En conséquence, à partir de 1998, ces montants sont mentionnés dans une note de bas de page à titre de rubrique « Pour mémoire » dans les tableaux des États membres de l'UE (partie III du Rapport) et ne figurent plus sous la rubrique 5123. Toutefois, ces montants sont inclus dans les grands totaux des recettes fiscales à la ligne supérieure pour toutes les années indiquées dans les tableaux.

105. Les ressources TVA qui sont déterminées par l'application d'un taux ne pouvant dépasser 1 % d'une assiette précisée dans la 6ème Directive des Communautés, constituent un cas particulier[21]. Elles ont en effet certaines caractéristiques d'une subvention (elles ne proviennent pas d'une source clairement identifiable de fonds effectivement collectés à cet effet) et certaines autres d'un impôt (le montant de la subvention est fixé par le sous-secteur d'administration bénéficiaire). Dans cette publication, ces ressources ne figurent pas comme un impôt de l'Union européenne (mais comme un impôt des États membres de l'Union) bien que les montants en question soient indiqués en note de bas de page dans la partie IV.

A.13. Classification provisoire des recettes provenant des prélèvements sur les banques et des contributions aux mécanismes de garantie des dépôts et de stabilité financière

106. L'OCDE a provisoirement adopté, depuis l'édition 2012 de ses *Statistiques des recettes publiques*, le principe suivant concernant l'enregistrement comptable des recettes issues des prélèvements sur les banques ainsi que des redevances acquittées au titre de la garantie des dépôts et de la stabilité financière. Il est recommandé que les montants concernés soient comptabilisés à la rubrique 5126.

- Les redevances de stabilité, les prélèvements sur les banques et les contributions à la garantie des dépôts, qu'il est obligatoire d'acquitter, doivent généralement être traitées comme des recettes fiscales lorsque les versements sont effectués au profit de l'administration publique et affectés au budget consolidé ou général des administrations de sorte que les pouvoirs publics soient libres d'utiliser les fonds sans délai aux fins qu'ils jugent opportunes. Ce principe s'appliquerait indépendamment du fait que l'administration promette ou non d'effectuer des versements pour garantir les dépôts des clients des établissements bancaires si la situation l'exigeait à l'avenir.

- Si les paiements obligatoires sont effectués au profit de l'administration publique et imputés à des budgets dont les ressources doivent être entièrement réaffectées au secteur de l'économie qui englobe les entreprises assujetties à ces paiements, ceux-ci seront toujours traités, en règle générale, comme des recettes fiscales étant donné que les fonds seraient disponibles pour l'administration et réduiraient son déficit budgétaire, que la redevance est sans contrepartie pour les entités individuelles et que les montants collectés pourraient être dissociés de tout versement en faveur des déposants ou de toute dépense visant à soutenir plus largement le secteur financier.
- Les contributions aux mécanismes traditionnels de moindre envergure destinés à garantir les dépôts de détail, contributions dont le montant est aligné sur le coût de la garantie, doivent être classées en tant que redevances pour services rendus.
- Tout versement au titre de la réalisation par une administration des actifs d'un établissement en faillite ou du recouvrement par cette administration d'une créance prioritaire sur les actifs de l'établissement en cours de liquidation, effectué en vue de financer l'indemnisation des clients ayant perdu leurs dépôts, serait traité comme une redevance par opposition aux recettes fiscales.
- Les contributions obligatoires aux fonds administrés en-dehors du secteur public et aux organismes non étatiques bénéficiant du soutien des institutions collectrices de dépôts ainsi que toutes les contributions aux mécanismes volontaires ne doivent pas être traitées comme des recettes fiscales.

Notes

1. Les références dans cette annexe aux chapitres ou aux sections de "ce rapport" sont issues de OCDE (2015), *Statistiques des recettes publiques* 1965-2014, Éditions OCDE, Paris.
2. Toutes les références au SCN concernent l'édition de 2008.
3. Se reporter à la section A.12 de ce manuel pour l'examen de cette notion.
4. Il est en général possible d'identifier les montants des cotisations de sécurité sociale et les impôts sur les salaires, mais pas les autres impôts payés par les administrations.
5. En revanche si un ou plusieurs pays considèrent comme un impôt un droit que la plupart des pays font entrer dans les recettes non fiscales ou qui procure des recettes substantielles, les montants ainsi perçus figureront dans une note de renvoi à la fin des tableaux par pays correspondants, même s'ils ne sont pas inclus dans le total des recettes fiscales.
6. Les appellations peuvent cependant être souvent trompeuses. Ainsi, une redevance de passeport sera normalement considérée comme une recette non fiscale, alors qu'un prélèvement additionnel sur les passeports (comme c'est le cas au Portugal), qui a pour but de procurer un montant substantiel de recettes eu égard au coût de délivrance du passeport, sera considéré comme un impôt du sous-groupe 5200.
7. La distinction prévue par le SCN 1993 est difficile à opérer dans la pratique.
8. On trouvera des précisions sur cette distinction dans l'étude spéciale intitulée « L'information sur les recettes fiscales : problèmes actuels », de l'édition de 2001 des *Statistiques des recettes publiques*.
9. On utilise parfois les expressions "non remboursable" et "remboursable" mais il peut paraître illogique de parler de "remboursement" lorsque rien n'a été versé.
10. Toutefois, dans les systèmes d'imputation de l'impôt sur les sociétés, les crédits d'impôts récupérables sont traités différemment (§ 32-34).
11. Il ne s'agit pas d'une véritable dépense fiscale au sens strict. De telles dépenses fiscales supposent que l'on identifie un système fiscal de référence pour chaque pays ou, de préférence, une norme internationale commune. En pratique, il n'a pas été possible de parvenir à un accord sur une norme internationale commune.
12. Sauf s'ils sont calculés sur le bénéfice résultant de la vente, auquel cas ils seraient classés parmi les impôts sur les gains en capital dans le sous-groupe 1120 ou 1220.
13. Dans certains pays, la même législation est applicable aux personnes physiques et aux entreprises dans le cas d'impôts sur le revenu particuliers. Cependant, les recettes procurées par ces impôts peuvent, en général, être ventilées et figurent donc dans les deux sous-groupes appropriés.
14. Ainsi, « celles qui sont suffisamment autonomes et indépendantes pour que leur fonctionnement soit comparable à celui d'une société... (y compris) la tenue de comptes complets » (2008 SCN section 4.44).
15. Au Canada — pays généralement considéré comme appliquant un système d'imputation — le crédit d'impôt (non récupérable) offert à l'actionnaire concerne l'impôt national sur les sociétés censé avoir été acquitté, qu'un impôt sur les sociétés soit ou ne soit pas dû. Comme, dans ces systèmes, il n'y a aucun lien complet entre l'impôt dû par les sociétés et le crédit d'impôt appliqué au montant de l'impôt sur le revenu, ces crédits pour les dividendes sont traités, comme les autres crédits d'impôt, selon les principes exposés au § 21.
16. Il peut en être ainsi lorsqu'un régime en faveur des agents des administrations existait avant l'instauration d'un régime général de sécurité sociale.
17. Dans le SCN 2008, ils sont considérés comme des transferts en capital et non pas comme des impôts (voir section G).
18. Système selon lequel l'Union européenne ajuste les effets des différences entre les taux de change utilisés pour fixer les prix des produits agricoles dans le cadre de la politique agricole commune, et le taux de change réel. Les paiements effectués selon ce système portent sur les importations ou les exportations; lorsqu'ils sont identifiables, ces montants figurent dans la rubrique appropriée (5123 ou 5124). Dans ce guide, sont inclus les montants bruts, c'est-à-dire sans déduction d'aucune prime payée par le SMC.
19. Les transferts de bénéfices de loteries d'État sont considérés comme des recettes non fiscales (voir aussi § 64).
20. Voir à ce sujet le § 26(c).
21. Au sommet d'Édimbourg (1992) les membres de l'Union européenne ont décidé de réduire le pourcentage de 1.4 à 1, et d'effectuer cette réduction entre les années 1995 et 1999. Pendant la période 1970-1983 ce pourcentage était également de 1.

ANNEX B

Interpretative guide to non-tax revenue in Revenue Statistics in Africa

Coverage

The definition of non-tax revenues and the main subcategories identified in this publication generally correspond to the concepts laid out in the 2014 IMF Government Finance Statistics Manual (GSFM). Non-tax revenues refer to increases in government net worth resulting from transactions other than tax revenues. They exclude funds arising from the repayment of previous lending by governments or from borrowing, or proceeds derived from sales of fixed capital assets, stocks, land and intangible assets or private gifts. Non-tax revenues are made up of grants, property income, sales of goods and services, fines, penalties, forfeits, other social contributions, miscellaneous and unidentified revenue.

Grants

The GSFM 2014 states "Grants are transfers receivable by government units from non-resident government units or international organisations without the receipt of any goods, services, or assets in return. Grants are normally receivable in cash, but may also take the form of the receipt of goods or services (in kind)". These transfers are un-refundable and unrequited. Grants exclude inter-governmental transfers.

Property income

This category includes income to government arising from their ownership of property, enterprises, financial assets, or intangible assets when government units place them at the disposal of other units. Sales of nonfinancial assets such as the sales of lands are not recorded as revenue because disposal of such an asset does not increase the net worth. Similarly, repayments on loans and loan disbursements are not revenue. Property income may take the form of dividends, interest, land rents, royalties, or withdrawals from entrepreneurial income. The main components are:

- Interest and dividends: Interest is the revenue earned by the government unit from a financial asset by putting it at the disposal of another institutional unit. Dividends are the revenue earned by placing equity funds at the disposal of a corporation (resident or non-resident corporation). This category also consists of profits of state-owned enterprises except those classified as fiscal monopolies (see §62-§64 of the OECD Interpretative Guide in Annex A), export and import monopoly profits (see §70-§71) or those providing public utilities such as rail transport, electricity, post offices and other communications. In this category are included revenue from public financial institutions such as the central banks' profits, profits transferred or distributed from the operation of monetary authority functions outside the central bank and the profits of state lotteries transferred to the government. Transfers from public utilities are recorded as non-tax revenue under "sales of goods and services" whereas profits for fiscal, export or import monopolies are classified as tax revenue.
- Rents or Royalties: Rent is the revenue generated from natural resources, such as land, mining, or oil resources, when a government unit places these at the disposal of private or foreign entities. The rents received relate to a lease-giving agreement for the exploitation and extraction of a natural resource by the lessee in return for a payment. Payments for exploration rights are also treated as rent. Rents should not be confused with other payments a government may receive related to the exploitation of subsoil and similar assets, such as severance taxes, business licences, or other taxes (e.g. value added taxes, excises, taxes on exports, etc.). They should also not be taken to mean incomes from the rental of buildings and

equipment, which are treated as sales of goods and services. Revenues from rents and royalties are in some cases difficult to establish and depend on the agreement between the government unit and the lessee. For example rents, royalties and taxes such as corporate income taxes and VAT are sometimes encompassed in a single payment to the general government. In such cases the revenue should be classified under the category to which the majority of revenue belongs.

- Other property income: This includes revenue earned by a government unit placing funds at the disposal of quasi-corporations.[1] Conceptually this source of revenue is equivalent to that of dividends from a corporation but by definition, quasi-corporations cannot distribute income in the form of dividends. This category of "other property income" also includes retained or reinvested earnings, i.e. the percentage of distributable revenue not paid out as dividends, but retained by the corporation or quasi-corporation on foreign investment; property income from investment income disbursements and unidentified property income.

Sales of goods and services

Revenue under the category "sales of goods and services" is reported on a gross basis, without deduction of costs. Since these costs can represent a significant proportion of revenues, they cannot be regarded in total as funds available for governments to finance their general activities. This contrasts with tax revenues, where the collection costs are usually a small proportion of revenue. This difference implies that it may not be meaningful to sum tax and non-tax revenues as part of a calculation of generally available funds.

The proceeds of sales of nonfinancial assets such as the sale of buildings or lands are not classified as revenues since their disposal does not increase the net worth.

Sales of goods and services consist of:

- Sales by market establishments.[2]
- Administrative fees for services (i.e. fees for drivers' licences, passports, visas; court fees and harbour fees; fees for birth, marriage or death certificates; patent registrations; and radio and television licences when public authorities provide general broadcasting services). Administrative fees that are sales of services associated with a regulatory function of government (such as fees for the inspection of premises before delivering a business licence) and are considered to be proportional to the cost of producing the service are included in this category. If the fee is disproportionate to the service provided by the government, then the fee will be classified as a tax. Specific examples of fees that are considered taxes include fees for permission to perform activities such as hunting, fishing and shooting; and fees for business registration where this is a legal requirement for the business to operate.
- Sales by non-market establishments such as fees at government hospitals, tuition fees at government schools and admission fees to museums and parks.
- Leasing of buildings and equipment.

Fines, penalties and forfeits

The GSFM 2014 states "Fines and penalties are compulsory transfers imposed by courts of law or bodies for violations of laws or administrative rules. Out-of-court agreements are also included (...). Forfeits are amounts deposited with a general government unit pending a legal or administrative proceeding, and that will be transferred to the unit upon resolution". For example traffic fines are included here. Fines and penalties charged on overdue taxes or penalties imposed for the evasion of taxes should be recorded in this category and not as taxes. However if it is not possible to separate the amounts paid in taxes and fines, the whole amount should be classified under the tax to which the fine relates.

Other social contributions

This category includes the actual and imputed contributions to social insurance schemes[3] operated by governments as employers on behalf of their employees, excluding the contributions that do create future defined liabilities. This category also includes the sum of the total voluntary contributions.[4] Excluded from this category are any contributions to funds in which the contributions of each participant and of his employer on his behalf are kept in a separate account earning interest and withdrawable under specified circumstances. Also excluded are any contributions to a pension fund autonomous to the general government. This category is not included in this publication as no such revenue streams were identified for the Revenue Statistics in Africa (RSIA) countries.

Miscellaneous and unidentified revenue

This category consists of unidentified non-tax revenues or revenues that do not fit into any of the other categories listed above. It includes revenue such as gifts and transfers from individuals, private non-profit institutions, nongovernmental foundations, corporations, or sources other than governments and international organisations. Major non-recurrent payments receivable in compensation for extensive damages or serious injuries not covered by insurance policies are also included, such as payments of compensation for damages caused by major explosions; oil spillages; or payments receivable for damage to property other than payments from an insurance settlement.

Notes

1. The latter are defined as unincorporated enterprises that function as if they were corporations.
2. A market establishment is an establishment that charges economically significant prices.
3. Social insurance schemes' benefits are directly related to contribution levels, which is not the case for social security schemes.
4. The IMF includes these contributions as part of their total of social security contributions.

ANNEXE B

Guide d'interprétation des recettes non fiscales dans les Statistiques des recettes publiques en Afrique

Champ couvert

La définition des recettes non fiscales et des principales sous-catégories décrites dans la présente publication coïncident en grande partie avec les notions retenues dans le Manuel des statistiques de finances publiques du FMI de 2014 (Manuel SFP 2014). Les recettes non fiscales désignent des augmentations de la valeur nette résultant d'une transaction et qui ne sont pas des recettes fiscales. Elles excluent les fonds relatifs au remboursement de prêts consentis par les administrations ou liés à des emprunts faits par ces mêmes administrations publiques, ainsi que le produit de la cession d'actifs immobilisés, d'éléments de stocks, de terrains, d'actifs immatériels et les dons à titre privé. Les recettes non fiscales incluent les dons, les revenus de la propriété, les ventes de biens et de services, les amendes, pénalités et confiscations, les recettes diverses et non identifiées.

Dons

Selon le Manuel SFP 2014, les dons sont des transferts qu'une administration publique reçoit d'une autre administration publique étrangère ou d'une organisation internationale, sans recevoir de cette dernière un bien, un service ou un actif en contrepartie directe. Les dons sont habituellement reçus en espèces, mais peuvent aussi prendre la forme de biens ou de services. Ces transferts sont non remboursables et sans contrepartie. Les dons excluent les transferts entre administrations nationales.

Revenus de la propriété

Cette catégorie regroupe les recettes publiques découlant de la détention de biens fonciers, de parts de sociétés, d'actifs financiers ou d'actifs immatériels que certaines unités administratives ont mis à la disposition d'autres unités. Les cessions d'actifs non financiers comme la vente de terrains ne sont pas enregistrés en tant que recettes parce que la cession de tels actifs n'a pas d'effet sur la valeur nette. De même, les remboursements de prêts octroyés et les déboursements de prêts reçus ne sont pas des recettes. Les revenus de la propriété peuvent prendre la forme de dividendes, d'intérêts, de revenus fonciers, de redevances, ou de prélèvements sur des revenus d'entreprises. Les principales composantes en sont les suivantes :

- Intérêts et dividendes : Les intérêts sont les revenus perçus par une unité administrative au titre d'un actif financier qu'elle met à la disposition d'une autre unité institutionnelle. Les dividendes sont les recettes perçues par une unité qui met des capitaux à la disposition d'une société (qu'elle soit ou non résidente du pays concerné). Cette catégorie recouvre également les bénéfices d'entreprises détenues par une administration, en excluant les monopoles fiscaux (voir paragraphes 62 à 64 du Guide d'interprétation de l'OCDE en Annexe A), les monopoles d'exportation et d'importation (voir paragraphes 70 et 71) ainsi que les entreprises qui fournissent des services publics comme les chemins de fer, l'électricité, les postes et autres moyens de communication. Sont regroupés dans cette catégorie les revenus provenant d'institutions financières publiques comme les bénéfices de la banque centrale, les bénéfices transférés ou distribués d'une administration publique assumant des fonctions d'autorités monétaires exercées en dehors de la banque centrale et les bénéfices liés aux loteries nationales qui sont transférés à l'administration. Les recettes émanant d'entreprises qui assurent des services publics sont comptabilisés dans la rubrique « ventes de biens et de services » des recettes non fiscales alors que les bénéfices des monopoles fiscaux, d'exportation ou d'importation constituent des recettes fiscales.

- Loyers et redevances : Les loyers sont des revenus générés lorsqu'une unité administrative met à la disposition d'autres entités privées ou étrangères des ressources naturelles, comme des terrains ou des gisements de minéraux ou de pétrole. Les loyers perçus sont liés à des accords de concession relatifs à l'exploitation et à l'extraction d'une ressource naturelle par un concessionnaire en contrepartie d'un paiement. Les paiements en échange de droits de prospection doivent également être traités comme des loyers. Les loyers sont à distinguer des autres paiements qu'une administration publique peut recevoir pour l'exploitation d'actifs du sous-sol et d'autres actifs du même type, par exemple les paiements de taxes d'extraction de ressources naturelles provenant de terrains appartenant à des entreprises privées, patentes ou autres impôts (taxes sur la valeur ajoutée, accises, taxes à l'exportation, etc.). Il ne faut pas non plus confondre loyers et revenus de la location de bâtiments et d'équipements qui sont classés dans les ventes de biens et de services. Les revenus liés aux loyers et redevances sont parfois difficiles à déterminer car ils dépendent de la nature de l'accord conclu entre l'État et le concessionnaire. À titre d'exemple, un versement unique effectué en faveur des administrations publiques peut regrouper le paiement de loyers, de redevances et d'autres obligations fiscales comme l'impôt sur les bénéfices des sociétés ou la TVA. Dans un tel cas, le paiement est classé dans la catégorie qui correspond à la majeure partie du versement considéré.
- Autres revenus de la propriété : Cette catégorie inclus les recettes perçues par une unité administrative qui met des capitaux à la disposition de quasi-sociétés[1]. Cette source de recettes est en substance équivalente à des dividendes versés par une société mais, par définition, les quasi-sociétés ne distribuent pas de bénéfices sous forme de dividendes. Cette catégorie englobe de plus les bénéfices non distribués ou réinvestis, à savoir la fraction du bénéfice distribuable qui n'a pas été versée sous forme de dividendes, mais conservée par la société ou quasi-société sur des investissements étrangers ; les revenus de la propriété provenant de versements de revenus d'investissements et revenus de la propriété non identifiés.

Ventes de biens et de services

Les recettes qui entrent dans cette catégorie sont enregistrées en valeur brute, sans déduction de coûts. Dans la mesure où les coûts peuvent représenter une part importante des recettes, le montant total des ventes biens et de services ne peut pas être considéré comme un montant dont l'administration dispose dans son intégralité pour financer ses activités générales. C'est une différence notable avec les recettes fiscales, auxquelles sont associés des coûts de recouvrement qui ne représentent le plus souvent qu'une faible part des recettes. De ce fait, le montant obtenu par addition des recettes fiscales et non fiscales ne fournit pas forcément une bonne évaluation des fonds généralement disponibles.

Le produit généré par la cession d'actifs non financiers tels que des bâtiments ou des terrains n'est pas enregistré en tant que recettes étant donné que la cession de tels actifs n'a pas d'effet sur la valeur nette.

Les ventes de biens et de services se composent des éléments suivants :

- les ventes des établissements marchands[2].
- les droits administratifs pour services fournis (droits sur les permis de conduire, sur les passeports, sur les visas ; droits de procédure ; droits portuaires ; droits pour l'établissement d'actes de naissance, de mariage, de décès ; frais de dépôt de brevet ; licences de radio et télévision lorsque les autorités publiques fournissent des services de radiodiffusion). Les droits administratifs qui sont des ventes de biens

et de services associés à une fonction régulatrice des administrations publiques (comme les droits perçus au titre d'une inspection d'installations menée en vue de la délivrance d'un permis d'exploitation) sont inclus lorsqu'ils sont considérés comme étant proportionnels au coût de la prestation du service en question. Lorsque les droits perçus en contrepartie d'un service fourni par l'administration sont disproportionnés par rapport aux coûts, ils sont considérés comme des impôts. Parmi les droits ainsi classés dans la catégorie des recettes fiscales figurent notamment les droits perçus pour l'octroi de permis d'exercer des activités telles que la chasse, la pêche et l'utilisation d'armes à feu ; et les droits d'enregistrement d'une société dès lors que les entreprises sont tenues par la loi de procéder à un tel enregistrement pour pouvoir exercer leur activité.

- les ventes par les établissements non marchands, comme les droits prélevés par les hôpitaux publics, les droits de scolarité des écoles publiques et les droits d'entrée aux musées et parcs.
- la location de bâtiments et d'équipements.

Amendes, pénalités et confiscations

Le Manuel des statistiques de finances publiques du FMI de 2014 définit les amendes et pénalités comme des transferts obligatoires imposés aux unités par des tribunaux ou des organismes pour infraction à la loi ou aux règlements administratifs. Les accords extra-judiciaires sont également inclus. Les confiscations sont les montants déposés auprès d'une unité d'administration publique pendant le déroulement d'une procédure judiciaire ou administrative puis transférés à cette unité au moment du règlement de celle-ci. À titre d'exemple, les amendes sanctionnant les contraventions au code de la route entrent dans cette catégorie. Les amendes et pénalités appliquées au titre d'arriérés d'impôts ou les pénalités pour fraude fiscale doivent également être comptabilisées ici et non comme des recettes fiscales. Toutefois, s'il est impossible de distinguer les montants qui correspondent respectivement à l'impôt et aux pénalités, la somme totale est rattachée aux recettes générées par l'impôt qui a motivé l'application des pénalités.

Autres cotisations sociales

Cette catégorie englobe les cotisations sociales effectives et imputées aux régimes d'assurance sociale[3] gérés par des administrations publiques en qualité d'employeurs pour le compte de leurs employés, excluant les contributions qui génèrent un montant pré-défini de prestations à verser dans des périodes futures. Cette catégorie inclut également la somme des contributions volontaires totales[4]. Toutefois, sont exclues les cotisations à des fonds dans lesquels les cotisations de chaque salarié et celles que l'employeur verse en son nom sont comptabilisées séparément dans un compte productif d'intérêts d'où elles peuvent être retirées dans des conditions biens déterminées, ainsi que les cotisations à des fonds de pension autonomes vis-à-vis des administrations publiques. Cette catégorie n'est pas incluse aux fins de la présente publication dans la mesure où de tels flux de recettes n'ont pas été identifiés dans les pays objet de l'analyse.

Recettes diverses et non identifiées

Cette catégorie regroupe toutes les recettes non fiscales qui ne peuvent être identifiées ou qui n'entrent dans aucune des catégories décrites précédemment. Elle englobe aussi des dons et transferts provenant de personnes physiques, d'institutions privées sans but lucratif, de fondations non gouvernementales, de sociétés ou de sources autres que les administrations publiques et les organisations internationales. Les paiements non récurrents d'un montant élevé reçus par les administrations publiques en compensation de dommages importants non couverts par des polices d'assurance sont également inclus, ainsi que des paiements d'indemnités en compensation de dommages causés par des explosions de grande ampleur, le déversement d'hydrocarbures, ou des paiements exigibles en cas de dommages matériels autres que les paiements au titre d'une indemnisation par une assurance.

Notes

1. Il s'agit d'entreprises non constituées en société mais qui exercent leur activité comme des sociétés.
2. Un établissement marchand est une entité qui pratique des prix économiquement significatifs.
3. Les prestations versées par les régimes d'assurance sociale sont directement liés au niveau des cotisations versées, ce qui n'est pas le cas pour les régimes de sécurité sociale.
4. Le FMI comptabilise ces cotisations dans le total des cotisations de sécurité sociale.

OECD PUBLISHING, 2, rue André-Pascal, 75775 PARIS CEDEX 16
(23 2016 12 3 P) ISBN 978-92-64-25190-8 – 2015

www.ingramcontent.com/pod-product-compliance
Lightning Source LLC
Chambersburg PA
CBHW061208240926
51846CB00006B/1147
* 9 7 8 9 2 6 4 2 5 1 9 0 8 *